BEYOND OCCUPATION

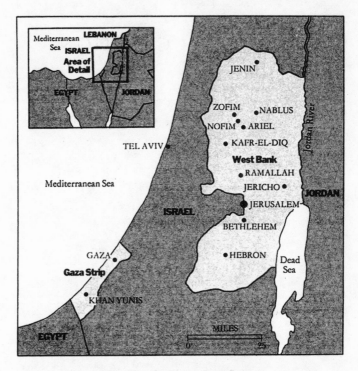

The West Bank and Gaza Strip

BEYOND OCCUPATION

AMERICAN JEWISH, CHRISTIAN, AND PALESTINIAN VOICES FOR PEACE

Edited by Rosemary Radford Ruether and Marc H. Ellis

BEACON PRESS : BOSTON

BEACON PRESS
25 Beacon Street
Boston, Massachusetts   02108-2800

Beacon Press books are published under the auspices of
the Unitarian Universalist Association of Congregations.

97 96 95 94 93 92 91 90   1 2 3 4 5 6 7 8

Text design by David Ford

Library of Congress Cataloging-in-Publication Data

Beyond occupation : American Jewish, Christian, and Palestinian voices
for peace / edited by Rosemary Radford Ruether and Marc H. Ellis.
        p. cm.
            ISBN 0-8070-6900-0
1. Jewish-Arab relations—Religious aspects—Judaism.   2. Jewish-
Arab relations—Religious aspects—Christianity.   3. Zionism—
Controversial literature.   4. Israel—Moral conditions.
    I. Ruether, Rosemary Radford.   II. Ellis, Marc H.
            DS119.7.B44   1990
        291.5′622—dc20   89-43078

To Jean Zaru and Felicia Langer
who as Palestinian and Jew have dedicated their lives
to a justice which one day will give birth to peace

Contents

Contents

Part 2: American Christians, Judaism, and the Israeli-Palestinian Conflict

Part 3: Palestinian Perspectives

Contents

Part 4: Concluding Thoughts

Introduction

MARC H. ELLIS AND
ROSEMARY RADFORD RUETHER

In January 1988, one month after the Palestinian uprising had begun, an Israeli captain was summoned to his superior. The captain was given instructions to carry out arrests in the village of Hawara, outside Nablus. The arrest of innocent young Palestinians is hardly out of the ordinary, but the further instructions given to the officer—what to do to those Palestinians after their arrest—was disturbing. His conscience would not allow him to carry out these instructions unless he was directly ordered to do so. Having then received the direct order the captain, with a company of forty soldiers, boarded a civilian bus, arriving at Hawara at eleven o'clock in the evening.

The local mukhtar was given a list of twelve persons to round up, which he did, and the twelve sat on the sidewalk in the center of the village, offering no resistance. Yossi Sarid describes what followed.

> The soldiers shackled the villagers, and with their hands bound behind their backs they were led to the bus. The bus started to move and after 200–300 meters it stopped beside an orchard. The "locals" were taken off the bus and led into the orchard in groups of three, one after another. Every group was accompanied by an officer. In the darkness of the orchard the soldiers also shackled the Hawara residents' legs and laid them on the ground. The officers urged the soldiers to "get it over with quickly, so that we can leave and forget about it." Then, flannel was stuffed into the Arabs' mouths to prevent them from screaming and the bus driver revved up the motor so that the noise would drown out the cries. Then the soldiers obediently carried out the orders they had been given: to break their arms and legs by clubbing the Arabs; to avoid clubbing them on their heads; to remove their bonds after breaking their arms and legs, and to leave them at the site; to leave one local with broken arms but without broken legs so he could make it back to the village on his own and get help.

The mission was carried out; the beatings were so fierce that most of the wooden clubs used were broken. Thus was born the title of the article detailing this action, "The Night of the Broken Clubs."[1]

1

Just months after the beatings, Marcus Levin, a physician, was called up for reserve duty in the Ansar 2 prison camp. When he arrived, Levin met two of his colleagues and asked for information as to his duties. The answer: "Mainly you examine prisoners before and after an investigation." Levin responded in amazement, "After the investigation?" which prompted the reply, "Nothing special, sometimes there are fractures. For instance, yesterday they brought a twelve-year-old boy with two broken legs." Dr. Levin then demanded a meeting with the compound commander and told him, "My name is Marcus Levin and not Josef Mengele, and for reasons of conscience I refuse to serve in this place." A doctor who was present at the meeting tried to calm Levin with the following comment: "Marcus, first you feel like Mengele, but after a few days you get used to it." Hence the title of an article written about the incident, "You Will Get Used to Being a Mengele."[2]

The references in these articles to the night of broken glass, *Kristallnacht*, and to the Nazi physician Josef Mengele, in the context of contemporary Jewish Israeli policy and activity is startling. The resistance on the part of the Jewish community to what one might call the Nazi analogy is understandable and so strong as to almost silence all such references. Yet during the brutal attempt to suppress the Palestinian uprising, in fact from the very beginning of the Jewish struggle for statehood in Palestine in the 1940s and continuing to the present, the connection between the Jewish experience of suffering in Europe and the Palestinian experience of suffering at the hand of the Jewish people in Palestine and Israel has been, and continues to be, repeatedly made by Jewish Israelis.

What are we to make of these references? First, it is important to see that they are not primarily comparisons between Nazi and Israeli behavior, though some of the behavior may in fact be comparable. Second, these references are not attempts to further political objectives, such as promoting one political party over another or delegitimating the state of Israel, though clearly they subvert partisan and bipartisan policies of Israel that lead to these situations. Rather, the force of the Nazi reference involves and moves beyond comparison and politics and represents an intuitive link between the historic suffering of the Jews and the present suffering of Palestinians. It further represents an implicit recognition that that which was done to Jews is now being done by Jews to another people. At the same time, the connection of Jewish and Palestinian suffering is prepolitical and preideological, that is, it operates in a terrain filled with the images of Jewish suffering that remains untouched by the "realities" of the situation, the need to be "strong," or even the communal penalties for speaking the truth. We might say that the Nazi reference represents a cry of pain *and* a plea to end a madness that was visited upon Jews for millennia and now is visited by Jews upon another people. Thus the vehemence with which such analogies are met when spoken, almost as if a blunt instrument is needed to repress the memories and aspirations of the Jewish people to be neither victim nor oppressor.

For over twenty years Jewish theology, and before that Zionist ideology, have functioned to a large degree to suppress this intuitive link, as well as other questions and traditions that challenge the forms of empowerment of the Jewish community in Israel. This is why the unpardonable sin—the only sin that warrants excommunication in the Jewish community today—is that which critically addresses Jewish empowerment in Israel. Since contemporary Jewish theology has as its basis a sense of Jewish innocence, especially in suffering, and the reality of empowerment in Israel as redemptive, and intuitive link between Jewish and Palestinian suffering undermines this basis. By repressing the intuitive connection, Jewish theology continues to articulate who Jews were—weak and helpless—rather than who Jews have become—powerful and too often oppressive. But the threatening aspect of Jewish intuition is not only that it calls into question the enterprise of state building from the beginning; it also warns us of a potential future. When Lieutenant General Dan Shomron recently remarked, "Whoever demands the wiping out of the *intifada* has to remember that there are only three ways to achieve it: transfer, starvation or physical extermination—that is, genocide," those words should be understood in the context of the company commander and the medical doctor quoted earlier as now truly possible. Such ruminations on the future are only a step away from possible public policy, and would, in the context of our discussion, be labeled "the final solution."[3]

If at a deep subconscious level Jews and others want to scream that such a policy is impossible, that Jews could never do such a thing, it is important to remember that the incidents recalled above were likewise once considered impossible for the Jewish people. Are we as Jews being prepared for the scenario that Shomron's words articulate, as we have now almost become accustomed to the policies of might and beatings that continue and even escalate daily? And will Jewish theologians who have helped, sometimes willingly, sometimes out of ignorance, and sometimes out of fear, to legitimate Israeli actions, speak before it is too late?

Of course, the political and theological realities of the Middle East, and

3

especially of Israel and Palestine, did not simply appear in the context of the Palestinian uprising. There is a long history that helps sharpen our perspective as the difficult path toward peace is considered.

Palestine lies on the crossroads of three continents of Asia, Europe, and Africa and has long been a contested area between empires centered in North Africa, Syria, or the Western Mediterranean. It has been continually settled by migrations of peoples, mainly of the Semitic world, since before the tenth millennium B.C.E. It has never been exclusively the land of the Jewish people, but, even during the brief periods of Jewish hegemony in antiquity, a land of several Semitic peoples. The land came to be called Palestine by the Romans in the first century, after one of these people who predominated in the coastal areas, the Philistines.

Because of expulsions and migrations, the Jewish population there dwindled, but never disappeared, by the end of the first century C.E., and the area became primarily Christian. It was conquered by the expanding Arab Muslim empire in the seventh century and gradually became predominately Muslim, both through the migration of Muslims to the area and the conversion of the indigenous population. Small groups of Jews continually migrated there during Middle Ages. They were welcomed by the Ottoman Turks in the sixteenth century, after the expulsion of Jews from Spain.[4]

All three religious groups—the large but dwindling Christian community, the growing Muslim community, and the tiny Jewish community—became Arab-speaking. Together they are regarded as Palestinian by the Palestinian national movement that arose in the early twentieth century with the disintegration of the Ottoman Turkish control over the region. Palestinian nationalism, in part because of its Christian leadership, has resisted an Islamic definition of nationalism. It has opted for a secular democratic definition of Palestinian peoplehood, based on indigenous Arab Palestinian culture, language, and history and encompassing Muslims, Christians, and Jews (the Arab-speaking Jews of the region prior to the European Zionist immigrations of the twentieth century).[5]

The Zionist movement arose in Eastern and Western Europe in the mid to late nineteenth century, because of the threats and failures of assimilation of Western European Jewry into the emerging European nation states. European Jewry had been persecuted and ghettoized throughout the centuries of Christian hegemony, following the Constantinian establishment in the fourth century, but particularly following the crusades in the High Middle Ages. Nevertheless, Christian theory accorded the Jews some minimal rights to communal and religious existence and protection, based on its view that the Jews must continue to exist pending their eventual conversion to Christianity, this conversion being seen as one of the necessary events leading to the return of Christ and the final salvation of the world.[6]

Within these hostile and often precarious parameters, European Jewry shaped a self-governing communal life in their own villages and neighborhoods. The Enlightenment and the emergence of secular European nationalism broke down this traditional Jewish communal life, based on Jewish religious law, in two ways. First of all, the new definition of civil society demanded the dissolution of all forms of feudal communal autonomy in order to assimilate the population to its concept of the citizen. In order to become French, English, or German, Jews had to dissolve their separate communal institutions. Judaism, like Christianity, had to be privatized, existing as personal religion, but no longer as quasi-political community.

In 1789 the Count Clermont-Tonnerre made a famous statement at the French Constituent Assembly: "Everything must be denied the Jews as a nation and everything granted to them as individuals. They must not form either a political body or an order in the state. They must be individual citizens." This was not a statement of special bigotry against Jews, as it has generally been interpreted. Rather, it reflects the formula by which liberal civil society was to be constituted by dissolving all forms of separate feudal communitarianism.[7]

Nevertheless, the long tradition of Christian vilification of Jews as Christ-killers and demonic agents was not to be so easily overcome by secularization. No sooner had the Jews of Europe begun to be incorporated into secular definitions of national citizenship than new forms of racial anti-Semitism arose, scapegoating the Jews as the cause of the various tensions of secularization, class conflict, and urbanization that accompanied modernity. Jews found themselves the targets of political anti-Semitic movements that blamed them for internal and inter-European national conflicts. Racial definitions of French, German, or other European nationalities arose that defined Jews as racial aliens, incapable of being true members of the national body politic.

Zionism was a response of European Jews to this double-bind of European racial nationalism; on the one hand, inviting them into European nationalisms at the price of dissolving their distinct Jewish communal identity and, on the other hand, rebuffing them as aliens. It sought to solve the problem of Jewish alienation, both from Jewish communal identity and from European national identity, by defining the Jews as a national community in terms similar to the other forms of European ethnic nationalisms. Jews, like other nationalities, must assert their national identity by reclaiming their language and building the cultural, economic, and political institutions of this national life in their homeland.[8]

For most Zionists, inspired by the long religious tradition of expectation of messianic restoration to the "land of Israel" in Palestine, this land was the only possible choice for a national homeland, although some Zionists toyed with the possibility of immigrating to other lands, for example, Africa during the time when European colonialists were carving up that continent among themselves. Led by this vision of building a Jewish homeland and nation state, Zionist groups, particularly from Eastern Europe, began to send settlers to Palestine beginning in the 1880s.

However, this Zionist option remained the position of a small minority of European Jews until after World War II.[9] Most Jews preferred to stay in Europe or migrate to America and to continue to pursue the liberal vision of Jewish existence in secular society. Only after the shock of the Holocaust during World War II did Zionism capture most Jewish institutions as the dominant ideology of world Jewry. Patriotic support of the Jewish state became de rigeur for all Jews as a way of expressing their collective Jewish identity and as a possible place of safety in case of a new genocidal attack in the West.

Yet, despite this ideological embrace of Zionism by the dominant Jewish institutions, most Jews have not chosen to immigrate to Palestine-Israel. Four-fifths of world Jewry continues to live elsewhere, particularly in North America. The Soviet Jewish population, targeted as an immigrant group by the Zionist movement in the 1970s, has also shown a marked preference for the United States over Israel as the goal of migration. As Israel becomes a nation of chronic conflict with its neighbors, a land where some 15,000 Jews (most of them soldiers) have died in the last forty years, a land of extreme inflation and economic dependency on American aid, a pariah among many nations of the world because of its violent repression of the Palestinians, the numbers of Jews wishing to emigrate has steadily increased over those wishing to immigrate. The Zionist dream is dying for more and more Jews.

The establishment of a Jewish homeland and state has, from its beginning, been fatally tied to European colonialism in the Arab world and dogged by a basic demographic problem. Jews were and remain a minority

6

among the Arab majority of Palestine. Only by the most forceful and sometimes manipulative efforts to get Jews to migrate to the region, together with the expulsion of Palestinians and expropriation of their land, has it been possible to create the appearance of a Jewish majority as the basis for the imposition of a "Jewish state" in the region.[10]

The first era of the Zionist-Palestinian struggle was shaped between the First and Second World Wars, during the period of British colonial rule in Palestine and in much of the Arab world. For the emergent Palestinian movement, both British rule and its sponsorship of Zionism represented profound betrayals of their own national rights. During the First World War the British persuaded the Arab armies, led by the sons of Sharif Husain of Mecca, to side with them against the Turks, allied with Germany, by promising them an independent Arab state. The British, however, had no intention of allowing such a united Arab state to emerge to challenge its own hegemony in the region. They intended rather to carve up the region for themselves, reserving part of it for their rivals, the French.

In the secret Anglo-French Sykes-Picot agreement of 1916, the Arab region was divided into British and French regions of control. At the same time the British made an agreement with the Zionists to sponsor a Jewish homeland in Palestine. The agreement represented a combination of British Christian biblical romanticism about the region and a hard-headed colonialist strategy that saw the European Jewish settlers as a population that would remain dependent on British control.

When the Arabs discovered after the war that their promise of national independence had been betrayed and that their lands were to be divided into a series of mandate areas under the British and French, they were outraged and began a struggle to make these regions into independent states. Thus there emerged a plurality of sub-Arab nationalisms—Lebanese, Syrian, Iraqi, Jordanian, and Palestinian—following the lines of the boundaries defined by European colonial subdivision. The Palestinians felt doubly betrayed, for not only was their region taken over by the British, but these rulers were also engaged in sponsorship of Zionist immigration aimed at displacing them from their national homeland.[11]

Throughout the twenties and thirties Palestinians continually protested both Zionist settlement and land purchase and demanded a Palestinian state. Between 1936 and 1939 there was a major Palestinian uprising against British rule and Zionist plans which took the form of a prolonged boycott and then an armed uprising. This uprising was repressed by the British with great brutality, with some 5,000 people killed or wounded and thousands more imprisoned. Draconian measures of detention without trial and collective punishment (e.g., blowing up the house of a whole family because of suspected insurrectionary activity by one member) were instituted. These military laws are still used by the Israeli military today to repress Palestinian resistance to Israeli Jewish rule. The Haganah, or Jewish army, got its first training under the British in this war against the Palestinians. Some of the major Israeli "Arab fighters," like Moshe Dyan, were trained in the techniques of total war against Palestinian villagers during this period.[12]

During the 1936–39 Palestinian revolt the British sponsored a series of commissions to study how to resolve the growing conflict. In 1937 the Peel Commission recommended a further partition of Palestine. (In 1922 the British, under Winston Churchill, had already separated the Transjordan into the separate state of Jordan, under the rule of the sons of Sharif Husain, who ruled with the help of a British-trained army.) The Peel Commission recommended a partition of the remaining region of Palestine into a small Jewish state (20 percent) and an Arab Palestinian state that would be attached to Jordan. The British would retain control of small strategic regions and roads. They further recommended that the Palestinian population be "transferred" out of the Jewish region into an enlarged Jordanian state. At this time Jews made up less than 10 percent of the population of Palestine.

The Peel Commission recommendation is important because it shaped what has remained the dominant Zionist solution to the "Palestinian problem"; namely, a partition of Palestine into an increasingly enlarged Jewish state and a dwindling Arab region, attached to Jordan, together with removal of most of the resident Palestinian population from the area designated as the Jewish state to the state of Jordan or other Arab states that might be persuaded to receive them. An independent Palestinian state and national identity are thus made impossible to achieve.[13]

In 1939, after prolonged Palestinian resistance and with a new world war looming on the horizon, the British abandoned the Zionist project that it had supported for twenty-two years. In an effort to prevent the Arabs from siding with Germany during the coming war, the British promised the Palestinians an independent state in five years. Meanwhile, Zionist immigration would be restricted to 75,000 over five years and land purchase would be limited. Both the Zionists and the Palestinian leaders rejected this British White Paper of 1939, the Palestinians because it still granted the Zionists too much and postponed Palestinian independence and the Zionists because it threatened to abandon them altogether at the very time when Hitler was sending European Jews fleeing for their lives.

Zionists saw this large, wealthy, and well-educated European Jewish population as the key to building the demographic and economic basis of a future Jewish state.[14] While they continually sought to open up the doors to immigration to Palestine that had been largely barred by the British, they also were anxious to discourage immigration of European Jews to North America or other regions, lest they become comfortable there and no longer be interested in going to Palestine.

The Zionist leaders, of course, did not envision that Hitler would actually seek to exterminate European Jewry. Like many others, they resisted this information when it was communicated to them. They simply assumed that European Jews would be made into refugees and thus could be tapped as the basis of building a Jewish state by the rapid transfer of four to five million Jews to Palestine after the war.

After the defeat of Hitler opened up the concentration camps to view, Jews, as well as most other Europeans and Americans, were horrified by the revelations of systematic human destruction. The millions of European Jews that Zionists had hoped would build the Jewish state had dwindled to a few hundred thousand starved and traumatized survivors. Zionist leaders threw their energies into forcing open the still barred gates of Palestine to these remaining European Jews and into using the horror of the Holocaust to persuade the leaders of the United Nations, particularly the United States, to compensate the remaining Jewish people by granting them a Jewish state.

In November 1947 the United Nations, under immense pressure from American Jews and American President Harry Truman, voted to partition Palestine into two states. Fifty-seven percent of the territory, including the best agricultural land, would go to the some 560,000 Jews, while 43 percent would go to the 1,320,000 Palestinian Arabs. At that time the Jewish *Yishuv* owned only about 7 percent of the land in the area designated for the Jewish state. The Zionists enthusiastically accepted this decision, and the Palestinians indignantly rejected it. Arab leaders announced that if this decision were not changed they would go to war.

It has been generally assumed in the West that Palestinians were totally unreasonable in this rejection. But it should be evident that such partition of what they regarded as their homeland was seen as completely unacceptable by Palestinians who were, at that time, still the majority population by some 70 percent. Also, for Palestinians, the European Zionist settlers were not an indigenous people "coming home," but a European population continuing the unjust Western history of colonial settlement and expropriation of land from the indigenous community, denying them their right to national self-determination.

Although the Zionist leaders accepted the U.N. partition plan as the legal basis of a Jewish state, in fact they did not intend to abide by its limits. Under the cover of war they hoped to expand its boundaries still more, remove as many as possible of the Palestinians from the Jewish area, and expropriate their land. To what extent this plan was fully formed before the actual outbreak of hostilities in 1948 has been the source of enormous debate. The general consensus of scholars today is that the general intention was clear in the mind of key leaders, such as David Ben Gurion, although the extent to which land could be appropriated and Palestinians expelled depended on the "opportunities" of war. Ben Gurion and other Zionists did not really want a peaceful settlement with the Arabs at that time, since this would have forced them to abide by the limits of the U.N. plan. They hoped for a war that would serve as the cover for the accomplishment of these goals. They were in secret negotiation with Jordan to occupy and annex what would remain of a Palestinian state.[15]

Despite great sword-rattling, only about 22,000 Arabs in five armies, fighting at cross-purposes with each other, actually entered the struggle during 1948–49.[16] After initial mobilization difficulties, the newly declared state of Israel was easily able to overrun these Arab armies with well-coordinated forces several times the size of the combined Arab troops. Under the cover of war the Israelis terrorized into fleeing or directly expelled at gunpoint some 780,000 Palestinians.[17] Israel also expanded its boundaries another 20 percent. This left only 23 percent of the Palestinian land remaining in two pieces: the Gaza Strip, under Egyptian occupation, and the West Bank, occupied and annexed by Jordan. Israel expropriated all the lands of those who left, and much land of those who remained, ending with more than 90 percent of the land under Jewish national control.

After the war, the state of Israel, together with the World Zionist Organization, sponsored mass immigration of Jews to the new state in order to expand the Jewish demographic base. Some 350,000 came from Europe. But since these immigrants were still too few, the Zionists turned to the Jews of the Arab world. Anti-Jewish reprisals against Arab Jews by the Arab world provided the opportunity to uproot many of these Jews, who previously had shown no interest in Zionism. More than 400,000 Arab Jews were "airlifted" to Israel during the 1950s.

Today the Israeli Jewish population has grown to over 3 million (usually listed as 3.5, but at least .5 million are resident abroad). The remnant of 180,000 Palestinians that remained in Israel after the 1948 expulsion has grown to 780,000. After the 1967 war, Israel also gained control of this large Palestinian population of the occupied West Bank and Gaza Strip, which today has grown to a million and a half. Another two million Palestinians, descendants of those expelled in 1948 and in successive wars, dwell in the surrounding Arab states. These Palestinians have refused to submerge their Palestinians national identity and "disappear" into the other Arab states, as the Zionists leaders expected. They have continued to demand their right to an independent Palestinian state and to return to the homes from which they have been expelled.

Thus the Jewish "majority," on which the claim to a Jewish state has been built, remains precarious. The combined Palestinian population of the region outnumbers Israeli Jews five to three, while the Palestinians within Israel and the Occupied Territories make up over 40 percent of the population.[18] Moreover, the number of descendants of Arab Jews has overtaken that of Jews of European descent and now comprises 60 percent of the Israeli Jewish population. So, despite a century of effort to shape Israel as a European Jewish enclave in the Middle East, it would seem that the long-term prognosis is that Israel will become a predominantly Arab Jewish state that must enter into cultural and political détente with its Palestinian Arab neighbors.

However, this development is being violently resisted by Israeli leaders, who are determined to hang on to their European dream of a Jewish state. In 1967, with the occupation of the remaining region of Palestine, Israel began a new process of Palestinian expulsion, Jewish settlement, and the expropriation of land and water resources of the region. The Palestinian population was not granted civil rights, but kept under draconian military repression in a way that has gone far beyond any rationale of security and has, as its primary purpose, the persuasion or forcing of as many as possible of this population to leave.

In December 1987, the Palestinians in the Occupied Territories began a prolonged revolt against Israeli rule. Israeli repression of this revolt has led to continual Palestinian deaths and injuries, as well as to the increase in the manifold violations of their human rights that have been detailed in other essays in this volume. Although in 1988 the Palestinian Liberation Organization finally accepted the principle of the partition of Palestine into a Jewish and a Palestinian state, Israeli leaders still resist this political settlement, hoping to be able to retain the major land and water resources of the whole of Palestine while persuading the Palestinian population either to acquiesce to Israeli rule or to depart. This stalemate, with its prolonged bloodletting, is likely to continue as long as the United States, which provides the primary funding for the state of Israel, declines to use its economic and political muscle to force a political settlement.

With the beginning of the Palestinian uprising in December 1987, the Israeli-Palestinian conflict has entered a new phase, one that precludes any return to the previous terms of discussion. Palestinians have developed a renewed hope that they will be free in their own homeland, even if that freedom is to be found in a part of historic Palestine on the West Bank and Gaza. For Jewish Israelis the uprising serves notice that the occupation, as they have known it, is over. The choices are now narrowed to perpetual military tyranny, Palestinian statehood, or an annexation of the territories that would mean Israel could no longer maintain its Jewish character.

The dilemmas experienced by Palestinians and by Israelis are agonizing, but in quite different ways. Palestinians in the occupied territories are paying a high price for their continued resistance. At this writing, over 900 Palestinians, mostly young adults and children, have already been killed and well over 80,000 injured. The strategies used by Israel to quell the uprising have expanded the types of repression used during the more than two decades of occupation: expropriation of land, demolition of houses, closing of educational institutions, imprisonment without trial, deportation of Palestinian leadership, beatings, torture, and death. For the Jewish community in Israel and around the world, these methods are shattering the pretenses of Israel's political and moral idealism.

The uprising has focused world attention on the struggle of the Palestinian people for self-determination. This new visibility of the Palestinian struggle, primarily in the form of nonviolent resistance, and the brutal methods used to suppress it, have thrown into question the myth of Israel's occupation as necessary and benign. A shift of relationship has begun between Israelis and Palestinians in Israel and in the occupied territories (or Occupied Palestine). This, in turn, is calling forth reevaluations in the relation of world Jewry to Israel and in how Western Christians understand their relation to Israel as a modern state. Many Western Jews and Christians have begun to hear the Palestinian voice for the first time. It has become more difficult simply to define the Palestinian as a stereotyped "terrorist" to be dismissed from discussion.

For Israeli Jews and for Palestinians under Israeli control, and also for Christians, Jews, and Palestinians in the West, the uprising is a watershed that has created a new possibility. It is evident to many that continued Israeli occupation of the West Bank and Gaza can only lead to more suffering and death of Palestinians, as well as to the progressive demoralization of Israeli Jews. At the same time, new factors have appeared that hold out promise of a resolution to one of the most costly and explosive conflicts in the world today. The meeting of the Palestine National Congress in Algiers in 1988, with its declaration of a Palestinian state in a framework that also recognized the existence of the state of Israel, allowed the United States government to shift its long refusal to talk with the PLO. The initiative of then-Secretary of State George Shultz in making contacts with the PLO, together with the increasing numbers of American Jews calling for a two-state solution, point to this as a time of new possibilities for the resolution of this conflict.

The negotiation of a resolution to the conflict will include many elements—diplomatic, military, and economic. This involves not only the immediate parties to the dispute, but the geopolitical context in which Western nations, particularly Britain and the United States, have long cast this issue. Most Jews of the world do not live in Israel, and now the majority of Palestinians also live outside historic Palestine, scattered throughout the Middle East and, in growing numbers, in North America as well. The Arab states each have a different perspective on this conflict, by no means identical with each other or with that of most Palestinians.

This volume focuses primarily on ideological, theological, and ethical aspects of the conflict and its resolution. Such a discussion of the mindsets that have blocked understanding necessarily involves much recounting of history as well. This is because one of the major barriers to peace has been disparate perceptions of what has happened since 1948. The Jewish Israeli community, and also the world Jewish community, on the one hand, and the Palestinian community, on the other, have had entirely different stories, entirely different pictures of reality. Dialogue must begin by bringing these stories together in one place where both can be heard.

In the Palestinian view, their story, their historical experience, has not been heard in the West. Their voices have been discounted and silenced. The Jewish Israeli interpretation of events alone has had authority for both Western Jews and Christians. Some of this disparity between the two views of reality has begun to be bridged by recent Israeli revisionist historians who have shown that some of the key "verities" about Israel's founding have been based on distortions and even deliberate fabrications. Israeli revisionist history has brought the Jewish Israeli story and the Palestinian story into greater harmony. But most Western Jews and Christians have yet to hear and understand the implications of this rethinking on the Jewish Israeli side or to give a hearing to the Palestinian story.

In this volume this gap between world views is not completely bridged, but we have tried to create a framework in which it can be begun. This framework brings progressive American Jews who are struggling to rethink their own world view to accommodate some room for Palestinian self-determination, together with key American Palestinians who present a revised Palestinian perspective that is ready to accommodate the existence of the state of Israel within a two-state framework. In the "middle" are American Christians who have been involved in Jewish-Christian dialogue and who also are concerned about justice for Palestinians. These Christians are seeking to sort out a revised Christian stance toward what many regard as agonizingly conflicting loyalties, to Jews and to Palestinians.

Any volume that seeks to bring together key voices to a dialogue necessarily involves selectivity. There are many areas of disagreement of world view involved in this conflict and thus many possible dialogues. There is an enormous spectrum of perspectives within the Jewish community, ranging from religious fundamentalist Zionists to secular leftist anti-Zionists. (There are also ultra-religious anti-Zionists.) There are big differences between how Western Christians (particularly those shaped by the history of the Holocaust and a wish to learn about the Jewish tradition) and Middle Eastern Christians have tended to see the issues. There are also areas of difference which we do not discuss here, between what has been the secular democratic perspective of westernized Palestinians and the more Islamic nationalist perspective that is emerging from the grassroots leadership of the uprising.

This volume does not represent all those voices. We have, first of all, limited it to an American discussion. All of the authors of these essays are American citizens. It does not include Middle Eastern Christians or Muslims, Israeli Jews, or Palestinians resident in the Middle East. These voices also are essential to the dialogue, but no one volume can do everything. The volume also does not include the full spectrum of American Jewish or Christian opinion. Christian fundamentalist pro-Zionists and more conservative Jewish religious Zionists have not been included.

We have limited the volume to American Jews, Christians, and Palestinians, not because this is the only or even, finally, the most important context of discussion. Ultimately the discussion must take place between Jewish Israelis and Palestinians who are to live together and side-by-side in Israel and Palestine. Such conversations are already underway. But the United States is a key actor in the conflict as the primary economic and ideological ally of Israel. Therefore a specifically American debate seemed to us an important piece of the puzzle. Secondly, we have selected thinkers coming from a progressive range of opinion because, in our opinion, they are the individuals most willing to listen to one another in the discussion.

We have included progressive Christians who have been involved in Jewish-Christian dialogue and Middle Eastern questions because we see the Christian churches as key shapers of moral opinion and the climate of public ethics in America. Therefore, how leading Christian thinkers sort out their concerns for more just relations to Jews and Judaism and their concerns with justice for the Palestinians can reshape the climate of American opinion. For such Christians, this discussion involves theological issues and ethical issues: how Christians relate to Judaism, to religious Zionist claims to the land, and to the relation of particularistic peoplehood and universal humanity.

For many Jews, theological issues are also involved, both in response to the Holocaust and to how Israel is understood in Jewish history, but the main framework in this volume is that of Jewish identity and ethics. For westernized Palestinians, whether of Christian or Muslim background, there is deep suspicion of religious terms of discussion since they have often experienced religion as divisive ideologies that block rational discourse. Thus the optimal framework of discussion for this group of American Palestinians is more in the realm of questions of historical truth and justice. By telling the Palestinian story, they call for the shaping of a new consensus about history and justice as the framework for ethical coexistence.

The volume is arranged in four sections. The first section contains American Jewish responses to the uprising, most of them written within its first months and shaped by the official Israeli response to the uprising, particularly by the shocking policy of lethal force and bone-breaking beatings. The writers, while selected from the liberal spectrum of American Jewish opinion, show some of the diversity of opinion and perspective of that community. However, the struggle with Jewish identity, the role of ethics in Jewish life and the difficult path of justice within the context of remembrance of the Holocaust, and the new realities of Jewish empowerment in the state of Israel provide common themes for these thinkers.

The second section contains essays by Christian theologians and ethi-

cists forced, in one way or another, to rethink their views of their relationship to Israel as a result of their growing recognition of Israeli injustice to
the Palestinians. These writers have been selected because they have all
been deeply involved in Jewish-Christian relations and thus have a longstanding commitment to overcoming anti-Semitism in Christian relations
to Jews. Several of these writers have also been involved in fighting for
Palestinian human and civil rights. The extent of their work in this second
area tends to shape their angle of vision. But each of these authors is struggling to distinguish between anti-Semitism and a critique of Israeli policies, and to find the just balance between concern for national security
and for Israel and Palestinian rights.

The third section features essays by leading Palestinian-American intellectuals. Most of these essays were also written in the first year of the
uprising, but reflect an integration of this event into a consciousness of
the Palestinian story that stretches back more than seventy years, to the
founding events of the conflict in the British Mandate for Palestine and the
Balfour Declaration. The perception that shapes these essays is that if
the West—both Jewish and Christian—were to recognize the injustice of
this story, they would recognize the justice of the Palestinian cause.

The volume concludes with three short reflections written by Marc Ellis
and Rosemary Ruether, editors of this volume and contributors to the Jewish and Christian sections, together with Ghada Talhami, an American
Palestinian of Muslim background who contributed an essay to the Palestinian section. These reflections attempt, from the three contexts, to
enunciate the emergent areas of common ground for discussion among the
three groups. But they also make clear that the discussion has only begun,
and many differences of viewpoint about both facts and values still remain.
Thus while this volume is not yet a dialogue, or even yet a common framework for dialogue, by bringing these voices together in one volume,
where readers can see their views side-by-side, we hope to have contributed something to an atmosphere of mediation in which consensus on
truth and justice can arise—an atmosphere that must be created if there is
to be just co-existence between Israeli Jews and Palestinians.

P A R T   1

Jewish Responses to the Uprising

One month after the Palestinian uprising began, with the announcement by the Israeli government that the *intifada* would be met with might and force, Rabbi Alexander Schindler, President of the Union of American Hebrew Congregations (which represents the Reform movement in the United States), sent an urgent message to the President of Israel. "I am deeply troubled and pained in sending you this message," wrote Schindler, "But I cannot be silent. The indiscriminate beating of Arabs, enunciated and implemented as Israel's new policy to quell the riots in Judea, Samaria and Gaza, is an offense to the Jewish spirit. It violates every principle of human decency. And it betrays the Zionist dream."[1]

This statement, released to the press by the president of a major Jewish organization, represented the beginning of an agonizing and often bitter debate within Jewish communities around the world regarding the state of Israel. But in a sense, the discussion both involved that state and went far beyond it. At stake were the central perennial questions of Jewish life, the centrality of ethical questions to Jewish identity, and the difficulties of a small and suffering community living in an often hostile world.

What Rabbi Schindler realized implicitly in his statement was that these questions were being asked in the context of Jewish empowerment, terrain unfamiliar to the Jewish people over two millennia. Moreover, this empowerment is haunted by the suffering of the Holocaust, which is almost beyond words and images.

It is hardly an exaggeration to suggest that with the stories and pictures of Jewish soldiers beating Palestinian youths, relayed daily in print and on television, the Jewish community in the United States had come face-to-face with the contradictions of being a long-suffering and recently empowered people. Could Jewish ethics survive the demands of a state whose occupation of the West Bank and Gaza was entering its third decade? Or were these ethics, developed during our suffering and victimization, out-

17

dated, even inapplicable to our situation of relative empowerment? The state of Israel and its role and priority in Jewish life also became a central issue. Was Israel, a small state, a refuge from European anti-Semitism, formed within Europe's progressive and democratic values, to become a powerful and expansionist state, brutalizing its neighbors and itself? And what was the role of Jews in America, those far from Israel who represented a community organized on behalf of the state, both financially and politically? What responsibility did American Jews have for Israel's governmental and military policies? Was this role one of silent supporter or mild critic, or did American Jews have the right to support, disagree with, or, in this dire situation, demand a course of action different from the one Israel was pursuing?

Most of the discussion in the American Jewish community that erupted in the wake of the Palestinian uprising has been conducted, at least in the public forum, in secular terms. But pained and sometimes fearful questions underlie the political rhetoric: What does it mean to be Jewish? Can a state sponsoring occupation and brutality claim to be Jewish? What is the Jewish mission in the world and can this—or rather *how* can this—be carried out within empowerment? These are intensely religious questions for any people to answer, but especially for the Jewish people, whose religious expression is bound to activity in history.

That is why we begin this section with an essay by Irving Greenberg, an Orthodox rabbi, whose earlier essays on Jewish history and theology seek to chart a path for the Jewish people in a time of God's silence, even God's apparent absence. According to Greenberg, the third era of Jewish history, beginning with the Holocaust, poses two fundamental shifts in Jewish consciousness and history: the movement from the sacramental to the secular in theological terms and from powerlessness to empowerment in political reality. Like other contemporary Jewish theologians, but with surprising honesty, Greenberg recognizes that the third era of Jewish history, with its components of secularity and empowerment, tests theological, ethical, and political presumptions developed among a previously more overtly religious and suffering people.[2]

Greenberg's essay "The Ethics of Jewish Power," written in the first months of the uprising, represents his further attempt to chart an ethical path for the Jewish people within empowerment. As he writes in his introduction, the assumption of power represents a fundamental change in the Jewish condition, and the Palestinian uprising forces Jews to "confront the profound challenge to religious understanding and ethical capacity implicit in this revolutionary change." Greenberg accurately describes the difficult moment facing the Jewish people:

Many people are devastated when they see Jewish hands dirtied with the inescapable blood and guilt of operating in the world. The classic Jewish self-image—the innocent, sinned-against sufferer—is being shattered. The traditional Jewish conviction of being morally superior, which has sustained our self-respect throughout centuries of persecution, is being tested. Who imagined the day that to re-establish order, Jewish soldiers would deliberately beat Arabs on the hands? Or smash arms and legs of some civilians, not just terrorists? Who anticipated that such a policy would be morally superior to the alternative in which clashes led to shootings with live ammunition and to deaths? Some recoil and wish Israel away; some lash out and blame particular leaders. Many yearn for an alternative to regain lost innocence. The truth is more painful and must be faced.

Rabbi Arthur Hertzberg, historian and former president of the American Jewish Congress, reminds us in his essay "The Illusion of Jewish Unity" that the Jewish community in America is hardly monolithic. In fact the community is divided in many ways, sometimes avoiding the hard questions, other times answering them in surprising ways. In his view, Israelis consistently misinterpret the depth of American Jews' loyalty to Israel and the independence of the Jewish community in America. Israeli Jews dangerously overestimate American Jewish support for the occupation. Hertzberg addresses tensions and misunderstandings between the state of Israel and the diaspora and exposes disparities between Jewish perception and reality.

If Greenberg analyzes the assumption of power and Hertzberg the divisions within the Jewish community, Judith Plaskow, a leading feminist scholar, suggests that the patriarchal concepts and structures of Israeli life are barriers to a transformation of power and division. Within Israel and between Israelis and Palestinians, the result of patriarchy in Israel is threefold, dividing Jewish men and women, European and non-European Jews, and Jews and Palestinians. Though the history and politics are complex, Plaskow charts a different way of viewing the Middle Eastern question so that oppressive power and divisive difference can be transformed into the building of a new communal ethos in Israel and Palestine.

Another voice included here is that of Michael Lerner, editor of the progressive Jewish journal, *Tikkun*. *Tikkun* was founded during the year before the *intifada* to provide a voice for the many Jews who resisted the neoconservative drift of the established Jewish community. Lerner's editorial "The Occupation: Immoral and Stupid," written in response to the uprising, crystallized the thoughts of individuals and movements within the

Jewish community who had felt voiceless in previous years. Lerner's concern is to demand the end of the occupation for practical and ethical reasons; his anger at Israel's current policies comes from moral outrage but also from deep concern about Israel's survival and the survival of the Jewish people. To Lerner, the contradiction is clear: "Israel is putting its supporters in the agonizing position of either rejecting its current policies or rejecting some of the central tenets of Judaism." His essay is passionate and nuanced. In a powerful statement of Jewish dissent, Lerner calls on the Israeli government to "stop the beatings, stop the breaking of bones, stop the late night raids on people's homes, stop the use of food as a weapon of war, stop pretending that you can respond to an entire people's agony with guns and blows and power. Publicly acknowledge that the Palestinians have the same right to national self-determination that we Jews have and negotiate a solution with representatives of the Palestinians!"

As a contemporary historian of religion Marc H. Ellis is attempting to reveal the contradictions, tensions, and possibilities within contemporary Jewish history that will inevitably lead to new Jewish theological expressions. As Ellis describes it, the normative theology of the Jewish community—Holocaust theology—arose within the context of the experience of suffering during the Holocaust and the struggle for empowerment in Israel and the diaspora. This theology crystallized in the wake of the June 1967 Six Day War, which held the possibility of destruction and ended in an almost miraculous victory. Yet because of the occupation, and in light of the uprising, the Six Day War is now entering its third decade. According to Ellis, Holocaust theology looked toward Jewish empowerment but, upon arrival at its goal, has been unable to analyze empowerment critically. Thus the Jewish community has a theology that tells Jews who we were—weak and helpless—but is in need of a theology to tell us who we have become—powerful and often oppressive. Theology is important here because in the uprising the question facing the Jewish people involves politics, military security, and economics but also the deepest theological presuppositions of post-Holocaust Jewry. The call here is for a movement of the Jewish people toward the Palestinian people, as difficult and paradoxical as this might sound at first hearing.

The final essay is written by Rabbi Arthur Hertzberg, "An Open Letter to Elie Wiesel." Here Hertzberg appeals to the leading Jewish spokesperson of our day, the Nobel laureate Elie Wiesel. Yet this letter is more than an appeal to a person whose voice and written word is respected around the world; rather, it represents a plea to the survivors of the Holocaust, which in a way is to all Jews alive today, to look honestly at the situation of Israel and speak the truth publicly. Surely for many, like Wiesel, it is not easy, but as Hertzberg reminds us, "We show the truest love of Israel and the Jewish people when we remind ourselves that, in strength or in weakness, we survive not by prudence and not by power, but through justice."

1

The Ethics of Jewish Power

IRVING GREENBERG

We are at the beginning of a fundamental change in the Jewish condition: the assumption of power. After almost two millennia, Jews are again exercising sovereignty in their own land. In the Diaspora and in Israel, the Jewish people is taking responsibility for its fate in the realm of politics and history. Only now are we beginning to confront the profound challenge to religious understanding and ethical capacity implicit in this revolutionary change.

Many people are devastated when they see Jewish hands dirtied with the inescapable blood and guilt of operating in the world. The classic Jewish self-image—the innocent, sinned-against sufferer—is being shattered. The traditional Jewish conviction of being morally superior which has sustained our self-respect throughout centuries of persecution is being tested. Who imagined the day that to re-establish order, Jewish soldiers would deliberately beat Arabs on the hands? Or smash arms and legs of some civilians, not just terrorists? Who anticipated that such a policy would be morally superior to the alternative in which clashes led to shootings with live ammunition and to deaths? Some recoil and wish Israel away; some lash out and blame particular leaders. Many yearn for an alternative to regain lost innocence. The truth is more painful and must be faced.

Power corrupts. But there is no other morally tolerable choice. The alternative is death. This is the lesson that the Jewish people learned from the Holocaust.

The Holocaust demonstrated that, thanks to concentrations of power created by modern culture and technology, there has been an enormous shift in the balance of power between the victims and the persecutors. The victims were always weaker but there were inherent limits in the power of the dominant groups. Now many of the limits on the aggressors—ranging from moral taboos on killing to technological limitations—have been shat-

22

tered. The total imbalance of power from 1939 to 1945 corrupted the murderers into ever more destructive behavior. Powerlessness encouraged the indifference of the bystanders. In the face of Jewish political passivity and weakness even great liberals like Franklin D. Roosevelt and Winston Churchill did little or nothing to stop the carnage. The overwhelming force tormented or broke many victims before they were killed. Thereby, Jews learned that power corrupts, absolute power corrupts absolutely, but absolute powerlessness corrupts even more.

Driven by the will to live, survivalist Jews have become overwhelmingly Zionist, even if they have no intention of ever living in Israel. Goaded by the absolute pain of the Holocaust, American public opinion became pro-Zionist and has stood by Israel ever since. All understand that Jews must have access to the kind of power and guaranteed haven that only a government and an army can provide. This lesson has been learned by others as well. Liberation movements have arisen in the former colonial world, as well as among women, blacks, and other minorities worldwide.

Erstwhile victims should not be romanticized. The moral purity of victims is often a function of the fact that they have no power to inflict evil. They are equally, sometimes more, subject to being corrupted by accession to power. Throughout history, when downtrodden classes would arise, they would often turn a murderous fury against the equally victimized neighboring Jews. Many a liberation movement has denied the Jewish right to liberation. It is delusion or self-righteous flattery to believe that Jews can avoid the same tendencies. The historical challenge of power must be taken on with eyes open.

The Bible recounts that when Israel's ancestral father paused in his flight and turned to defend himself against the oncoming armies of Esau, "Jacob feared and was greatly distressed" (Genesis 32:7). Said the Rabbis: "'Jacob feared' that he might be killed, 'and was greatly distressed' that he might kill others." The costs of power are always both human and moral.

1. The Moral Philosophy of Power

Renouncing Power

For almost two thousand years, Jews and Christians have glorified the renunciation of power. The original moral insight of Judaism was that might does not make right and that power itself must be judged by its results. Over the ages, the original morality principle was steadily extrapolated until it became an idealist code of the powerless. (This is what Nietzsche mocked when he dismissed the two religions as slave morality.) Jews went into exile and a state of powerlessness. Living on sufferance, Jews had to accept the political order as given and seek to accommodate to it or serve it. Christianity interpreted redemption to be a spiritual rather than a political/economic matter and made the exercise of power irrelevant or a distraction from the ultimate goal. The principles "turn the other cheek" and the inherent wickedness of any force or violence replaced the prophetic demand for social justice. Power itself became identified as the source of evil by people who taught that it was better to save one's soul and give up activity in the world.

A good expression of this tendency was incarnate in the growing Jewish culture of passivity. The medieval Jewish Mussar (ethical) literature treated anger in any manifestation as an extreme sin, even as idolatry. Jews, who in biblical times were warriors, now focused on the talmudic idea that God made Israel swear not to revolt against the nations in whose midst it served its term of exile. Jewish actions to redeem the world were turned inward to individual and community concerns or were directed to mystical, cosmic realms. The concept of the Jews as a merciful, compassionate people was extended to the idea that the Jew will not or even cannot shed blood. Gentile persecution seemed all the more evil by comparison with Jewish helplessness.

The idealistic tendency of Western culture was adopted and greatly strengthened by the liberal/progressive/utopian wing within modern culture. Liberal idealization of human nature and repugnance for war or *realpolitik* sometimes lead uncritical liberals to confuse the dream of worldwide peace and the ultimate victory of ideals with the actual facts. Such ethicists tend to see the use of force as atavistic behavior and the moral ambiguities of statecraft as ethically inferior—both doomed to die out. The views of this wing have been particularly attractive to Jews and other Americans as well.

When, under the influence of modern values, Zionists set out to create a Jewish state, most Jews were neutral if not opposed. Traditionalists said it was impious to take power into one's own hands and that the state was premature (the Messiah not having arrived). Modernists said it was unnecessary to take power into one's own hands and that the state was too late (universal modern culture having arrived). The sledgehammer blow of the Holocaust smashed these constellations of beliefs and changed the course of Jewish history. The Jewish people determined not to yield up hope, but to recreate life and human dignity. The consensus was that Jews must take power into their own hands in order to live. The State of Israel was established. Jews set out to shape a society in which justice and *tzedakah* would govern. Thus, they reaffirmed the ancient Jewish belief in the call to perfect this world and took up the classic Jewish role of modeling a society on the way to that final redemption for all humanity.

Taking Power

The creation of the State of Israel places the power in the hands of Jews to shape their own destiny and to affect and even control the lives of others. This is a revolutionary 180-degree turn in the moral situation. The dilemmas of power are far different from the temptations and problems of powerlessness. Jews have been fond of contrasting Christian persecution of Jews with Jewish innocence. Modern Jews often juxtapose Christianity's failure to lead the fight for social justice in the medieval world with the Hebraic prophetic passion for helping the oppressed. Christian implication in upholding an unjust status quo and abusing Jews is contrasted with Jewish martyrdom, and Judaism's high moral standards. These short-hand images incorporate elements of self-flattery. You need power to do harm as you need power to do good. It remains to be seen whether Jewry's innocence reflects its past powerlessness or some intrinsic higher moral performance. The test will come now in Judaism's relationship to Jewish sovereignty and Jewry's ability to ethically elevate the Jewish exercise of power. The entire issue must be addressed with absolute seriousness. We are dealing with a matter that is an historic turning point. The costs are already staggeringly high; the moral risks are even higher.

2. The Human Costs of Power

The Jewish people has been paying the costs of the assumption of power for more than forty years. Thousands of *halutzim* (Zionist pioneers) voluntarily declassed themselves, gave up hearth and home to go struggle with hostile authorities, swamps, malaria, and flinty soil to build the infrastructure of the future Israel.

Hundreds of thousands of survivors, after going through hell and losing everything, chose confinement in D.P. camps or internment in Cyprus under primitive conditions for additional years rather than yield their part in building a Jewish homeland. More than half a million Oriental Jews were stripped of their wealth and fled the Arab lands to join in the formation of the Jewish state. Thousands of their families lived in shacks for years and suffered the loss of their native cultural and geographic guide-posts until they rebuilt their lives. The price of parental authority lost, of children deracinated, of old people dying in an unfamiliar place, or the normal existential difficulties compounded by uprooting and migration was enormous—but Jews paid it to build a new Jewish society.

When the State of Israel was declared, it was invaded, precipitating the first of the "Wars for Israeli Independence." During this first war, Israel had neither the armaments nor the trained soldiers that it needed. At one battle, near Latrun, hundreds of survivors were rushed from shipside and thrown with inadequate arms and no training into a desperate battle against the Jordanian Legion. Most died. Individually, they were the remnant—one from a family, two from a city. With each one, whole worlds died. They should have been treated like whooping cranes or some other re-mainder of life so rare that its surviving exemplars must be sheltered from normal history. But the pressure was too great. Jews were too weak and nothing could be held back. When the war ended, Israel's losses stood at 6,000 dead—almost 1% of the Jewish population. The equivalent today in the United States would be 2,000,000 people.

Every Israeli has been on permanent service ever since. From 1950 to 1956, there were 3,000 armed clashes with Arab regular or irregular forces outside Israeli territory and some 6,000 acts of sabotage or theft by infil-trators. Israeli men and women serve for two years in the army, followed by reserve training up to the age of forty-nine. Behind these deceptively simple statistics is an infinite chain of human cost.

Every year, thousands of students miss examinations and have to rear-range their lives; stores and artists' galleries close for weeks because the sole proprietor is away for *miluim* (reserve duty). How many fathers miss births or birthday parties? How many children do not get put to bed by their fathers? How many wives sleep alone? And all these people are the lucky ones because their lives go on. How many widows lie awake night after night in the isolation of their torn lives?

In every decade, the costs have been paid again. I think of two close friends, American families that went on *aliya*. Their turn came in the Lebanon war. One lost a twenty-three-year-old son, a student in Yeshiva, handsome, full of life, full of plans for the future. The other's son-in-law was one of two pilots who did not survive the downing of his plane on the mission that uncovered the Syrian introduction of Sam-8s into Lebanon. He was a young father, and brilliant, a warm person who had extraordinary promise as a scholar. He put that aside to stay in the professional Air Force because that was where he was needed. He left behind a young wife, two small children, and grieving parents and in-laws.

These are the people that I, a sheltered American Jew living six thousand miles away, know. Who can chronicle the rest—the Israeli family that lost a father in 1948, a child in 1967, a grandchild in 1982? . . . A relative's brother who was killed by a random terrorist bomb placed on a bus of travelers in Jericho? . . . A friend attended a funeral in which the bereaved father was the only survivor of his family from Europe. The father told the mourners that one son was killed in 1967, another in 1973, and with the loss of his final child in 1982, the family was now permanently cut off.

Of course, in this generation, even paying these terrible costs of power is a betterment. Once we stood in a group, shell-shocked at the final tabulation of more than 2,500 dead in the Yom Kippur war and asked ourselves: will Israel be able to live with such ongoing costs? Edward Luttwack restored our perspective. Said Luttwack: only thirty years ago, the Nazis killed 10,000–15,000 Jews a day with *Einsatzgruppen* (shooting squads) or gas chambers and every death weakened Jewish security, leaving the other Jews more vulnerable to destruction. The Yom Kippur loss was staggering. But with their deaths, the 2,500 reversed a dangerous invasion, secured the lives of their loved ones, and left every Jew in the world safer. And their inheritance went for their children and their people and not to enrich their murderers . . . But this contrast does not stop the pain.

To arrive at a rough appraisal of the human cost of power, one would have to take each of the ten thousand dead from the five Israeli wars and multiply them by the lives cut off, the families left behind, the worlds unbuilt. Then one would have to multiply the total by three or four: for thousands who were wounded or disabled in those past forty years. For every paraplegic, handicapped, or permanently scarred soldier, one would have to add the interminable hours of struggling and living with the physical and psychic costs of going on. Then multiply all this by the countless families sharing or touched by those lives. Who but God can measure the oceans of tears that have been shed in this process?

Despite these terrible costs of assuming power, there has been an overwhelming consensus in the Jewish community that this people must pay the toll and proceed. For one, the alternative to power would be death. Then, too, the consciousness of the rectitude and morality of the Jewish cause sustained the people. Despite a continuing series of wars and a universal draft, the State of Israel, over the course of its forty years, had very few conscientious objectors; before the Lebanon war, hardly any. (The objections to women serving in the army and the demand for exemptions for religious scholars are connected to issues of modesty and sheltered cultural existence rather than to the ethics of war and violence.) Despite heavy casualties, the morale and willingness to fight of Israeli soldiers has remained high; they feel they are fighting for home, family, and life itself. And as they overcome their initial dependence on maximal acceptance and approval from gentiles, diaspora Jews also grew more and more steadfast in support of Israel.

But the issue of the moral costs of power has grown ever more pressing over the past few decades. The widespread sense that Jews must hold themselves to a higher standard of ethics has increasingly come into conflict with the morally compromising situations that Israel has entered. The types of allies that Israel sometimes works with make some uneasy. The links to South Africa have drawn the most attention in recent years as the anti-apartheid movement has grown. But the Somozist connection in Central America also became highly controversial in the 1970s as the Sandinistas drew the support of the world's left. From a moral perspective, the Lebanese war was the most marginal war Israel fought. Unlike the Six Day and Yom Kippur wars, the existence of a clear and present danger to actual Israeli survival was not beyond argument, leaving the moral side effects (such as civilian casualties and destruction of local society) open to severe challenges. Willingness to criticize Israeli policy has grown—especially among American Jewish leadership. This phenomenon has been portrayed as a weakening of the Israel-Diaspora bonds. I believe that criticism properly done represents not a backing away from Israel but an important piece of the Jewish ethic of power currently in creation. Still, many people feel that any criticism is betrayal so the conflict over the moral costs of power has escalated.

"Moral" delegitimation of Israel has grown in certain radical circles. At the height of the outcry over the Sabra-Shatila massacres, it appeared for a few days that Israel might have been implicated in instigating the massacre. A leading American Jewish theologian, in an anguished *cri de coeur*, lamented that if this was the cost of the Jewish state, then the cost was too high! My personal reaction was: I do not believe that Israel would do such a thing. But let us assume the worst—what if it had organized the massacre (God forbid). The action should be condemned unequivocally. However, the United States of America was made possible in part by a systematic genocide of the Indians, pursued over the course of centuries. This was shameful and it remains a permanent moral blot on America's record. But did anybody suggest that the cost was too high and it were better that there had never been a United States? The Soviet Union has enslaved hundreds of millions, has persecuted Jews, has engaged in a genocidal invasion of Afghanistan. Does anyone seriously propose that it has lost its legitimacy as a state?

It seems clear that without some context of a Jewish ethic of power to guide us along our historical way, we may lose our moral compass. Dangerous alternatives tempt us at every step: undermining Israel or abandoning it through excessive criticism and faulty judgments—or betraying Israel by giving it a moral blank check and uncritical love.

3. The Moral Costs of Power; or, Toward an Ethical Jewish Power

Reality and Morality

When the vast majority of believers have little say in their own fate, religions legitimately play their classic role of comforting the afflicted by focusing on such teachings as the dignity of the powerless, the preciousness of suffering, the moral heroism of renunciation and asceticism. On balance, Judaism and Christianity moved toward more idealistic moral codes as their power diminished. Morality standards were developed by people with little ability to carry them out. This led to more utopian and absolute standards—standards relatively unchecked by reality. Worldly power was generally left to those who had it. They had fewer qualms about exercising it. This increased inequality and the corrupting effects of power. But the religious community prided itself on its moral purity and blamelessness.

The new rules cannot be identical with the old. Operations in the real world are affected by human error and vested interest. There is no one moral policy carried out but an endless series of judging specific situations and reconciling conflicting claims and shifting facts. This means linking ultimate ends and proximate means in a continual process; it cannot be done without involvement, partial failures, guilt. Since real policy rarely meets the absolute standard of the ideal, those who exercise power are in constant tension with the prophets who denounce their moral failures. The contrast is not always in favor of the prophets. If those in power are responsible people, they must renounce prophetic stances. Prophets can rely on spiritual power and make absolute demands for righteousness.

Governments have obligations to protect people. On the other hand, when governments ignore prophets, they usually end up abusing the people they are supposed to protect.

What appears to be moral in the abstract may work poorly in actual practice. An alternative, more compromising approach may achieve its goals brilliantly and come out ahead. This is why reality eventually disciplines moralism. Says the Talmud: Those who are merciful to people who deserve cruelty will end up being cruel to people who deserve mercy. Often the punishment for failure to take reality into account is to do the opposite of what was intended. In the 1930s, an underground religious group considered assassinating Hitler but decided against it on the grounds that there is no moral right to kill a bad ruler. The millions of innocent victims of Hitler's later murderous war on the Jews and others could well claim that the righteousness of the German underground paved the way for the cruel sadistic war on them. Similarly, in 1967, the absolute radical demand for justice of many in the American New Left led them to denounce the all-too-human, bourgeois Israel with its social imbalances. As a result, they ended up supporting slaveholding and feudal Arab oil sheiks intent on genocide. Those murderous designs were frustrated by Israel's strength, no thanks to the uncompromising radical moralism that only led its practitioners to de facto collaboration with attempted mass murderers.

Some Principles of Power

The beginning of ethical wisdom is the recognition that in an unredeemed world, one must be able and willing to exercise power to protect or advance the good. Yet, power is not self-validating; giving power that kind of respect is tantamount—or will lead—to idolatry. All exercises of power must be judged by the standard of perfecting the world and the triumph of life that such exercises seek to advance. However, any exercise of power, no matter how well-intentioned, will have inescapable "immoral" side effects. Yet, if doing nothing leads to greater evil than doing something, then failure to act is moral default. Those who refuse to use such "immoral" means are guilty of placing their moral image above the suffering of others—which is a form of selfishness.

The truly moral do not avoid stain by not exercising power. They act, but only when necessary and they seek to reduce suffering caused by their actions to the minimum. The firm moral principle is that *given the evil that cannot be avoided, there is still an ideal way of exercising power.* A moral army uses no more force than necessary. If it uses less force than necessary, and fails, it betrays those it seeks to protect or its own soldiers who died in vain. If the amount of force necessary is unclear, then willingness to take losses to avoid causing innocent suffering is the ethical test.

Sometimes, there is a deadlock that can only be broken by an action which has immoral elements (civilian casualties, etc.). But the justification for causing innocent suffering—that greater suffering will be prevented by this action—is not assured. In such cases, only the outcome will decide if the action was morally right (on balance). In other words: If it works, it is moral. If it fails [to yield less suffering on balance], it is immoral. In abstract ethical systems, morality is independent of success; in actual life, it is not. In a perfect world, there will be no gap between reality and principle, which is why Judaism strives to bring the Messiah. In the interim, the good is often advanced by a morally ambiguous process.

Moral acts producing immoral side effects are intermixed with flawed acts yielding good effects. The historical record shows that participation in power often leads to the weakening of conscience unless there is some continual refreshment of judgment through exposure to prophetic norms. Happy is the people which learns to reconcile prophetic demands with the compromising arts of governance and real policies. Those who care inescapably take on guilt—and they know it. Show me a people whose hands are not dirty and I will show you a people which has not been responsible. Show me a people which has stopped washing its hands and admitting its guilt, and I will show you a people which is arrogant and dying morally.

4. On Being Normal

The exercise of power is unrelenting; in history, one cannot take up one's marbles and go home—this is especially true when, as in the case of Israel, the state is surrounded by a sea of unreconciled enemies. Power is corrupting, and the Jewish people's relative weakness (compared to larger powers) narrows the margins for purely magnanimous, morally idealistic behavior even more. The net effect of constant struggle and involvement in morally ambiguous situations can be readily projected. Over time, the gap between the ideal and reality is reduced; the movement is in the direction of the demands of reality. The behavior of all people in history can be fit within a bell-shaped curve of moral performance. Inevitably, the continuous exercise of sovereignty will narrow the spread between the behavior of Jews and of other people.

This is what classical Zionists meant when they glorified the "normalization" of the Jewish people. They recognized that many pathological social phenomena were absent among Jews because there was no Jewish holistic political society. The price of an organic Jewish community—one not confined to urban ghetto areas or money lending professions by discrimination, or absent a proletariat because it had no means of production—would be crime and prostitution and a host of ills of modern life. The price was inescapable—but, in light of the greater good, more than worth it.

In dreaming about the future reality, the founding Zionists could romanticize and soften the hard edges of the unborn pathology. Now that we are back in history, we see, up close, the hard edges of social sickness and corruptible power. Jewish military force is not exempt from killing innocents or skewing lives or officers' privileges or attracting camp followers. Only "how much" can be modified by Jewish action and ethical will.

This is a painful admission for most Jews. But to believe otherwise is to commit a "genetic fallacy" and assume that Jews are intrinsically more moral than other people. Such a belief bespeaks a covert racism. After all, Jews are like other people—only more so. The Bible portrays the Jews as no better inherently than other nations. Its picture of Jewish sovereignty shows a deeply flawed record. "Not because of your righteousness does the Lord your God give you the good land to inherit, for you are a morally stubborn, recalcitrant people . . ." (Deuteronomy 9:6). The illusion of ethical perfectionism grows out of the record of millennial powerlessness whose results are projected incorrectly into the new reality. It also happens that in coming out of an extended period of heightened moral consciousness, initial behavior may be more ethically sensitive. The memories of suffering are fresher and the moral energy released by the shift from potential to actual behavior is unusually high. But such releases are temporary phenomena. They are abnormal; they can be utilized once or twice but are not automatically self-renewing.

While this truth is sad, it should not be a cause for depression or moral recoil. In actual history, excellence is contextual—and always possible. Exercising heroic self-control, within the give and take of self-interest and political/military pressures, utilizing ethical restraints of a particularly demanding nature—such as the Jewish covenantal ethic of *tikkun olam* [perfection of the world]—will yield a record that is the highest achievement; one worthy of honor and celebration. Five or ten percent better than the other nations—that is what it means to be "a light unto the nations." To be perfect is the light that never was on land or sea. The Promised Land is a normal land whose inhabitants are raised to a heightened awareness of God and human ethical responsibility. The chosen people is a normal people called to an intensified commitment to create a moral community as part of a human-divine partnership to perfect this world. Even if it were possible to set up a perfect society, it would have a limited impact. For the most part, it would be so far beyond the capacity of others to imitate that it would be dismissed out of hand. (As it is, the five-percent-better model has evoked anti-Semitism, the most sinister, protean, and wide-ranging, social pathology in human history. If the Jews really were perfect, they would be insufferable.) Perfection is better than life but non-existent. In history, less is more.

5. The Building Blocks of an Ethic of Power

Once it is recognized that an ethic of Jewish power must be established within the parameters of normal politics, it becomes clear that Jews cannot be beyond criticism. It will take a struggle to prevent Jews from lowering their guard and yielding to all the corruption of history. Since moral erosion and/or compromise is inevitable, the key question is: what can be done to uphold an ethical standard? The first answer is a paradox. Sin is inevitable; therefore, the ethical health of a society is judged not so much by its ideal procedures or potential ability to do good but by the excellence of its corrective mechanisms. Every moral person and society will misbehave. "There is no righteous person in the world who will do good and never sin" (Ecclesiastes 7:21). The truly moral person and society will be willing to admit the error and organize to correct it.

One cannot depend only on good will for moral reparation. There must be built-in mechanisms to challenge and test the exercise of power. When the will to do good falters, the structure is there to encourage correction. It follows that the fundamental building block of an ethic of Jewish power is a structure not a principle. The most effective ethical structure in any situation is a balance of power. To put it in classic Jewish theological terms: only God's power should be absolute (and God has waived exercising that degree of power through commitment to operating through covenant!)

To relativize human power, one must distribute it widely. One-sided force corrupts both the governors and the governed, the aggressors and the victims. The more one-sided power is, the less likely it is to be challenged on its merits. Countervailing force, exercised independently, checks

33

the tendencies to abuse the other—for the other has the power of self-protection. Being in a situation when one cannot act with impunity (or being forced into better actions by the ability of the other to retaliate) usually brings out the best behavior in people.

The ethical ideal would be a balance of power in the Middle East in which Israel cannot dominate the Arab nations and the Arab nations cannot dream of destroying Israel by force. Ideally, the Palestinian Arabs should have their own state and should treat the Jews living on the West Bank with dignity. They should respect Jews' rights and cultures just as the internal Arab minority in the Jewish state has a vital inner life and real political power to protect itself. Arab sovereignty should check potential Israeli excesses even as Israeli might should check Arab aggressiveness. The interaction of balance of power combined with cultural and religious openness creates the best setting for the flowering of ethical relationships and true brotherhood. (According to the Bible, God gives up absolute power and enters into covenantal self-restrictions for the sake of loving and being loved by humanity.)

There is a serious flaw in this statement of the ideal. Major elements in the Arab world are unreconciled to Jewish sovereignty and would gladly destroy Israel if they could. Under such circumstances, a balance of power is not morally acceptable. A situation of approximate equality of force tempts the aggressors to try for one strategy, one breakthrough, that can tilt the balance in their favor. There should be no equation between one people threatened with extermination and one people fearful, at worst, of expansionism. Therefore, the ethically ideal balance of power must be a dynamic one. As acceptance of Israel goes up, the balance should be adjusted toward greater military and political parity.

In the interim, Israel should seek maximum Arab autonomy in Judea and Samaria by encouraging the emergence of indigenous leadership willing to live in peace with the Jewish state. Let the word go out unequivocally from Israel that Palestinian Arabs can earn autonomy and even a state by seeking peace and taking risks for it. In theory, the PLO also can earn the status of a negotiating partner with Israel. The PLO would have to disavow its call for the destruction of Israel and purge its "rejection front" elements—preferably by military confrontation—to make clear that it really intends to live in peace with Israel. Of course, this will not happen until the Arab nations and the world stop romanticizing and encouraging the murderous elements in PLO leadership.

Internal sources of moral balance of power are equally crucial. Religious pluralism will prevent any one group from seizing control and imposing its unchecked will (in the name of God) on policy. A free press and independent media are major sources of moral criticism and of evaluation of policies from within. Whatever the excesses of media sensationalism, infantile leftism, etc., the costs are well worth it. The channels of communication are indispensable to moral regulation and to insure that prophetic voices are heard throughout the society. Plural sources of values—synagogues and churches, universities, the private sector, wide distribution of economic power, separation of business and unions, mediating agencies and institutions—are all major contributors to a moral and political balance of power.

World Jewry also can play a role in establishing standards of behavior. Since Israel is wielding sovereignty, its moral responses will be skewed toward realism. World Jewry's responses, being those of observers on many issues, will be skewed toward "idealist" models. These tendencies can be mutually corrective. As loving critics, world Jewry can be truly helpful to Israel in its effort to keep on the moral path. However, the key is to avoid stereotypical positions and extreme polarization. A conventional diaspora idealist critique of Israeli policy will not be very useful. It could undermine Israeli viability and Israel would be well advised to dismiss it as "armchair generalizing." It would be far more helpful if world Jews showed deep understanding of the pragmatic parameters of policy and offer morally realistic advice and criticism. Similarly, it would be healthier if Israeli society generated internal prophetic criticism side-by-side with a mainstream policy blend of Jewish ideals and Jewish realities. The balance of king, priest, and prophet was the glory of Biblical covenantal, ethics and politics—when it worked. As the prophets taught us, loving criticism is the highest loyalty and failure to make judgments is a betrayal of the covenant and of the policy makers. On the other hand, extreme polarization on policy between kings and prophets led to ethical breakdown and disastrous policies.

Another major source of moral parameters for a Jewish ethic is the internal culture, its paradigms and memory. Jews are committed to the redemption of the world. But the covenantal process mediates this utopianism by encouraging a step-by-step progression toward the ideal goal. The ideal of freedom was achieved by a gradual narrowing and improving of the conditions of slavery. Thus entrenched injustice and vested interests could be dealt with realistically and overcome gradually. A contemporary ethic of Jewish power also should combine moral utopianism with a pragmatic methodology of perfection. The balancing models of the Exodus and the covenant can serve as guiding principles for power when they are yoked to hard-headed analysis and practical steps toward the desired goals. And, as the classic tradition reminds us, the memory of Jewish suffering is supposed to increase empathy for those who are oppressed or those who will suffer because of Jewish exercise of power.

The memories of being a slave in Egypt or isolated in ghettoes in Nazi Germany should be ever present when Israel makes judgments on policy vis-a-vis South Africa. Memories of being a stranger in Egypt, in medieval Europe, in a Muslim *mellah* should be guiding Jews who set policy vis-a-vis the Arab minority in Israel. The memories are specifically intended to create greater concern for the other. Thus Meir Kahane correctly summons Jews to keep the memory of the Holocaust vividly before them in setting policy. But he reverses the ethical direction of the classic tradition in allowing the pain of remembered suffering to deaden Jewish conscience. To encourage Jews to turn Arabs into refugees or into victims of violence is to continue the Holocaust, not oppose it.

6. On Being Normal: Case Studies in Ethical Judgments

On Kahanism

Some people are shocked by the emergence of Meir Kahane and are surprised by the widespread hearing, if not sympathy, that he has won. The sense of shock reveals the underlying presence of the "genetic fallacy," the belief that Jews are intrinsically morally pure. Jews are as capable of racism or mafia morality as any other people. Kahanism should be fought but it should not come as a surprise. Nor should it be the occasion for hand wringing and claims that Israel democracy is about to go down the tubes. In any normal society there are people prone to lashing out in anger and frustration at unending war and economic disadvantage and turning to simplistic solutions at the expense of others. Kahane's appeal is particularly strong among disadvantaged Sephardi youths and teenagers (especially in development towns where unemployment is high and opportunities are limited) facing disruption of their lives by military service, possible war, and four decades of future reserve service. Correction of the underlying problems to undercut the appeal of demagogues is the way democracies respond to such phenomena.

Given forty years of war, the uprooting of Sephardi Jews from Arab lands, and the disadvantages they suffered in living their lives in Israel, the percentages who follow Kahane or even Sharon is lower than one would expect. Add the number of Israeli soldier casualties in four wars (at least 50,000—dead and wounded) to the direct civilian casualties of the terrorism of the last forty years. The total number involved is over 70,000. Include those injured in army service and the total exceeds 100,000. Consider that each of these casualties has an immediate family. This means that close to half-a-million Israelis have experienced direct casualties in their own lives or families. Kahane's vote in 1984 (25,907—1.2 percent of the votes cast) constitutes a fraction of those who should hate Arabs irrationally, simply for reasons of personal loss. Kahane himself admits that individual acts of terror as well as extended periods of intense conflict and terror feed directly into his support. Given the countless other reasons for rage and frustration to which a vote for Kahane offers some outlet, so low a vote for him is testimony to an extraordinarily high level of emotional self-restraint and mature electoral behavior on the part of the Israeli voter.

In 1932, facing a great depression (but not genocide!), the American electorate gave the Socialist and Communist parties 984,736 votes, about two and a half percent of the total votes cast. In 1936, bogged down in that same depression (but no violence) the American voters gave William Lemke's National Union Party—a coalition of populists angry at business, and anti-Semites like Father Coughlin and Gerald L. K. Smith—two and a half percent of the vote. This occurred in an election in which a highly popular incumbent was running and in a system which, unlike Israel, deters the potential voter for a third party by giving marginal votes no representation at all in Congress. Thus, the Kahane phenomenon—as sad and dangerous as it is—is testimony to the *strength* of Israeli democracy under great strain rather than to its collapse.

In 1968, George Wallace won a plurality of the votes in the Democratic presidential primary in Michigan. After the furor, many came to see that this was a low-cost way for blue collar workers to get the attention of the establishment and air their grievances at the weakening of the industrial base of America and at the radical challenge to American social values. In fact, these workers reverted to normal Democratic candidates (or voted for Nixon to get a more conservative policy in Washington) when the vote really counted. The surge in support for Kahane in Israeli public opinion polls in 1986 was a similar "low-cost" exercise, hitting the mulish establishment over the head with a two-by-four. Instead of placing the gesture in context, there was a deluge of apocalyptic pronouncements on the death of Israeli democracy. After the painful devastating clashes over Gaza, even a jump to ten percent of the votes for Kahane would not be out of line with a functioning democracy. This ugly phenomenon is being fought tooth and nail. The Israeli political leadership has treated Kahane as the moral pariah that he is—but he (and Israel's political system) must be judged in the proper perspective.

What all this attention to Kahane really proves is that "covert chosenness"—the conviction of unreal Jewish exceptionalism is alive and well in American Jewry, American media, and Israel. This expectation leads to a dangerous, continuing, excessive harshness in judging Israeli behavior and a proneness to believe the worst about the decline of Jewish moral fiber. It is a shame that in the generation after the Holocaust there are Jews who lump all Arabs together and advocate expulsion and violence against them. It is a kind of posthumous victory for Hitler that the memory of Jewish suffering is used by some to give legitimacy to such horrors. But all it proves is that Jews are a normal people with hatred and violence-prone members—like all the others. Once the reality of Jewish normality is grasped, and the contextual nature of special moral behavior is admitted, then Israel—and Jewish power—will obtain a fair judgment.

The Lebanon War

Israel's first four major wars were all preceded by Arab assaults combined with unvarnished threats to wipe out Israel. In two cases an Arab first strike invasion further underscored the unquestioned self-defense nature of the wars. This created a totally one-sided moral ambience, in which there was no room for moral equivocation or even ambivalence. The focus of attention was on Israeli suffering, heroics and ethical self-restraint. The essence of this period is confirmed in the classic quote in Golda Meir's name: "some day we will forgive the Arabs for killing our boys but we can never forgive them for turning our boys into killers." The quote wraps a romantic haze around the Israeli reality, obscuring the torn and mixed feelings that bereaved parents are likely to have. At the same time, the Arabs in this quote exist as highlights for Israeli heroism, certainly not as flesh and blood casualties. (Even though the Israeli boys are "killers," they are not really killers.)

Sooner or later this situation of moral purity was bound to change. As power is exercised over a period of time, a situation was bound to arise in which war was not purely defensive or self-evident but rather a judgment call. In Lebanon, a PLO infrastructure came into existence that threatened the long-term viability of the Northern border settlements; their collapse, in turn, could ultimately unravel the Israeli security situation. Allowed further to entrench itself, the PLO could have matured into a dominant sovereignty wielding military force. In Menachem Begin and Ariel Sharon, the Israeli government found people who made the judgment to scotch the snake in its lair and took the initiative to do so. This step represented not a moral breakdown but the arrival of more normal parameters of military choice and judgment.

Because the necessity of war was a matter of judgment—a departure from the clear-cut predecessor wars—the Lebanon War evoked enormous criticism and resistance in Israel. As Israeli troops went beyond the twenty-five mile limit, the criticism escalated with a major media focus on the civilian casualties and Arab human costs of the invasion (to the point of obscuring the frequent PLO military presence in civilian settings). This war in other contexts would have been judged as an optional war (a moral success if ultimately it reduced more suffering than it caused; a moral failure if not.) This distinction of types of war grows naturally out of the classic *halachic* distinctions between *milchemet mitzvah* (commanded war, or self-defense) and *milchemet reshut* (permitted/optional war, in which the threat is not as immediate and is subject to the judgment that there are alternative strategies available). In a *milchemet reshut*, both positions (for and against) deserve to be treated as legitimate moral policy alternatives even if ultimately one side is proven wrong by the unfolding events.

The Lebanon War turned out to be based on a gross misjudgment of what could be accomplished to rearrange the balance of power. The Israelis did inflict civilian casualties in Beirut and elsewhere. Shellings and bombings caused the death of innocent people. On the other hand, the Israeli army took casualties again and again in the effort to spare civilians. Residential buildings in which PLO guerillas had dug in were usually not shelled broadside although the costs in Israeli soldiers' lives of house-to-house searches was much greater.

In historical situations in which sovereign, force-wielding nations wage wars, wars like the Lebanon invasion are likely, almost inevitable. In the Israeli context, the War was bitterly criticized and opposed. This is a tribute to a higher standard of morality being applied by the Jewish people— the opposite of the standard interpretation offered by the media and others. The Lebanon war is often described as a complete breakdown of Israeli morality and democracy—which is a tribute to the excessive judgments bred by the continuing influence of the ethic of powerlessness. The war was wrong but well within the parameters of error and breakdown which characterize normal, healthy, moral democracies.

Afterwards, the Israeli political process reasserted itself. The government of national unity withdrew the Israeli army from Lebanon with a minimum of backlash and none of the hysteria or scapegoating that erupted after the United States' withdrawal from the Korean War. Of course, excessive judgment is not altogether bad—it is better than pure amorality— but in the context of threatened delegitimation of Israel, it could have tragic results.

The Shin Bet and the Landau Commission

The Shin Bet scandal which surfaced in 1986 reflects the ongoing struggle to use power to resist evil without becoming corrupted. A miscarriage of justice—a frame-up of a Circassian Israeli army officer by some Shin Bet officers—was uncovered and corrected by judicial review. This case led to the discovery that for more than a decade some Shin Bet agents had been extracting confessions by force from Arabs, later convicted of terrorism, without informing the courts of the use of those extra-legal tactics. Many critics, inside and outside of Israel, cited this revelation as proof that Israel's moral fiber was rotting away.

For forty years, Israel has been assailed by terrorism, organized and abetted by Arab powers and by other world powers. As anyone who has lived in a democracy like America knows, an open society is particularly vulnerable to acts of violence. Democracies cannot keep tight control over population movements or monitor conspiracies and the flow of information in the way that police states can. Due to the atmosphere of communal conflict, terrorists have the potential advantage of being sheltered by fellow Arabs by appealing to ethnic solidarity of Arabs against Jews. Yet, Israel has kept terrorist activity to a minimum inside the country. Incredibly, the level of terrorist activity has not disrupted everyday life nor led to the erosion of civil liberties that often occurs in a society at war.

In a talk in Israel in September 1987, Supreme Court Justice William Brennan pointed out that situations of extended siege and intense war typically lead to fundamental restrictions of liberty, even in democracies. Brennan cited the American record from the Alien and Sedition Acts of 1798 to President Lincoln's denial of habeas corpus during the American Civil War to deportation and internment of Japanese-Americans in California during World War II. Yet, after forty years of continuous wars and extended terrorist siege, Israel has maintained normal life with full legal rights basically upheld for its Jewish and Arab citizens. It even lifted the restrictions on Arab population movement that had been imposed in the forties and fifties.

The Israeli commitment to democracy and law combined with the overwhelmingly loyal behavior of the Arab population of Israel made this achievement possible—that and the work of prevention. For every terrorist attack, hundreds of attempts were detected and failed, never surfacing to disrupt Israeli life. This was the work of the Shin Bet. Fighting a shadowy enemy, one with no moral compunctions and for whom no targets were off limits, the Shin Bet succeeded by diligence, heroism, and an unrelenting pursuit of intelligence and reports on would-be attackers.

How many times did questioning a suspect leave a margin of hours or minutes to prevent a massacre? How often would following the normal legal process have meant that the plot went undetected and the evil deed was done then or later? Of course, democratic legal systems operate on the assumption that better a guilty person escape than an innocent person be convicted. But this principle can and should operate unqualifiedly in a society at peace, not in a situation of war. How many times did use of force—or the implied threat of use—make the difference between silence and innocent deaths *or* confession and thwarting an attack? In that situation, true morality consisted of taking responsibility and forcing the confession. One who would insist on never going beyond the legal norms (of a peaceful society) during war or wartime could be compared to the famous Talmudic description of the *hassid shoteh*—the "moral idiot saint." Seeing a woman drowning, the "saint" covered his eyes and turned away—letting her drown—lest he see a woman's body immodestly clothed.

Think now of the Shin Bet agents. To succeed they must deal with all kinds of people—including paid informants, criminals, terrorists, double agents, etc. If they fail, countless innocents die. If they do not get their hands dirty, more innocents will die than if they do. Yet, at the same time, they must strive to sift accurate from imagined plots. They must distinguish when someone they have detained is hostile but innocent of planned violence. They must use force but only as a last resort. And they have to make sure that all this does not deaden them ethically or lead them to undermine the integrity of the overall legal system.

Did some innocent Arabs get pulled in? Did someone who was in fact not involved in a plot ever confess under duress? Did any agent become so hardened as to become careless of others' freedom or lives? As with any human system, we can say for sure that some failures had to happen. On balance, legality and civil rights were strongly preserved. There was no summary judgment, all defendants were given trials. Even Arabs tried in special courts for suspected terrorist activity were given legal rights, including access to counsel. As time went on, both Israeli and Arab lawyers built up practices in this area. Defendants' access to rights became broader and procedures more monitored. In the course of this work, the Shin Bet did not invade or undermine the normal legal processes of Israel.

One of the keys to the integrity of the system was that when confessions—even those validated by other evidence—were obtained with use of duress, the judges were so informed.

But the atmosphere of the war on terrorism darkened. The last decade and a half included the Munich massacre, hijackings, Entebbe and assassination of ambassadors. The war ranged from the coastal plain massacre to the Achille Lauro and the Neve Shalom massacre in Istanbul. Terrorists caught abroad were often released with impunity by appeasing governments. At some point in the last decade and a half, some agents became so hardened or so determined to convict that they crossed the line and stopped reporting when duress was used. This was wrong because it raised the probability of innocent people being convicted.

Clearly, the judges and the senior cabinet ministers who oversee the Shin Bet became less careful in supervision. Was this a reflection of normal hardening of any policy that goes on for a long time? Was it due to the rise of politicians on the right less concerned for Arabs and more convinced that toughness saves lives? Probably it was a mix of all these factors plus the success of the Shin Bet in itself—and the distractions of everything else going on in government that created the circumstances for such a departure from legal norms.

Did this development prove that Israel's moral standards had declined? The test came in the uncovering of the frame-up of the Circassian officer. Although he was sentenced unjustly and served time in jail, his appeal—based on the claim of a coerced confession—broke through. True, Israel's senior cabinet ministers were disappointing in their apathetic, self-serving response to the scandal. But the people and press of Israel made certain there would be corrective action. When the concealment of the use of force was uncovered, the uproar led to the appointment of a national review board, the Landau Commission. The Commission's report—as the Kahan Commission on Sabra-Shatila—is a foundation document of the developing ethics of Jewish power.

The Landau Commission had to find a moral balance. It dared not yield its concern for a deterioration in the legal and moral standards of the Shin Bet (suggested also by the killing of the two terrorists captured after the coastal plain bus massacre). The Commission also had to avoid shattering the Shin Bet. Disabling the Shin Bet would lead to many more innocent lives lost and to a backlash that could weaken legal restraints even more. The Commission reasserted the rule of law and the integrity of the court system, upheld the need to report all uses of force in obtaining confessions, and directed restructuring and more careful supervision for the Shin Bet. At the same time, it fully recognized that limited but appropriate use of force and extra-legal means are a necessary evil in this underground war.

The heart of a viable code of ethics of power is taking proper steps, even those that incur guilt *when morally necessary*, but restricting and regulating such departures from moral norms so that they do not pollute the entire system, and then correcting when matters get out of hand.

The sweeping condemnatory judgments in the Shin Bet affair, claiming that Israel has forfeited the rule of law, betray the ethics of powerlessness and of the double standard. There is even an element of hypocrisy in such words for they constitute no-cost moral exhortations by critics, but carry powerful risks to the lives of others.

It is true that over the long haul, there is a risk of a coarsening of the moral fiber of a people who wields power in history. One cannot escape the feeling that such a coarsening in the attitude toward the Arabs is shown by the emergence of the Jewish underground and by Kahanism. The incident in which Shin Bet officers beat two terrorists to death after their capture also shows how covert action that often inescapably goes beyond normal process and civil liberties can lead, by extension, to the breakdown of norms of legality and respect for the law. Yet, here too, the good news is that the matter was uncovered and became a *cause célèbre* in Israel thanks to an alert press; that despite the morally negligent and legally insensitive response of Ministers Shamir and Peres, the law triumphed. When President Herzog was manipulated into pardoning those who had covered up the killing of the terrorists, members of the Attorney General's Office and others treated the exempted officers as pariahs and forced a further process of investigating and cleaning up the Shin Bet.

After more than forty years of war with no-holds-barred terrorism, the margin of legality and zeal to uphold the integrity of judicial institutions has narrowed. The situation calls for a higher degree of alertness lest the corruption spread. Adding it all together, the processes of democracy and legal, moral norms have kept the problem within the parameters of a

healthy moral society—judged by the ethic of power. The alternative—
the claim that force never should be used to extract a confession or that all
terrorist suspects should be handled by standard civilian courts and procedures—is not a real-life, higher moral standard but a double standard that
is not realizable in an actual historical situation. Extreme criticisms of
Israel's moral standing drawing on this unreal standard only abolish the
difference between the better, i.e., the Israeli system and the worst, i.e.,
the genocidal totalitarian system that the terrorists would run if they overthrow Israel. The best can be the most dangerous enemy of the better—
unless moral standards are applied in the real world.

The Gaza/West Bank Uprising

The Palestinian uprising on the West Bank and Gaza will go down in history as a classic example of the new moral situation of the Jewish people.
The experience of this period proves the dilemmas of trying to use restraint in the exercise of force, the inescapability of guilt, and the urgency
of trying to exert moral control over power.

The Uprising: Evolution of a Policy. Israeli public opinion is relatively evenly
split between those who are willing to trade territory for peace despite the
security risk of reducing Israel's strategic depth and those who hope to
maintain control of the occupied territories—for reasons of national/
religious grandeur or greater security. Probably a majority of the group
favoring retention would accept giving up the territories if it were absolutely necessary—but only in return for a dependable assurance of peace
and security. Since there has appeared to be no serious Arab leadership
able and willing to make such a peace, this group has remained firmly in
favor of Israeli control. Hence the deadlock in public opinion and policy.

As long as the costs of maintaining occupation were not unacceptably
high to the bulk of the Israeli population, the stalemate could not be
broken. Occasionally doves would argue that the growth of Israeli settlements and suburban housing on the West Bank would soon foreclose any
future compromise. Most Israelis did not agree. The prospect of a non-
existent Arab peace leadership coming into being some day was not worth
the extreme internal division that would be the price of blocking highly
motivated settlers or of not meeting the housing needs of young couples.
The relative passivity of the Arab population made the financial costs of
occupation minimal; some argued that Arab taxes more than paid those

costs. To most Israelis, the human costs, i.e., the occasional victims of terrorism, were bearable and even the moral costs of occasional suppression of Arabs were tolerable.

Israeli authorities turned down suggestions to organize a special border police to enforce law and order on the West Bank. A group with special training in curbing civil disorder would be more likely to stay calm when trouble flared and better able to suppress troublemakers while using non-lethal methods. Still, the idea was rejected. Given the low level of Arab resistance, the Israelis feared that the creation of a permanent professional riot control group posed a greater moral danger than any possible mishandling of riots. A permanent police group, dedicated to controlling Arab civilians and often in contact with violent people, ran a greater risk of erosion of attitudes toward Arabs and of proper procedures over the long term. Its members would more likely become callous or even brutalized because of the premium on suppressing disorder quickly. Since its members would associate primarily with fellow professionals, there would be less likelihood of peer condemnation of the spread of bad attitudes.

The government concluded that it was better to use regular citizen soldiers serving temporary army duty to patrol the West Bank. The limited time of service and the rare incidents of suppression made it more likely that they would remain morally uncompromised by control duty. There are standing orders against excessive use of force and strong, widely shared moral norms in the armed forces. Because the Israeli army is a citizen army with eighty percent of its soldiers (i.e., its reservists) moving back and forth between civilian life and army duty every year, the shared values are closer to civilian than military norms. In the army, there is much less danger of developing a moral/psychological attitude that in a war situation, "anything goes."

Out of such "innocent" miscalculations do morally compromised situations grow in history. That is the essence of what happens when power is exercised. Of course, this is not an "excuse"—for calculations of the unexpected must be factored into policy projections and judgments. The fact is that Israel drifted into a long-term occupation.

In retrospect, the chemistry for an explosive uprising on the West Bank was always there. It was a compound of unhappiness with the occupation, of people in relative poverty reacting to the sights of affluence encountered via television or working amidst the Israelis, of the presence of a high percentage of teenagers in the population with a high degree of unemployment, of a growing fundamentalism, and continuing hatred and resentment of the Jews. This volatile mixture was kept under the threshold of explosion by the passivity of the population, the isolation of the terrorists and the sense of awe at Israeli prowess in defeating all Arab assaults over the past decades.

The rioting was ignited by two adventitious events. One was a crash between an Arab and a Jewish motor vehicle in which Arabs were killed. Rumors spread that the crash was deliberate, in retaliation for a terrorist knifing of a Jew. (Similar rumors that Arab vehicles, which have killed Jews in vehicular accidents, were deliberately operated to kill have obtained wide currency among Jews, particularly on the West Bank.) The other incident was a "successful" terrorist operation in the Galilee. A guerilla riding a motorized hang glider penetrated Israel's security zone with Lebanon and landed near an army base. Aided by the element of surprise, he shot and killed six soldiers before being cut down. The blood spilled, the fact that soldiers were killed, electrified many in the West Bank population. Rumors spread that the guerilla or a group with him had fought and held off an Israeli army for hours and killed tens if not hundreds.

Feelings of rage and triumph and the consequent weakening of awe for Israelis inspired demonstrators to defy the occupation. Some teenage *shabiba* [Palestinians] started to throw rocks . . . and stumbled onto a low-cost, no-lose policy. They could throw rocks or burn tires; the soldiers they faced were not allowed to fire back. Sometimes the soldiers were injured or retreated under the hail of projectiles. The worst that happened to demonstrators was that they were scattered by tear gas; sometimes they could throw the canisters back. Demonstrators were being arrested but most of them would be arraigned and back in the streets in short order. Neither prison nor confinement held much terror—Israel's military prisons were not that abusive. Occasionally soldiers panicked; sometimes they lost their nerve or were in dire straits. They fired and wounded or killed people. This happened rarely enough and so was not perceived as a high probability risk. In an environment where life is difficult and short, and martyrdom glorified, the risk was not sufficient to keep the demonstrators down. Soon pride, peer group pressure, and a growing sense of solidarity combined with some outside help and growing media attention to override all the old restraints. The riots had become a movement.

The uprising caught everyone—including the Palestinians—by surprise. There were preceding signals of erosion of Arab passivity in the increasing incidence of individual, spontaneous, terrorist actions. Few dreamt of a fundamental transformation of Palestinian consciousness such as crystallized in a few months. When the riots started, Defense Minister Rabin did not cut short his trip to America. He assumed that normal procedures would suffice. It turned out that the limited number of soldiers on duty in the West Bank were unable to restore order. They were unprepared for the new situation. Most Israeli soldiers are eighteen to twenty years old. They were facing angry mobs throwing heavy and dangerous rocks. Yet, under their standing orders, they were not allowed to shoot unless and until their lives were endangered. Untrained in riot control, they occasionally retreated, and often did not act effectively until they had to shoot (or, in a situation of great emotional tension, concluded that they had to shoot).

Since shootings were occasional and largely unpredictable, Arab casualties were not certain enough to serve as an intimidating factor. On the contrary, when Palestinians were killed or wounded, the population was further inflamed and media attention aroused. Within a couple of weeks the genie of Arab political activism, pride, solidarity, and rage, was out of the bottle and seemingly impossible to recapture. Israeli authorities heard Americans urging the increased use of non-lethal weapons, rubber bullets, etc., but these tactics seemed even less likely to restore calm. The rising toll of civilian deaths increased the moral costs and damaged Israel's standing in world opinion without changing the equation that made rioting pay in Arab eyes.

At this point, Rabin returned determined to restore order. Behind him was a consensus in Israel that retreat was not viable because the enemy (identified as the PLO) sought the liquidation of Israel. Rabin concluded that existing policy exacted too high a toll in human lives and in respect for Israel in the West without achieving any deterrent effect. He decided that a more focused use of force—a policy using beatings—more certain to inflict pain on the Palestinian activists was the only way to restore order. The decision had to be made in a volatile situation with day-to-day fluctuations of violence and enormous worldwide attention. The pressure was compounded by reports of occasional outbursts of rage by Israeli soldiers out of fear and frustration and occasional panics by yet other soldiers undergoing rock barrages. The Israeli soldiers, after all, were used to fighting armed soldiers in wartime and not children heaving rocks. Rabin himself expressed the rage of frustration and chagrin as he expressed the new policy: "force, beatings, might" was his outcry.

The decision to use beatings to restore order, the deliberate breaking of bones of another human, is in itself a deeply troubling cut in the standard of moral living of the Israelis. The news was particularly shocking to Jews conditioned by memories of pogroms and by centuries of Jewish moral innocence. Yet, it must be said, this policy was ethically preferable to shootings. If it worked quickly, it would result in less loss of life and fewer injuries than a long, drawn-out, ineffective policy of suppression. People can recover from broken bones; death is irreversible. If the authorization to beat had been restricted to actions taken in hot pursuit of violent demonstrators, then the choice was the least obnoxious alternative available. But Rabin's anger only dramatized the thin ice on which Israeli policy was skating. Beatings introduced an element of harshness and cold blood not present before. Rabin's declamation was wrong. Cynics argue that Rabin's sin was to talk too bluntly and thus damage Israel's moral image. Most Jews believe that Rabin's statement was wrong because it sinned against the principle of inflicting the least evil possible. In fact, his words were an invitation to excess and to lashing out blindly in a situation already rife with explosive fear, anger, and hatred.

Exercising Power: Directions, Dilemmas, Dangers. What are the actual guidelines for Israeli army behavior? In the course of a three-month *tironut* (basic training) program, one full week is set aside for special study and lectures on the principles of the army. These include ethical guidelines, stress on the Army's relationships and obligations in a democracy, and the moral parameters of behavior. In addition, officers are required to give regular weekly sessions on such issues. Soldiers are instructed not to obey any officers' orders which are "manifestly illegal." They even explore the contingency of distinguishing between an order that the soldier feels is illegal but involves a borderline judgment call and an order that is manifestly illegal. In the first case, soldiers are told that they should obey but should complain afterwards to higher authority. They are assured that a full-scale investigation will follow and that the officer—but not the reporting soldier—will be punished if the order is found to be illegal. In the case of a manifestly illegal order, soldiers are instructed not to obey and are warned that both the officer who gave the order and any soldier who carried it out will be punished. Soldiers are all under standing orders not to fire unless they are in life threatening situations and there are strict inquiries whenever shooting takes place. The soldiers perceive the inquiries to be deadly serious. They even complain that they find them intimidating and a significant deterrent, a pressure against shooting even when it is felt to be a necessary action.

The instruction to use beatings introduced morally compromising actions. For many soldiers, the beating of another human being is emo-

48

tionally devastating and morally agonizing whatever the justification. There is a real danger of brutalization or, at the least, moral callousing as time goes on. This threat was compounded by another risk. In addition to direct pursuit (not always possible when large mobs are operating), squads of soldiers raided homes or camps at night in places where intelligence reports identified the presence of violent demonstrators or Palestinians active in leading the riots. Arrests and beatings were used in this situation also. Given the pressures, the difficulties of getting intelligence in a situation where the Arab population is showing strong solidarity against the Israelis, the risks of harming innocent bystanders, of people mistakenly identified, of scores settled by informers are greatly increased. The real key to the army's performance lies with the lower rank officers and their emotional stability and moral self-control in carrying out the new orders. Rabin's outburst was all the more culpable because it weakened restraint and served as rationalization for misbehavior by officers whose anger at Arabs was great or whose personal inhibitions against violence were weak.

The ethical dangers of the situation were shortly exemplified in an incident in which some Israeli soldiers dumped dirt from a bulldozer on four demonstrating Arabs, burying them alive. (The victims were saved by their relatives.) When the story broke, it caused a nationwide protest and front page headlines in the Israeli press. The army's investigation held the soldiers and the officers involved responsible. Furthermore, in response to earlier protests in Israel, and by American Jews and others worldwide, the government gave assurance that it was not going to allow an indiscriminate policy of beatings.

Whatever one feels about the justification for the policy even when properly applied, the potential for being on a moral slippery slope is self-evident. The beatings policy constituted a drastic step beyond due process of the law—conviction without trial, carrying out of sentences in a setting that increases the probability of abuse or error, and use of corporal punishment, a method not accepted in Israeli law. In the past, abuses were the outcome of individual breakdowns or deviations from the norms of military ethics. This policy framework meant that it was inevitably likely that some officers or groups of soldiers—in the heat of daily clashes or in the cold blood of rage released—would seize Arabs, guilty of rioting or not, and beat them after arrest and beyond any security concern. This also raised the question whether such a policy of breach of legal norms can exist side-by-side with a democratic political and legal system without undermining it.

For the Israelis, however, the basic fact was that the Palestinians were waging war. It is no less war for being pursued by teenagers using methods—rock throwing, burning tires, gasoline bombs—that kill or maim few Israelis. True, the sides are ill-matched in fire power but Israel's internal moral and political controls restrain it from using the bulk of its available fire power and force. Above all, the situation is no less war because the goals are the destruction of the state of Israel by attacking its legitimacy, its support, its capacity to defend itself. Given the tender mercies of the Middle East, loss of Israel's sovereignty would mean loss of the right to live for the Jewish population of Israel.

The objection that this policy will undermine Israel's moral and legal system is mistaken in the judgment of the policy makers. This was an emergency policy, a short-term action, designed to check revolution before it got out of hand. War is always cruel and potentially brutalizing. To drop bombs from a distance is less shocking than face-to-face bayoneting, but war demands that soldiers attack and even kill others without those behaviors being brought back home afterwards. Israel has not brought its anti-terrorist war tactics home; there was no reason that this should be any different.

Yet, at every step down this road, Israel's moral costs and risks escalate. Soldiers cannot beat people without dissonance unless they convince themselves that the victims are evil. There is a real danger of spreading hate or dehumanization of the Arabs. Every incident deepens the Arabs' rage. The collective punishments such as curfews or restriction of entry of food or supplies radicalize Arabs who might have remained relatively passive. On the other hand, when Israeli soldiers were caught beating an Arab prisoner (the film was shown worldwide and caused great damage to Israel's reputation), the soldiers were arrested and the supervising officer suspended. The commanding general on the West Bank required his top officers to view the film of the beatings from start to finish to feel the shame and the pain and the awfulness of the situation. General Mitzna then gave unequivocal instructions that such behavior would not be tolerated from soldiers or from supervising officers.

The principle remains. All exercise of power results in some abuses. Therefore, all exercise of power involves guilt. That is the price of being able to accomplish good. However, there is excess guilt incurred in this case due to the authorization of beating, which is prone to generate more abuse than usual. But the measure of a moral system is not that there is never an abuse. The key test of a truly moral system is that it correct its errors. Israeli authorities and Israeli public opinion have repeatedly shown that the moral capacity to correct error and misbehavior is unimpaired. By now, there should be more trust in Israel and a more mature awareness that moral ambiguities and tragic choice are the typical unavoidable options in most historical situations.

Policy Alternatives: Actions and Reactions. But is this all out war? Is suppression of the uprising the only alternative? Would not withdrawal constitute a less morally risky policy? The answer lies in the interpretation of Palestinian behavior. Is this uprising the Palestinian demand for the right to live unoccupied or their denial of the Israelis' right to live? The witness of the Palestinian youths who defied the risk of beating or shooting is a powerful one. If it aims for self-determination, it has a right to be heard. If it aims for destruction of Israel, it must be defeated.

From day one, Rabin himself defined the process as restoring order so that negotiations for a political settlement could be started. Throughout this period, no recognized leader of the Palestinians or the PLO or even of the Arab nations spoke out unequivocally that Palestinian self-determination be combined with full and unqualified acceptance of Israel's existence. In the initial mood of triumphalism and rage fulfilled, many Palestinians are talking instant sovereignty on the West Bank—and beyond. True, Sari Nusseibeh called for mutual recognition in the Sunday *New York Times Magazine*—and even Nusseibeh asked "Is it absolutely necessary . . . to *have* two separate states?" In any event, no one believes that Nusseibeh or Hanna Siniora or any moderate Palestinian can exercise an independent leadership role in this matter in contravention of PLO instructions—and live. Nor did any leader even hint that Arabs engage in negotiations with Israel that would recognize its right to security by exhibiting a willingness to adjust boundaries somewhat to provide defensibility. From the Israeli government's perspective, then, the presumption that the Arabs were trying to destroy Israel, not just free the West Bank, was the proper policy guide. At the least, suppressing the uprising would convince the Palestinians that visions of destroying Israel were self-defeating illusions. Any errors or violations of Israeli moral norms could be corrected afterwards.

Like any organism under attack, democracies have the right to narrow their moral focus and concentrate on repelling the enemy and survival. It is instructive that the bulk of American popular opinion and policy makers, despite their disapproval of the beatings policy, remained relatively firm in support of Israel. This showed that most Americans had come to the same general policy conclusion. Most people reserved final judgment, looking to see if the Palestinians would choose a leadership committed to a realistic process of developing self-determination—or to undermining Israel. Further negotiations will reveal whether the Israelis were fighting for security or for a "grandeur" that would require an occupation that of necessity would become more repressive and even brutal as time went on.

A significant minority within Israel disagreed with the government policy from the beginning. Israeli doves, particularly, were critical. They felt that had the government followed their advice to trade the territories for peace earlier, it would not now have been backed into a morally compromising situation. For its part, the Israeli press reported on and criticized the beatings. An important group of psychologists and social workers attacked the policy as creating impossible moral conflicts for the soldiers.

Finally, Attorney General Harish wrote a stern letter to Minister Rabin reporting widespread complaints about beatings. He charged that Rabin was fostering a breakdown in the moral norms that were fundamental to Israel's army and its national values. There were too many cases, he said, where people not actually engaged in violence were beaten for those incidents to be dismissed as "exceptions." The Attorney General demanded corrective action, issuance of explicit instructions that "it is forbidden to use force as punishment, torment, humiliation or shaming." Rabin himself repeatedly insisted that the policy had never been one of random beatings but only for use of force to suppress rioting and restore order, where unavoidable.

The Israel Defense Force had been monitoring the operation of the Rabin policy including sending psychologists in to assess the impact on the soldiers carrying it out. IDF now recognized that abuses were occurring. On February 23, 1988, Israel's Chief of Staff, Dan Shomron issued instructions designed to stop them. Shomron's orders were:

> The use of force is permitted during a violent incident in order to break up a riot, to overcome resistance to legal arrest, and during pursuit after rioters or suspects—all within the confines of the time and place where the incident occurs . . . Force is not to be used once the objective has been obtained—for example, after a riot has been dispersed or after a person is in the hands of our forces and is not resisting . . . In every instance, the use of force must be reasonable, and one should refrain as much as possible from hitting anyone on the head or on other sensitive parts of the body. No steps should be taken to humiliate or abuse the local population, nor should property be intentionally damaged . . . Under no circumstances should force be used as punishment.

General Shomron presented the orders as a clarification to stop misinterpretations by soldiers and supervising officers who acted as if they were free to apply physical force at their own discretion. Clearly they represented a response to Israeli public opinion, the remonstrances of Israel's friends, and bad publicity. Shomron captured the dilemmas of the ethics of power when he commented that maintaining law and order in the territories was a "distasteful task" but one that was morally justified. The alternative—a unilateral withdrawal now—would lead to the establishment of a Palestinian state in a form and on a basis that would pose a serious threat to Israel. Therefore, Shomron said, the soldiers should not allow their task to create moral confusion either by weakening ethical restraint or by undermining the legitimacy of the army's mission.

The key to the proper outcome lies in the army's proper behavior. As Shomron put it in his orders: "The fulfillment of this task requires the use of force. IDF soldiers must act aggressively and decisively but with self-restraint and sensitivity in accordance with the high behavioral norms demanded of the IDF's soldiers and commanders."

In the long run, the only sure way of keeping Israel's moral order intact is to find a political settlement that can reduce the conflict between Jews and Arabs. But, in an era of power and sovereignty, it is easier to get into morally equivocal situations than to get out of them. One policy option being widely bruited in Israel is to get out of at least Gaza unilaterally. The opposing concern is that this could pave the way for radicals to seize control and use Gaza as a staging ground for assault on Israel. The most plausible alternative is an American proposal for elections in the hope that a responsible leadership willing to make peace would emerge. However, initial reactions of the Palestinians, the PLO and the other Arab governments suggest that as long as the uprising is winning the battle for public opinion, such moderation will not be allowed to emerge.

Initial reaction to the United States peace initiative in the Middle East showed that the Palestinians would allow no one to represent them who was open to a settlement accepting Israel's legitimacy. They are not likely to moderate until the uprising is stopped or begins to lose the battle for public opinion. This strengthens Rabin's policy analysis that only suppressing the uprising can pave the way for a political settlement. Awareness of the risk and the limited chances that a moderate Palestinian leadership will emerge at the end should temper the criticism of those who strongly disagree with Israel's current policy. On the other hand, the initial reactions of the Israeli right suggest that they are not so chastened as to be willing to give an unequivocal signal of readiness to trade territories for peace. This strengthens the Palestinian conviction that the violence must continue until Israel is exhausted. This, in turn, strengthens the Israeli left's position that the only way out of this morass is for Israel, unilaterally, to pull its troops on the West Bank back from the Palestinian areas.

If all three policy analyses are strengthened by current events, then what is to be done? On balance, I find Henry Kissinger's conclusions the most plausible. To get to some stage of positive negotiations, Israel probably will have to hang in there, gradually suppress the disturbances, and drastically curb press coverage so as to starve the uprising of its publicity fuel. Yet, these steps are bound up in heavy public relations costs around the world. Interestingly, Chief of Staff Shomron opposed closing the territories to press and television coverage because he feared that would mean closing out Israel's citizenry from the knowledge they need properly to direct policy. Shomron felt this would be morally regressive; better there be damage to Israel's image than damage to the underlying capacity of the society to exercise democratic political and moral control over policy.

Whatever steps Israel takes, the drawn-out nature of the uprising runs the risk of radicalizing Israeli Arabs as well as strengthening the hands of the bitter-enders in the West Bank as various forms of collective responsibility are inflicted on the population of Judea and Samaria. The appeal of extremist policies that bring with them grave moral and political dangers grows in Israel. One of the main inescapable outcomes of the uprising is that whatever policies are pursued henceforth, the costs—at least short term—will go up.

How to Make Judgments. In retrospect, the drift of the past twenty years was not a viable policy for the long run. Given the deeply conflicting impulses of the Israeli public, the absence of Arab peace leadership, the internal Israeli policy stalemate was understandable and nothing to apologize for. The unknown is risky particularly with a country surrounded by enemies. The status quo was not that morally compromising, not compared to the risk of war and genocide. Once the riots exploded, the ethic of power standard justifies some but not all of the policy options chosen.

On the other hand, once the issue flares up, judgments must be made all over again. The ethics of power standard demands that friends, not just foes, must make judgments. No one can be given moral carte blanche. Despite legitimate hesitations—especially the fact that diaspora Jews do not bear the human costs of Israeli policies—all Jews are bound by covenant and love to share their judgments and criticism with Israel. Most committed Jews were troubled but did not criticize publicly. Some committed pro-Zionist Jews did speak out publicly. Some of the harshest language used was wrong; the standards were drawn from the ethic of powerlessness.

Rabbi Alexander Schindler's past record, both of moral concern and of leadership for Israel, entitled him to criticize Israeli policy. But his language (describing the policy as "an offense to the Jewish spirit" that "betrays the Zionist dream") and his public release of the statement was excessive. Similarly, the Central Conference of American Rabbis' Executive Committee statement that "the policy of deliberate beatings . . . [is] . . . beyond the bounds of Jewish values" was excessive. A fairer statement might have been: "From the perspective of our Jewish view which is heavily weighted toward a liberal and idealist position in foreign policy and which leans toward holding Israel to the same standards that Jews held themselves to when we were powerless, we feel that Israel went too far." The policy may be judged to be wrong ethically, on balance, but it is not beyond the bounds of an ethic of power.

These two examples are cited with some diffidence for fear that they may be read as an Orthodox Rabbi's critique of Reform Rabbis qua Reform. The concern for Israel and commitment to its moral performance is too important to be dragged into the denominational politics of Jewry. Indeed, Rabbi Alfred Gottschalk, President of the Hebrew Union College, dissociated himself from the CCAR statement. It will be helpful if there are Orthodox doves and Reform hawks, etc. so that we can concentrate on the issues, painful as they are.

Friends of Israel must help each other navigate very treacherous waters, between the Scylla of double standards that jeopardize Israel's ability to function and, ultimately, Israel's support and the Charybdis of ethical blank checks that jeopardize Israel's moral standing and, ultimately, Israel's support. Let us stipulate the good will and concern for Israel—at least of most Rabbis. Those who think that criticism went too far should console themselves with one thought. The rest of the world is impressed by the fact that democracies and morally upright societies generate self-criticism. Even when criticism is excessive, it is perceived as a sign of moral health. On balance, self-criticism adds credibility to the cause (that is, if it stops short of self-destruction).

Ideally, diaspora Jews should express their concerns to Israel behind the scenes—albeit in no uncertain terms—to minimize any aid and comfort to those who would use their critique to harm Israel. Correspondingly, there is need for more channels of two-way conversation between diaspora Jews and Israel with provision for both partners to be really heard. Most American Jewish leaders do not feel that Israel listens enough. Most accept this situation on the grounds that Israel carries the security risks and that Israel's government is elected by a democratic electorate where American Jewish leaders are not. In the long run, the better instrumentalities and institutions for two-way dialogue of diaspora Jewry and Israeli are a necessity.

On balance, the present Israeli policy can be defended as a necessary evil or criticized as a morally flawed policy that grows out of the failure to resolve the future of the territories. The key to the moral outcome lies in the future policies. One key to a positive future lies in the hands of the Palestinians. If the Palestinians define their "victory" in the uprising as Sadat did in his initial victories in the Yom Kippur war and declare their honor upheld and generate leaders ready to make peace now, then these events will prove to be a blessing for all. If the harm inflicted on Israel's standing leads the Palestinians to believe that they can now demand untrammeled sovereignty and a chance to swallow all of Israel in stages, then the political and moral future is far grimmer. In such a case, Israel will have a far more restricted set of moral choices.

When the alternative is survival, then the most likely policy choice is to hang in there, suppress the uprising and extend the occupation indefinitely. If the choice is between standing pat and destruction for Israel, then an overwhelming majority of Israelis and of diaspora Jews and indeed of American non-Jews will stand by Israel when it chooses to live—even if that means a harsh occupation regime.

Toward New Policies: Right Lessons and Wrong Lessons from Gaza. If the Palestinians open the door to peace by generating a leadership willing to articulate Israel's right to exist and to negotiate a process of letting Palestinian self-rule grow, then a decisive majority of Israelis will respond positively. Before Sadat's trip to Jerusalem, a strong majority of the Israeli public opposed giving back the Sinai. Once Sadat came, the public switched. Ideally, the Palestinians should earn their way—all the way to statehood—by peaceful behavior and policies. Israel's fears are real and Israelis will want to watch Arab performance at each stage of the way. For the Arabs to accept such realities, they must be convinced that American support for Israel is not wavering. Secretary of State Shultz has correctly said that when the Arabs become convinced that "nothing can separate the U.S. from Israel" they will move to make peace. In short, a lot of the outcome of the uprising will depend on whether each of the groups involved draws the right lessons rather than the wrong lessons from the events.

For Palestinians, the wrong lessons would be to surrender to the passions and rage released by the resistance especially in light of the temptation to create internal solidarity by turning all frustration and hatred against the Israelis. The right lessons would be to feel vindicated for having taken their fate into their own hands but to appreciate that the uprising was made possible by Israeli restraint in not following the model of the Syrians in Hama or the total suppression that Hussein inflicted on the Palestinians in 1970. Drawing the right lesson would lead to a reciprocal cycle of peace moves.

For Israeli hawks, the wrong lessons would be the belief that if only Israel were tough enough, it could regain easy possession of the West Bank. In fact, Israel's government, soldiers, and supporters are bound by conscience in a way that restricts Israel's policy options. Israeli soldiers are not up to a policy of unlimited cracking of heads and bones. This "softness" is exploited by some Arab strategists. It even costs Israeli lives. But that is the makeup of Israelis and the price of democracy—and the source of much of Israel's support in the United States. The right lessons would be to recognize that hope of peaceful, low-price annexation of the West Bank is gone. Absorbing 1.4 million Arabs with the high birth rates that characterize Gaza and the West Bank would undermine the Jewish character of Israel within a generation.

True, there are those who believe the Arabs can be driven out, but the overwhelming majority of Israel and of world Jewry rejects such morally repugnant, anti-democratic "solutions." Any attempt to carry out such a policy would split Israeli society, alienate world Jewry and repel American support. New decisions will have to be taken by the moderate right in Israel. (This constitutes 40 percent of the electorate.) An inescapable policy of tragic moral choices, taken for the sake of survival, incorporating only necessary evils, can sustain the loyalty of the large majority of Israeli and diaspora Jews and of decent people worldwide. A policy driven by illusions of grandeur that by choice puts Israel on a collision course with Arab self-determination and generates high probabilities of abuses will lead to moral fatigue inside and outside of Israel. This means that the cost of trying to hold down the Arabs in Gaza and the West Bank for the sake of the land will be horrendous—the creation of multiple Beiruts, unrelenting and brutalizing use of force, radical polarization within Israeli-Jewish society, a risk of alienating the loyalty of the Arabs inside the green line whose cooperation has made Israeli life infinitely more livable in the past four decades. The path is likely to lead down the road to Kahanism and moral perdition—even if unintended.

All this does not mean that the settlements on the West Bank will be uprooted. If the Arabs want peace, then Jews can live on the West Bank with dignity and security even as Arabs live within the green line with a flourishing culture and political rights. Once full trust is established, there are creative ways in which Jews and Arabs on different sides of the line can choose which government they wish to be part of, and to which to pay taxes. Jews have a right to dream of Hebron, to live there and to pray there. There is something deeply moving in a people realizing its dreams and reconnecting to its historic roots after 2,000 years. However, historical memories cannot justify suppression of another people's need for dignity and political self-realization.

In the 1930s, Zev Jabotinsky—the founding father of the Revisionist-Herut-Likud tradition—acknowledged the clash of Jewish and Arab destinies. He argued that Jews had the overriding moral claim and historic right. Jabotinsky reasoned that for the Jews, the Land of Israel was a matter of survival; this was their only possible state. For the Arabs, Palestine was a matter of strong preference and of national/religious ambitions, but not of necessity; they had other states.

Herut, Gush Emunim, Tehiya followers must heed Jabotinsky's wisdom. If the Palestinians are willing to live in peace with Israel, then some Jews' desire to control Hebron or Shechem becomes a matter of strong preference and of national/religious ambition. These concerns must take second place to the needs of Palestinians to live in self-determined dignity—on the condition that Israel's life and right to exist are not being challenged or undermined. The difference between being host or guest at the cave of Machpelah (the burial cave of the Patriarchs) cannot justify suppression of Palestinian political existence.

The *shabiba* are feeling their oats, denying the need to negotiate and dreaming of taking Tel Aviv and Haifa for themselves. They have not yet grasped that Israel cannot be forced to leave Judea and Samaria against its will. Perhaps the passage of time or American firmness or Israeli strength will bring them closer to accepting the limits of historical existence. Then they will see that their own national dignity would best be expressed in a joint venture with Israel to create model societies and good neighbors.

There are Israelis swept by Messianic dreams and vast visions. This is a redemptive age. But the greatest Messianic testimony which Israel could now offer would be to accept present historical limits and work within them to create a peaceful paradise in the area in cooperation with the Arabs of the Middle East. Arab autonomy or sovereignty is not the maximum dream of Jews—even as a demilitarized state is not the maximum dream of Palestinians—but such a reconciliation can pave the way for an era of peace and life for both. Rabbi Aharon Lichtenstein, the distinguished *Rosh Yeshiva*, is reported to have said: "If the price of peace is that I must present a passport every day as I travel from my home in Jerusalem to Yeshivat Har Etzion on the West Bank, then I am willing to do so." This is true moral leadership. Ultimately Rabbi Lichtenstein can be given an even greater assurance. He can put away the passport. It will not be needed. The two societies are located so close to each other that a system of peace and open borders, even better than the situation between the United States and Canada, will have to evolve to make it livable. This is a realizable goal—if taken one step at a time with firm purpose and determination to let each live within the other's dream.

For Israeli doves, the wrong lesson is that an offer to make peace can create counterpart Arab peace leadership. Good will in itself cannot overcome the pent up rage released by the Arab struggle for self-determination and modernization. The right lesson is that Israelis are starting a process that will take a generation and more—but that now is the time to start.

For diaspora Jews, the wrong lesson would be to denounce Israel as a brutal state. It is equally wrong to blame the whole uprising on media incitement. The wrong lesson is to give in to cheap macho or murderous fantasies as do those who underwrite Meir Kahane from the safety of America's shores. They write neat checks and keep their hands clean while Israeli hands would have to do that bloody dirty work they are supporting. President Chaim Herzog has complained repeatedly that without American money, Kahane could not survive politically in Israel. The right lesson is to refuse to surrender all ethical judgments, to express our deepest moral concerns, and to stand by Israel as friend and family. The right lesson is that Israeli strength is the key to peace but "the strongest one is the one who exercises self-control" (Ethics of the Fathers, 3:1).

The Terms of the Policy Debate; or, The Judgments Of Power. A word should be said about the language of the debate now going on in diaspora Jewry over Israeli policy. After forty years of remarkable moral performance, Israel is entitled to some credit. Israel has earned the ethical credibility that if it embarks on a policy that is leading to an ethical dead end, the policy will be corrected. It has earned the trust that if immoral acts are committed in the exercise of power—as they inevitably are in any functioning government or army—the evil-doers will be punished and the system corrected. The right to the benefit of the doubt has been earned by four decades of democracy pursued under the most trying conditions. Compare the outbreak of McCarthyism in the United States and the military stalemate in Korea in which the U.S. found itself after only one decade of cold war.

Israel's trustworthiness has been hard earned over forty years by sacrificing soldiers', even generals', lives because the army would not resort to all out shelling of civilian homes where guerillas were hiding; by arresting and punishing officers for abuse of civilians; by heavily penalizing government officials and politicians for not anticipating and preventing abuses. The record is not perfect; no human system can be. But the rush to apocalyptic dismissals and the harsh denunciations of Israel's policies are not true judgments. They are reliable indicators of the presence of the ethic of powerlessness or, worse, of the application of an impossible-to-live-up-to standard. At worst, Israel is a democracy engaged in an erroneous war. After maintaining extraordinary moral norms under siege and after herculean efforts to maintain its human face and full legal rights for all in a situation of war and terrorism, Israel's whole political system should not be dismissed nor the worst moral scenarios projected forward as if they are already here. An actual record should carry more weight than futuristic scenarios.

This caution applies to Israel's supporters also. After four dynamic decades of building a society, Israel is not a frail blossom that can be blown away by a few months or even a few years of bad publicity or bad behavior. This means that friends must bear with and share the normal ups and downs of government policies and societal functioning in the real world. True friends must challenge and express criticism. They cannot absolve themselves of this responsibility by pleading that Israel is too fragile to sustain a shock to its self-image or to its sense that diaspora Jewry admires it unqualifiedly. In the ethic of powerlessness, the self-image is that of moral perfection; one major failure can jeopardize the whole system. In the ethic of power, reality operates. The incredible infrastructure built in the past forty years can outlast even grave policy errors that stretch over decades. In plain truth, Israel is not as fragile as its enemies hope or its friends fear.

Polls taken in January 1988 show that the bulk of Americans had not shifted their support of Israel even after two months of unsympathetic media portrayals of Israeli soldiers putting down the "underdog" Palestinians. This reflects the public's judgment that on balance Israel is a democracy primarily motivated by the desire to stay alive rather than by the drive to dominate the Palestinians. The public knows that democracies sometimes pursue policies that are morally ambiguous or flawed. As long as democracies remain democracies, the public understands and waits. It sorts through the policies, identifies the right principle and upholds it even if it feels that the wrong policy application is being made.

These polls should be no source of complacency to Israel. If in fact a fundamental change is taking place and the Palestinians are ready to renounce genocide and Israel persists in a policy of dominance and annexation, then the American public will be open to switching its support. On the other hand, Israel's friends should see beyond the surface distortions of the media. If the Palestinians remain unreconciled to Israel's existence, then all the exaggerated criticism of Israel will fail.

For their part, the media must come to grips with the double standard and the danger it poses to Israel's survival. The wrong lesson is to portray Gaza as Soweto and Israel as South Africa. To show Gaza's poverty without revealing the 120 percent rise in the standard of living, the drop in infant mortality of 60 percent, the growth of life expectancy from 42 to 63 since 1967 is to bear false witness. To dramatize acts of suppression of rioting without giving historical background or a portrayal of the steps that led to that moment is to abolish all distinctions. True, it is more dramatic when the past moral hero is "unmasked" as guilty of acts that are all too human, defensive, and even morally culpable. Democracies' behaviors are always subject to more minute analysis and their errors open to more sweeping criticism than that of dictatorships. But unrelenting application of the double standard can lead to the collapse of partial evil and its replacement with greater evil. Witness what happened in Vietnam, in Cambodia, in Nicaragua.

Democracies make errors—sometimes these are fundamental policy mistakes; sometimes these are errors in carrying out a correct policy. Media highlighting can lead to correction of errors. In Vietnam, the media coverage forced the United States to face up to its mistakes quicker than otherwise. But the unrelenting criticism left a legacy of policy confusion that cost America dearly. The United States is big enough to recover, to reassert itself, and to find new foreign policy capacities. Israel is far more vulnerable and its margins far more limited. Sufficient one-sided coverage could endanger its very existence. The double standard in exaggerated form could turn out to be not a fight for the victimized but collaboration with genocide.

Diaspora Jews must learn to discount media coverage more than they do currently. The built-in "underdog" bias (which flattered Israel in the past), the skewing of perspective, the ability to criticize without responsibility for consequences—all create a gap between media coverage and policy responsibilities. Anybody who has exercised power knows that there are often stretches of time when policies that are unpopular must be pursued. Sometimes there are mistaken policies that cannot be dropped overnight but must be reduced gradually. Power wielders learn to live with criticism, unpopularity, error, fallibility, ambiguity. Israelis who wield sovereignty will automatically adjust for these differences. Diaspora Jews who do not exercise power in the same way will be tempted to go with the emotions and images generated by the media and to recoil when bad news persists. Failure to sift news reports and transcend pressures will make all diaspora Jews' policy recommendations suspect in Israeli eyes.

Sometimes the shrill criticism approaches asking Israel to take excessive risks because we cannot take the heat. Many diaspora Jews are reacting to the present bad news from Israel with the disillusion of frustrated idealists. Some exhibit the rage of parents accustomed to getting only *nachas* (gratification) from a child who suddenly turns into an adolescent or a problem. Some threaten to "take their money and go home." This betrays the continuing presence of the perfectionist self-image from the days of powerlessness. One is tempted to say: if you can't stand the heat, don't go into the kitchen of history. But that is too flip. The deeper truth is that taking power in history, like taking on parenthood, is a covenantal commitment; one's life is on the line and the liability is unlimited. A parent who will accept only *nachas*, a lover who will accept only perfection, is unfit—morally and humanly unfit. The goals of resuming existence as a sovereign Jewish nation were elemental and infinite: to achieve basic dignity such as the right to live free, to attain mastery of one's fate, to grasp the privilege of shaping one society as a model toward building a better world. The society and the constructive building needed to accomplish such goals cannot be turned on and off. They require the dedication of lives and energy over the span of generations. They deserve and demand realistic love and a commitment that can function in the face of frustration, setback, deviation and failure. This buck cannot be passed to the Israelis or someone else in the middle of the journey. Part of the responsibility—and risk—for taking power must be borne by all Jews.

At the same time, diaspora Jews must resist the temptation to dump on the media—to "shoot the messenger." The light of public disclosure keeps democracies and moral codes strong. It is important to listen to the media, to critique, and to ignore them in appropriate proportions as is necessary and morally right.

It will take great self-control by all the parties to curb the powerful emotions—fear, rage, revenge, polarization, martyrdom, protection of one's people and family's right to exist—that have been unleashed by the uprising. It will take great maturity to resist the simplistic answers. Israelis will be tempted to seize upon Kahane's, the Palestinians upon Jibril's. In each case, people are grasping at a straw, at a solution that neatly removes the other. In fact, going down those paths leads to the darkest recesses of history and the human soul—genocide, expulsion, the triumph of tyrants and demagogues, the evaporation of support. The other will not disappear; rather conscience will shrink and decency and liveability go first. Many times, humans face situations from which there appear to be no satisfactory exits. The difference between failure—or suicide—and true resolution often lies in finding the patience to start or persist in policies with no immediate end in sight. Life—and history—are open ended; one cannot always see the end. Frequently it happens that only when the first leg of the journey has been completed does the next way station or the final goal come into sight. Patience combined with urgency, persistence combined with openness to the other will ultimately get us there. In the Talmud's language, this is "the long way that is [in reality] the short way." The alternative, lashing out with full force in frustration at all who stand in our way in the hope of knocking them out with one big blow, is "the short way that is [in reality] the long way."

Possessing power enables one to inflict harm on real people; therefore, it brings with it the obligation to exercise strong, moral controls and a willingness to suffer frustration. Rabbi Israel Salanter once defined the three basic qualities that one who exercises power must exhibit: not to get angry, not to get impatient, not to expect to finish the job. No one person is that saintly. But, as a collective, people can approach that standard—by self-control, by checks and balances, by filtering out the influence of extremists. Otherwise the evils inflicted by power will outweigh the good for whose sake power was taken. Ethical power exercised by people willing to get their hands dirty, willing to do the best possible under the circumstances, can turn the most hopeless situation around eventually. Normal people must reach beyond themselves for greatness to turn this moment into a breakthrough for peace. Given some courageous leadership, this could be one of the moments of forging and maturation for the ethic of Jewish power.

7. Identifying Anti-Semitism; Another Judgment of Power

In the past, anti-Semitism has been an ever-present factor in others' responses to the Jewish situation, and the phenomenon persists. The very fact that Jews were excluded from power justified the assumption that discrimination was a *prima facie* factor when Jews were denied their needs. Now that Jews are involved in governmental and political processes on a day-to-day basis, a host of differences and legitimate conflicts of interest and needs are bound to occur. Operating in the realm of power, Jews must resist the tendency to invoke anti-Semitism as the explanation for opponents' behavior.

In going to Bitburg in 1985, Ronald Reagan was guilty of moral insensitivity by equating victims and murderers. He should be faulted for offering premature reconciliation and shallow forgiveness—but not for anti-Semitism. By meeting with Kurt Waldheim in 1987, Pope John Paul II was guilty of tawdry associations and of putting Vatican *realpolitik* considerations ahead of moral concerns—but not of anti-Semitism. All the more so, those who vote against Jewish interests or specific societal, legislative, or governmental policies should be presumed innocent of anti-Semitic intent unless they prove otherwise. Premature or excessive invocation of the specter of anti-Semitism can cripple Jews' capacity to see their own inevitable errors or pretensions and deaden their sensitivity to inflicting pain on others.

In normal political processes, groups and even good friends disagree intensely on specific policies from time to time. People of good will need the assurance that they can disagree with Jews without incurring spiritual "nuclear retaliation," i.e., an escalation to the ultimate denunciation that they are guilty of anti-Semitism. Anti-Semitism is still stigmatized by association with past hatred and the Holocaust. When Jews were powerless, this obloquy was a verbal weapon to be hurled at persecutors when there was nothing else to do. Now that Jews have other levers to evoke proper treatment, so grave a moral charge as anti-Semitism is best used with great restraint. Stamping others' behavior with this absolute seal of disapproval blinds judgment; in fact, the other side may have a point. Too quick a resort to the charge of anti-Semitism weakens the future impact of such a finding. It alienates the innocent and overlooks the fact that today's opponents may be tomorrow's supporters.

The most problematic application of this principle is in dealing with opposition to Israel's policies. There is legitimate disagreement with Israel but it has not been easy to separate it from anti-Semitism.

First of all, many anti-Semites seek to mask and dignify their behavior by defining it as anti-Zionism. Most such haters betray their true colors by their language or actions, as when Russia's anti-Zionist rhetoric turns to libeling the Talmud or when hijackers segregate all Jewish passengers, not just Israelis, or when terrorists open fire on synagogues in France or Turkey. Jews have to be on guard against semantic smokescreens. This makes it even harder to separate out legitimate opposition to Zionist policies. In any event, blanket condemnation of Zionism as against opposition to specific Zionist policies is *ipso facto* anti-Semitic. Generic anti-Zionism opposes the Jewish right to national self-determination in contrast to the treatment of other nationalisms where people condemn specific acts or policies but do not deny the basic right to peoplehood and sovereign dignity.

However, not every Israeli policy touches upon fundamental existence. As Israel's use of diplomacy and military force becomes more the expression of statecraft than of immediate self-defense or survival, there is more room for legitimate criticism and opposition. Open debate is as important to Israel's moral health as to the development of accurate intelligence and effective policy formation.

On the other hand, since Israel is functioning in the real world, its morality must be exercised and judged in that arena. A normal country—let alone one like Israel that is continually threatened—will not survive if it ties its hands with absolute moral strictures and does not adjust to the pressures of power and the threats posed by its enemies. Using this reasoning, the United States Supreme Court ruled that those dedicated to the overthrow of the system are not entitled to all the constitutional guarantees. To rule otherwise would be to turn constitutional rights into a cover for an assault designed to destroy them. Those who insist that Israel must live by absolute morality are similarly perverting morality, turning it into a battering ram for destruction. If you insist that Israel's right to exist *depends* on its being perfect then you are making common cause with the anti-

Semites. If your self-image as a Jew demands that Israel *never* be morally compromised, in whatever way, then you are making common cause with the anti-Semites. Obviously, there is a difference whether the individual making those absolute judgments is a sworn enemy of the Jewish people or a devoted and spiritual Jew who cannot abide the limits of the flesh. Imposing absolute messianic demands on flesh and blood people in an unredeemed world does not bring the Messiah closer; rather it endangers the fragile first blossoms of Jewish redemption.

Why is this moral absolutism deemed to be "anti-Semitic" rather than "immoral"? Because this insistence discriminates against Jews. Israel is the only nation that is expected to always live only by the highest moral standards. Since it is impossible to survive with these standards in today's world, Israel, by its very existence, must inevitably be condemned as a guilty nation. Israel then becomes the only nation whose right to exist is denied on the grounds that it has not lived up to ideal standards. What makes this all so insidious is that some individual moralists who profess a love for Israel as well as committed Jews push these standards, as do overt anti-Semites. The sponsorship makes the judgments harder to resist. Those who weaken respect for Israel through judgments based on these standards of perfection are, *de facto*, collaborating with those who seek to destroy Israel for less noble motives. Noble fellow-travelling with anti-Semitism may be more dangerous than ignoble anti-Semitism because it is more persuasive. By making total demands, moral absolutists destroy the partial good that is possible. The ultimate immorality is to obliterate the difference between the righteous-but-flawed and the wicked, and by moral exaggeration, pave the way for the destruction of the righteous.

8. On Being Special

One question remains: Why the continuous insistence that Israel and Jews not be held to an absolute ethical standard? Is not the Jewish covenant that has guided Jewish existence throughout history, that is the great source of Jewish influence on the world, a covenant that imposes special expectations on the Jews? Did not the prophets hold Israel to this higher standard? "Of all the families of the earth, I have known you singularly, therefore I will call you to account for all your sins" (Amos 3:2). Did not the Torah make it unequivocally clear that failure to live up to the covenant will lead to expulsion from the land of Israel?

The answer to all these questions is: yes. But the prophetic demand operates in a covenantal context. Demands and commandments are not external; they are ethically rooted in the relationship and behavior of their covenantal partners. Otherwise, law is coercion and torment instead of blessing and love. In the Biblical period, the prophet could legitimately assure Israel that those who obeyed the Lord's instruction would be saved even from world powers and overwhelming force! (cf. Isaiah 37:5–7, 33–38) Correspondingly, those who violated the covenant would be spat out by the land that is uniquely the locus of divine presence. Because the land is in the eye of God, the land's capacity to maintain life is sustained sacramentally. (Deuteronomy 11:12–25) In turn, the land responds to Israel's behavior by blessing or cursing, accepting or expelling the Jewish people.

Today we live after the Holocaust. This event is a clear signal that the Divine will not intervene to save miraculously. In this tragic event is a divine call to humanity to take up full responsibility for accomplishing the covenant and for stopping the forces of evil. The Divine decision not to intervene to save the righteous morally invalidates any Divine right to expel a people that does not live up to the covenant fully. There are people whose religious fervor leads them to disregard reality considerations in their actions—including calculation of the balance of power and the effects of policies. There are people who in the name of God or covenant, make absolute moral judgments on Israel—while ignoring the pragmatics of ethical standards or the impact of their words on support for Israel. In the light of the Holocaust, both types are guilty of irresponsibility and of deafness to divine instruction. Repeating the prophetic dicta that make possession of the land conditional on obedience and a pre-set standard of perfection, constitutes not upholding Divine authority but an attempt to hold God to an earlier stage of relationship. Such views are regressive in that they forego a responsibility now being offered to humans and pass it back to God. This borders on clinging to infantilization or child-like behavior in the face of being called to adulthood. Such clinging is often motivated not by love of the other but love of one's self or the desire to be cared for by others.

But did not Israel's unique quality and higher morality garner special support for its existence from the world, particularly the United States, and, above all, from the Jewish people? The answer to this question also is: yes. Therefore, Israel should not lightly give up the special moral standards that have always guided its actions. It would be foolish to dissipate the enormous fund of good will and respect that its moral stature and traditional Jewish norms have given Israel. But what Israel does voluntarily because of its internalized moral values dare not be demanded of it on pain

67

of delegitimation. After the Holocaust, neither humanity nor God have the right to require that Israel justify its existence by a perfect morality.

It was miraculous enough that Jews chose to live and recreate life after experiencing total degradation and death. To speak of Israel's "mere survival" or to dismiss it if it becomes just a "Levantine state" is to miss the incredible significance of its witness to life and redemption just by existing normally. The old Zionist ideal of normalizing the Jews is finally coming true. In a true Jewish twist, the normality is not only challenged and isolated abnormally, but it witnesses to the world in extraordinary fashion. Those who insist on an absolutely spiritually superior Israel and are embarrassed by the moral ambiguities of the actual Jewish body politic show how little they understand spirituality. There must be a body to embody ideals. Even in its cloddish or earthiest moments, this particular body's existence in defiance of the forces of hatred and history is a testimony to the Hidden God's concern and a tribute to the infinite commitment to life of a people. By existing and overcoming death, the survival of Israel's body points to the legitimacy of covenantal hope and the power of the transcendent.

Israel has the right—and thus far it has the record—to act by a higher moral standard in accordance with past norms of Jewish values. But now that it is a flesh-and-blood state, it can only act and be judged in the context of the real world. Israel can be five percent better, or ten percent more restrained, perhaps twenty percent more judgmental of its own behavior than the rest of the world. Achieving such a level would make Israel one of the greatest nations in the world morally—but this begins to approach the limits of survivability. Put it this way: If Israel proves to be ten percent better ethically than the rest of the world, it will be "a light unto the nations." If it proves to be twenty-five percent better, it will bring the Messiah. If it is fifty percent better, it will be dead.

No one and no group can survive in this world if they act fifty percent better than the rest of humanity. Therefore, to insist on perfection—that Israel must never fail the highest standard—is to deny its right to exist. Since Israel is practically the only country in the world that is continually delegitimated by armed neighbors and whose legitimacy is continually assaulted by overwhelming majorities at the United Nations, insistence that it act perfectly constitutes incitement to destruction. The double standard applied to Israel constitutes a particularly vicious form of anti-Semitism— collaboration with attempted genocide—in the name of morality! Jews must be particularly alert to resist this double standard because it appeals to a deep-rooted instinct and a two-thousand-year-old conditioned response that was appropriate in a different, i.e., powerless, context.

9. The End of the Double Standard

In the summer of 1982, Senator Joseph Biden was asked why he spoke so critically to Menachem Begin, then Israel's Prime Minister, when he visited Washington, D.C. Biden explained that predecessor liberals, like Hubert Humphrey, had viscerally supported Israel because they had experienced the Holocaust through first hand encounter. He was a member of a new generation that judged Israel more by the cooler standards of *realpolitik* and its congruence with American interests, so he felt no inhibition in criticizing it. Biden failed to grasp the other consequence of his judging Israel by the standards of *realpolitik*—that is: Israel had the right to use force and strategic considerations to meet those tests. Israel recovered from the debilitating effect of judgments made according to the double standard during the Lebanon war. The recent relentless attacks on Israel in the media and in the university world prove that we must make an end to the double standard before it collaborates with the enemies who seek to make an end of Israel.

If anything, the fading of the absolute taboo power of the Holocaust, which is also manifest in various outbreaks of anti-Semitism worldwide, means that Israel should be granted greater moral leeway. Israel remains a country which, if it loses a war, would be wiped out. The Jewish experience in the Holocaust shows that this is no idle threat. The model of the breaking of the killing taboos vis-a-vis Jews continues to influence behavior. Were this threat removed, more criticism of Israel would be proper. As long as Israel's basic legitimacy is not beyond contest or threat, well-meaning people with impressive moral agendas (or media trying to cheer on the underdog) can be paving the way for a new Holocaust by playing on the double standard and weakening support in its lifeline country, the United States of America.

Israelis continue to judge their own moral performance by a higher standard because the memories of Jewish suffering and of the Holocaust are still vivid and motivating. This is as it should be. The Holocaust should not be invoked just in self-serving ways. Its ethical implications must be used to judge Israel's behavior as well.

One of the deeply disappointing aspects of Menachem Begin's response to the Beirut massacre in 1983 was his failure to see the incident in the light of the Holocaust. He was so busy fending off the hypocritical and dissembling attacks on Israel that he failed to summon up the Holocaust memories of innocents killed while others remained apathetic. To paraphrase Golda Meir, one day we may forgive the anti-Semites for applying the double standard to Israel, but we will not forgive them for turning us into defensive rationalizers when something really went wrong.

In 1983, the overwhelming bulk of the Jewish people reacted as they should have—with anguish at the sight of the bodies of Palestinian men, women, and children mercilessly slaughtered, with shame and anger at those who did it and those who may have been guilty of permitting it. The Israeli population insisted on an inquiry. They refused to allow the hostility of those who seek only to indict Israel to distract the Jewish state from correcting its sins of omission or commission.

It took America, one of the great countries of the world, years to overcome the obstacles to a Watergate inquiry. It took the people of Israel one week to get the government to investigate the slaughter. Not a single general was held accountable for the My Lai massacre, although it was carried out by an American battalion. The Kahan Commission found no involvement by Israelis in planning or executing the Sabra-Shatila massacre. Yet, for the sin of omission, or failing to anticipate, the Defense Minister was forced to resign his post and three generals—the Chief of Staff, the Director of Military Intelligence, and the Division Commander, Beirut area— suffered irreparable damage to their careers. The Head of the Mossad, the Foreign Minister, and the Head of the Northern Command of the Army were censured. All this shows the vitality of Jewish conscience and Israel's democracy—which is the opposite of what the anti-Semites and the false prophets claimed. One must have confidence that any errors made in dealing with the uprising in Gaza will be similarly dealt with.

This same standard of ethical memory suggests that Israel must seek ways of finding room for the Palestinians' dignity and national identity. Whether this takes the form of local autonomy or an Israeli-Jordanian condominium or an independent Palestinian state is a secondary question. The form should grow directly out of historical process, direct negotiations and the ability of the Palestinians to win the confidence of the Israeli public and world Jews. The Holocaust standard suggests that the Palestinians must earn this trust by getting rid of their murderous leadership and making crystal clear beyond doubt, by actions and words, that they intend to live in peace with Israel.

To ask Israel to allow Palestinian self-expression in return for anything less than ironclad, Israeli-enforced arrangements with new leaders, is again to apply a double standard to the Jewish state. No other state in the world whose ruling population is a majority of the inhabitants would be asked to turn over land or power to enemies sworn to destroy it. The tragic clash of Jewish historical destiny and Arab nationalism continues. To incite to suicide in the name of morality or sympathy for the underdog is grotesque.

10. To Strive Together

There are no easy solutions in sight. Taking power has opened the door to an endless chain of struggles and decisions. Survival of the body and survival of the soul are at risk every step of the way. This is a task that can only be properly undertaken by a partnership of Israel and the Jews of the world, with the United States and with all decent non-Jews of the world.

American and other diaspora Jews have gotten a relatively free ride on this long march to power. For a long time, diaspora Jews thought of Israel as their surrogate for the Jewish assumption of power. Now, the recognition is growing that they cannot pass the buck. In the last two decades, American Jewish political action has become a major factor in United States policy. And if there were any diaspora Jews who "imagined to themselves that they would escape to the royal sanctuary from the fate of all the Jews" (Esther 4:13) then they, too, are increasingly disabused of this notion by the dynamics of history.

During the struggles over arms packages for Arab countries, both Presidents Carter and Reagan were not above trying to intimidate American Jewry. Both Presidents (or front men for them) dropped open hints that American Jews had a conflict of loyalty in the matter. True, the charges were not followed up and, later, were even repudiated by designated spokesmen. But the Pollard Affair raised the issue all over again. Pollard acted as an individual and his actions have been repudiated almost universally by American Jews. Still, there have been reports of Jews excluded from certain areas of foreign or defense policy. This is wrong morally and offensive to democracy—but the bottom line remains. Whether tacitly or openly, the legitimacy and acceptance of American Jews in the United States will be on the line in the struggles over American support for Israel.

For decades, diaspora Jews basked in the sunshine of approval for Israel; with every triumph of the "new Jews" of Israel, Jews all over the world gained standing and respectability. Now, if diaspora assumes some of the burden of vulnerability in Jewish history, morally that is only right. The attacks on French Jewry and its synagogues, the murderous assault on the Neve Shalom synagogue in Turkey, the upsurge of anti-Semitism in Italy in the wake of the Gaza-West Bank clashes, show that, in fact, the risks of being Jewish go beyond the shores of the state of Israel. Similarly, Russian Jews who have stood up in solidarity with Israel have been isolated and punished. Inevitably, they opted to return to the body of world Jewry, thereby bringing down on themselves further persecution and a general assault on the loyalty and integrity of all Russian Jews. One fate and one destiny is the logic of Jewish unity and the price of Jewish power.

There are many Jews who will be unnerved by this prospect. Some will distance themselves because of indifference and lack of commitment and seek only to cover themselves. Others will evoke moralistic judgments on Israel to come to the same conclusion. Jewish history shows that the real dividing line will not be drawn by Israel's behavior or even by whether one agrees with that behavior or not, but by a simple principle: whether one is prepared to pay the costs of Jewish destiny.

What then can a Jew who has embraced Jewish destiny say? Israel remains the central theater of collective Jewish action. It is *the* place where Jewish religion and Jewish morality is put to the test because there a Jewish majority decides policy. The results can neither be evaded nor denied nor can responsibility be divided and diluted. Nothing can separate me from Israel. It is my people's statement of life and the vehicle to the future of a world perfected. I will be active to assure its safety and will intervene to help it perform as morally and humanely as possible. It is not a matter of "us" and "them." Some of the battles of Jewish power and life will be fought in the diaspora. Let there be a covenantal partnership between all Jews—and all people who care—to assure that the power is exercised for life and with full respect for the lives of others.

My unqualified support means that I am responsible when Israel's force is misapplied or hurts others. I cannot pass the buck. I will remonstrate and criticize when Israel acts wrongly; I will plead for change, particularly "within the family" and in a manner that will not endanger its existence. I have confidence that Israel will err, but like all democracies, that it will correct itself. I cannot withhold my money, my visits, sending my children, because its travail is my travail, even as its triumphs are my triumphs. Building Israel is not a one-year campaign—or a one-lifetime mission—because the goal is nothing less than redemption, the perfection of life. This is not a one-time pledge because there is no one achievement to resolve the challenge of *tikkun olam* (the transformation of the world). This is a calling to life and power. Ahead lie lifetimes of work for myself, my children and generations yet unborn.

The bulk of committed Jews have made the challenge of assuming power their premier concern. They have proven their seriousness by their pattern of philanthropic giving and political activity, by the way they express religious loyalties and moral response. They ask only for help in confronting the issue together.

Here, then, are the parameters of the new condition. Jewish powerlessness is absolutely incompatible with Jewish existence. But Jewish power is incompatible with absolute Jewish moral purity.

Moral maturity consists of grasping both these truths without evasion or illusion. Moral responsibility consists of the continuous struggle to contain both truths without letting them paralyze either the will to power or our moral faculties. To take power is to give up innocence and take up greater responsibility. If we understand that we are pledged to the covenant of life for everyone and that we are accountable to a Divine covenantal partner who dwells "with the oppressed and the humble in spirit," then we will be more self-critical and humane in the exercise of strength.

By any objective measurement, taken in the context of the real world where Israel operates, Israel is—and is struggling to remain—a model of taking power without abusing neighbors, of resisting assault without turning cruel or yielding democracy, of building a humane and fairly distributed society without tyranny and without uprooting the traditional values of a people. On the other hand, there have been sufficient errors and failure along the way to show the human limitations of Israel and its moral imperfections.

The growth of Palestinian nationalism and of Jewish attachment to the West Bank have generated growing friction, hostility and reaction, suffering, and a sense of clash of destiny. The extended Gaza and West Bank riots and the Israeli efforts to suppress the violence have created a powerful force for hardening of heart on both sides. This means that all those determined to link power and ethics, to reconcile Israeli life and Arab rights should redouble their efforts to make room for the security and dignity of all. Nor is this a time for despair. At some point, Arab rage or fundamentalism will come up against the limits of reality—Jewish power, United States support—and choose the road of peace and life together. At some point, Jewish anger and fundamentalism will shift to acceptance of peace and sacrifices for the sake of living as neighbors—as occurred when Sadat came to Israel in peace.

At one point in history, hatred and loathing were the dominant attitudes of Frenchmen and Germans toward each other. This was the outcome of three consecutive major wars between the two nations. Now stable structures of peace and trade and culture between them have brought a new alliance and widespread mutual regard into being. The geographical and demographic closeness of Israel and the West Bank suggests that the ultimate scenario for peace will be more open borders, more flexible citizenship, more religious pluralism than anywhere else in the world. Isn't that the way the Promised Land should be special? At present, that ultimate situation is further away than in most places in the world, but that is only the measure of the task to be done, of the greatness to be achieved.

With all, Israel has made remarkable progress since 1948. Should Jewish sovereignty be reconciled with social justice and Arab dignity in peace, then the whole world will learn a lesson in taming nationalism and turning it into a blessing. Should Jewish, Muslim, and Christian religious/national needs all find fulfillment in Jerusalem, then this will be a model of how renewal of faith is a blessing to the world. It will show the way that tradition can increase communal love instead of civil strife. This will be a Torah for humanity that goes forth from Zion, a healing word of God that sounds from Jerusalem. The alternatives—genocide or regression to an earlier human passivity, back to the age of acceptance of a status quo of suffering, poverty and oppression—are not acceptable. We must believe that once the divine word of redemption and perfection goes forth, it will not return in vain. Once humans have taken on the task of freedom their hopes and conflicts must be realized—for good. The task is to persist with hope and realism until the final perfection.

In meeting the challenge of power, the Jewish people again is the embodiment of humanity. In its body and history, the dilemmas of humanity are reflected and illuminated. There is no political security for Israel yet, and there are no moral guarantees, either. Jews are not immune to the errors and corruptions of the human condition. I would venture my life that by its total behavior Israel will be a model and a light unto the nations.

Jewish hands have grasped the wheel of Jewish destiny. Jews will bear the shame and the glory. But the blessing will be for all the nations of the earth.

2

The Illusion of Jewish Unity

ARTHUR HERTZBERG

1

In the political drama playing on Israeli television, American Jews are shown as largely supporting Israel's hard line. During Yitzhak Shamir's visit to the United States in March 1988, he addressed two national Jewish conferences: first, of the "young leaders" of the United Jewish Appeal in Washington, then of the leaders of the American Jewish organizations in New York. He was cheered at the first meeting, and there was only a scattering of opposition to his views at the second. American Jewish leaders were demonstrating their solidarity with Israel at the very moment, in fact, that polls were showing that most American Jews were critical of its policies. But that criticism was not perceived in Israel.

After the meetings with Shamir, Gideon Samet, a columnist for *Ha'aretz* who had been its Washington correspondent in the early 1980s, protested that American Jews had betrayed their liberal convictions and had let Israel down. Samet was upset because he knew that the film clips of those meetings on the Israeli nine o'clock news, which the entire country stops to watch, would be interpreted as Shamir's triumph. He would be seen to have persuaded American Jews to support the position that it was better to remain at war with the Palestinians than to have to surrender any part of the "undivided Land of Israel." Since Israel itself is split between hawks and doves, the doves needed direct and unmistakable support from American Jews to help them influence opinion. At the very least, they hoped for television images that would show the average Israeli that a serious confrontation had taken place with Shamir.

Israel's left wing should not have been surprised: they have been disappointed before. In the years before he came to power in 1977, Begin used to argue that American Jews were capitalists, that they were, indeed, among the greatest beneficiaries of the free enterprise system. He ap-

75

pealed to the Jews in the diaspora to put their weight on the side of capitalism in Israel, and thus create a world Jewish majority against the socialism of the Labor party. Begin even went so far as to propose a second chamber to advise the Knesset—he called it, with a dose of melodrama, a Jewish "House of Lords"—to which leading figures in the diaspora would be appointed along with their peers in Israel. This body was to act as a brake on the leftist policies of the Israeli government and give it advice from on high. Of course, nothing ever came of Begin's suggestion. So long as Labor was in power, it did not want such highly placed *kibitzers*. When Begin himself became prime minister, he never said another word about the "House of Lords." He made it even clearer than Golda Meir had before him that what he expected of Jewish leaders of the diaspora was not advice but agreement.

The truth is that Israelis do not understand American Jews. Most Israelis, including some of the most sophisticated, want to believe that American Jews think of themselves as managers of a large warehouse that furnishes political influence and money, and even people, to serve Israel. Israel persists in asking only one question of the news from America: Is it "good or bad for Israel"? Is the news of yesterday's meetings of Jews in Washington or New York, reported on the front pages of Israel's newspapers, good for Shamir or good for Peres?

This is a grave misconception of American Jews. Most of them are committed to helping Israel, but this commitment does not dominate their lives in the way Israelis think it does. If that were so, hundreds of thousands of American Jews would have gone to settle in the Jewish state, to help build and defend it. Many Israelis I have talked to believe that most of the money that is raised by the annual Jewish appeals throughout America is given to Israel, but it is not. Less than twenty years ago, Israel received roughly 60 percent of the total, and it now receives 40 percent. The leaders who conduct these drives in the several hundred organized Jewish communities in America loudly proclaim their loyalty to Israel. One sees them on their annual "missions to Israel" shouting "We are one!" from their tour buses, but in committee meetings back home they have allocated funds to build community centers and hospitals and old-age homes and day schools for the benefit of Jews in America.

It is also not true, as most Israelis want to believe, that many American Jews support Israel as an "insurance policy" for themselves, that is, as a haven that they are keeping in reserve for the day when they might feel threatened by anti-Semitism in America. Jews in New York and Los Angeles may sometimes say such things, especially when raising money for Israel, but they do not mean them. American Jews simply cannot imagine a truly murderous anti-Semitism in the United States. If they could, they would be more circumspect than they have been in forcing the issue of Israel to the very center of American domestic politics.

American Jews have become a "one issue" lobby in Washington. In the climate of a strong pro-Israel opinion in America, they have succeeded in establishing Israel as the major recipient of American foreign aid, now some $3 billion a year. This success has made it easier for them to spend most of the charity dollars that American Jews raise on their own on institutions in the U.S. The public display of passion for Israel represents not the fear of anti-Semitism and the need to prepare a refuge from it, as many Israelis think, but, on the contrary, an almost complete denial of the possibility of such a backlash.

Israel is, indeed, the center of Jewish loyalty for most American Jews, but not in the way that the Israelis imagine. For many American Jews, Israel is not only a cause to be supported but a place whose existence helps to make them more comfortable and secure in America. Jews in America are the only ethnic minority that does not have a homeland, a country of origin to which they can trace their roots. On trips to Europe, John F. Kennedy and Ronald Reagan each made a sentimental journey to the village in Ireland from which his ancestors came. German-Americans claim the past of Goethe and Beethoven, and skip over the Nazi years. The Jews cannot claim as their homeland czarist Russia or the Poland of Colonel Beck in which they were persecuted, especially since most of these Jewish communities were destroyed by the Nazis; and those communities that still exist in the Soviet Union do not remind American Jews of the towns from which their grandparents came. After 1948 Israel became the homeland. The connection with Israel has been an important element in making Jews seem a "normal" part of the American scene.

The need for a homeland of which American Jews "could be proud" has had many consequences. In the earliest years of the state of Israel it was possible for American Jews to learn something about the moral ambiguities that came with power, but they preferred not to do so. Little notice was taken in the United States of a novel by Yigal Mossinsohn, *Khirbet Khiza*, written as the War of Independence was ending, which spoke with pain about Jews with machine guns lording it over Arabs, or of the poems by Nathan Alterman, in which he berated Israelis for their failure to behave decently toward the Arabs they had just conquered.

American Jews preferred to see Israel as it was depicted by Leon Uris in *Exodus*, in which Israelis were painted as totally noble and Arabs were the Middle Eastern equivalent of the murderous Indians of Hollywood Westerns. American Jews preferred to see Israel as unquestionably good. Jews recalled that even in America they were, in accordance with the faith of their ancestors, the "chosen people." When support for Israel became the "secular religion" of most American Jews, Israel had to be presented as a homeland that was superior to all other homelands.

Therefore, through the years, most American Jews have not wanted to know what was really happening in Israel. They could take pride in the kibbutzim as a "great social experiment," and resolutely ignore the fact that fewer than 5 percent of Jews lived in them, while most of Israel was trying to become more bourgeois, "just like America." After the Six Day War in June 1967 American Jews did not have to think about the occupation of the West Bank and Gaza, not even after Menachem Begin came to power a decade later. By definition, among American Jews the "homeland" was simply the one peace-loving state in the Middle East. If they heard echoes from Jerusalem of statements about the "undivided Land of Israel," such remarks could be dismissed, in a very American way, by claiming that the Israelis who made them didn't really mean them: they were only trying to stake out a hard bargaining position from which they could achieve the best deal. By saying that the Likud does not mean what it says, one does not have to face the uncomfortable fact that there is a right wing in Israel that is so insistent on its ideology that it would rather live amid violence than search for compromises.

2

So far I have used the phrases "most American Jews" or "many American Jews," and not the usual phrase "the American Jewish community," because there is no such thing as an American Jewish community. American Jews are divided into three unequal, sometimes overlapping, parts.

On the right, a minority of no more than 15 percent of American Jews are convinced, undeviating hard-liners. Most are Orthodox in religion, and many come from the small element of American Jewry that arrived after World War II; they tend to be Holocaust survivors or the children of survivors. The experience of ultimate powerlessness in the Nazi death camps has made the survivors particularly susceptible to the appeal that Menachem Begin made his own: "never again." Even among the American

Jews who remember the death camps, there are some with moderate views. For example, Menachem Rosensaft, the founding chairman of the Children of Holocaust Survivors, is an outspoken dove, even though many of the most vocal people in his group are hawks. But for most of those whose lives were deeply affected by the Holocaust, the memory of powerlessness translates into the assertion that Jews cannot show any weakness to their enemies, that only power counts. And the major enemies of the Jews, now, are the Arabs.

The other component of the right-wing minority is the neoconservatives. This right-wing intelligentsia makes considerable noise, because it produces countless articles and makes many speeches, but it has no substantial number of foot soldiers. In a poll of American Jewish opinion by the *Los Angeles Times*, the results of which were reported on April 12 and 13, 56 percent described themselves as belonging to the Democratic party and 27 percent described themselves as political moderates. Only 17 percent described themselves as conservatives: not many more than the 10 percent of American Jews who were Republicans in the Roosevelt era. And many of today's Jewish Republicans are Orthodox believers, few of whom are subscribers to *Commentary* or *The Wall Street Journal*.

The neoconservatives identify the cause of Israel with their campaign against détente with the Soviet Union. They are upset by Ronald Reagan's new policy of accommodation, for they continue to see the Soviet Union as the "evil empire," and they want Israel to be America's bastion in the Middle East, the only country in the region on which America can depend. They argue that it is in the American interest that Israel have "strategic depth." In light of these "strategic necessities," of what account are the deaths and humiliations of Arabs on the West Bank? Local riots make little difference to pundits who see themselves as the masters of geopolitics.

The Israeli politician whom the neoconservatives most admire is General Ariel Sharon. They join with him in continuing to insist that Israel's invasion of Lebanon in 1982 was well conceived, and that if only he had been allowed to finish the job he could have redrawn the strategic map of the Middle East. They ignore the violent internal conflicts within Lebanon and they conveniently forget the frightful cost in lives that street fighting in Beirut would have exacted. Even though Ronald Reagan was the American president who pushed Israel to end the siege of Beirut, the neoconservatives have already joined with Sharon in adding Lebanon to the list of military ventures that failed because the home front, both in America and in Israel, became chicken-hearted.

There can be little doubt that the "stab in the back" theory is waiting to be used again by the right wing in Israel and America should a compromise between Israel and the Palestinians ever emerge. It is almost inevitable that the moderates will be accused of lacking the guts to secure the undivided Land of Israel, which was supposedly in the grasp of Israel and its American ally if only they had stood fast.

The largest group of American Jewish opinion is in some conflict with itself. According to the *Los Angeles Times* poll, American Jews, by a majority of at least four to one, want some formula that would quell the violence. Two thirds of those polled favored some form of political accommodation with the Palestinians.

Almost half of those who expressed opinions, 41 percent, were willing to admit that "there is an attitude of racism involved in the attitude of Israelis towards Arabs," and 47 percent denied this. By a margin of two to one, those polled opposed negotiation by the United States with the PLO. Thirty-one percent said they were willing to give up "the occupied territories in exchange for Arab recognition as part of a settlement of the Middle East conflict." Forty-three percent said they were not willing to give up the territories, and nearly 25 percent did not give an opinion. That is, a substantial minority of American Jews who have expressed an opinion are now willing to give up even "the territories," that is, *all* of the West Bank and Gaza, with some minor rectifications of borders. More than 60 percent are for the Shultz plan, which calls for an international peace conference with a view to trading "territories for peace."

In keeping with this result, 57 percent of the American Jews polled said they were favorably impressed by Shimon Peres, who endorsed the Shultz plan, while 49 percent said they were impressed by Yitzhak Shamir, even though Shamir now has the prestige that comes with being prime minister of Israel. Perhaps most striking of all is that more than a quarter of those polled were willing to say that the "foreign and domestic policies of the State of Israel have become less acceptable to them," while only 11 percent, the bedrock constituency in America of the Israeli right wing, found Israel's recent policies to be more acceptable.

The basic findings of this most recent poll—that a clear majority of American Jews support moderate policies in Israel and that they are increasingly uneasy with Likud hard-liners—are consistent with other available evidence. All the recent studies of the attitudes of American Jews toward Israel have shown that a majority by at least two to one rejects the hard-line policies of the Likud.

The results of the Democratic presidential primary in New York on April 19 would suggest the same views. Albert Gore ran in that primary as a pro-Israel maximalist, whose views did not differ much from those of Yitzhak Shamir. Jesse Jackson said he favored a Palestinian state on the West Bank and Gaza, although in the last days of the campaign he said he would not talk directly with Arafat. Michael Dukakis embraced the Shultz plan; he was perceived as holding views that were nearly identical with those of Shimon Peres, that territories had to be traded for peace. Jackson received about 6 percent of the Jewish vote; Gore got only 16 percent; at least 75 percent voted for Dukakis.

No doubt some Jews would have preferred to vote for Gore and probably voted for Dukakis to insure a heavy loss for Jackson. Right-wing Jews insist that Gore would otherwise have done far better among Jews. But in the light of all else that we know about the preferences of American Jews, this explanation is not convincing. It would explain the shift to Dukakis of no more than 10 percent of the Jewish vote. Dukakis is viewed by most Jews as a middle-of-the-road urban liberal, close in many respects to their own image of themselves. Had a contest been held between him and Gore on the issue of Israel alone he would have gotten nearly two thirds of the Jewish vote, which is the proportion of Jews who have consistently, and undeviatingly, expressed their distaste for the Likud's intransigence.

As American Jews are losing some of their illusions about Israel and are being forced to think about the real Israel, and to begin to make hard choices from among the clashing political factions, they remain predictably committed to its security. The researchers for the *Los Angeles Times* found that 85 percent of American Jews continue to "favor strong United States support for the government of Israel"; only 3 percent were opposed, and 12 percent said they did not know—roughly the same results as in other polls of the last thirty years. But there is one radically new note: the respondents were evenly split over whether those who privately disagree with Israeli policies should nevertheless publicly express their support. Younger Jews, those under forty-one, by a margin of 60 percent favored public criticism of Israel. An Israeli government that continues to resist political compromise can therefore expect open disaffection to increase among American Jews, and especially among the younger generation.

If Yitzhak Shamir wins the Israeli election in November, as he very well may, he is likely to maintain a tough, repressive policy toward the Palestinians, while opposing any attempt by a new American president to revive the Shultz initiative. Since returning home from his visit to the United

States in March, Yitzhak Shamir has left no doubt in Israel about his political intentions. On Sunday night, April 24, speaking to the Central Committee of the Likud party in Tel Aviv, he was cheered when he said that "the Arabs must understand that we will never part from Judea, Samaria, and Gaza." He added that the Palestinians would have an autonomy plan under which they would be able to run their own lives. As Israelis know, this means, at most, the right of Palestinians to run the local fire department and sanitation services, while the government of Israel controls the disposition of land, water, and virtually everything else of any consequence. Shamir announced this policy as his election platform against the Labor party, which has accepted Shultz's formula of "land for peace."

In Israel, Shamir's declarations are understood against the background of his repeated insistence that the riots and the continuing civil disobedience by the Palestinians can be suppressed. Shamir has called the rioters "grasshoppers" by comparison to the Israel Defense Force.

Shamir's views are opposed by some of the country's leading generals. Perhaps the most striking of all such statements was reported on the front page of *Ha'aretz* on April 1. Eleven retired generals—among them Aharon Yariv, a former head of military intelligence, and Motti Hod, a past commander of the Air Force—insisted that the future of Israel requires withdrawal from the territories. The generals want the West Bank to become a demilitarized region under Palestinian control, with a few Israeli observation points on the highest ground. The declaration of these generals, most of whom have been lionized repeatedly on the platforms of the American Jewish organizations, was ignored in all the American Jewish establishment publications I have seen.

When the refusal of Israel's hard-liners to deal politically with the uprising can no longer be explained as the negotiating tactics of tough bargainers who really want to compromise, American Jews will find themselves facing wrenching choices.

A movement toward open disaffection with Israel's right wing seems all the more likely because of one seemingly strange result in the latest *Los Angeles Times* poll. Half of the American Jews surveyed report that their major concern as Jews is not support of Israel but "social justice." Support of Israel is the main issue for 17 percent, and another 17 percent give religion as their prime concern. At first glance these figures seem to contradict the overwhelming support for Israel (85 percent) that these same respondents demonstrated when asked if they would continue to press the American government to support Israel—but the two results are really not contradictory. Among American Jews, as I have noted, Israel is supported by the majority as a homeland in which Jews take pride; only a minority is undeviatingly devoted to Israel "right or wrong." Therefore, the mainstream of American Jewish opinion, which is essentially identical with the third and fourth generations of Jews who descend from the mass migration that began in the 1880s—i.e., the most "Americanized" elements of the community—will struggle to depict the homeland as virtuous by the standards of liberal, democratic opinion that they share. The breaking point will come when they can no longer do so, and that this moment may be arriving is worrying for most American Jews and especially for the young.

Why, then, was Shamir cheered in Washington this March before a large gathering of "young leaders" of the United Jewish Appeal? Some were, no doubt, really on his side, inspired by a defiant assertion of "Jewish power." Many wanted to imagine that the Israeli leader was acting like an American politician, posturing as intransigent as a way of preparing for an inevitable compromise with the Palestinians. Here the fundamental difference between Israeli and American Jewish perspectives was apparent. The same political performance had different meanings for two different audiences. In Washington younger American Jews were asserting their pride in their homeland. In Tel Aviv and Jerusalem the standing ovation they gave Shamir was seen as support for the tough ideologue known to the Israelis, not for the "reasonable" Shamir of the Americans' imagination.

3

The most visible representatives of American Jews are the leaders of the national organizations, who gather together as a bloc in support of Israel in the Conference of Presidents of Major American Jewish Organizations, and the official lobby in Washington, the American Israel Public Affairs Committee (AIPAC). Both groups, and especially the "Presidents' Conference," are widely regarded as the elected spokespeople of the American Jewish community. This is to exaggerate their representative character.

To begin with, the Jewish organizations, including religious groups, have an enrollment of fewer than half of the Jews of America. Since Jews can leave or join these organizations as they please, those who become disaffected are more likely to drop out than to stay and fight for their views. When they leave the organizations, however, they do not leave Jewish life. Most of their children have bar or bat mitzvahs and are married as Jews, and most are deeply concerned about Israel, especially at moments of crisis. That few unaffiliated Jews rejoin Jewish organizations to fight the hard-liners creates an anomaly: the Jewish establishment claims to speak for an American Jewish community, but the real opinions of American Jews can be discovered only through opinion polling and not through the pronouncements of the presidents and executive directors of the national organizations. On the contrary, as moderates leave the establishment organizations, or do not join, or find no way to express their views, and hard-liners remain, these organizations give a more and more false impression of American Jewish opinion.

This false impression is particularly damaging in Israel, where the pronouncements of the "Presidents' Conference," or the kind of reception that it gives an Israeli leader, are taken as a reliable measure of the mood of American Jewry. Israelis tend to think that American Jews have elected these leaders after vigorous public debate on policy, because they themselves come, most of them, from Europe and the Arab world, where Jews were organized in *kehillot,* that is, in community councils that held periodic, and usually hard-fought, elections. Most Israelis imagine that American Jews are organized in roughly the same way. The Jewish organizations are listened to in Israel as if they were the elected representatives of American Jewry, and as if they had deliberated on the differing party platforms in some kind of national referendum.

Nor are most of the "establishment" leaders in the drama of the relationship between Israel and American Jews unaware of the effect they create in Israel. The American managers of such events as Yitzhak Shamir's speech in March to the "Presidents' Conference" know that Israelis will interpret their cheers not as respect for the prime minister but as backing for the leader of the Likud party. Why are they willing and even eager these days, in the face of majority American Jewish opinion, to oblige Shamir?

Most of the leaders of Jewish organizations believe that such displays of unity are necessary in order to strengthen Israel's prestige and position in America. Many share the dominant American-Jewish myth that even an ideologue like Shamir is a politician comparable to American political leaders and that he will ultimately negotiate a compromise. The counterargument, that public support for other, more moderate, Israeli politicians is of far greater help to Israel than supposed unity behind an intransigent ideologue, has in the past been silenced by a cadre of presidents of organizations and of professional managers. But the solid front of the Jewish establishment, which was briefly shaken by the events surrounding the invasion of Lebanon in 1982, was broken by the Palestinian uprising that began in December 1987.

An important sign of a crack in the unity of Jewish opinion is the strange and continuing silence of AIPAC, an independent membership organization that claims to represent the interests of Israel in the U.S. and that is not directly controlled by the Jewish national organizations. In recent years, it has often been even more tough-minded and maximalist than the establishment organizations in the pressures it has mounted in Washington on behalf of Israel. The strategists of AIPAC differ from the other Jewish leaders in that they are in close touch with a great many politicians in Washington, and especially in Congress. AIPAC's lobbyists, therefore, know that support for Israel in American opinion has been decreasing. According to the *Los Angeles Times* poll, while Jews have remained overwhelmingly in favor of strong American support for the government of Israel, non-Jews were in favor of it by 27 percent, opposed by 23 percent, and 50 percent answered "don't know." For the AIPAC lobbyists such results would indicate that Israel should move quickly toward a negotiated political solution of the conflict with the Palestinians.

AIPAC has not dissented from the hard line merely by remaining silent. Its office in Washington has also acted, indirectly but with strong effect. The now-famous letter sent in March by thirty senators to Secretary Shultz in support of his peace initiative could not have been written without the knowledge of AIPAC. The signers of the letter included five of the seven Jewish senators and the majority of Israel's most vocal Senate supporters. It is even more striking that the thirty senators who signed the letter were those who have received most of the money allocated by the pro-Israel PACs. A letter of support for the Shultz plan could not have circulated in the Senate without most of the strongly pro-Israel senators sooner or later discussing the matter with AIPAC. That these men would have signed such a letter immediately before Prime Minister Shamir's visit to Washington if AIPAC had objected vigorously is very unlikely. AIPAC has denied that the letter of the thirty senators was drafted somewhere within AIPAC itself, and there is no point in trying to disprove its claim. What is clear is that the signing of the letter—and AIPAC's apparent decision not to try to stop it—was an act against Yitzhak Shamir, and he understood it correctly as a warning of disaffection not only in Congress but within American Jewry itself.

Shamir came to the United States in March to silence such views, and he moved adroitly. He deplored the letter of the thirty senators, but rap-idly changed the subject. It was best, from his point of view, to suggest that these great friends of Israel had simply made a mistake, for which he benignly forgave them. He did not confront AIPAC.[1]

The turning point came at the beginning of March. A "mission" of the "Presidents' Conference" went to Jerusalem to confer with the prime minis-ter before his visit to Washington. He told his guests that he had no inten-tion of accepting the Shultz plan; in fact he had announced, in advance of their coming, that there was not a single line in it that he found true ex-cept the signature. The leaders of the American Jewish establishment re-turned from that meeting knowing that their urgings since December for Israel's right wing to be reasonable—that is, to behave like De Gaulle in Algiers, or Nixon in China, or Begin at Camp David—had not succeeded. The organization presidents heard Shamir out, and most of them chose to go along with him.

Shamir, in Washington, did not want any more expressions of public disagreement, and he could use the "Presidents' Conference" to create the image of a consensus backing him, even though the various organization leaders, when polled privately, have long shown a majority of somewhere between three and four to one on the side of moderation.

True, almost every one of these leaders tells stories of how firmly he has spoken, and continues to speak, to Israel's leading politicians of all shades of opinion about the need for political compromise with the Palestinians. The tales of these conversations are repeated in the U.S., and not only "off the record" to Jewish groups. They sometimes leak, and not always by accident, to the press in Tel Aviv and even in New York. But these leaders protect their positions by being publicly circumspect. To be in open conflict with a sitting prime minister, even one of a divided government, is a disaster for any leader within the Jewish establishment. He will be treated coolly in Jerusalem. He will not be able to return home to tell his board of trustees of his intimate conversation with the prime minister in Jerusalem, or carry messages of supposed importance between Jerusalem and Washington.

What the prime minister requires in return for listening privately in his Jerusalem office to a polite, perhaps even pained, disagreement with his policies is the staging in America of public support. Both the prime minis-ter and the Jewish organization officials who give him a standing ovation while the cameras roll know what the bargain is all about. Shamir's posi-tion is built up in America, and especially in Israel, not only as prime minister of all Israel but as the triumphant Likud party leader. At the same time the Jewish organization leaders cheering Shamir are confirmed by the prime minister as the legitimate representatives of American Jewry—and never mind the polls or the other Jewish leaders who speak for the moderate opinion of most Jews.

And yet, despite this seeming unity in public, the opinions of American Jews are inherently unstable. Uneasiness is growing even within the organizations, as the quiet defection of AIPAC from support of the hard line proves. So far, a few of the organizations within the Presidents' Conference have already dissented from Shamir's line. These include the American Jewish Congress and the Union of American Hebrew Congregations, as well as the American affiliates of Israel's Labor party. In mid-April 1988 there was a mass rally in New York of some five thousand people who wanted to show their solidarity with moderate policies in Israel and to protest the views of the Likud. This virtually unprecedented gathering was co-sponsored by twenty of the American Jewish organizations to which political moderates belong, among them the Labor Zionist Alliance, the Progressive Zionists, and the Children of Holocaust Survivors.

Perhaps most significant, mainstream organization leaders, the very people who support the prime minister in public, have recently been returning from visits to Israel deeply concerned about what will happen after the Israeli and American elections this fall. They are fearful that a confrontation will take place between the right-wing majority in Israel and the United States government. In this case an open break with Israel's policies could occur even within the establishment organizations. That such a confrontation may well be coming was suggested by Reagan's praise of Shimon Peres on May 17, 1988, and his criticism directed at Shamir.

Most American Jews certainly remain loyal to the homeland in Israel, but they are less and less willing to allow the organization leaders who have been speaking for them to say what they will. A growing debate has been taking place among American Jews and in the press between the spokespeople of the organizations and the leaders who speak for the majority of Jews, who hold moderate opinions. The claim that American Jewry is largely united behind, and controlled by, the organizations is becoming exposed as an illusion. If the political confrontation between Israel and the United States does indeed become sharper after the two national elections in the fall, then the principal Jewish organizations will, I believe, have to face an unprecedented challenge: to reflect the reality of Jewish opinion in America.

3

Feminist Reflections on the State of Israel

JUDITH PLASKOW

For the last twenty years, Jewish feminists in the United States have been calling the American Jewish community to a truly pluralistic egalitarianism. We have demanded of the community not simply equal access for women to all the rights and responsibilities of Jewish life but, more importantly, equality in and through our particularity—a particularity that women ourselves will articulate and define. Jewish texts and Jewish religious and communal institutions have too often taken maleness as normative, dropping women's unique history and spiritual insights, attitudes, and feelings from the long chain of Jewish memory. Jewish feminists declare that this is no longer acceptable. We ask that the Jewish tradition become *wholly* Jewish, that it incorporate the suppressed history and experiences of women into the memory and ongoing life of Judaism and, in doing so, transform the tradition.

The fact that this demand of Jewish feminists is analogous to the demands both of minority feminists and of Jews in the modern West brings into focus the enormous obstacles to creating communities rich in diversity and accountable to different perspectives. The projection of women as Other and the insistence on the part of liberal Jews that Jewish women adapt ourselves to a male tradition echoes the Otherness of the Jew in the larger society and the insistence that Jews "melt" into the prevailing culture as a condition of our citizenship. Similarly, the feminist community, despite its explicit commitment to inclusiveness, has repeatedly offered accounts of women's experience that falsely universalize a white middle-class (race and class) perspective and expected minority women to conform to its generalizations. It seems that in so many contexts, difference is perceived as something to be feared; the recognition of difference is fraught with guilt;[1] and community-building is identified with the eradication of difference and the fostering of uniformity.

To this human heritage of difficulty with diversity, Jews bring our own long history of suspicion and ranking of difference. Thinking of itself as a "kingdom of priests and a holy nation," the Jewish people from its beginnings understood its own holiness partly in contradistinction to the beliefs and behavior of the surrounding nations. The key notion of *chosenness*, so central to Jewish self-understanding, expressed itself both in shunning foreign gods and morality and in setting up a host of internal separations that set apart distinct and unequal objects, states, and modes of being. On a religious level, to be a holy people was both to be different from one's neighbors and to distinguish between pure and impure, Sabbath and week, kosher and nonkosher, and male and female. On a social level, the Otherness of women was the first and most persistent among many inequalities that have marked Jewish life. Differences in wealth, learning and observance; differences in cultural background and customs; differences in religious affiliation and understanding have all provided occasions for certain groups of Jews to define themselves as superior to different and non-normative Others.

The challenge of overcoming this heritage and creating communities that respect and nurture particularity without hierarchy is the very heart of the feminist project, and it is in light of this project that I approach the question of the state of Israel. Committed though I am to a diaspora context, I cannot as a late twentieth century Jew think about the transformation of Jewish community without taking into account the place in the world where Jews have deliberately and self-consciously sought to create a Jewish society. The persistent human difficulties in dealing with difference, the social implications of traditional Jewish attitudes toward difference, the continuities between the modern Jewish construction of difference and historical Jewish treatment of Others all emerge with special vividness in the context of the state of Israel. The crucial issues of community and diversity with which feminism is concerned take on new urgency in relation to the national community that Jews have created.

The early Zionist vision of an abundant and self-determined Jewish life in continuity and contention with tradition has much to commend it to the feminist imagination. This vision was rooted in awareness of the importance of community and the desire for a community that could nurture its members. Growing out of the experience of emancipation and its failure to end anti-Semitism, Zionism knew the issue of difference and the importance of particularity. In providing an opportunity to bring renewed life to traditional Jewish values while taking seriously the lessons of the modern world, the establishment of a Jewish homeland challenged Jews to create a culturally rich and diverse society on the basis of a new understanding of difference. The fundamental feminist question concerning the state of Israel is whether it has found fresh ways to accommodate particularity or whether it has instead perpetuated the same hierarchical construction of difference that has hitherto shaped Jewish communal existence.

While the early Zionists imagined an egalitarian community in Palestine formed by Jews from the many lands of dispersion, numerous factors in the development of Israel have conspired against the realization of their vision. The complexities and conflicts of Zionist ideology and history, and the story of the many forces at work in shaping the state are well beyond the scope of this essay.[2] But what is important from a feminist perspective is that the enduring inequalities of the Jewish community have found new and complex embodiment in the laws and structures of a nation-state struggling to secure its existence and survival.

With reference to women, for example, the establishment of a Jewish homeland provided an unparalleled opportunity to "start afresh," building a community and nation in which women would define and shape Jewish history side-by-side with men. Since most early Zionists had little sympathy with the strictures on women's roles delineated by religious teaching, their understanding of Jewish community seemed to promise a new beginning for women who wanted to live full Jewish lives and at the same time free themselves from traditional Jewish restrictions. Yet while the *myth* surrounding Jewish Israeli women is that their aspirations for liberation were realized, in fact sexual equality never was taken seriously in Israel as an important social goal.[3] The image of pioneer women draining swamps, changing the face of the land, fighting enemies alongside male comrades, projects as *reality* the *hopes* of the first Zionist women settlers. These women envisioned a society in which differences would be treated equally, in which they could bring their full physical and intellectual capabilities to all aspects of common life.[4] The Labor Zionist movement with which they identified, however, subordinated women's emancipation to the overriding project of establishing a Jewish home. Just as was the case with many liberal Jewish institutions in the diaspora, sexual equality was taken for granted in principle and ignored in the concrete. Women found that many male settlers simply could not comprehend or take seriously women's desire to build the land side-by-side with them. Even in the communes that were forerunners of the kibbutz, women were assigned limited, primarily domestic, roles and were considered to work for the men rather than being full members of the collectives.[5] Indeed, on the kibbutzim themselves, while there were women who fought for and won the right to do men's work, no one ever suggested that men ought to be in the kitchen and nursery; the sexual division of labor went unquestioned.[6]

With the establishment of the state of Israel in 1948, important new factors came into play that served to consolidate and intensify sexual inequality. The role of Orthodox parties in the formation and governance of the state guaranteed that, even for the non-Orthodox majority, important areas of women's lives would be shaped by Orthodox patriarchalism. Israel has a declaration of independence granting "equal social and political rights for all citizens, irrespective of religion, race, or sex"—but this declaration functions only as a statement of general principles that does not have the force of law. Lacking a constitution, Israel insures the rights of its citizens through statutes that are open to ongoing modification. In 1951, Israel passed a Women's Equal Rights Law, but within the law itself severely limited its application by exempting marriage and divorce. When in 1953 the Orthodox establishment was granted complete control of these areas, equal rights for Jewish women were effectively annulled.[7] While secularist compromises with Orthodox parties have had a profound effect on many areas of Israeli life, in the case of women, they have functioned to give institutional and legal sanction to some of the most disabling aspects of *halakhah* (Jewish law).

Another factor that has profoundly shaped women's lives is Israel's ongoing concern for survival and the consequent emergence of its citizens army as a major institution in the Israeli state. While in this case also, myth would have it that Israel is one of the few countries in the world to include women in the military on equal terms, here too myth obscures a very different reality. Of the fifty percent of women who serve at all in this major socializing institution, the majority do the same kind of office work they perform in the civilian market. Rather than serving alongside men, women replace them in clerical, switchboard, and social services so that men are freed for combat. Women's jobs in the army accord with a traditional understanding of female roles. The name of the women's corp— *Chen*, meaning charm—indicates the expectation that women are to humanize the military, strengthening the morale of male soldiers and making the army a "home away from home." Sexual relationships, formally ignored, are informally encouraged, and women are to provide amenities and forms of support that men are accustomed to in a patriarchal family.[8]

This supposed humanizing and softening effect of women on the armed

91

services signals the presence of a "cult of true womanhood" at work in Israel.[9] In a situation of continuing profound insecurity, women and the home come to be constructed as antidotes to, and havens from, the harsh realities of Israeli life. As the exemption of married and pregnant women from national service indicates, the role of women in the country's defense is less important than their role in the home. Or rather, the crucial role of women in Israel's survival is the role of mother. Living constantly in the fear of war and concerned that a growing Palestinian population threatens the Jewish character of the Israeli state, many in Israel see procreation as women's most important contribution to the Israeli future.[10] Thus the vision of equality in difference that was shared by at least some of Israel's founders has given way to traditional forms of women's subordination, now shaped and colored by the exigencies of an embattled nation-state.

The subordination of women is not the only hierarchical differentiation in diaspora Jewish life that has found expression in Israel. The relationship between Ashkenazim (Jews of Eastern European origin) and Mizrachim (Jews from Africa, Asia, and the Middle East) is also hierarchically ordered, with the "first" Israel (Ashkenazim) setting itself up as normative and expecting the "second" Israel to adapt to Ashkenazi standards. Like the subordination of women, this hierarchy is also a product of the diaspora, with the politics of statehood giving new form to older class and ethnic divisions. In the diaspora, Jews of different cultural and national backgrounds regarded one another as Other! There were hierarchies within the Eastern European Jewish community and also between that community and outsiders. Jews from Lithuania looked down on Jews from Galicia and also the religiously different Mizrachim. Sephardim in turn saw themselves as superior to Jews of Eastern European origin. In addition, each community had its own class structure, based on inequalities in wealth and learning. In Israel, traditional ethnic and cultural differences came to coincide with class differences in a way that realigned and solidified the divisions of the diaspora community.

Zionist belief in the fundamental unity of the Jewish people was put to the test quite soon after 1948 by the influx of great numbers of oriental immigrants from many Arab lands. Viewed with consternation and contempt by the Ashkenazi founders of the state, these "primitive" people from "backward countries" were expected to modernize and westernize, acculturating to Israeli society by taking on European customs and values.[11] Since this process was not to be reciprocal—Ashkenazi Israelis were not to learn from or be influenced by the culture of Middle Eastern Jews—

Ashkenazim effectively identified their own interests with the interests of the state. The resulting glaring social and economic discrimination against Oriental Jews and their exclusion from Israeli leadership have been important items on the Israeli national agenda for many years.[12] While the relationship between Ashkenazim and Mizrachim has shifted and been complicated by the oriental community's important role in the election of Likud (in 1977), this shift has not fundamentally altered the discomfitting role of ethnic pluralism in the Jewish state. In a situation in which many activist oriental Jews have themselves been ambivalent about whether they are claiming equality within an Ashkenazi state or demanding recognition of a separate oriental Jewish identity,[13] Israel has been no more effective in mining the creative possibilities inherent in differences among Jews than have Jews in the diaspora.

It is the Palestinians, however, rather than the Mizrachi Jews, who pose the most fundamental test of Israel's capacity to deal with difference, and whose situation highlights the connection between the creation of hierarchies within the Jewish community and between that community and others. Palestinian Israelis constitute a segregated and peripheral underclass whose grievances, unlike those of the Mizrachim, seldom capture the attention of the wider society. Formally granted equal rights by the same Declaration of Human Rights that gave equality to women, Palestinians are in fact excluded from the central symbols and institutions of the Jewish state. Both the ordinary operation of Israel's major institutions and specific government programs and policies have fostered the isolation and internal fragmentation of the Arab community and its economic dependence on the Jewish majority.[14] While the operation of these dynamics is complex, massive, and subtle, the barring of Moslem Arabs (the vast majority of the Arab population) from military service can serve as a symbol of the Palestinian population's isolation and lack of access to important resources. The question of Palestinian army service is a difficult one, tied up with broader questions of Jewish Israeli security and self-definition. Yet since the army is a key institution in building a sense of Israeli identity, transmitting a wide range of skills, and providing entrée to jobs and public assistance programs, the exclusion of Palestinians from the army means they are "cut off from the major dynamic processes of social integration and mobility which exist in Israel."[15]

The contradictions of a democracy in which seventeen percent of all citizens are suspected as a fifth column and subjected to discrimination are vastly intensified by Israel's direct military rule of over a million and a half

Palestinians on the West Bank and in Gaza. In the occupied territories, there is no pretense of democracy. Palestinians have no control over the government that determines the conditions of their existence, no right of appeal against the judgments of military courts, no secure rights to the land on which they live.[16] While these conditions are supposedly temporary, pending a permanent peace settlement, the Palestinian uprising has dramatized the untenability and injustice of such rule and the profound effects of twenty years of it on Jewish Israeli attitudes and values. Those Jews who favor annexing the occupied territories do not imagine offering Palestinians equal rights within a "Greater Israel." An increasingly vocal and militant religious right claims divine sanction for Israeli expansion—expansion that leaves no room for non-Jewish citizens within a Jewish state. As some religious nationalists understand it, equality of rights is at best an alien, i.e. European, democratic principle, and at worst, a violation of the biblical commandment to exterminate Amalek. Thus twenty years of military rule has created a situation in which Israeli government policy is to treat occupied Palestinians as intruders in their own land, and in which some Jews are actually advocating expelling or killing Palestinians in the name of chosenness.[17]

While the conflicts and inequalities between Jews and Palestinians, and Eastern European and oriental Jews have their own distinct origins and manifestations, they are also interstructured with the inequalities between women and men. As a few examples can make clear, the fact that many Israeli women are Palestinians or oriental Jews means that the relations between men and women are shaped partly by these other rifts; conversely, the subordination of women means that anti-Arab or Mizrachi discrimination falls differently on women than on men. Thus when Palestinian society was radically disrupted by the creation of Israel in 1948, one reaction of Palestinian men was to maintain cultural stability by increasing their traditional control over Palestinian women. As this control has relaxed and Palestinian women's independence has increased over the last twenty years, Israeli politicians have sought to control Palestinian women's political activism by appealing to the traditional Arab value system in relation to women.[18] Or, if we look at the role of (Jewish) women in the Israeli army, it is striking that of the approximately twenty-five percent of women exempted from service for lack of basic qualifications (insufficient level of literacy, inability to tolerate discipline), almost all are oriental. Just as most Palestinians are excluded from the important integrative and social functions the army performs, so are large numbers of oriental Jewish women.[19]

Or, as Israeli occupation of the West Bank and Gaza has brought the number of Palestinians under Jewish Israeli control to thirty percent of the population, the pressure on Jewish women to bear large numbers of children has increased greatly. The Jewish Israeli woman must serve as a breeder not only to supply future soldiers to the army but also to do her part in the "demographic war" for a continued Jewish majority in the state.[20]

As we look at this picture of interstructured hierarchical differentiations in Israeli society, a striking analogy emerges. The embattled Israeli Jew ignoring the inequities of Israeli society bears a disquieting resemblance to the oppressed ghetto Jew ignoring the internal inequalities in the Jewish community.[21] In the ghetto situation, God was believed both to vindicate Jewish suffering and to define and justify the subordination of women within Judaism. The rage engendered by male powerlessness was projected onto women who become the doubled Other in a community of Others. In Israel, Israeli Jews wish to see themselves as new and free people, but in fact are as surrounded by enemies as the Jews of the diaspora. In this situation, they claim a struggle in which they have "no choice" as warrant for oppressive policies toward Palestinians and for diversion of financial and moral resources from the resolution of internal social conflicts to the military budget. As in the diaspora situation, struggle with the enemy outside also fosters the oppression of women, whose theoretical equality is sacrificed to the needs of a beleaguered state.

It seems that the Jewish experience of oppression has led not to the just exercise of power by Jews in power, but to the Jewish repetition of strategies of domination. The many forms of oppression to which Jews have been subject, from denial of fundamental rights and outright expropriation of resources, to lack of respect for Jewish culture, to discrimination in housing and employment, are recapitulated within and between various groups in Israel. Not only has the Jewish historical experience not served as a lesson and warning, but past oppression has even been used as a justification for the right to oppress others. Past Jewish suffering is presumed to confer a moral purity that covers over and excuses moral weakness and rage.[22]

If this cycle in which oppressed becomes oppressor is psychologically comprehensible and historically familiar, it is, nevertheless, not inevitable. While the Israeli government often has set aside internal debate about the nature of Israel in the name of building and protecting the state, Israel's citizens have shown a persistent and remarkable willingness to discuss and reassess the purpose of Israel's existence and to question the values that have informed its actions.[23] Books and articles examining and criticizing various aspects of the State are widely read and vigorously debated, and numerous organizations have been formed to deal with the inequalities of Israeli society. Thus alongside discrimination against women and Mizrachim, there exist battered women's shelters, the Israeli feminist movement, numerous self-help organizations for Mizrachim, and groups working to facilitate Mizrachi and Ashkenazi cultural integration.[24] Alongside the multi-faceted discrimination against Israel's Arab citizens and governmental unwillingness to consider the existence of a Palestinian state, there exist literally dozens of organizations working for peace and Arab-Jewish reconciliation, trying to create a future in which Jews and Palestinians can peacefully and respectfully coexist.[25] Moreover, just as the various forms of discrimination in Israel are interstructured, so efforts toward ending discrimination seek to form coalitions across various structural lines. In numerous woman-to-woman dialogue groups, for example, Jewish and Arab women attempt to speak to one another directly of the conflicts between them and the pain and complexity of their lives. At the UN Decade for Women conference in Nairobi, Jewish and Palestinian women from Israel and the diaspora sponsored a public workshop on the Arab Israeli struggle attended by four hundred women from around the world.[26]

These groups and organizations working toward a new vision of community shift the boundaries of community, creating out of the multiple allegiances and identities that define the modern experience communities committed to a common purpose, able to address the issues that unite and divide them. Rather than leaving Ashkenazim and Mizrachim, Jews and Palestinians confronting each other across an abyss, projects for justice, peace, and dialogue forge—however temporarily—a shared Israeli, or woman's, or Middle-Eastern identity that, without denying differences, places these groups in a new context. Projects like these enact the conviction that difference need not be expressed in dominance or strife. If people work to make it so, shared oppression and resistance to oppression can be a bridge to mutual understanding and joint action. There may be no guarantee that the oppressed will not become oppressors, but it is nonetheless possible to forge links between oppression and the commitment to justice by careful and conscious insistence on remembering and using one's experience precisely for that purpose.

While the impulse toward self-questioning that characterizes many in Israel has sometimes been connected to the notion of chosenness, it is more appropriately linked to particular values central to Jewish memory and to the historical experience of oppression. The recent history of the religious right in Israel would seem to suggest that belief in chosenness can go hand-in-hand with the worst idolatry of the state and the willingness to justify any sort of abuse of the non-Jewish Other.[27] Over against this willingness lies the pain of oppression experienced in one's own flesh and the injunction of memory: "You shall not wrong or oppress a stranger, for you were strangers in the land of Egypt" (Exodus 22:20, altered). The multiform wrongs that the Jews have experienced, the commitment to remembering these wrongs as part of the struggle against them, and the continuing quest for integrity and self-definition as a community fuels questions about what kind of society the state is fighting to protect and whether there are forms of self-defense that undermine what supposedly is being defended.

If the state of Israel is to find modes of self-preservation compatible with and productive of a just society, it must learn from the whole Jewish experience what makes a society just. Surely, a just society is one in which the rights of minorities are not simply promised but guaranteed in law and in practice, in which the resources of the society are available to and shared by all its members, in which citizens are free from religious coercion, even if it be the coercion of their own tradition. It is a society that recognizes not simply the individual citizens who dwell within it but also the diverse communities, that acknowledges the different needs and traditions of these communities and expects that all will contribute to shaping the character of the nation as a whole. Such internal justice is not possible, moreover, unless a society recognizes the rights of its neighbors and has done its utmost to live in peace with them. The economic, social, and moral costs of military occupation make it incompatible with equity within one's own boundaries. The rightful claim of Palestinians to a land of their own renders occupation profoundly unjust.

Sometimes it seems that the realities of the Israeli occupation are only marginally related to the central agenda of Jewish feminists. Yet if we recognize that different forms of hierarchy and oppression intersect with and reinforce one another, then we must know that none will be abolished until all are addressed. Jewish feminists must apply the vision of community in which difference is nurtured and respected to all communities and all differences with which Jewish feminists are involved. When one group in a community has had the power to rule or speak for all within it, acceptance of difference entails dislodging long-fixed patterns of dominance. Such transformations are never easy, but they promise much, and not simply to those whose experience is obscured or denied by the reigning order. An Israel that honored diversity might transform itself from a fortress state into a country enjoying the energy and resources of a remarkably rich and varied multicultural citizenry, just as diaspora communities respecting particularity might find themselves with both a broadened and enlivened Jewish memory and present spiritual resources of unexpected depth. If difference is threatening, it also holds power. The struggle to find new models for relating to difference is a struggle to bring the manifold riches of a complex human heritage to the careful nurturing of communal and individual life.

4

The Occupation: Immoral and Stupid

MICHAEL LERNER

The widespread moral outrage at Israel's policies in Gaza and the West Bank—the sense that Israel is violating the basic ethical values of Judaism—is coupled with a growing realization that these policies are also bad for Israel and bad for the Jewish people. Granted, some of Israel's current critics have been unfair, both in their failure to acknowledge the role of Palestinian leaders and Arab states in creating the conflict and in their tendency to judge Israel by standards that they rarely apply to the rest of the world. Nevertheless, from the standpoint of Jewish ethics and Jewish survival the occupation is unacceptable. There are plausible solutions to the Palestinian problem that must be tried. But they won't be tried unless American Jews unequivocally tell Israel that the occupation cannot continue. This message must be conveyed forcefully to Prime Minister Shamir and to the Israeli public.

The pain and sorrow many American Jews feel about Israel's policies on the West Bank and Gaza are rooted deep in our collective memory as a people. Israel's attempt to regain control of the refugee camps by denying food to hundreds of thousands of men, women, and children, by raiding homes and dragging out their occupants in the middle of the night to stand for hours in the cold, by savagely beating a civilian population and breaking its bones—these activities are deplorable to any civilized human being. That they are done by a Jewish state is both tragic and inexcusable. We did not survive the gas chambers and crematoria so that we could become the oppressors of Gaza. The Israeli politicians who have led us into this morass are desecrating the legacy of Jewish history. If Jewish tradition has stood for anything, it has stood for the principle that justice must triumph over violence. For that reason, we typically have sided with the oppressed and have questioned the indiscriminate use of force. We, who love Israel, who remain proud Zionists, are outraged at the betrayal of this sacred legacy by small-minded Israeli politicians who feel more comfortable with the politics of repression than with the search for peace.

Any policy that requires the immoral tactics currently being used against an unarmed and militarily subjugated population must be rejected. If the activities of the Israeli army since December 1987 really are necessary, that in itself is sufficient to discredit the occupation. We do not diminish our loyalty to our own people by acknowledging our profound sadness at the suffering of Palestinians. Those who have grown up in camps or in exile have experienced homelessness in much the same way that Jews have experienced it throughout history. Even if this suffering were the absolutely necessary consequence of our self-preservation, we would still be deeply upset by the pain that thereby was caused to another group of human beings. We have been too sensitized by our own history of oppression not to feel diminished when others are in pain. That is why we dip drops from our wine cups at the Passover seder in memory of the pain of our Egyptian slaveholders. But when that pain is largely unnecessary, we feel not only sadness but also anger and a deep determination to do what we can to stop the suffering.

Our outrage is shared by many Israelis. Over fifty thousand of them gathered in Tel Aviv on January 23, 1988, in one of the biggest antiwar demonstrations in Jewish history to protest Israel's policies. Joined by hundreds of thousands of others who could not attend the demonstration but who share their outrage, they are asking American Jews to speak out. To be silent, or keep our criticisms safely "in the family," would be to betray our Israeli brothers and sisters.

That is why we say in unequivocal terms to the Israeli government: stop the beatings; stop the breaking of bones; stop the late night raids on people's homes; stop the use of food as a weapon of war; stop pretending that you can respond to an entire people's agony with guns and blows and power. Publicly acknowledge that the Palestinians have the same right to national self-determination that we Jews have, and negotiate a solution with representatives of the Palestinians!

But our anger at Israel's current policies comes not only from moral outrage but also from deep concern about Israel's survival and the survival of the Jewish people. From a strictly self-interested position, the occupation is stupid. Here's why:

1. The longer the occupation exists, the more angry and radical young Palestinians will become. The possibility of negotiating a two-state solution will decrease since these young Palestinians will come to regard a

West Bank state as a "sell-out" of their dreams for a fully liberated Palestine, and PLO leaders willing to settle for such a state will be seen not as "moderates" but as betrayers of the struggle. This attitude is becoming more prevalent, but it has not yet achieved dominance. Yitzhak Rabin's policy of "the iron fist" only quickens this radicalization. In years to come we may wish that we had dealt with the PLO before the Palestinians embraced some radical form of Islamic fundamentalism that makes it a religious sin to live in peace with Israel.

2. Even those Palestinians who now live within the pre-1967 borders of Israel are being drawn into the struggle. Faced with the repression of their own people in the occupied territories, they participated in the general strike in December. Some have rioted in protest of Israeli military action. The longer the occupation lasts, the more they will be drawn into the struggle—with disastrous consequences for Israel. Unless the occupation is speedily ended, Israel may soon resemble Beirut or Northern Ireland.

3. As the occupation continues, the logic of domination and repression of Palestinians will require that Israelis adopt an increasingly insensitive view towards those whom they must control. Israelis will inevitably be pushed to the political right. In the past few years we have seen the right-wing Tehiyah party and even some sectors of Likud advocate Kahane-like ideas. Today, right-wing members of the Labor party such as Yitzhak Rabin act in ways that would have made them scream at Ariel Sharon only a few years ago. This move to the right is likely to accelerate the already large emigration (*yeridah*) rate plaguing Israel—only this time those who leave will be going, not to find their "fortune" in America, but to escape a political situation that they cannot morally justify. Increasingly, it will be the scientific, technical, and professional personnel who leave—people whose contributions have been essential to the defense technology, economic strength, and intellectual creativity of the country.

4. Because most of the pro-Zionist Jewish leadership in the United States has remained quiet, the only voices articulating clear moral criticism have been those of Israel's enemies. For the anti-Semites and the anti-Zionists these are wonderful times. Reports already exist of campus demonstrations with posters denouncing "Jewish murderers"—and many Jewish college students, ashamed of the images of the Jewish state being portrayed in the media every day, are willing, for the first time, to listen to the anti-Zionist propaganda being disseminated. Previously lacking any rational foundation for their attacks on Jews, the voices of hate have gained

credibility by their association with legitimate criticisms of the Jewish state. Israel's current policies give credibility to the worst lies about Judaism. And, in the years ahead, the Jewish people may face hard times based not simply on lies and distortions of anti-Semites, but on the justified indignation of many people who see the Jewish state embodying a viciousness and moral callousness that they would find repugnant anywhere.

5. The occupation threatens to erode the popular base of support for Israel in the United States. As America's economic problems intensify in the coming years, people will inevitably question any large-scale military and economic aid given to any foreign country. Moreover, major American corporations have never been happy with the government's tilt toward Israel. Most corporations understand that their long-term economic interests are better served by friendlier relations with the various Arab autocracies. Opportunities for investment and trade have been limited by America's alliance with Israel. The United States' policy of military support to Israel is one instance in which popular forces, using the democratic mechanisms of the electoral process, have countered corporate interests. Even the power of AIPAC is based less on its fundraising capacities (does anyone seriously doubt that Arab oil companies could, if they so chose, raise more cash for political candidates than AIPAC?) than on its ability to mobilize a political constituency of Israel's supporters. Yet many of Israel's supporters would be much less committed if Israel were perceived as having repudiated its commitment to democratic values and human rights. If Americans continue to be barraged by images of Israelis beating, teargassing, shooting, and starving a civilian population, they will be much less likely to stand up to the Arab and corporate interests that argue for "evenhandedness" in American policy.

Make no mistake about it—what is at stake for Israel is not only its Jewish soul but its survival. Once the perception fades that Israel stands for moral values, those of us who want to provide for Israel's defense may be unable to convince the United States to supply the latest and most sophisticated military hardware, and Israel may be unable to keep up with Arab armies supplied not only by the Soviet Union but also by Japan and Europe. As a result, Israel may become vulnerable to serious military attack. There is no more pressing Israeli security need than its need to maintain its image as a society committed to just values.

6. The occupation is also a threat to the survival of Judaism and the Jewish people in the diaspora. The breakdown of authoritarian communal structures increasingly makes every Jew a Jew by choice. In the past two

decades there has been a dramatic revival of interest in Judaism from Americans who have found the individualistic and competitive values of American society unfulfilling and morally vacuous. They have turned to Judaism because they rightly sense Judaism's moral sensitivity and its transcendent vision, which stands in sharp opposition to the logic of domination and mean-spiritedness that permeates life in most competitive market societies. The occupation may reverse this trend, since increasing numbers of Jews will begin to dismiss much of Judaism's moral vision as pious moralizing that lacks substance. A Judaism that has lost its moral teeth and becomes an apologist for every Israeli policy, no matter what its moral content, is a Judaism that not only betrays the prophetic tradition, but also risks losing the adherence of the Jewish people.

Israel is putting its supporters in the agonizing position of either rejecting its current policies or rejecting some of the central teachings of Judaism. While Israel's policies in the West Bank and Gaza are anathema to Jew and non-Jew alike, to secular as well as religious people, they are especially upsetting to those who take Judaism seriously as a guide to life. No rules in the Torah are repeated as frequently as those that, in one form or another, warn us not to respond to being oppressed by oppressing others. Using the term *ger* (stranger) to refer to anyone who is part of a relatively powerless minority, just as *we* were in Egypt, the Bible commands us over and over again: "When you come into your land, do not oppress the *ger* who dwells in your midst." "One law shall be for you and the *ger*." And always the haunting reminder: "Remember that you were a *ger* in the land of Egypt!" (Exodus 23:9; Leviticus 19:33–34)

The wisdom of the Jewish tradition is deep. It recognizes the temptation to do unto others what was done unto us, to engage in a kind of collective repetition compulsion in which we attempt to achieve mastery over the traumas of the past by identifying with our oppressors and becoming like them. We can see this dynamic in many people who were traumatized as children, and who then as adults seem to replicate, in their behavior towards others, much of what was done to them when they were young and powerless. The Torah seems to recognize that this same dynamic can affect an entire people, and it insists that freedom means breaking out of this pattern by consciously resisting it. For the Children of Israel, political freedom from slavery was only the first step. In order to be entitled to the Land of Israel, they had to accept the yoke of moral responsibility not to pass on to the next generations the evils of the past. For that reason, the

Children of Israel were required to wander in the desert for forty years until the generation that was crippled by the mentality of slavery died off. The psychological traumas of oppression cannot be made the basis for building a Jewish society. We must transcend this dynamic: we must not do to others what was done to us. God's voice here is unequivocal: there is no right to the Land of Israel if Jews oppress the *ger*, the widow, the orphan, or any other group that is powerless.

The Torah insists that both physical and psychological/spiritual slavery must and can be broken. This is the liberatory message of Passover. To the extent that Judaism has kept alive this message of hope, it has been a revolutionary vanguard, insisting that the logic of the past, the logic of oppression, is not the only possible reality, that there exists a transcendent and liberating Force that we must foster. For this very reason, Jews must reject every effort to turn Judaism into a cheering squad for Israeli policies. We also must resist the arguments of those who say, "We Jews were hurt so badly in the past and have such a residue of anger for our past oppression that you must understand why we act as we now do." On the contrary, the essence of Judaism is to resist that argument.

Nevertheless, we must have compassion for the people who feel this way. We cannot ignore the specific features of Jewish history that may have conditioned Israeli soldiers to act like a classical colonial force trying to subjugate a rebellious citizen population. The rage that these soldiers exhibit when they beat civilians they suspect have been involved in rock throwing may be understood, in part, as a response to the two thousand years during which the world systematically denied their right to exist as a people, a denial that culminated with extermination in gas chambers and crematoria. This oppression occurred not only in Europe; many Jews also had to flee Arab lands after hundreds of years of oppression and delegitimation. This same process of delegitimation has been further perpetuated by the Arab states in their refusal to relocate Palestinian refugees in 1948, in their insistence that these refugees stay in camps in Gaza and the West Bank, and in their failure to follow the lead of other countries that resettled much larger refugee populations, such as Pakistan's resettlement of nearly ten million Moslems after the struggle for Indian independence. This conduct by the Arab states was a loud proclamation: "You Jews don't really exist for us. Your presence here is temporary. We don't have to resettle the Palestinians or deal with this problem because you will soon be gone."

For two thousand years the Jews had to scream in silence, fearful that protesting their delegitimation would lead to an escalation of oppression.

Now, with the existence of the State of Israel, these Jews have begun to unleash their pent-up anger on the Palestinians—not a people of innocent bystanders, but a people that refused to accept the state of Israel in 1947, a people whose leadership still views a state as a transitional entity to a "second stage" in which Israel will be destroyed. One can understand the rage of some Israeli soldiers by recognizing this history of delegitimation.

A people this deeply wounded deserves compassion. Yet love for Israelis requires us to do our best to stop them from hurting themselves and others. Just as we understand the frustration that leads Palestinian youths to throw rocks even as we criticize their conduct, so too do we express deep care for our brothers and sisters in Israel even as we reject their actions.

We do not have to be reminded that the Palestinians themselves played a major role in creating the present conflict. When they were the majority in Palestine and *we* were refugees, they would not allow refugees to share the land. When Jews were desperately fleeing Christian Europe as well as Islamic Asia and North Africa, the Palestinian refusal to grant Jews a haven convinced many Zionists that Palestinian self-determination is incompatible with Jewish survival. When the media focus on Israel's treatment of the Palestinians, they paint an incomplete picture to the extent that they fail to inform their audience that the Palestinians are heirs to a tradition that to this day continues to reject the legitimacy of Jewish claims to a state. Those who throw rocks today may be justifiably frustrated, but if they do not have the courage to match their rock throwing with the political will to accommodate Israel, if they wallow in their fantasies of eliminating the Jewish state, they simply will prolong their homelessness.

So we say to the Palestinians: stop the rock throwing; stop the talk of violently overthrowing Israel; reject the rejectionists; and publicly proclaim your willingness to live in peace with Israel. Begin to talk publicly about peaceful coexistence. You will not be granted genuine self-determination until you allay the legitimate fears of many centrist Israelis that you still are committed to destroying Israel.

Along with many people's failure to recognize that the Palestinians bear part of the responsibility for the present crisis has come criticism of Israel that simply is out of proportion, criticism that makes both Israelis and American Jews defensive and prevents them from recognizing the genuine injustice of Israel's policies. The worst example of such criticism is the comparison between Israel and South Africa. Israel is not South Africa, and what it is doing is not apartheid. It is true that Israel, like South Africa, is inflicting needless suffering on a population that seeks self-determination. But when it does this, it acts as a colonial oppressor in ways more similar to the Soviet Union's oppression (on a much larger scale) in Afghanistan, or China's in Tibet, or the United States' (acting through local proxies) in much of Central America.

Apartheid is a racist system under which blacks are discriminated against simply because they are black. In Israel the picture is different. Arabs who have remained within the pre-1967 Israeli borders have the same political rights as any other Israeli and are represented in the Knesset. Though Israeli Arabs rightly complain about unfair allocations of the budget and discrimination in housing and employment, these are practices that more closely resemble the unfair realities of black life in the United States than the formal legal discrimination of apartheid. The fact remains that an Israeli Arab with large amounts of money does not face the kind of discrimination that remained legally instituted against blacks in the United States until thirty years ago. Israeli Arabs play on the same beaches, eat at the same restaurants, attend the same movie theatres, and are free to stay at the same hotels as other Israelis.

The situation in the occupied territories is terrible, but resembles colonial oppression much more than racist apartheid. First, even if the territories were annexed into Israel, we would not be faced with the South African situation of a minority ruling a majority. Israeli Jews would remain a majority oppressing a minority the way Sikhs are oppressed in India, or the Kurds in Iran and Turkey, or the Miskito Indians in Nicaragua, or the Irish Catholics in Northern Ireland, or the Basques in Spain. Second, unlike typical colonial oppressors, many Israelis still favor a solution under which they would rid themselves of the West Bank, provided that they could guarantee Israel's security. Israel's good faith already has been shown in its withdrawal from the Sinai in return for peace with Egypt. This is not the behavior of a colonial power, much less of a South African-type regime. In short, the South Africa analogy distorts reality and allows right-wingers to focus on its flaws instead of dealing with the justified criticism of Israel.

There are solutions to these problems. A demilitarized and politically neutral Palestinian state can be established on the West Bank and Gaza in precisely the same fashion that the Russians and Americans agreed to give Austria independence after World War II. Demilitarization would be guaranteed by the United States and the Soviet Union, and the treaty that established this Palestinian state would also recognize Israel's right to intervene militarily in order to prevent the introduction of tanks, heavy artillery, or airplanes. The United States, the Soviet Union, and Israel would create a unified force to protect the Palestinian state from attack by Syria, Iraq, Iran, or other hostile powers, and the United States would enter into a collective security agreement with Israel guaranteeing the full power of American military might to defend Israel against attack. The Palestinian state would renounce all claims to the rest of Palestine and would police those remaining Palestinians still desiring a further struggle with Israel. Israel would agree to enter into economic confederation with this Palestinian state after a specified period of peaceful coexistence.

Who could negotiate for the Palestinians? Any group that is willing to recognize Israel's right to exist. If Israel claims that the PLO doesn't represent the Palestinians in the occupied territories, let it immediately hold a plebiscite to determine whom West Bank Palestinians want to negotiate for them. And Israel must set no restrictions on who can be a candidate.

What if no Palestinian leadership is willing to accept a demilitarized Palestinian state? Then Israel loses nothing by having offered, and actually gains a great deal. Instead of Israeli rejectionism, we would be back to a clear picture of the Palestinians as the obstacle. It is reasonable for Israel to insist on its own security. If, in the 1930s, Jews had been offered a state under a similar plan guaranteed by all the great powers, they certainly would have accepted it, even on a considerably smaller piece of land. Ultimately, a totally demilitarized Middle East is optimum, but for now a demilitarized Palestinian state is the only kind of state likely to be accepted. We hope the Palestinians prove the skeptics wrong by accepting a demilitarized state.

Israel should publicly offer the Palestinians such a state now. This proclamation will help ensure Israel's political and military survival. It probably also will provoke a crisis in the Palestinian world and bring to the fore the unresolved conflict between those Palestinians who really are willing to accept Israel's right to exist and those who desire a state on the West Bank simply as a launching pad for the total destruction of Israel. If the rejectionists win the struggle, Israel has proved itself reasonable without weakening itself militarily. We hope, however, that the forces of reason among the Palestinians will win and that the kind of peace that most Israelis want can be achieved.

Anything less than such a public proclamation will be seen as stalling—and rightly so. Prime Minister Shamir's attempts to revive Camp David "autonomy" talks clearly are delay tactics. The autonomy being proposed is a sham—the opposite of genuine self-determination. But even an international conference will have limited impact if Israel is unwilling to commit itself to a demilitarized Palestinian state. A "solution" that proposes anything less than this—for example, a Jordanian confederation on the West Bank under which the Palestinians still do not have self-determination, their own flag, or their own passports—will give extremist Palestinians the incentive to expand the struggle. The psychology of the situation is clear: until the Palestinians feel that they own something, which limited autonomy cannot provide, they have no real incentive to stop the struggle. Once they achieve this sense of ownership, those who advocate continuing the struggle will be seen by fellow Palestinians as putting their own state in jeopardy. If, however, Israel commits itself publicly to a demilitarized Palestinian state, it need not yield an inch of land until the demilitarization is firmly in place.

Americans, particularly American Jews, have an extraordinary historical responsibility at this moment. The path of least resistance—privately criticizing Israel but publicly supporting it or remaining silent—is actually a dramatic betrayal of the interests of our people. Americans must use every possible means to convey to Israelis—in private communications, in letters to Israeli newspapers and to members of Knesset, in petitions to the government of Israel, in public rallies and teach-ins, and in statements issued by synagogues and communal organizations—that Israel is in deep jeopardy and that the occupation must end.

What we do now actually may make a significant difference. Israeli centrists are under the illusion that American economic and political support can be taken for granted. Conservative leaders from the American Jewish world have fostered this fantasy. Many of these centrists can be moved to support peace proposals if they are made aware of the precariousness of their position. The ordinary Israeli has no idea how deep American disaffection has become or how such disaffection may threaten Israel's military security in the future. The only way she or he will "get it" is through a combination of public protests and private communications. Since we can't count on Jewish leaders to convey this sense of urgency, we need to do it ourselves.

Many American Jewish leaders have displayed shortsightedness and cowardice in dealing with the current difficulties. Little in their past style of operation or in their intellectual approach gives them the tools necessary to provide leadership now that it is needed most. The neoconservatives, the "Israel is always right" crowd, the people with moral blinders—

none of these people can provide an analysis or a strategy that will speak to the American Jewish public. A very large number of American Jews are in a state of deep personal crisis. Their identification with Judaism, Israel, and the Jewish people is being fundamentally challenged. This is the moment when they need to hear a different kind of voice from the Jewish world. Let them hear our voice.

The crisis in Israel is a moment of truth for all of us. We should respond to it with the deepest seriousness and with the full understanding that the choices we make now may have consequences that reverberate for centuries to come.

5

The Occupation Is Over:
Perspectives from a Jewish Theology
of Liberation

MARC H. ELLIS

With the decisive victory of Israel in the June 1967 Six Day War, certain trends in Jewish theological understanding crystallized. It might be said that the war itself posed both sides of a dialectic present in Jewish life since the discovery of the death camps and the emergence of the state of Israel: the dialectic of Holocaust and empowerment. Because of the perpetual diaspora situation over the last two thousand years and the difficulty of humanly absorbing the Nazi attempt to impose a "final solution" to the Jewish question, theological responses to this new dialectic were naturally slow in coming. A revolution in theological thought was needed to match the revolutionary change in the Jewish condition, i.e., the loss of European Jewry, the shift of diaspora Jewish power to North America, and the reality of a Jewish state. After the Six Day War, that philosophical transformation was solidified and articulated by Holocaust theologians who, in despair and courage, charted a theology that is now normative for the Jewish community throughout the world.[1]

In its beginnings, Holocaust theology, as pioneered by Elie Wiesel, Emil Fackenheim, Richard Rubenstein, and Irving Greenberg, was radical, incisive, and controversial. It spoke about and named the collective trauma the Jewish people had experienced as a, or often as *the*, formative event of Jewish history. Holocaust theologians juxtaposed the Holocaust with the biblical origins of the Jewish community to pose the question of God's fidelity to a covenanted people. They challenged the Rabbinic tradition both in its theological analysis of the diaspora condition and the type of leadership, or lack thereof, it provided in the moment of great adversity.

110

At the same time Holocaust theologians critically analyzed the dark side of modernity with its landscape of mass dislocation and mass death.[2]

While the formative event of the Holocaust encouraged retrospective probing of traditional Jewish understandings in the theological and political realms, it demanded even more urgently the development of a framework for sustaining Jewish survival in the present. For if Holocaust theologians understood anything with great clarity it was that the Holocaust was the most disorienting event in Jewish history. Thus in the midst of broken lives and shattered faiths, Holocaust theologians needed to articulate a future for the Jewish people.[3]

The genius of the Holocaust theologians was that they understood that the prospective search needed to be as radical as their retrospective probings. And that somehow within the radical questioning of past and future, the Jewish people would need a sustaining faith, one no longer overtly theological, in the present. Hence, in order to survive in the face of a disorienting event, a redefinition of what it meant to be Jewish was the task before this emerging theology. Defining a practicing Jew as one who engaged in study, ritual, and observance of the law was no longer adequate, and Holocaust theologians knew it. They also understood that religious affiliation or nonaffiliation would be an insufficient test of fidelity to the Jewish people. What they offered instead was a framework to integrate diverse experiences and outlooks into a strong solidarity with the future of the Jewish people. No longer would the primary commitment to synagogue, to liberal/radical politics, or to an assimilationist indifference suffice. What was needed was a broad and energetic commitment to the commands of the Holocaust experience: memory, survival, and empowerment, especially as embodied in the state of Israel. It was these commands that allowed for the continuation of the people so that at some point in history there would be a context for the resolution of the questions posed by the Holocaust. In a sense, Holocaust theologians gathered the people together for the only kind of Sinai experience possible after the Holocaust.[4]

The task of charting the future of the Jewish people was even more complex than its internal community components. The new Sinai, in gathering Jews of different persuasions into a transformed covenant, demanded a radical probing of the diverse worlds Jews lived within, including the worlds of Christianity and modernity. Indictment of historical Christianity was simple enough, at least in its overt institutional capacity; apathy toward, complicity in, and solidarity with the murderers was the order of the day. The "righteous gentiles" were clearly a minority to be mentioned, though often in passing and surely as exceptions. The collapse of European culture and values, the need to emphasize the dark side of the ideology of progress, the failure of the democracies to respond to massive Jewish refugee populations—these were more difficult issues to face. Modernity, as a promise to the world of human betterment and freedom, and especially emancipation for the Jewish people, needed a radical analysis as well. Thus Holocaust theologians confronted a dual crisis of massive proportions involving the shattering of the Jewish people and modernity.

Just as they responded to the crisis of Jewish life by creating a framework for solidarity among the Jewish people, Holocaust theologians responded to the crisis of modernity by envisioning a solidarity for those consigned to the other side of a century of progress. Richard Rubenstein and Irving Greenberg have crystallized this struggle to articulate a theological thesis for our time: "The passing of time has made it increasingly evident that a hitherto unbreachable moral and political barrier in the history of Western Civilization was successfully overcome by the Nazis in World War II and that henceforth the systematic, bureaucratically administered extermination of millions of citizens or subject peoples will forever be one of the capacities and temptations of government." They explain further that "the victims ask us, above all, not to allow the creation of another matrix of values that might sustain another attempt at genocide." The terrible tragedy of the Holocaust thus lay in the future as much as in the past.[5]

The Limitations of Holocaust Theology

By 1975, just eight years after the conclusion of the Six Day War, Holocaust theologians had addressed the crisis of the Jewish people and modernity, proposed a framework for solidarity among the Jewish people and others suffering around the world, and thus had outlined the essential dimensions of Holocaust theology as we inherit it today. Holocaust theologians had succeeded in the task that faces all theology: to nurture the questions that allow us to understand the history we are participating in and creating. Yet it was at this moment, the time when Holocaust theology became normative for the Jewish people, that its critical edge became elusive. Holocaust theology was succumbing to that to which all theologies inevitably succumb: it no longer could address the questions critical to the history the Jewish people were creating. The reasons for this failure are complex and beyond the scope of this essay. Suffice it to say here that Holocaust theology emerged out of a situation of powerlessness that demanded a mobilization of psychic energy and material activity toward empowerment; the dialectic of Holocaust and empowerment acted as a counterbalance and a critique of weakness and empire. However it did not have within it a way of analyzing power once it had been achieved. Because of the experience of Holocaust, the theology lacked objectivity regarding power in Jewish hands. It could not address the cost of our empowerment.[6]

In fact as the situation in Israel changed over time, with expanded borders, two decades of occupation, the invasion of Lebanon, and an increasing role in global arms sales and foreign policy intrigue, Holocaust theology's dialectic remained as it had crystallized at the moment of the 1967 triumph. What did change was its emphasis on empowerment. The critical role of the Holocaust diminished. We might say that in this process the Holocaust became the servant of power, called upon to legitimate activity that hitherto was seen as unethical, even immoral. Jews in the United States were in the most difficult situation of all diaspora communities: maintaining a highly visible support of Israel and creating the climate for an expanded U.S. role in support of that state as necessary for its survival, while being relatively powerless to affect Israeli domestic and foreign policy even when in profound disagreement.[7]

As Holocaust theology lost its ability to enter critically into the contemporary situation of the Jewish people, its reliance on empowerment became more and more obvious. A strange paradox ensued that continues today: a theology that poses the most radical religious and ethical questions functions politically in a neoconservative manner. Not only are the most articulate Holocaust theologians neoconservative in their political stances, they help to legitimate the shift of Jewish intellectuals from the left to the center and right of center on the political spectrum. Even Holocaust theologians with previous liberal credentials bear analysis. By the 1980s Irving Greenberg, who wrote so eloquently about the prophetic call of the victims of the Holocaust in the 1970s, was essentially supporting the reemergence of American power under Ronald Reagan. At the same time, he warned against the misuse of the prophetic to undermine the security of the state of Israel: "There is a danger that those who have not grasped the full significance of the shift in the Jewish condition will judge Israel by the ideal standards of the state of powerlessness, thereby not only misjudging but unintentionally collaborating with attempted genocide." The subliminal if not overt message is clear: those who dissent carry a heavy burden even to the point of creating the context for another holocaust.[8]

However, because of the Palestinian uprising, increasing numbers of Jews are beginning to understand that our historical situation has changed radically in the last two decades and that something terrible, almost tragic, is happening to us. With what words do we speak such anguished sentiments? Do we feel alone with these feelings so that they are better left unspoken? Do such words, once spoken, condemn us as traitors or with the epithet, self-hating Jew? Or does articulating the unspeakable challenge the community to break through the silence and paralysis that threatens to engulf us? And those of us who know and empathize with the Palestinians, can we speak without being accused of creating a context for another holocaust? Can we be seen as emissaries of an option to halt the cycle of destruction and death?[9]

This is the challenge that faces the Jewish people. And with it lies the task of creating a new Jewish theology consonant with the history we are creating and the history we want to bequeath to our children. When all is said and done, should it be that we are powerful where once we were weak, that we are invincible where once we were vulnerable? Or would we rather be able to say that the power we created, necessary and flawed, was simply a tool to move beyond empowerment to a liberation that encompassed all those struggling for justice, including those we once knew as enemy? And that our power, used in solidarity with others, brought forth a healing in the world that ultimately began to heal us of our wounds from over the millennia?

New movements of renewal within the Jewish community that have developed or expanded during the uprising point the way to this theology. In Israel, the Committee Confronting the Iron Fist, made up of Israelis and Palestinians, whose first publication carried the provocative title "We Will Be Free In Our Own Homeland!", creates dialogue situations and stages demonstrations to end the occupation. Members of the anti-war movement Yesh Gvul, or There Is A Limit, made up of Israelis who refused to serve in the Lebanese War and today refuse to serve in the West Bank and Gaza, are courageous in their willingness to say "no" to the oppression of others, even at the expense of imprisonment. Women in Black, made up of Israelis who hold vigils in mourning dress, and Women Against Occupation, who adopt Palestinian women political prisoners and detainees, are just two more of many Jewish groups protesting the occupation and expressing solidarity with the Palestinian uprising.[10]

Since the uprising, North American Jews are increasingly vocal about justice in the Middle East. New Jewish Agenda, a movement of secular and religious Jews, continues to argue for Israeli security and the just demands of Palestinian nationhood. *Tikkun*, the progressive Jewish magazine, is in the forefront of vocal argument and organizing for a new understanding of the Israeli-Palestinian situation. And now with the recent crisis, Jewish intellectuals, such as Arthur Hertzberg and Irving Howe, and institutions, including the Union of American Hebrew Congregations, have voiced their horror at Israeli policies in the occupied territories.[11]

What these individuals and movements represent is a groping toward a theological framework that nurtures rather than hinders expressions of solidarity. It is almost as if a long repressed unease is coming to the surface, breaking through the language and symbol once deemed appropriate. Of course the risk is that if the crisis passes without fundamental change, the language of solidarity will recede and the more familiar patterns will reassert themselves. And it is true that even the movements cited are often limited in their scope and vision, equivocating where necessary to retain some credibility within the Jewish community still dominated by a Holocaust theology framework.

Still the drift is unmistakable and the task clear. The theological framework we need to create is hardly a departure, but a renewal of the themes that lie at the heart of our tradition, the exodus and the prophetic, interpreted in the contemporary world. A Jewish theology of liberation is our oldest theology, our great gift to the world, that has atrophied time and again only to be rediscovered by our own community and other communities around the world. A Jewish theology of liberation confronts Holocaust and empowerment with the dynamic of solidarity, providing a bridge to others as it critiques our own abuses of power. By linking us to all those who struggle for justice, a Jewish theology of liberation will, in the long run, decrease our sense of isolation and abandonment and thus begin a process of healing so necessary to the future of the Jewish community.

If it is true that we cannot go back behind empowerment, we now know that we cannot go forward alone. Could it be that the faces that confront us somehow contain the future of the Jewish people? This is why a two-state solution is only the beginning of a long and involved process that demands political compromise and a theological transformation that is difficult to envision. For if our theology is not confronted and transformed, then the political solutions will be superficial and transitory. A political solution may give impetus to this theological task; a theological movement may nurture a political solution. However, a political solution without a theological transformation simply enshrines the tragedy to be repeated again.

Here we enter the most difficult of arenas. The presupposition that in the faces of the Palestinians lies the future of what it means to be Jewish, that at the center of the struggle to be faithful as a Jew today is the suffering and liberation of the Palestinian people, is *hardly considered in Jewish theological circles*—despite the uprising. At some point, though, an essential integration of Jew and Palestinian in a larger area of political, cultural, and religious life is integral to a Jewish future. However, this assumes that a fundamental confession and repentance of past and present transgressions is possible and a critical understanding of our history developed.

The Occupation Is Over

Since the beginning of the uprising we have awakened to reports of the torture and death of Palestinian people, mostly youth, in the occupied territories. This raises a strange and disturbing question: if Palestinians cease to die, will the uprising—at least for North American Jews and Christians—cease to matter? A horrible thought follows: for the Palestinian cause, it is crucial that they continue to die in ever increasing numbers to drive home the understanding that the occupation, as we have known it, is over. Unable to accept this conclusion, I approached a Palestinian acquaintance and a Christian who had just returned from the West Bank: both had the same thought. The Palestinian leadership—as well as the Palestinian villagers—understand this tragic fact: the uprising is dependent on the continuing torture and death of Palestinian youth.

Can Jewish Israelis continue to torture and kill Palestinian youth ad infinitum? Can North American Jews continue to support these horrible acts? And can Christians, especially those who have chosen to repent of the anti-Semitism of the Christian past and who have accepted Israel as an integral part of the contemporary Jewish experience, remain silent on the uprising and Israeli brutality? Or, are we all hoping that somehow the situation will dissipate, go unreported, or better still, disappear? This much seems clear: the willingness of Palestinians to endure torture and death and the willingness of Israel to inflict such brutality, point to the most difficult of situations, which many choose to ignore: that some basic themes of post-Holocaust Jewish and Christian life are being exposed in a radical and unrelenting way.

If it is true that the occupation of the territories is over, that it has moved beyond occupation to uprising and civil war, then the theological support for the occupation in Jewish Holocaust theology and Christian theologies that lend uncritical support to Israel must end as well. The core of both types of theologies has been shattered. The uprising, therefore, is a crisis on many fronts. It is, at its deepest level, a theological crisis. Of course, like any crisis the uprising presents us with both tragedy and possibility. By demonstrating the truth, even at the price of broken bones and lives, the children of Palestine force us to think again and to break through ignorance, half-truths, and lies. Will we have the tenacity and courage in safe and comfortable North America that the Palestinian children have on the streets of Gaza and the West Bank? Or, will the inevitable allegations of Jewish self-hate and Christian anti-Jewishness deter us? Are we willing to reexamine our theological presuppositions as particular communities and in dialogue with each other, or will we attempt to pass over the question in silence?

It is not too much to say that the uprising presents the future of Judaism in stark and unremitting terms. The tragedy of the Holocaust is well documented and indelibly ingrained in our consciousness: we know who we were. But do we know who we have become? Contemporary Jewish theology helps us come to grips with our suffering; it hardly recognizes that today we are powerful. A theology that holds in tension Holocaust and empowerment speaks eloquently for the victims of Treblinka and Auschwitz yet ignores Sabra and Shatila. It pays tribute to the Warsaw Ghetto uprising but has no place for the uprising of ghetto dwellers on the other side of Israeli power. Jewish theologians insist that the torture and murders of Jewish children be lamented and commemorated in Jewish ritual and belief. It has yet to imagine, though, the possibility that Jews have in turn tortured and murdered Palestinian children. Holocaust theology relates the story of the Jewish people in its beauty and suffering. Yet it fails to integrate the contemporary history of the Palestinian people as integral to our own. Thus, this theology articulates who we were but no longer helps us understand who we have become.

So some Jews who are trying to understand the present become a contradiction to themselves, while others simply refuse to acknowledge the facts of contemporary Jewish life. A dilemma arises: awareness of Jewish transgressions has no theological framework in which to be articulated and acted upon; ignorance (albeit preferred rather than absolute) insists that what is occurring is impossible, that torture and murder are not in fact happening at all, that Jews could not do such things. Jews who become aware have few places to turn theologically, and the ignorant become more and more bellicose in their insistence and in their anger. Meanwhile, despite increasing dissent, Holocaust theology continues as normative in the Jewish community, warning dissident Jews that they approach the terrain of excommunication and continuing to reinforce the ignorance of many Jews as a theological prerequisite to community membership.[12]

As Israel and Jews in diaspora communities become more empowered, this neoconservative trend remains, buttressed by fear, anger, and by a deepening sense of isolation. Anyone who works in the Jewish community recognizes this immediately, the almost uncontrollable emotional level that criticism of Israel engenders. To be accused of creating the context for another holocaust is almost commonplace, as are charges of treason and self-hate. It is as if the entire world is still against us, as if the next trains depart for Eastern Europe, as if the death camps remain ready to receive us after an interval of almost half a century. This is why though the entire world outside the United States and Israel understands Yasir Arafat to be a moderate, there is no *other* name linked by the Jewish community so closely to Adolf Hitler. This is why Prime Minister Shamir spoke of the plans to launch a ship of Palestinian refugees to Israel as an attempt to undermine the state of Israel, as an act of war.

Years after the liberation of the camps, Elie Wiesel wrote, "Were hatred a solution, the survivors, when they came out of the camps, would have had to burn down the whole world." Surely with the nuclear capacity of Israel, coupled with the sense of isolation and anger, Wiesel's statement remains a caution that may yet be exercised. Is it too much to say that any theology that does not understand the absolute difference between the Warsaw Ghetto and Tel Aviv, between Hitler and Arafat, is a theology that may legitimate that which Wiesel cautioned against?[13]

Christians who have entered into solidarity with the Jewish people are similarly in a dilemma. The road to solidarity has been paved both by Christian renewal, which since Vatican II has been profoundly affected by the recovery of Hebrew Scriptures and the Jewishness of Jesus, and by Holocaust theology, which advised Christians of their anti-Jewishness and their complicity in Jewish suffering and allowed a repentance through recognizing the centrality of Israel to the Jewish people. Understanding the beauty and suffering of the Jewish people as a call to Christian repentance and transformation hardly prepares the community for a confrontation with Israeli power. How do Christians respond now when, over the years, the centrality of Israel has been stressed as necessary to Christian confession in the arena of dialogue, and no words of criticism against Israel are countenanced as anything but anti-Jewish? Also, Christian Zionism, fundamentalist and liberal, is ever present. What framework do Christians have to probe the history of the state of Israel, to understand the uprising—to question the cost of Jewish empowerment? The challenge for Christian theologians is to articulate a solidarity with the Jewish people that is a critical solidarity, one that recognizes the suffering *and* the power of the Jewish people. By doing this Christian theologies in the spirit of critical solidarity can open themselves to the suffering of the Palestinian people as a legitimate imperative of what it means to be Christian today.

Clearly the Palestinian struggle for nationhood poses more than the prospect of political negotiation and compromise. For Jews and Christians it presents fundamental theological material that lends depth to the inevitable (though long suffering) political solutions. Without this theological component a political solution may or may not appear. However, the lessons of the conflict would surely be lost and thus the political solution would tend toward superficiality and immediacy rather than depth and longevity. A political solution without a theological transformation would simply enshrine the tragedy to be repeated again. An important opportunity to move beyond our present theologies toward theologies of solidarity, which may usher in a new age of ecumenical cooperation, would be lost. Could it be that the struggle of the Palestinian people—their struggle to be faithful to their history and peoplehood—is a key to the Jewish and Christian struggle to be faithful in the contemporary world?

The torture and death of Palestinian children calls us to a theology that recognizes empowerment as a necessary and flawed journey toward liberation. It reminds us that power in and of itself, even for survival, ends in tragedy without the guidance of ethics and a strong sense of solidarity with all those who are struggling for justice. Today, the Palestinian people ask the fundamental question relating to Jewish empowerment: can the Jewish people in Israel, indeed Jews around the world, be liberated without the liberation of the Palestinian people? If we understand the question posed by the Palestinian people, the occupation can no longer continue. What remains is to build a theological framework which delegitimates the torture and the killing—a theology of liberation that sees solidarity as the essence of what it means to be Jewish and Christian.

A New Theological Framework

The development of a theological framework is crucial to delegitimate torture and murder—that is, to end theologies which promote a myriad of occupations including, though not limited to, the West Bank and Gaza. In this case we focus on the Israeli occupation as the breakthrough point for Jewish theology. The theological framework which legitimates occupation also, if we look closely, forces Jews to take positions on other issues which would be questioned, even abhorred, if the framework were different. If our theology did not support the occupation, its vision of justice and peace would be transformed. Thus we turn again to the prospect that the uprising represents a culmination and a possibility, if only we seize the moment.

An essential task of Jewish theology should be to reassess the centrality of the state of Israel. To see Israel as an important Jewish community among other Jewish communities, with a historical foundation and evolution, is to legitimate theologically what the Jewish people have acted out with their lives: the continuation of diverse Jewish communities outside the state. Thus the redemptive aspect of Jewish survival after the Holocaust is found in a much broader arena than the state of Israel. Reassessing the centrality of Israel hardly means its abandonment. Instead it calls forth a new, more mature relationship. Jews cannot bilocate forever, and the strain of defending policies implemented by others, of criticizing without being able to influence directly, of supporting Israel financially, and of being made to feel guilty for not living there, is impossible to continue over a long period of time. With this new understanding responsibilities between Jewish communities assume a mutuality which includes a critical awareness of the centrality of our ethical tradition as the future of our community. Therefore, the present crisis and any future crisis moves beyond the call for unquestioned allegiance or disassociation from Israel to a critical solidarity with responsibilities and obligations on all sides. To say that we are responsible for one another individually and corporately is, like the centrality of ethics, among our oldest traditions, one that needs to be recovered in a critical way.[14]

A parallel task is to deal with the Holocaust in its historical context and to stop brandishing it as a possible future outcome to issues of contemporary Jewish life. The constant use of the Holocaust with reference to Israel is to misjudge and therefore refuse to understand the totally different situation of pre- and post-Holocaust Jewry. Pre-Holocaust European Jewry had no state or military; it was truly defenseless before the Nazi onslaught. Israel is a state with superior military ability. Pre-Holocaust European Jewry lived among populations that varied in their attitudes toward Jews from tolerance to hatred. Post-Holocaust Jewry, with its population concentrations in France, England, Canada and the United States, resides in countries where anti-Jewishness is sporadic and inconsequential. Pre-Holocaust Jewry lived among Christians who had as a group little reason to question Christian anti-Jewishness. Post-Holocaust Jewry live among Christians who have made repeated public statements, writings, even ritual affirmations of the centrality of the Jewish people and Christian culpability for an anti-Jewish past. The differences between pre- and post-Holocaust Jewry can be listed on many other levels as well, which is not to deny that anti-Jewishness continues to exist. As many Jewish writers have pointed out, the paradox is that the most dangerous place for Jews to live today is in the state of Israel rather than the Jewish centers of Europe and North America.

Even in relation to Israel the application of Holocaust language is clearly inappropriate. Israel has been involved in two wars since 1967 and can claim an undisputed victory in neither; no civilian life was lost outside the battlefield. The great fear, repeated over and over again, is that one day Israel will lose a war and that the civilian population will be annihilated— i.e., will experience another holocaust. It is important to note here that, if the situation continues as it is today it is inevitable that one day Israel will lose a war and face the possibility of annihilation. No nation is invincible forever, no empire exists that is not destined to disappear, no country that does not, at some point in its history, lose badly and suffer immensely. Can our present theology exempt Israel from the reality of shifting alliances, military strategies, and political life? *The only way to prevent military defeat is to make peace when you are powerful.* Of course, even here there is never any absolute protection from persecution. But if military defeat does come and if the civilian population is attacked, the result, though tragic, will not be, by any meaningful definition, another holocaust. And it would not, by any means, signal the end of the Jewish people, as many Holocaust theologians continue to speculate. It would be a terrible event, too horrible to mention, except that we must discuss it in order to prevent it. The differences between the Holocaust and any future military defeat of Israel would be too obvious to explore, and would hardly need exploration, if our present theology was not confused on this most important point.

To reassess the centrality of the state of Israel and distinguish the historical event of Holocaust from the situation of contemporary Jewish life is imperative to the third task of Jewish theology, the redefinition of Jewish identity. This is an incredibly difficult and complex task whose parameters can only be touched upon here. Yet it is the most crucial of areas, raising the essential question that each generation faces: what does it mean to be Jewish in the contemporary world?

There is little question that Holocaust theology is the normative theology of the Jewish community today and that at the center of this theology is the Holocaust and the state of Israel. Rabbinic theology, the normative Jewish theology for almost two millennia, initially sought to continue as if neither the Holocaust nor the state of Israel were central to the Jewish people. Reform Judaism, the interesting, sometimes shallow, nineteenth century attempt to come to grips with modern life, also sought to bypass the formative events of our time. Yet after the Holocaust and especially since the Six Day War in 1967 both theological structures have been transformed with an underlying Holocaust theology. Secular Jews, as well, often affiliated with progressive politics and economics, have likewise experienced a shifting framework of interpretation. Though not explicitly religious, their aid has been solicited by Holocaust theologians to build the state of Israel as *the* essential aspect of belonging to the Jewish people. In sum, both those who believed in Jewish particularity and those who sought a more universal identification have increasingly derived their Jewish identity from the framework of Holocaust and Israel. And there is little reason to believe that any of these frameworks—Orthodox, Reform, or secular humanistic—can ever again return to its pre-Holocaust, pre-Israel position.

We can only move ahead by affirming the place of the Holocaust and Israel as important parts of Jewish identity while insisting that they are not and cannot become the sum total of what it means to be Jewish. The point here is to take the dynamic of Holocaust and Israel and understand it in new ways. In both events there is, among other things, an underlying theme of solidarity, which has been buried in our anger and isolation. This includes solidarity with our own people—resistance in the Warsaw Ghetto, for example, as well as the mutual support found in the empowerment of the Jewish people after the Holocaust—as well as others who have come into solidarity with us, including the small, though courageous, minority of Christians during the Holocaust who helped Jews at the risk of their lives, and those Christians who supported Jews in the difficult post-war years. As importantly, if we recover our own history, there is a theme of Jewish solidarity with others, including Palestinians, even in times of great danger. The latter includes some of the early settlers and intellectuals involved in the renewal of the Jewish community in Palestine, well-known figures like Albert Einstein, Hannah Arendt, Martin Buber, and many others.[15]

Even during the Holocaust there were voices, the Dutch Jew Etty Hillesum, for one, who argued that Jewish suffering should give birth to a world of mutuality and solidarity so that no people should ever suffer again. As she voluntarily accompanied her people to Auschwitz, Hillesum was hardly a person who went like a lamb to her slaughter. Rather, she chose a destiny as an act of solidarity with her own people and the world. Is it possible that those who affirmed human dignity where it was most difficult and those who argued, and continue to argue today, for reconciliation with the Palestinian people even with the risks involved, represent the only future worth bequeathing to our children? By emphasizing our dignity and solidarity we appropriate the event of the Holocaust and Israel as formative in a positive and critical way. Thus they ask us once again to embrace the world with the hope that our survival is transformative for our own people and the world.

The key to a new Jewish identity remains problematic unless we understand that deabsolutizing Israel, differentiating Holocaust from the contemporary Jewish situation, and recovering the history of solidarity within our tradition and with those outside it, leads us to a critical confrontation with our own empowerment. To celebrate our survival is important; to realize that our empowerment has come at a great cost is another thing altogether. Can we at the fortieth anniversary of the state of Israel realize that the present political and religious sensibilities can only lead to disaster? Can we argue openly that the issue of empowerment is much broader than that of an exclusive Jewish state and that other options, including autonomy with confederation, may be important to contemplate for the fiftieth anniversary of Israel? Can we openly declare that as American Jews we can no longer ask our government to support a foreign policy that contradicts the ethical heart of what it means to be Jewish? Can we, in good conscience and faith, appeal to Christians, Palestinians, and people of good will around the world to help us end the occupation and, if we do not heed the call, to force us to stop for our own sake?

For this is the place we have arrived, well beyond the pledge of loyalty and the private criticism that has abounded for so many years. The uprising challenges the power of the Israeli government and the heart of the Jewish people. But the power to inflict injury and death remains. And therefore the power to change our history, to redefine our inheritance, to alter what it means to be Jewish, continues in the hands of those who would see the occupation continue. And with the occupation are a myriad of policies around the world that bring only shame to those who invoke the victims of the Holocaust to legitimate terror.

With the uprising we have lost our innocence; Jewish theology must begin with this loss. A weak and helpless people has arisen with a power that surprises and now saddens us. A people set apart returns to the history of nations less as a beacon than as a fellow warrior, living at the expense of others, almost forfeiting its sense of purpose. The commanding voice of Sinai and of Auschwitz beckons us to struggle to reclaim the ethical witness of the Jewish people.

6

An Open Letter to Elie Wiesel

ARTHUR HERTZBERG

Dear Elie,

You and I met almost half a lifetime ago, in the late 1950s, when you had just written your first book, *Night*, and I had just finished my own first book, *The Zionist Idea*. In those days very few people in America were much interested in either the Holocaust or in Zionist ideology, and so we established a comradeship of the ignored. Much more important, we were among the few who still spoke Yiddish, as we continue to do when we meet, for neither of us can let go of the world of our childhood.

You will remember what I told you when you asked about my own family. My mother and her children were the only survivors of her family. Her father, all of her brothers and sisters, and all of their children were murdered in Poland. On the eve of Yom Kippur, in 1946, when it was certain that all were dead, my mother lit thirty-seven candles in their memory. I entered your life, so you told me, because I carried with me, then and to this day, the guilt of my good fortune, for my parents emigrated from Poland in the mid 1920s and brought me to the United States as a child; I was spared what you suffered and what you saw. We are, both of us, part of what is left of the Hasidic communities of your birthplace in Vishnitz and of mine in Lúbaczów. What have we learned from the murder of our families? How must we live with their memory? You and I read and reread the Bible and Talmud: What do the sacred texts command us to think, to feel, and to do?

Many Jews are deeply troubled these days by Israel's behavior in response to the *intifada*, the uprising of the Palestinians against their occupation by Israel. Both in Israel and in the Diaspora many—you and I among them—have been expressing our deep distress in public (and some even more so in private) over the rocks and firebombs hurled by Palestinians and the beatings and shootings by Israelis. You have expressed sympathy for the "anger of young Palestinians," writing that the Palestinians are

125

"treated as nonpersons," as "objects of pity, at best." "Why," you say, "shouldn't they have chosen violence as a means of attracting attention to their existence and their dreams of obtaining a national identity?" (*The New York Times*, June 23, 1988). You have deplored "the extremists in both camps."

I know of no one in the Jewish community who would not agree with your appeal to the Palestinians to "stop using stones and start using words." But you do not accompany such an assertion with an appeal to the Israelis to do anything at all—in particular to move away from the policy of repression and toward negotiation. In those of your statements that I have seen, you seem to have avoided saying anything about the content of Israel's policies. In a speech in Washington on March 13, after saying that American Jews behave "appropriately" when they question actions by Israel, you quickly added that "I am afraid of splitting the Jewish community with regard to Israel." How appropriate are the questioners, in your view, if their questions "split" the community and thus, so you clearly imply, do harm to Israel? You have reduced the political questions before Israel to all-or-nothing choices. You condemn the "right-wing Israeli fanatics" for the "disgraceful suggestion" of transferring all the Palestinians immediately to Jordan; you are equally critical of "some liberals who are ready to give up all the territories immediately," for there is, in your view, no one to whom to give them. Thus you are able to throw up your hands, as you have done repeatedly in interviews and statements since January, and say, "What are we to do?"

The effect of what you have been saying is this: the present situation is deplorable, and Israel has even behaved badly on occasion, but for Jews abroad to say so is less an act of conscience than a sign of weakening resolve. All of the currently discussed political choices, from "territories for peace," the policy of both the Labor party and the US administration, to movement toward a demilitarized Palestinian state (which at least some Palestinian leaders are willing to discuss in public), you do not mention. For all the nuances in your statements, and the distress that you feel as a Jew and as a moral human being, your position amounts to an elegant defense of the Likud hard line. When it comes to policy, you have said little that Yitzhak Shamir could not countersign. When you refer to opposition to Israeli policy you simply ignore the measured criticism that comes from the moderate half of Israel and you refer mainly to "malicious attacks," and to "left-wing Jews who oppose Israel or its recent policies."

I have looked in your statements that deplore the "extremists in both camps" for a definition of who these extremists are, and I have found many paragraphs about Arabs who practice terrorism. You have even quoted from a Palestinian poet, Mahmoud Darwish, who has "recently stirred up angry passions in Israel" with a poem that has been read as demanding that all the Jews get out and leave Palestine, including Haifa and Tel Aviv, to the Arabs. These passages of yours seem to require some balancing comments. You know of the incantations by Meir Kahane and his followers in which the Jews are commanded to expel Muslims and Christians from the Holy Land. That a former chief of staff, Rafael Eitan, called the Palestinians "drugged cockroaches" has, surely, not escaped your attention. I wonder whether you, and I, would have been silent if a Russian general had uttered a comparable slur about Jews demonstrating in Red Square. You know that the prime minister of Israel, Yitzhak Shamir, has been saying that he will not return a single inch of the West Bank to Arab sovereignty; he has thus stalled even the beginnings of negotiation.

A basic premise of your position is that "Israel is the only country that feels its existence threatened." This, too, is a staple argument of Israel's hard-liners; because Israel feels endangered, it must use force to protect itself, even if the excesses of this force are sometimes deplorable. The same rhetoric is often used by the Likud and the parties to the right of it, in order to excuse intransigence. On this issue, Israel's moderates take a different view. Abba Eban knows as much about Israel's strategic position in the region as anyone else, not least because he serves as chairman of the Foreign Affairs and Defense Committee of Israel's Knesset. Speaking in March 1987 in Jerusalem to a meeting of the New Israel Fund, Eban said:

> We have reached a point at which we can say that Israel has never been stronger in power and in quantitative measure. Never has Israel been less existentially threatened. Never has Israel been more secure against external assault and never more vulnerable to domestic folly. The major perils that now face us come from within ourselves. And they would emerge from the stupendous folly of attempting to enforce a permanent Israeli jurisdiction over the one and a half million Arabs in the West Bank and Gaza.

Eban went on to argue—and he has said this repeatedly since, in speeches both in Israel and in the United States—that all who care about Israel will help her best by uttering the very criticisms that you, Elie, do not acknowledge.

You have suggested that some of the Jewish critics of Israel's conduct, and especially those who live outside the state, are "intellectuals who had never done anything for Israel but now shamelessly use their Jewishness to justify their attacks against Israel." This may be true of a few, but is that all that you, who have been morally so sensitive, have heard in the outcries of Israel's critics? You have found no place, so far, in any of your writings or statements that I have seen to suggest that there are Jews in the world who have been devoted to Israel for many years and who have expressed outrage at such actions as dynamiting houses in the Arab village of Beta. Some of these villagers had tried to protect a group of Jewish teen-agers who were on a hike against stone throwers. In the melee a girl was shot by accident by one of the group's Jewish guards. The army then blew up fourteen houses in the village. According to accounts in the Israeli press, this was done not to punish anyone who was guilty but to appease the angry hard-line settlers in the West Bank. You were not among those who said anything in public after this and all too many other such incidents. Are such figures in the Diaspora as Sir Isaiah Berlin, Philip Klutznick, Henry Rosovsky, and the president of Yeshiva University, Rabbi Norman Lamm, and hundreds of others like them, who have spoken up in criticism of actions that they could not countenance, simply to be written off as people whose public statements endanger Jewish unity?

"No one says," you write, that Israel should "be above criticism." Yet when you refer to public criticism you mainly warn of the "risk" it poses to Israel. But the view of many Israelis who have fought for their country is different. Are the reserve generals and colonels of Israel, more than 130 of them, who have launched a public campaign for territorial compromise to be discredited because they are pointedly critical of the occupation of the West Bank? They keep saying that only compromise can end the conflict, and that repression is unworkable. Four of these generals have recently been on tour in the United States, to enlist support for such views among all those who care about Israel. Is it a betrayal of Israel to take seriously what these men say?

As you know better than anyone else, silence is a form of interference. In all your writings you have insisted that no one has the right to be silent in the face of injustice, any injustice. Those who throw up their hands and who, to use your own recent words about Israel, can say no more than that they "would like to believe in miracles" appear to have abdicated responsibility. This seems all the more an abdication now, because there is no authoritative demand from Israel that the Jews of the Diaspora be silent. On the contrary, the leaders who speak for the more moderate half of Israel have been saying over and over again that it is perfectly legitimate for Jews who care to speak their minds.

On May 18, Shimon Peres made the point unmistakably when he spoke to the leaders of the Jewish establishment organizations in New York: "Whoever wants can be involved. We are a free people." He made it clear beyond any doubt that dissent and criticism do not in any way weaken one's commitment to Israel. Nor has the half of Israel that is led by Prime Minister Yitzhak Shamir really asked the Jews of the Diaspora to leave decisions to Israel. The most effective device of these hard-liners has been to suggest that *any* criticism of their position is a self-hating assault on the state when such criticism is uttered by Jews, and that it is a form of anti-Semitism when it is spoken by non-Jews. This strategy is used in Israel itself. The Likud likes to call itself the "national camp"; it insists that moderates are not sufficiently patriotic, that they are enemies of the Jewish people. You, Elie, do not believe such canards. But I must ask: Are you not lending aid and comfort to this view?

To your repeated question "What are we to do?" there are two orders of answer: political and moral. If, as you have written, "self-determination is a sacred principle," one that you believe should apply to the Palestinians, then how and where is it to express itself? If the Palestinians were to take the step that you have suggested of choosing to talk rather than throw rocks or Molotov cocktails, are they to leave the West Bank and go to Jordan? But you have ruled out, on moral grounds, the forced transfer of Palestinians from the West Bank to the East Bank. On your own premises, Palestinian nationalism and self-determination require from the Israeli-Jewish side a counterstatement that the two peoples involved will finally enact peaceful partition, that Jews will agree that Palestinians have a right to a territorial base for their national life. It is this principle that your own statements make unavoidable—but you have avoided it. I cannot help thinking that you know, at least as well as I, that there are rhetoricians in the mainstream of Israel's right wing who manage to find ways of asserting that they will give the Palestinians very limited local autonomy (this they now call national rights) while retaining control of land, water, and everything else that matters in the West Bank. "What is Israel to do?" It must accept the principle of partition—but to say this is to put oneself on the side of Israel's moderates and to break one's ties to the Likud.

Morally, Jewish tradition commands us to act justly, especially when actions seem imprudent and embarrassing, and never to be silent, even to protect Jewish unity. This Jewish morality has taken one form, recurrently, throughout the ages. Even in bad times, when Jews were under fierce attack, their moral teachers gave no exceptions. The prophets knew that Assyria and Babylonia were far more wicked than Judea, but they held Judea to account, even as the Assyrians and the Babylonians were advancing. "Only you have I known among all the nations of the world; therefore I will hold you to account for all your sins."

There were other voices in the days of the prophets. The prophets Amos, Elijah, Isaiah, and Jeremiah, and all the rest, were opposed, generation after generation, by prophets who belonged to the royal courts, who assured the king that his conduct was beyond reproach. The biblical prophets were harassed as traitors who weakened the resolve of a small people—but it is their "treason," and not the prudence of the court prophets, that is our unique Jewish tradition. While the official soothsayers denounced the enemies of the king, the prophets whom we revere followed after Nathan, who dared to confront King David with murdering Uriah and stealing his wife. Nathan defended this Hittite stranger against a divinely appointed Jewish king: "You are the man," he said to David: you are morally responsible.

In the memory of the Holocaust we have been reminded by you that silence is a sin. You have spoken out against indifference and injustice. Why are you making a special exception of Israel? Do you think that our silence will help Israel? The texts that we study and restudy teach the contrary. "Israel will be redeemed by righteousness, and those who return to it, by acts of loving kindness." To be silent is an act of misplaced love. Such silence gives free reign to the armed zealots of ages past, and of this day. Several times in our history, armed zealots have led the Jewish people to glorious disasters. Encouragement by silence, of the kind some of the rabbis gave the zealots when they declared war on Rome in the first century, has a long history of being tragically wrong. We dare not repeat this mistake.

The excesses of the zealots may succeed today, briefly, as they succeeded for a moment several times before, but such excesses are likely to lead again to disaster. Teachers of morality must not indulge the zealots of today, and not only because zealotry does not work. To suppress the weak because of our own supposed weakness is against the very essence of our tradition. When we were a group of hunted former slaves in the desert, Moses proclaimed, as divine teaching, that we should not oppress strangers, for we had been oppressed as strangers in the land of Egypt. This injunction is unconditional.

We should both be haunted by one recent image. Several days after the incident in Beta, an Israeli patrol tried to stop some Arab youths to question them. The youths were unarmed; they had not been throwing rocks, and they were guilty of nothing except not wanting to be interrogated. These young men were fired on, and one was killed. Now I know, as you do, about the dangers for Israeli soldiers in the West Bank and Gaza. I have nieces in Israel's army, and I have said to them that their moral obligation does not include allowing themselves to be slaughtered. But killing those who are simply unwilling to be questioned is another matter entirely. How can we be silent?

I agree with you that *ahavat Yisrael*, the love of the Jewish people, is a great virtue, but I can find little trace in all the Jewish texts through the centuries that this love must be uncritical. Even Levi Yitzhak of Berdichev, the eighteenth-century Hasid who wrote in defense of the conduct of the Jews, was not silent about their misdeeds. He accepted the moral responsibility to lead. "Love can bend a straight line": it can mislead the lover, so that, with the highest motives, he does grave injury to his beloved. You, Elie, care far too much about the Jewish people, and about Israel, to indulge falls from grace and, de facto, to lend comfort to zealots. If you are persuaded that the policies of the Likud are right, say so, but, in fairness, cease treating so dismissively the political and moral views of the many moderate Jews who reject the politics and morality of the hard line.

I keep thinking these days of the saying that both of us have quoted many times, and sometimes at each other, especially in those early years when we were closest. Menachem Mendel of Kotsk, the tortured Hasid of the last century, once said that when the Evil One wants to destroy us, he tempts us not through our wicked desires but through our most virtuous inclinations; we do good deeds at the wrong time, with the wrong intensity, and in a setting in which they do devastating harm. I fear that for all your love of Israel, you, in what you say, sometimes risk falling into the moral trap that Menachem Mendel described.

You belong among those who speak the truth, even to Jewish power, and who do not look away because of real or invented Jewish weakness. We show the truest love of Israel and the Jewish people when we remind ourselves that, in strength or in weakness, we survive not by prudence and not by power, but through justice.

Your friend,
Arthur Hertzberg

PART 2

American Christians, Judaism, and the Israeli-Palestinian Conflict

The four essays by Christian theologians and scholars in this section do not illustrate the whole range of Christian views on the Israeli-Palestinian conflict. Rather, in keeping with the concerns of this volume, they illustrate some of the diversity of views among that group of American Christian scholars who are concerned both with Jewish-Christian dialogue and with justice in the Middle East. Yet, even within this group of Christians, there are sharp conflicts. These conflicts relate to the way Western Christians make connections between issues that are typically seen as opposed to each other: just relations between Christians and Jews and just relations between Christians and Palestinians.

In order to interpret the types of responses to the connections between these two issues found in these essays, it is useful to put them in some historical context. It is important to examine the ways in which Western Christians have tried to "balance" their new sensitivity to Christian anti-Semitism, on the one hand, and their views of Zionism and the state of Israel vis-à-vis the Palestinians, on the other. We speak here only of Western Christians, because, until recently, Middle Eastern Christian voices have either been almost unheard by Western Christians or dismissed as irrationally anti-Semitic.[1]

The two major types of responses to Judaism and to Zionism by Western Christians can be broadly catagorized as the liberal response and the fundamentalist evangelical response, although a careful examination of these two groups reveals a range of nuances and diversities within them. The liberal response can be found in statements of the National Council of Churches on relations to Judaism and to the Israeli-Palestinian conflict.[2] The fundamentalist evangelical response is expressed in groups such as Christians United for Israel and the National Christian Leadership Conference for Israel.[3] The position taken by the Vatican is similar to that of the World Council of Churches, but the thinking behind the Vatican's views tends not to be well known or understood by American Catholics.[4]

Liberal Christians have sought to address the issues of relationship to Judaism and relationship to Israel without putting the two issues together in a single Biblical and theological schema. In discussions of relationship to Judaism, liberal Christians have sought to repent and make amends for a millennium and a half of institutionalized and theologically legitimated anti-Semitism which played a key supportive role in allowing the Nazis to carry out their genocidal program against European Jewry without a major outcry from Christians.

Western Christians have sought to make some statement on the Jews and Judaism as part of the policy position of their denominations or ecumenical bodies. The general line of such revised views of Judaism is to back off from suggestions that Judaism is an inferior and superceded religion (as had been taught by Christian theological training in the past) and/or that it needs to accept Jesus as the Messiah in order to be complete. Instead, these revised statements not only express gratitude and a sense of renewed positive relation to the Jewish roots of Christianity, but wish in some way to recognize the ongoing validity of Judaism as a religion of authentic relation to God and vehicle of redemption in its own right.

The litmus test of such a changed relation to Judaism is whether the Christian body is willing to renounce a mission to the Jews, i.e., the organized effort to convert Jews to Christianity. Because such a rejection of mission to the Jews threatens the Christian belief in the universal nature of redemption in Christ, most liberal denominations have been somewhat ambivalent about reaching this conclusion. Most liberal Christian statements attempt to recognize the ongoing validity and spiritual authenticity of Judaism without a full and complete rejection of mission to the Jews.[5]

Liberal Christian statements about relation to Judaism are theological statements that are based on a searching of the Bible and an effort to rethink the relation of the two religions scripturally and theologically. In contrast, liberal Christian statements about relation to Israel are based on a more secular set of principles of political and social justice. Such statements, particularly from the National Council of Churches, also represent a balancing of the diversity within these bodies, ranging from views close to those of fundamentalist evangelicals, on the one hand, to Christians with more positive first-hand experience with Middle Eastern Christians and Muslims in general, and with Palestinians in particular, on the other.

Eastern Christians are also represented in the membership of the World Council of Churches. The failure of both the World Council and National Council to place the statements about justice in the Middle East in a more comprehensive theological and Biblical context is largely due to the difficulty of reconciling these conflicting viewpoints within their memberships.[6]

Liberal Christian statements on justice in the Middle East have sought to balance a recognition of Israel's right to exist and its need for territorial security with an affirmation of the injustice that the creation of the state of Israel has posed for Palestinians, who have been made refugees or people oppressed under occupation by the development of this state. The emergent liberal solution to this conflict has been the two-state solution, i.e., an affirmation both of the right of Israel to exist in secure borders and the right of the Palestinians to a Palestinian state in the West Bank and Gaza.

The conservative evangelical Christian view is in marked contrast to this liberal view. By and large fundamentalists have not dealt in the same depth with Christian anti-Semitism. Their view of the Bible as inerrant and their belief in the universal necessity of salvation through Christ does not allow them to make the same concessions, theologically, to the separate validity of Judaism or to admit serious error in a Christian theological anti-Semitism rooted in the New Testament. Thus fundamentalists continue to believe that Jews, and all non-Christians, must be converted to Christ, and indeed converted in the fundamentalist, "born-again" sense, in order to be saved.

Also, in contrast to liberal Christians, fundamentalists put the existence of the modern state of Israel in a Biblical and theological world view. For them this state represents the promised restoration of the Jews to their homeland that is part of the promises of God. These Christians believe that God gave this land to the Jews in Biblical times, and this means that Jews have a God-given right to this land for all time. They also see the founding of the modern state of Israel as part of the redemptive work of God promised in the Last Days.

These redemptive actions of God include the return of the Jews to Palestine, the refounding of a Jewish state on the promised land, the rebuilding of the Jewish temple (possible only by destroying the very sacred Muslim mosque presently on that site), the conversion of 144,000 Jews to Christianity, and the return of Christ to punish the wicked and vindicate the Elect. Thus for fundamentalist evangelicals militant support for the present state of Israel, including its expansion into the West Bank, is an integral part of a theological eschatology.[7]

Although liberal Christians of the kind represented in this book would not share this theological eschatology in its total and explicit form, such views color the feelings of many Western Christians outside the fundamentalist camp. Many Christians who do not share this eschatology nevertheless believe in a more general way that the Jews have a God-given right to the land of Palestine and that their return there in modern times is in some way a redemptive event.

Most liberal Christians concerned with justice in the world also have a desire to make reparations for the Holocaust and for the centuries of Christian anti-Semitism. Support for the state of Israel is seen as something the Western Christian world owes the Jewish people in reparation for these Western crimes.

From the Palestinian perspective, such attitudes negate the historical reality of Palestinian Christians and Muslims who have been living in this region for one to two thousand years. Such notions also uncritically make the Palestinians, who had nothing to do with these Western crimes, pay the price for these crimes by losing their homeland and becoming refugees and colonized people. Most Western Christians have missed these points, mainly because they don't know the Palestinian story. In addition, they have grown up with deep prejudicial stereotypes against "Arabs" that condition them against efforts to understand that story.

The four Christian authors in this section of the book represent two divergent tendencies among liberal Christians. All four authors have been involved in Jewish-Christian dialogue and have been deeply concerned to overcome Christian anti-Semitism and to revise Christian theology to take account of the full validity of Judaism as a redemptive religious path in its own right. However these concerns have lead the authors in somewhat different directions.

Two of the authors, John Pawlikowski and Robert McAfee Brown, have been led by their deep concern to overcome Christian anti-Semitism to a feeling that the state of Israel must be affirmed, in some sense, as a redemptive event. Christians are seen as owing Jews a moral debt to be paid by compensatory support for Israel as a Jewish state. Support for the Palestinians seems like a kind of disloyalty to this commitment to the Jewish people.

Sister Miriam Ward and Rosemary Ruether, on the other hand, have incorporated their concern for anti-Semitism into a concern for the Palestinian people. These two authors have experienced the reality of the Palestinian people under occupation and in the Middle Eastern and Western diaspora first-hand. They have come to the view that Jewish-Christian dialogue, in the context of the Western experience, is an inadequate framework for discussion of the Middle East conflict.

There is a need for a three way religious dialogue of Jews, Christians, and Muslims in its Middle Eastern context. And there is the need for a political solution to the Israeli-Palestinian conflict that more explicitly takes account of Palestinian national rights. Although the second position can be stereotyped as the pro-Palestinian, over against the pro-Israeli view, this would be a distortion of the concerns of all four writers.

All four Christian authors are concerned with justice for both Jews and Palestinians. Their differences lie in where they place the weight of their emphasis. John Pawlikowski and Robert McAfee Brown express concern for Palestinians and accept some version of the two-state solution. But their emotional attachment and concern is dictated by their intense loyalty and commitment to the Jewish people in compensation for Christian anti-Semitism.

Sister Miriam Ward and Rosemary Ruether are concerned for the welfare and security of Israeli Jews and for the state of Israel. But they question whether this security is truly served by expulsion and repression of Palestinians. For them Palestinians are not an abstraction, but a suffering people whose faces they know. They seek to affirm both experiences of suffering, Jewish and Palestinian. But they feel that, at the moment, it is necessary to hear that story that has been less heard by the West, namely that of the Palestinians.

Thus the differences among these four Christian authors are less differences in theology than differences of experience. Whose story have you heard? Whose pain has entered your consciousness? It is these differences that make the plumb-line in their essays fall in different places in what all four hope to be genuine expressions of balanced justice for both Israeli Jews and Palestinian Arabs.

7

Christians in the West Must Confront the Middle East

ROBERT MCAFEE BROWN

> Why can't Jews and Arabs sit down at a table
> together and work out their differences like
> Christian gentlemen?
>
> —Warren Austin, former U.S. ambassador to the
> United Nations, whose suggestion fortunately died
> for want of a second

It starts out supportively: "You have been fairly outspoken on issues like civil rights, Vietnam, Nicaragua, racism in South Africa, and racism at home," people say. And then comes the change of pace: "Why are you so silent on the Middle East?" (This, if truth be told, was the tenor of the invitation to contribute to the present volume.)

There is an even more pointed way to pose the question. It goes, "Why have you been so reluctant to criticize the policies of the state of Israel?" I shall conflate the two questions, since they seem to me two ways of engaging in the same query, but I shall use the imagery of the second as a way to discuss the first, not to condone past silence, but to reflect on my reasons for it (both good and bad), and then point in some new directions that speech must move when silence has been disavowed. I write partly to clarify matters for myself, but even more to think aloud with readers like myself who have also come to realize that whether or not silence in the past could be justified, silence in the present and future cannot be.

For the last twenty years I have been trying to see the world through the eyes of victims—particularly of Jews as victims of genocide in World War II, the violence emanating from centers of power in a so-called "Christian culture," and also of third world peoples as victims of capitalist imperialism, most of the violence emanating from centers of power in my own country. The Holocaust has focused my vision in relation to the Jewish people, liberation theology in relation to third world peoples. While I have tried to read widely in the literature of both realities, it has been having colleagues and friends, some who are both victims and articulators of the plight of victims, that has been most important. As a result, my previously intact white, male, middle-class Christian worldview has been shattered, and I have been trying to reshape the remnants in new ways ever since. For the record, those who have contributed most not only to the shattering but also to the rebuilding have been Elie Wiesel and Gustavo Gutierrez.

In probing these two areas I have discovered that they often mutually illuminate one another, as I shall try to illustrate later in this essay. But because of my own starting point, there has been a tilt in relation to Middle East questions that made me reluctant to be publicly critical of the state of Israel. Since this meant silence and consequent lack of involvement in relation to the plight of Palestinians, I need to explore some of the reasons for this:

1. The history of the Holocaust, from 1933 to the present, reveals a high degree of Christian complicity in the murder of six million Jews. It has cast a heavy shadow over my view of the world, my understanding of God, my estimate of human nature and my theology of the church. This history convinces me that the creation and survival of the state of Israel has been one of the few affirmations of Jews and Judaism in a world almost devoid of such affirmations, and one therefore deserving of support. For the state of Israel to be destroyed now would be for Jews a "second Holocaust," a definitive effort to rid the world of Jews once and for all, or at least relegate Jews to an existence that could have no meaning for them.

This relation of Holocaust to Israel is a very delicate one, even apart from the questions of Palestinians, Arabs, Muslims and the balance of power in the Middle East. Even to imply that the creation of the state of Israel is somehow a "compensation" for the loss of six million Jews suggests either the blasphemous notion that Jews can be "bought off" after their unparalleled suffering, or the trivializing notion that suffering does not entail permanent wounds. Those who see the state of Israel as the consequence of God's intervention on behalf of the chosen people need to ponder the comment once made to Elie Wiesel, "For it to have been a miracle, it would have had to happen a little sooner." Even so, I think we can say that the awful reality of the Holocaust at least slightly quickened and sensitized the conscience of the world to the moral and political appropriateness of a homeland for Jews, and that the injustice of gentile dealings with Jews over the centuries was at least slightly redressed. This is one reason that many people like myself have been supportive of Israel's right not only to survive but to thrive, and to insist that its borders remain secure.

The shortcoming of this approach is that it fails to take with equal moral seriousness the rights of Palestinians, their displacement from land they had held for centuries, and the oppressive conditions under which they have been forced to live ever since.

2. However, the Holocaust is only the culmination of policies toward Jews that go back to the very beginnings of Christian history. There have been almost twenty centuries of so-called Christian-Jewish relations in which the "relations" were at best demeaning to Jews and at worst physically and psychically destructive. In the light of this history, for Christians to challenge the existence of the state of Israel could hardly be interpreted by Jews as anything but a continuation of a consistent anti-Jewish posture that should have ended with the horrors of the Holocaust.

Put gently, Christians aware of that history did not want to alienate further whatever Jewish friends they still had by challenging the one remaining thing that Jews could now believe would be stable and enduring. Put sternly, Christians did not relish the opprobrium of being called "anti-Semitic" as a consequence of criticism of policies of the state of Israel.

The shortcoming of this approach has been the failure, on both sides, to distinguish clearly enough between Judaism as a religious faith and the state of Israel as a modern political entity. Much discussion of this distinction is still needed, since many Christians assume they are making the distinction when in fact they are not, and some Jews refuse to make the distinction at all, since for them the survival of Judaism and the survival of Israel have become indistinguishable.

3. Alongside a desire not to jeopardize Jewish-Christian relations by attacks on Israel has been a Christian desire not to speak or act in ways that give aid and comfort to enemies of Israel who are anti-Semitic, terroristic, chauvinistic, unreasoning, or all of the above. Because of the many strident assertions over the years that Israel had no right to exist, the choice to support Israel against unfair attacks seemed clear. As Jews often say, "Israel has plenty of critics; it needs more?"

The shortcoming of this approach is its failure to distinguish between fanatical criticism and creative criticism. One must be able to voice a criticism without automatically being linked to those who voice criticism from radically different perspectives. The terrain for public discourse must not be defined by those who hold the most extreme views. There must be other options to support than Palestinian displacement or Israeli annihilation.

4. A further reason why critical reflection on the Middle East has often been neglected is that with dozens of issues clamoring for attention one has to decide which shall hold "center stage" when the "stage" is not nearly big enough for all of them. Vietnam, Nicaragua, and South Africa have been my international concerns; racism, anti-Semitism, and injustice to powerless minorities have been my corresponding domestic concerns. While I cannot defend the notion that these should be central issues for all, I believe I can defend the notion that it is better to work on a few issues about which one can become reasonably knowledgeable than to have an infinite agenda concerning which one can only be a dilettante at best. To make any impact, one must do a lot of homework, go to a lot of meetings, explore all sides of a question, and find ways to put oneself publicly on the line with those being victimized.

As far as determining priorities goes, Christian church bodies have usually been more supportive of Palestinian than Israeli claims, not only because they feel that justice points that way, but because Palestinians who are not Moslems are usually Christians. This means that Christian voices on behalf of Israel need to be heard within Christian councils when decisions are being made.

The shortcoming of this approach is a failure to recognize that one's choice of priorities might be wrong, and that issues relating to the Middle East should be higher on the scale than those mentioned above.

But the dilemma is not easily resolved. Elie Wiesel's first book (a Yiddish version of what eventually became *Night*) was a long treatment of the Holocaust with the title *And the World Remained Silent*. The silence of the world is reprehensible. But without denying the uniqueness of the Holocaust, which cannot be "reduced" to only one of a number of instances of terrible evil, a book might be written about the plight of blacks in South Africa, or *campesinos* in Nicaragua, or labor organizers in Southeast Asia, or blacks in the United States, or women in any culture, or displaced persons who are Palestinians, and employ the same title with equal force.

Gregory Baum has helpfully summarized the plight in which many Christians find themselves in relation to the Middle East; they find themselves caught between two concerns, both legitimate. They are (1) commitment to the state of Israel because of past Christian sins against Jews and Christianity's historic roots in Judaism, and (2) commitment to the liberation of all oppressed people because of the nature of our faith—a commitment that must include not only Jews historically but Jews and Palestinians in the present. And it is this tension, Professor Baum declares—commitment to the cause of the Jews and commitment to the cause of the

Palestinians—that must define our posture toward the Middle East in the future.[1]

One of the first times I spoke publicly about the need to be able to criticize Israel without automatically being branded anti-Semitic was in November 1987, about a month before the uprising of the Palestinians in Israel. I was the last speaker in a four-day conference of Christians and Jews, and the fact that tensions in the Middle East had not even obliquely been referred to during the previous sessions persuaded me that ignoring these issues was unrealistic. I mention this because I felt then that I might be expending whatever "capital" I had accumulated through years of participation in such dialogue.[2] The response at the time was more affirmative than I had anticipated. But within a few weeks, as a result of the uprising, the right and even the duty to speak critically of Israel's policies had not only been asserted but was being vigorously practiced by both American non-Jews and American Jews, many of them for the first time.

This may be the one positive thing that has emerged from all of the violence in the interval since then. The violations of human rights, the beatings, the civilian deaths, the acts of terrorism on the part of some of the Israeli army, have been so egregious (and so vividly present on nightly television) that no one—Jew, Christian, Muslim, agnostic, or whoever—can either pretend they have not happened or condone them.

This has been a difficult and bitter time not only for Jews and Palestinians in the Middle East, but for American Jews as well, who until the uprising had usually avoided criticizing the state of Israel in public, however much they might have deplored its shortcomings in private. To many Jews the necessity of criticizing Israel represents a terrible loss. But I want to argue that the right to do this is finally not a loss but a gain. It is not to Israel's benefit (nor to that of any other state) for portions of the world community to provide it with a kind of moral blank check that says, in effect, "Whatever you do, we will continue to support you uncritically." It is far more creative to realize that when we criticize Israeli actions we do so not only because we bleed for the Palestinian victims (although this would be a sufficient reason), but also because we fear for the Israeli victimizers; for what shall it profit the state of Israel to gain the whole of the Middle East and lose its own soul? And while the Israelis may not want to have gentiles adjudicating the status of its soul, a reminder even from outside that certain kinds of action are beyond the moral pale and are sure to lead to moral censure can be a positive deed. Such criticism is an act of loyalty, not disloyalty, to the vision of all that Israel should be.

If this has been a difficult transition for American non-Jews who have been supportive of Israel, it is immensely more difficult for American Jews, who have a multitude of reasons for being more concerned about Israel than the rest of us. It is a mark of great moral maturity that increasing numbers of Jews have set a clear and courageous example in this regard. For, as Albert Vorspan, senior vice-president of the Union of American Hebrew Congregations, has put it, "We owe Israel our support, yes, but we also owe it our best judgment, our honest disagreement, and our conscience." The basis for such a conclusion has been luminously stated by Arthur Hertzberg: "We show the truest love of Israel and the Jewish people when we remind ourselves that, in strength or weakness, we survive not by prudence and not by power, but through justice."[3]

At times the Jewish judgments have been based on an interweaving of moral and pragmatic considerations, once again motivated by a love of Israel and a concern that Israel not fail in crucial times of testing. Michael Lerner, in an essay contained in this volume, states: "From the standpoint of Jewish ethics and Jewish survival the occupation is unacceptable . . . These activities are deplorable to any civilized human being. That they are done by a Jewish state is both tragic and inexcusable. We did not survive the gas chambers and crematoria so that we could become the oppressors of Gaza . . . Our anger at Israel's current policies come not only from moral outrage but also from deep concern about Israel's survival and the survival of the Jewish people."[4]

The moral right to criticize is surely unexceptionable, particularly in light of occasional tendencies, as one rabbi puts it, "to substitute absolute devotion to Israel for absolute devotion to God," which is a violation of the first commandment. But that being said, all parties need zealously to guard against using the new situation as a device for pushing demagogic and merely malicious criticism. This happens whenever commentators draw parallels between Israeli actions in the present era and Nazi actions in the Hitler era. No matter how worthy of condemnation certain specific acts of Israeli soldiers may be, or however ill-conceived certain Israeli policies, they are simply not comparable in their magnitude or evil to the carefully crafted Nazi plan for the total extermination of an entire people by any means calculated to achieve that end. Such a policy remains awesomely and terrifyingly unique.

In 1988 Israel celebrated its fortieth anniversary as a nation-state. That is a short span as the history of nation-states goes, hardly time to build up a backlog of experience out of which to make the complex day-to-day decisions that are part and parcel of modern statecraft. As Irving Greenberg has convincingly argued above, it is not as though Israelis were able to feel their way gradually into the exercise of power and then emerge from an apprenticeship seasoned and ready to assume control. Indeed, there has probably never been a people in human history with less experience in the exercise of power than Jews since the destruction of the Temple in 587 B.C. Jews in recent centuries have not been tempted to abuse power since they had none to abuse.

And then, after two millennia of being ground under by all the great powers of the world, the Jews suddenly found themselves immersed in governance in a trouble-prone area of the globe, called upon daily not to a simple exercise of doing justice, loving mercy, and walking humbly with God, but of participating in all the complexities of a power-directed world, expected from the first moment to play by universally acknowledged rules of the game that can be reduced to a single maxim: "In the interests of national security, do whatever is necessary to survive." Since all other nations operate by that maxim, it is hardly surprising that Israel has done the same, since failure to do so would have illustrated the truth of another universal maxim: "Never let down your guard, even for a moment; if you do, somebody will destroy you."

In front of this backdrop of entrance into the world of *realpolitik* are two further interrelated facts: (1) To many Jews the creation of the state of Israel represents the fulfillment of a promised historical destiny in a land that they had long felt was theirs either by legal or divine right. (2) To some non-Jews the creation of the state of Israel represented a lessening, however slight, of the sense of guilt that "western civilization" felt for complicity in the Holocaust. Both groups saw something "special" about Israel as a nation-state in relation to other nation-states; when these perspectives were combined the impact was powerful.

However, this has been far from an unmixed blessing in Israel's forty year history, for it has meant that Israel is often assessed from the perspective of a double standard.

1. Some say, "Since the Jews have been through such terrible times, it is understandable for them to be suspicious of those who claim to be their friends, and to overreact against those whom they perceive to be their enemies. Throughout two millennia they have discovered that they dare not trust anyone. They can be excused, therefore, from occasional excesses in their struggle for self-preservation." In other words, because of the special circumstances of its coming into being, Israel can be held to less

exacting standards of collective behavior than other nations, at least during the growing pains of its historical adolescence.

2. A more widespread view (employed with different nuances by both Israel's friends and enemies) goes like this: "Israel is not just any old nation-state. Its people understand themselves to be in a special relationship to God, entrusted with the task of being a light unto the gentiles. Since their God is a God of mercy they are called to special enactments of mercy in their human dealings. As a result, more can be demanded of them than we demand or expect from other nations who claim no such allegiance and are bound by no such imperatives of conduct." Israel's friends, in other words, want it to be better than other nations so as to be a moral beacon in a dark world, while Israel's enemies, counting on it not to be better than other nations, find themselves with a handy ethical yardstick by which to criticize Israel for hypocrisy and dissimulation. In both cases, Israel is judged by standards that are not applied to other nations.

Is there a way out of the dilemma of such a double standard? There would seem to be at least two responses.

One denies the appropriateness of the analysis. "Away with the double standard," its advocates would urge, "judge Israel in the same way as all other nations are judged, no better, no worse, no more nor less accountable for its actions than other nations." This commonsense verdict implies that past hardships cannot be invoked as a basis for relaxation of judgment, nor can data derived from revelation be employed to heighten the standard of judgment.

A second response, however, keeps a tension between putting Israel in a special category and insisting that Israel is just like everyone else. It seeks to understand Israel's actions even if it doesn't condone them. It seeks to understand Israeli fears of annihilation, for example, in light of the fact that annihilation was expressly decreed for the Jews within their living memory by the sophisticated and modern German culture and with the tacit support of the rest of the world. Such a collective memory can induce justifiable paranoia on the part of the intended victims, and make it understandable that any state created by the survivors of such a proposed calamity will be anxious about the possibility that the annihilation that failed in the recent past may be replaced by a successful annihilation in the near future.

There *is* a "special" dimension because of what Jewish memory builds into the state of Israel that should be acknowledged by all who were guilty parties in the creation of that memory. But in dialectical tension with such an acknowledgement must go an ongoing reiteration that when it comes to issues like waging war, dealing with refugees, or invading other countries, Israel is fully accountable, like all nations, to whatever remnants of the rules of modern warfare still exist, to internationally agreed-upon standards for the care of prisoners, to avoidance of torture, and so on. If Israel has provided arms to white South Africans with which to kill black South Africans (which it has), or sent arms to the contras to engage in terrorist actions against Nicaraguan peasants (which it has), then Israel is as accountable for those actions as any other nation.

And it is from within this dialectical tension that I make a plea to Israel: "You, more than all the other peoples of the earth, know what it is like to be refugees, sojourners, displaced persons, people whose lands have been overrun time and again by invaders. Your psalms and liturgies invoke that sense of homelessness as something to be overcome. The Torah calls on you to welcome the sojourner, to feed the hungry, to care for the sick and dying. Could you not exercise that kind of concern for the Palestinians 'within your gates' today?"

Is that an unfair demand? Of course it is, if it is demanded only of Israel. It is morally legitimate only if we simultaneously direct such a moral imperative not only to the Palestinians but even more to ourselves, recognizing, for example, our need to help rebuild the Nicaragua we have so ruthlessly destroyed, to cease funding "low-intensity warfare" in El Salvador, to stand unequivocally with South African blacks against South African whites, to remove our military bases from the Philippines. (A full agenda would be much longer.) Not only is *Israel like us*, as a modern nation-state; but *we are like Israel*, in that moral demands are placed on us as a nation-state, and we cannot escape from them by insisting that Israel respond to a higher moral standard than we impose upon ourselves.

As Gregory Baum has suggested, the bind for many Christians is that we take seriously the inexpungeability of the Holocaust and consequent need for loyalty to Jews, and take with equal seriousness the cries of the oppressed who work for their liberation and ask our help. In many situations, these two concerns reinforce one another. But in the Middle East, as he has further suggested, the first loyalty translates into a strong concern for the state of Israel, while the second translates into a strong concern for the plight of the Palestinians. How can these two concerns, each legitimate, be brought into creative rather than destructive tension? How, in other words, can there be a theology of liberation that takes due account of such a complex context? To deal with this question I want to look first at one

approach to the contemporary world, and the role of Jews within it, that
has been central in recent theological exploration—the role of Holocaust
theology—and then deal with ways in which themes from "liberation theology" could resonate in the Middle East.

In his essay in this volume, Marc Ellis argues that "Holocaust theology,"
which he sees as normative in most Jewish circles today, is unable to speak
a word *of* power or a word *to* power, since it is backward-looking and
grows out of a situation of utter Jewish powerlessness. Today, he argues,
Jews must look ahead rather than back, and cope with something foreign
to "Holocaust theology," namely the awesome acquisition of power represented by the state of Israel, which must now engage in all the complexities of statecraft, such as establishing a permanent "place in the sun," deciding whether to build and detonate nuclear weapons, trafficking in arms
to tyrants and so on.[5] The *prima facie* evidence in support of such a claim is
strong.

And yet, granting that the ability to use massive power for good or evil
is hardly an issue with which inmates of the death camps had to cope, I
suggest that "Holocaust theology" can still make an important contribution to the present discussion. For if the Holocaust did not instruct Jews
on how to use power creatively, since they had none, it did provide an
indelible example of how others exerted power destructively when they
had too much. We at least discover some ways power should *not* be exercised, and in playing the power game in geopolitical terms today, it is no
small achievement to see clearly some ways of using power that must never
again be permitted. The reverse image of Nazi policies, in other words,
provides help in dealing with the use of power in the present.

Elie Wiesel's novel *Dawn* illuminates this point. Elisha, a youthful survivor of the Holocaust, enlists to go to Palestine and fight for the expulsion
of the British, a necessary prelude to the establishment of the state of
Israel. He is trained in the art of guerilla warfare, and after his first com-
mando raid, in which many British are killed, he has an uncomfortable
flashback to a scene in which the SS troops were doing to concentration
camp inmates precisely what Elisha and his compatriots were doing to the
British. But this dilemma, agonizing enough on its own terms, is compounded almost beyond his ability to cope when after the British have
seized and announced that they will execute a Jewish hostage, the Jewish
army similarly seizes and announces that it will execute a British hostage in
reprisal. And to young Elisha falls the task of killing the British soldier,
John Dawson, in cold blood.

After a visitation from "ghosts" of his past, who point out to him that he is repudiating the Jewish tradition by such an act, and after a conversation with John Dawson, whom he cannot hate and realizes he could like, Elisha nevertheless pulls the trigger as ordered. And as John Dawson falls, Elisha reflects that he has killed not only John Dawson but a part of himself as well. Murder thus becomes a form of self-inflicted destruction. Rather than being a victim, he is now an executioner, and the moral problem has not been resolved, but only exacerbated.

Just as Elisha discovered that he could not take on the role of death camp executioners but had to discover other tactics, so we, too, as we seek appropriate modes of action in the Middle East, can employ the negative example of the Nazis as a way of outlawing certain tactics:

Nazi ideology	*Contrary conclusion to be drawn*
1. Jews, without exception, can be treated as objects to be destroyed.	1. All persons, without exception, must be treated as subjects to be affirmed as having infinite worth.
2. Any means to achieve the glorious end of the triumph of the Third Reich is legitimate.	2. All means to achieve the triumph of justice that are themselves unjust are illegitimate.
3. A *lager* (concentration camp) can be run most efficiently on a structure of lies, shame, brutality and murder.	3. No community can be run morally or even (in the final analysis) efficiently unless the enduring communal values are truth, respect, compassion and sanctity of life.
4. Children are a special threat, since they might grow up to oppose us; they are therefore appropriate targets of extermination.	4. Children are a special blessing, since they can grow up and carry on our values; we must therefore create a society in which they can grow up without fear and with hope.

Holocaust survivors and their children, along with all people who have tried to sensitize themselves to what went on in the camps, have a moral obligation to challenge any people or nation-state if their actions begin to mirror, no matter how dimly, the actions of the SS guards. Only thus can society establish "early warning systems" to preclude future repetitions of the Holocaust.

Clearly we need more direction than this exercise alone provides, however. There are ways of approaching ethical issues, common to most liberation theologies, that can help us. Four examples are provided below.

1. Theological reflection should grow out of the immediate situation rather than out of abstract truths that are then "applied" to the circumstances. The witness of people caught in unjust structures is the starting point, and the authority of their witness has nothing to do with academic

qualifications, lists of publications, or membership in learned societies. Only after hearing their stories is it appropriate for theologians to employ tools of sociological or political analysis as a means of relating what is going on to the whole heritage of the faith.

In Elie Wiesel's novel, *The Oath*, Toli reports, "Grandfather says that when a Jew says he is hurting, one must believe him, and when he is afraid, one must assume his fear is justified."[6] In the context of the novel, which is set during a pogrom, this truth is almost self-evident. Without doing an injustice to Wiesel we can go on, I believe, to broaden the statement: "When *any* persons say they are hurting, we must believe them." The claim to be suffering, in other words, is *prima facie* evidence of the right to a hearing. Jews who were suffering in the Holocaust cried out that they were hurting, and those who heard them doubted, or denied, or refused to listen. Similarly, Palestinians who have been suffering in the Middle East cry out that they are hurting, and those who hear them doubt, or deny, or refuse to listen.

Are the two situations, Jewish and Palestinian, as parallel as I suggest above? In one sense, no: the deliberate Nazi extermination of an entire race is of a greater magnitude of evil than even the worst Israeli-Palestinian military clashes. But in another sense, the situations *are* parallel: the common denominator in both of them is intense human suffering, and it would be cruel and inhumane to close our ears to any human suffering on the grounds that there was not enough suffering to merit our attention and help. The immediate suffering of a child whose chest has been lacerated by a bullet is neither augmented nor diminished by a knowledge of the politics of the one who fired the rifle. Children bleeding to death are children bleeding to death, no matter what the context. The common element is suffering and the common obligation is to relieve the suffering.

The moral right of the victims to be heard and taken seriously is further increased if the victims not only say "we are hurting," but go on to add, "and you are the cause of my hurting." In this case, there is not only the direct charge of the hearers' complicity in inflicting pain, but also a proposal for alleviating pain: "You, the hearers, have it in your power to cease inflicting pain. In the name of God, use that power."

It may be that the victims are wrong, and that the targets of the anguished cry are not in fact guilty. But those toward whom the charge is leveled must nevertheless take it seriously. Perhaps they will discover that someone else is responsible; if so, steps may be taken to disarm the assailant. Or those to whom the complaint is addressed may discover a greater degree of their own complicity in inflicting suffering than was initially apparent.

The locus of Toli's statement as we saw, was the imminence of a pogrom in which Jews suffered as they suffered in pogroms throughout history. Jews know what it is to be the recipients of pain. But let us propose a different locus. Can Jews hear the cries of others, in this case Palestinians, who in pain and anguish cry, "we are hurting," and even, "we are hurting, and it is you, Jews, who are hurting us?" We know that there are Jews who *do* respond to such outcries, just as there are Palestinians who respond sensitively when Jews cry, "we are hurting, and it is you, Palestinians, who are hurting us." However, as far as Jews are concerned, we must also remember another part of Toli's comment: "When a Jew says . . . he is afraid, one must assume his fear is justified."[7] No non-Jew can measure the depth of Jewish fear that Israel will be isolated, invaded, annihilated, i.e., that the Holocaust will be repeated. The history of the Jews makes such fear reasonable, and there is not yet enough convincing evidence from the rest of the world that the fear is unfounded.

My most telling exposure to the justifiably deep-seated fear of Jews for their survival came in conversation with a Jewish friend. A synagogue had been desecrated in Paris and I commented that this must raise Jewish fears of similar outbursts elsewhere. "Yes," came the response, "every time there is a public expression of anti-Semitism I tremble." And then, with hardly a pause, my friend said, "And when there are *no* public expressions of anti-Semitism, I tremble even more."

We must start with the immediate situation if we hope to create a relevant theology.

2. A second contribution that liberation theology might make to solving the crisis in the Middle East lies in its recognition that liberation is no respecter of persons, parties, or causes; unless liberation is achieved for all, rather than for some at the expense of others, it is not true liberation.

Idealism and realism join forces here; the statement may sound like a high, unrealizable hope, but it is also a hard, descriptive truth. Israel will not be liberated from its present fears as long as Palestinians live under occupation and rebel against it. Palestinians will not be liberated from their present fears as long as Israelis feel themselves under daily threat of destruction of their country, and mobilize to protect it.

Stated in down-to-earth terms, this means that neither party to any future negotiations will get everything it wants. There will be a long, often dismal, and frequently discouraging, process, in which compromise rather than victory will be the condition of any settlement. That in turn will be followed by years of testing each other's sincerity and resolve, during which both sides will have to learn to settle for a little rather than a lot, since the only other possibility will be to settle for nothing. But it is only out of such long, hard struggles that any liberation worthy of the name will finally be achieved.

3. One of the most pervasive concerns of liberation theology is a "preferential option for the poor." This theme, first articulated by the Latin American Catholic bishops at Medellin in 1968, was repeated and elaborated at their Puebla conference in 1979, a decision that was particularly important since there were strong pressures from the Catholic right to eliminate the theme. A similar set of circumstances surrounded its adoption by the United States Catholic bishops in their pastoral letter on the economy, issued in 1986. In every case, the "poor" referred to are the *materially* poor: the indigent and the marginalized, who lack both possessions and power. In the light of this principle, two questions must be asked of any proposed program or legislation: (1) will it help to alleviate poverty among the poorest of the poor? and (2) will it lead to the *empowerment* of the poor, so that they are not simply the recipients of handouts but can play an increasing role in shaping their destiny?

This issue of empowerment gives the theme particular relevance to the Middle East, where "poverty" is not simply a paucity of material goods (though many Palestinians have lost all their possessions), but a paucity of political or economic control by Palestinians over their own lives. As long as that remains true, there is an ongoing need for liberation.

In an important sense, however, the same is true of Israel. Although it possesses an imposing array of arms and sophisticated weaponry, which it can unleash at a moment's notice and with devastating results, Israel is not as "free" as it appears, for at least two reasons: (1) It lives with the recognition that coalitions of Arab forces in the area have the potential to wreak almost total physical devastation on Israel, no matter how militarily strong it may be, and (2) Israel's dependence on the United States for weaponry, financial resources, and ongoing viability in the face of hostile neighbors means that Israel can never stray too far from the wishes, expressed or implied, of its benefactor.

In the Middle East, therefore, to call for a "preferential option for the poor," which in this context means a preferential option for the powerless, involves determining how the powerless on both sides can gain sufficient power to escape from situations of dependency, yet not gain their own liberation by denying liberation to others.[8]

This is an almost impossible conundrum for the participants; there are few precedents for nations relinquishing power, nor for those desiring to become nations foregoing the acquisition of as much power as they can get, preferably leading to a diminution of the power of the nearest adversary. Both Israel and the Palestinians have legitimate aspirations to power—at least to enough power to insure their survival in the face of threats from each other.

The question becomes: can each side develop enough trust, or wisdom, to forego amassing inordinate power? Each will want a sufficient surplus of power so that the other side will feel too intimidated to attack, isolate, or seek to annihilate. But no situation that is too asymmetrical can bring any assurance of peace. Perhaps never before in human history have people needed to achieve so delicate a balance with so little experience of creating the trust necessary to make the risks endurable. Such a balance can never be achieved if it is imposed from the outside—by the United States, for example—in such a way that either party feels it is beholden to forces beyond its control. And yet the stakes are so high that the well-being of the entire planet is affected by whether or not Israel and the Palestinians can work out a settlement in which each escapes from powerlessness yet does not accumulate too much power. Only an acknowledgment of the limitations that must accompany their respective empowerments can yield a situation in which both can be liberated.

Just how these forces can be calibrated into a successful settlement is beyond the scope or competence of this essay. But I believe that only if a settlement is explored in the context of a true quest for liberation as a preferential option for the powerless can we expect significant progress.

4. Any discussion of power and powerlessness suggests a further theme of liberation theology that is important in the Middle East. This is a realization of the inherent risk in the liberation struggle. The risk is not so much that of losing as of winning too decisively. There is always a danger that as oppressed people gain liberation they will deny liberation to others. Ignacio Silone, the Italian writer, who saw both the fascist state and the communist party succumb to this temptation, formulated the concern in novel after novel. In the words of one of his characters, a disillusioned revolutionary, "Why have all revolutions, every single one of them, begun as movements of liberation and ended as tyrannies?"[9] Paulo Freire, who has worked in the forefront of the liberation struggle in South America, has likewise called attention to the ease with which, for example, a peasant who is chosen out of the ranks to become an overseer all too frequently becomes tyrannical toward those who were once his companions in misery.[10]

This realization is often used by conservatives as a justification for opposing all revolutionary movements, since they may replace a tyranny of the right with a tyranny of the left. However, this is a curious employment by self-avowed free market capitalists of a view of historical determinism that would make Karl Marx blush at its rigidity. I would like to suggest that the best way to avoid succumbing to the temptation is to be aware of it at every step along the way.

It is a temptation to which many feel the nation-state of Israel has been succumbing with increasing frequency. There have been so many instances, particularly since the *intifada*, of Israeli soldiers capturing, torturing, and killing innocent Palestinians, that the lineaments of the oppressor have frequently been observed in those who until recently were clearly among the oppressed.

This is not yet a central problem for the Palestinians, with the important exception of the degree to which the threat or practice of terrorism has been a bargaining chip in their arsenal of weapons. But let us suppose that world opinion builds around them, and that the PLO, long the *bete noire* of Israel, becomes a major party in a worldwide peace conference, thereby gaining a credibility it has heretofore lacked. Surely the moment of truth for the Palestinians will not be just the achievement of nationhood and a piece of real estate to validate the claim, but the way it subsequently relates to the Israelis. Will it, even with only one foot in the door of power, seek subtle and not-so-subtle vengeance against the nation to which it was beholden for so long? Will the unleashing of long-suppressed energies result in vindictiveness and retribution against individual Israelis? To be forewarned might mean to be forearmed against excesses of "victory" that could rapidly tear to shreds whatever delicate fabric the negotiations might painstakingly have built up.

There is no ironclad law decreeing that the oppressed must become oppressors when they acquire power, however many precedents there may be for the likelihood of such an outcome. The great hope for peace in the Middle East does not lie solely or even primarily in the terms of a settlement, but in the degree to which, after a settlement, both parties can refuse to embrace the role of oppressor.

I can write no "conclusion" to this essay. For the moment there are only the most tentative beginnings. It is not the task of this essay, or this book, to provide a blueprint for peace in the Middle East. Such an aim would be not only foolhardy but futile. Even if we included specific proposals in these pages, the necessary gestation period in bringing the book to birth would render most of them dated by the time they were published. All that can be stated with assurance is that the search for peace in the Middle East is an ongoing process that will take years, perhaps decades, and that in that interval, however long or short, the process will remain volatile—full of ups and downs, charged with almost uncontrollable emotions on all sides, replete with recriminations and rebuffs, as well as occasional unanticipated breakthroughs. The great hope for success in this precarious stretch of human history is that the conflict will become more verbal and less physical, and that respect for life will count for more than unilateral expansion by either party.

However, I can offer my own tentative list of the ingredients that must be part of a final adjudication, however much they may need refinement along the way: a homeland for both Jews and Palestinians; a safeguarding of the rights of all minorities; a solution that (however much the international community participates) is the work of those who live in the area; a firmly established respect for one another's borders; bilateral de-escalation of the military forces; a willingness to have all parties judged by the same moral and political standards; an acknowledgment from the beginning of the process that everyone will have to settle for less than initially hoped for.

The geographical area in which the disputes have taken place for so long is a spiritual and physical home to three of the world's great religions—Judaism, Islam, and Christianity. Those three faiths pledge allegiance to the same God, however different their interpretations have become. When all the conferences have been held, all the negotiations entered into, all the decisions reached, it will surely be by the power of that one God, and the willingness of the adjudicators to profess ultimate loyalty to such a One, that a measure of the divine will can be achieved. For although all parties have the power to thwart that divine will momentarily, none has the power ultimately to defeat it. Prayer embodied in human deeds may finally be the instrument that transforms a present wistful hope into an ultimate reality.

8

Ethical Issues in the Israeli-Palestinian Conflict

JOHN T. PAWLIKOWSKI

It is important to preface the reflections that follow on ethical questions in the Israeli-Palestinian conflict with some indication of the basic context from which these reflections flow. For nearly two decades I have been an active participant in the national and international Christian-Jewish dialogue with some recent outreach to the developing Jewish-Christian-Muslim encounter. My contacts have been mainly with Jews and Israelis (of all stripes), though not exclusively. As a member of the Executive Committee of the National Christian Leadership Conference for Israel I have endorsed (though on a somewhat qualified basis) such controversial positions as the transfer of the US embassy to West Jerusalem. So I may be rightly judged an Israeli partisan of sorts, though certainly not an uncritical one, whose fundamental commitments definitely lie with those diaspora Jews and Israelis who desire a negotiated solution to the current crisis which will guarantee Israel's survival while assuring the Palestinian people territorial integrity. My commitment to Israeli nationhood remains as strong and enduring as ever, as does my rejection of the infamous UN resolution 3379 equating Zionism with racism.

Having confessed my basic partisanship, however, I must also point out that I have maintained a continuous commitment to dialogue with Palestinians and to the absolute need for some form of Palestinian entity. I first laid out this position in a 1974 article in *Worldview*,[1] where I also clearly rejected the "Jordan equals Palestine" thesis advocated by certain Israeli political leaders. More recently I have become associated with the US Interreligious Committee for Peace in the Middle East, whose goal is to insure continuing US involvement in pressing for a negotiated settlement of the present conflict that will guarantee territorial integrity for both Israelis and Palestinians.

The above confession of fundamental perspective is important because in my judgment no evaluation of the moral issues in the current Israeli-Palestinian struggle can be totally objective. Every person coming to such an evaluation undoubtedly brings presuppositions and experiences that may be valid, yet limited in terms of the overall problem. My experiences have largely been with the Israeli side. Thus the issues I raise reflect what I have observed through that lens. I see nothing especially wrong in this. I would naturally expect a parallel situation to prevail among those who speak primarily from experiences with the Palestinian community. In a complicated moral issue such as the present Palestinian-Israeli conflict, where there clearly exists a clash of basic rights, I would be automatically suspicious of anyone who too easily claimed total neutrality.

With the above point of departure in mind let me begin the analysis with the unqualified assertion that the vicious cycle of violence that has plagued the history of the relationship of the Israelis and Palestinians and that has greatly intensified since the beginning of the uprising on the West Bank/Gaza in December 1987 must be brought to a halt as soon as possible. Its potential for further escalation, even to the point of a superpower collision, remains high. And its destructive effects on the moral and spiritual fiber of both communities is beyond calculation. Neither side can emerge totally victorious. Both will suffer grave distortions, especially among their younger generations, if the hostility drags on indefinitely. The only sane path is that of substantive negotiation.

Speaking as a Christian ethicist I must direct a word of caution at my Christian colleagues. Our historical baggage, for which we must accept responsibility, does not allow us to assume an overly "moralistic" tone with respect either to the Jews or the Arabs. Our historical treatment of both, but especially the Jews, has been such that our moral voice as representative of the churches must be measured. This does not mean that we should remain silent. But we are in no position to lecture to either side. Our role, in my judgment, is primarily that of reconciler. Under this rubric we certainly have an obligation to present some moral evaluation, but careful consideration of the tonality of that evaluation is important if it is to receive any hearing whatsoever given our historical liabilities as a faith community with respect to both parties to the conflict. Somehow we must find ways of helping those Israelis and those Palestinians who wish to negotiate come together despite the many barriers their respective communities continue to place before them. The plea of some six hundred Israeli professors (a highly significant number given the small size of the country)

for a negotiated end to the conflict because of the deterioration of the Israeli national fiber they claimed to be witnessing among their students
must be heeded by those who profess to support Israel. And equal concern
must be shown for those valiant Palestinians who maintain a peace perspective in the face of even greater odds and who desperately fear their
approach may soon be totally submerged in the sea of Islamic fundamentalism that is on the rise throughout the area, especially in Gaza.

Additional reasons may also be cited for necessary Christian involvement in a peaceful resolution of the Palestinian-Israeli conflict. First, there
is little doubt that Israel has become a cornerstone of Jewish identity, both
in Israel proper and among diaspora Jews. This is evidently related to the
rediscovery of the cardinal role that the "land tradition" plays in the Jewish
Scriptures. One does not have to fall into biblical fundamentalism to acknowledge a basic linkage in this regard. Well-respected Christian scholars
such as W. D. Davies[2] and Walter Brueggemann[3] have asserted this on the
basis of responsible contemporary research. And recent documents in the
Christian-Jewish dialogue, such as the 1974 Guidelines for the implementation of Vatican II's *Nostra Aetate*,[4] have insisted that Christians must come
to understand and appreciate how Jews define their own identity. Secondly, the presence of a small, struggling Christian community that often
finds itself squeezed between larger forces must be of concern to the
churches at large. This includes both the Arab and Hebrew-speaking
Christian communities in the area. Closely allied to this reason for continuing Christian involvement is the historic interest of the Christian
world in the land of its origins. The churches need to insure their ongoing, viable presence in the region in the face of possible threats both from
Islamic fundamentalism and extreme forms of Jewish orthodoxy. And this
presence needs to be manifested in a living community, not merely in historical shrines. Christians know very well that they will be a minority in
this land. The Crusader flag will not fly again over Jerusalem. But the minority community must be a vibrant one, and not a dying relic of the past.
Finally, many of the central documents on Christian-Jewish relations issued
during the last two decades clearly name peace and justice as the heart of
the interreligious dialogue. While this peace and justice concern ought to
embrace global dimensions, it certainly cannot exclude the pivotal Israeli-
Palestinian conflict.

With this rationale for involvement by the churches in trying to establish peace in the region we can turn to a related question: how should we
Christians think about this involvement? Two respected ecumenists and

social activists, Robert McAfee Brown[5] and Msgr. George G. Higgins,[6] have offered some important cautions.

In response to the uprising, Brown articulated a series of principles for Christians to follow in engaging the Israeli-Palestinian issue. His first principle involves the unequivocal affirmation of the right of Israel to exist and prosper. Along with the resolution of legitimate Palestinian national identity claims, this right continues to be a centerpiece of the ongoing conflict. There is still insufficient basis for assuming that this issue is now behind us. Nothing is further from reality. There has been some constructive movement of late—including the implicit recognition of Israel that seems part of the Palestine National Assembly's Algiers declaration, proclaiming its own state in the West Bank/Gaza—to warrant some hope that a sufficient number of Palestinian and other leaders are finally willing to rid themselves of the goal of destroying the Jewish national homeland. But the Palestinian and Arab press, as well as Muslim religious leaders in the affected areas, are hardly preaching such acceptance of Israel to the masses. On the contrary, the Arab popular media is still strongly dominated by a "we shall destroy Israel" mentality. Until such a turnabout occurs, as it has in Egypt to a very modest extent, no Jew will rest easy, and rightly so. The right of Israel to exist must very explicitly remain an essential ingredient of any framework for a moral evaluation of the Israeli-Palestinian crisis.

Two further observations suggest themselves relative to this basic question of Israel's right to exist. The first is whether Jewish religious nationalism or fear of national annihilation constitutes the principal block to peace from the Israeli side.[7] The evidence is strong that "fear of national annihilation" is the prevailing obstacle to the creation of a peace mentality within the general Israeli population.

Extensive conversations with Israeli peace activists, including leaders of the largest peace organization, Peace Now, yield the clear conclusion that until something constructive is done about removing the basis for this fear among Israelis, Peace Now's efforts to promote a national willingness to enter serious negotiations with the Palestinians will falter. Even the Egyptian ambassador to the United States, in an address to a convocation on Middle East Peace at the Washington National Cathedral sponsored by the U.S. Interreligious Committee for Peace in the Middle East in January 1988, directly confronted the Palestinian side on this issue, insisting that the Palestinians must take steps to help alleviate Israeli fears in this regard. A poll commissioned by the Anti-Defamation League and conducted as a joint endeavor by a US and an Israeli polling firm in the late summer of

1988 showed that sixty-five percent of the Israeli population favored major concessions for peace. The poll also showed that sixty percent of the Israeli population supported relinquishing territories for peace if this would guarantee the nation's security. The 1988 national elections in Israel, at least in my opinion, continued to confirm that a majority of the population remains committed to a peaceful resolution of the current conflict that involves territorial concessions.

These figures, while substantial, are not overwhelming. This is a legitimate cause of concern for the future as the fervor of the Jewish religious nationalists who demand incorporation of the occupied territories into a Greater Israel escalates. It is important to pursue the peace effort with vigor while this basic openness remains present. But the peace process cannot be effectively promoted unless the "fear" question is addressed adequately, most especially by the Palestinians. Parading convicted terrorist killers before international television cameras and holding press conferences in which Palestinian leaders fail to state in unambiguous fashion their acceptance of Israeli national sovereignty do nothing to allay Israeli fears that the section in the Palestinian covenant calling for the destruction of Israel is still very much in force. Though recent statements made by Palestinian leaders seem to be less ambiguous about the existence of the state of Israel, there still seems to be an unwillingness on the part of Palestinian leaders to prepare their people for a moderate line toward Israel in the Arab popular media. One of the realities that convinced the Israelis several years ago that the Egyptian government was serious about negotiating a peace agreement was the significant change they noted in descriptions of Israel in the Egyptian popular media. If Israelis, some of whom understand Arabic, are to be convinced that Palestinian attitude on Israel is moving away from the Palestine covenant's call for Israel's disappearance, then the basic information channels serving the Palestinians and the other Arab nations must become less hostile towards Jews, Zionism, and the state of Israel.

At this point, it would be well to add a word or two about the issue of religious nationalism and Middle East peace. Too many Western commentators make the mistake of assuming that all interjection of religious perspectives into the Palestinian-Israeli conflict automatically corrodes ethical values. And when this happens Jewish religious nationalism becomes a special target.

It would be naive not to recognize the tremendous dangers in many forms of Jewish religious nationalism as they are being played out currently in the Middle East. But this judgment has to be made with equal force regarding Islamic religious nationalism, as well as the residue of the classical Christian anti-Judaic view that Jews have forsaken all rights to the land of Israel by virtue of their failure to accept Christ, which still surfaces from time to time among Christian Arabs. But it is wrong to assume that religious nationalism must (or can) be totally cast aside in any resolution of the Israeli-Palestinian struggle, as though a purely secular approach to political ethos and structure could work for either party. Religious tradition is an integral part of all the cultures of the Middle East. Of necessity it plays a pivotal role in the self-consciousness of all states in the region for the foreseeable future.

Any attempt to factor religious tradition out of the picture altogether is to build on quicksand. That does not mean encouraging fanatical forms of religious nationalism that make no room for religious pluralism. Nor does it mean simplistically settling borders on the basis of religiously-based maps. What it does mean, for example, is that anyone desirous of promoting an ethically based peace among Israelis and Palestinians needs to find ways in which Islamic, Christian, and Jewish attachments to the land can be honored as far as possible. Such a recognition of Jewish claims would not be acquiesence to fundamentalist biblical interpretation but, as was said above, acknowledgment of the serious research by such scholars as the Christian exegete W. D. Davies, who has written of the "umbilical," eternal connection between the Jewish people and its land.[8] Attempts to impose a purely secular solution on the Palestinian-Israeli conflict in the name of supposed high morality end as nothing more than a form of Western cultural imperialism.

There is one form of biblical interpretation practiced by some fundamentalist Christian supporters of Israel that should be repudiated. Such fundamentalists approach the current political crisis in the Middle East through Armageddon scenarios. In my judgment, many of them take a totally uncritical moral posture on the Palestinian-Israeli situation, believing that the Israelis, as the representatives of the forces of good fighting ultimately against the Devil, can do no wrong. They conceive of the state of Israel in such an exclusively theological fashion that the Palestinians are reduced to mere pawns in an apocalyptic drama. Jewish leaders who support the application of such morally dangerous biblical literalism to the concrete political decision-making in the Middle East deserve to be criticized as roundly as those who initially advance such claims in the name of the New Testament.

Clearly Western Christians interested in a morally based peace in Israel and Palestine should be prepared to take issue with simplistic biblical or Koranic approaches to the present conflict. But their primary contribution must be to help Jews, Muslims, and Christians find a way of maintaining a healthy religious influence in the respective states.

We come now to the second basic question regarding Israel's right to exist as a cardinal principle for any just Middle East peace settlement. It concerns the very establishment of the state, especially the events surrounding the 1948 war. Nearly all pro-Palestinian commentators on the conflict have strongly argued that the heart of the crisis, morally speaking, was the creation of hundreds of thousands of Palestinian refugees through military action and terror tactics on the part of the Jewish military.

Recently several volumes by Jewish authors have endorsed all or part of this argument. Three that have received attention of late are Benny Morris's *The Birth of the Palestinian Refugee Problem, 1947–1948*,[9] Simha Flapan's *The Birth of Israel*,[10] and Michael Palumbo's *The Palestinian Catastrophe*.[11] Palumbo's volume is the most extreme in its critique. Its basic bias against any form of Jewish nationalism shows through in its analysis even though many of its particular details are accurate. It has generally not received favorable notices save from already convinced pro-Palestinian sources. Far more reliable and nuanced, and attracting considerably more positive attention in Jewish circles, is the Morris volume. The Flapan volume is somewhat closer in its claims to Palumbo, but shows a much greater willingness to acknowledge the importance of Israeli nationhood despite the serious injustices endured by the Palestinians in its creation.

Morris recognizes a highly complex and varied set of developments in the Israeli-Palestinian struggle during the 1947–49 period. The situation differed markedly from place to place. As a result, he insists, "a single-cause explanation of the exodus from most sites is untenable."[12] He does recognize a certain shift in the spring of 1948 away from the dominance of internal Arab factors, such as lack of leadership and severe economic conditions, to Israeli-induced reasons for Arab flight, especially Haganah/Israel Defense Force attacks and expulsions (or at least the fear of these), as Jewish public opinion hardened in its stance towards the Arabs. But even in this period the Israeli factors, though often decisive, were not exclusive. Lack of assistance from the Arab world, a pervasive feeling of impotence and abandonment, and orders from Arab institutions and commanders to flee the territory continued to play an important role.

This growing research by scholars, including Jews, on the history of

1948 must be taken seriously in any moral evaluation of the current Middle East situation. But it must also be put into proper perspective. Certainly enough evidence has now come to light from a variety of sources to undercut earlier Israeli claims about total victimhood in 1948. Clearly a significant measure of injustice was perpetrated against Palestinians in the establishment and consolidation of the state of Israel.

Admittedly, many Jews and pro-Israeli partisans are strongly tempted to dismiss these Jewish historians. However those who have taken strong advocacy positions in behalf of the Palestinians over the years feel their cause has been morally vindicated. Neither posture is justified nor conducive to a peace between Israelis and Palestinians.

Recognizing the human rights violations against Palestinians and the right to national self-determination of the Palestinian people intensifies the moral obligation toward Palestinian nationhood, even if the national entity results in some form of freely chosen political liaison with Jordan. The evidence increasingly being brought to our attention by responsible Israeli critics such as Benny Morris compels us to acknowledge that Palestinian sovereignty carries a claim equal to Israeli sovereignty in any Middle East moral equation. It likewise forces us to speak of the Palestinians as the primary Arab group involved in the conflict, and not merely of Arab refugees. It renders morally bankrupt all calls for a "Jordan equals Palestine" solution or for the transfer of population, every bit as much as the inherent right of Israel to national self-determination renders morally bankrupt the UN declaration equating Zionism with racism. However, placing emphasis on the Palestinians does not imply that the rest of the Arab world remains incidental to Middle East peace. Without question, Egypt, Syria, Lebanon, Saudi Arabia, Jordan, Iraq, and Iran will remain crucial actors in any stabilization of the situation of the Middle East. There exist deep conflicts among the powers in the present Arab world, who often use extreme anti-Israeli rhetoric as a front. Such conflicts will hardly disappear on the day when the Palestinians and the Israelis reach an accord.

Some additional points need to be made in light of the recent research on the origins of the Israeli-Palestinian struggle. Palestinian identity is something that has developed fairly recently. Without subscribing to many of the rightly contested claims that Palestinian settlements are of recent origin by Joan Peters in *From Time Immemorial*,[13] evidence shows that a fair number of the families now living on the West Bank/Gaza do not have long-time Palestinian roots. Rather, they came at the end of the last century or throughout this century as Jews began to settle and improve living conditions to the point where they were among the best in the Middle East. And even families who can trace their roots for untold generations in the region tend to identify themselves principally in terms of their villages or cities, not in terms of a larger Palestinian identity. This fact is important for any overall evaluation of the current conflict.

We cannot forget that some six hundred thousand Jewish refugees were also forced from Arab countries where most often they too suffered serious human rights deprivations. The existence of Israel as a solution for the realization of basic human dignity for Jews of Middle Eastern background (which admittedly has not been fully met in the state to date but is continually improving) adds basic moral weight to Israel's right to exist as a cardinal ethical value in the current Middle East picture. These Israelis, who were part of the Arab world for centuries, are no more outsiders to the Israel/Palestine area than many of the people who now consider themselves Palestinian, an identity which, while of fairly recent vintage, must be honored in any just peace settlement.

How do we treat the new critical materials on the 1947–49 era? Do we simply use them to imply somehow Israel's de-legitimation as a nation-state or do we place them in the broader perspective of the checkered history of the rise of every present national entity? Only the latter choice will take us in a constructive direction. Hopefully Israel now possesses sufficient maturity as a nation to handle a critical assessment of its origins, just as people in the United States have begun to explore its history of slavery and its treatment of native peoples. Just as this has been done in the United States without suggesting that national existence of the United States rests on a foundation bereft of all moral justification, so too must the case of Israel be handled, as the new information generated by Morris and others is gradually incorporated into the national ethos. Critics of Israel should not use this new data to suggest grounds for questioning Israel's basic right to national existence. Such application of the 1947–49 data would constitute applying a moral criterion for Israeli nationhood that has been used in no other case. It would also feed the fears of national annihilation that remain strong in the Israeli consciousness.

In considering solutions to the Israeli-Palestinian conflict, it is helpful to examine current ethical approaches to the nation-state concept. One strain of moral thinking, flowing out of nineteenth-century German idealism, has espoused universalism and global community as the only sane, ethical choice for contemporary humanity. In this mind-set any form of nationalism automatically stands in conflict with the highest ethical values and represents a threat to the survival of humanity.

The power of the universalist ethic, in which the nation-state is inherently downgraded, has been reduced considerably in recent years. The primacy of national identity is clearly affirmed even though many recognize it must be combined with some sense of global interdependence. But the reality is that the enhanced appreciation of the nation-state, usually expressed through the principle of national self-determination, has often been applied only to moral justifications of the Palestinian cause. Zionism, whatever its stripe, is criticized as being, by its very nature, morally corrupt. This is total inconsistency and leads to the often-voiced Jewish complaint about a double moral standard. If one holds to the primacy of the universal ethic and thus regards nationhood in a negative light, then this principle must be applied with equal vigor to both Israeli and Palestinian nationalism. And if nationalism with interdependence is affirmed, then the satisfaction of both Israeli and Palestinian national claims should be viewed as inherent to the achievement of ultimate human dignity by each community. Thus we must be prepared to give a sympathetic ear to Jewish arguments both from the biblical tradition and from modern Jewish philosophers such as Abraham Heschel[14] and Manfred Vogel[15] about the integral link between nation and people in the Jewish vision.[16]

Clearly there is a high degree of moral complexity in the current Middle East conflict. Raised to the level of ethical model, what we have before us is another clear example of something that the late Reinhold Niebuhr staunchly maintained: in international politics only relative justice, not absolute justice, is possible. There are always conflicting claims, none of which are totally realizable, and inevitably serious ambiguities (even contradictions) arise in the affirmation of these moral claims. One example of this is the issue of terrorism. Some pro-Israeli partisans advance the argument that heavy reliance on terrorism has mitigated whatever legitimate claims Palestinians might have to national sovereignty, because it poses a fundamental threat to Israel's right to exist. Without defining the exact nature of terrorism and whether any Israeli actions may legitimately also be labeled "terroristic," it is clear to me that the PLO's use of terrorism, accompanied by a visible smugness about its effects, constitutes a serious problem in any moral judgments on the Israeli-Palestinian struggle. Here Niebuhr's distinction is absolutely crucial. Relative justice can still affirm Palestinian national rights despite the resort to terrorism. But it can be done with integrity only if such an affirmation is accompanied by an equally clear judgment on the terrorist activities of the Palestinians. Unfortunately, people either totally reject Palestinian national claims, using terrorism as a prime counter-argument, or they champion Palestinian self-determination, never uttering a word about the immoral use of terror in the overall drive for nationhood.

Frequent silence on the issue of terrorism is but one example of an almost total lack of criticism by those who espouse the Palestinian cause. Some of the silence even verges on outright hypocrisy. People who are otherwise committed to non-violence sometimes embrace the Palestinian cause without in any way mentioning the use of terror as a tool of the Palestinian national struggle. Some Palestinians have even wrapped themselves in the cloak of the great practitioner of nonviolence, Dr. Martin Luther King, which gives them a sympathetic hearing among many American social activists. As those who worked with the King movement in such diverse places as Montgomery and Chicago know, Dr. King's commitment to non-violence was profound. At key moments in the civil rights struggle, King demonstrated this unwavering non-violent resolve when he broke with other black leaders such as Rap Brown and Stokely Carmichael over the issue of non-violence. We have yet to see those who claim Dr. King's mantle in the Middle East conflict on the Palestinian side do the same with respect to the PLO which, whatever else one might say about it, is by self-admission not committed in principle to non-violence.

Because of the inability of Palestinians to commit themselves to non-violence, Christians should have a deeper understanding of why Jews of the diaspora are reluctant to criticize the state of Israel publicly. Such criticism has often fueled the arguments of pro-Palestinian sympathizers who have been totally unwilling to engage in any similar critique of ethical abuses on the part of the Palestinian leadership. I am convinced Jews must begin to engage far more in constructive public criticism of Israeli policy on the current impasse with the Palestinians. But for this expectation to be met there is need for some reciprocity from the Palestinian side. At the same time, Christians must be able to criticize a particular policy decision by the state of Israel without fear of automatically being classified as anti-Semitic. Also, Jews should understand that Christian disagreement with certain Israeli policies entails a theological as well as a political judgment. It is not part of the prophetic tradition, as Christians read it, to say that there can be criticism of all states save one, Israel.

Still, there is the danger that Christians may overdo the prophetic role in this complex situation. To recall the point made earlier in this essay, Christians come to any discussion of the current Israeli-Palestinian conflict with their own very blemished record throughout history, especially with respect to Jews and Muslims. So a prophetic posture, if adopted by Christians in this situation, needs to retain a certain measure of modesty. Also, in principle, there exists in Christianity the persistent danger of restricting moral behavior to the realm of the "prophetic." This is certainly an honored Christian role historically and remains an integral part of any Christian perspective. But it is not the only possible posture in the Middle Eastern situation. The delicate, painstaking mission of reconciliation and peacemaking may prove far more decisive in the end. Such a task usually requires great patience and a somewhat more muted voice. However, it is no less an exercise of moral leadership than the prophetic option. Clearly, inflammatory language will take us nowhere. The description of Israel's repression of the Palestinian uprising as a "vendetta" comparable to Jewish suffering in the Nazi Holocaust is such an example. Such comparisons are obscene.

Authentic peacemakers do not attack something that has become pivotal for the self-identity of one of the groups they are trying to reconcile. Like it or not, for most Jews the Holocaust has become a centerpiece of their contemporary self-identity. However serious the injustices connected with the Israeli occupation of the West Bank and Gaza, particularly during the period of the *intifada*, they do not constitute Holocaust. Such comparisons, coming from Christians whose own churches must bear considerable responsibility for the success of the Nazi effort, sound utterly repulsive to Jewish ears.

A far more constructive approach in connection with the Holocaust would be to argue, as Marc H. Ellis does, that the experience of the *Shoah* ought to make Jews especially sensitive to the plight of the Palestinians and should engender a spirit of solidarity relative to their cause. Should the Holocaust primarily generate an *ethic of survival* or an *ethic of solidarity?* Irving Greenberg lays strong emphasis on the survival pole with balanced use of power a cardinal feature of such ethic. Ellis, while seemingly no pacifist in principle, argues with equal vehemence for the primacy of solidarity. As a Christian ethicist viewing this internal Jewish debate, it appears to me that both make critical points. What Greenberg is ultimately saying is that after the *Shoah* we cannot rely on divine intervention in human history to protect us, even if we consider ourselves a covenanted people. The *Shoah* has shattered the foundations of any such divine-human relationship. Post-Holocaust morality must respond to this unparalleled situation. The Jewish community, and by implication all of humankind, must assume a far greater responsibility for its continued survival. This can only be accomplished through the judicious use of power—accompanied by the development of self-correcting mechanisms for preventing unwarranted application of this power. Ellis, on the other hand, is as strongly convinced that Jewish survival, human survival, after the *Shoah*, can be insured only if Jews tie their destiny to other oppressed peoples of the world. He leaves little doubt that he would include the Palestinians within the ranks of the oppressed.

I believe Ellis has put power aside far too easily. Despite recent events, there remains a serious threat to Israel's national existence from certain parts of the Palestinian movement and from other forces within the larger Arab world. Ellis ignores this very real, continuing threat. I am quite prepared to side with Irving Greenberg on the basic contention that with Israel's survival remaining far from certain, it must maintain a strong power capacity to defend itself. And since I cannot see simple, unilateral Israeli withdrawal from the West Bank and Gaza as a viable option, Israel has a responsibility to maintain public order in the region until a peace agreement can be negotiated.

But, while endorsing the basic thrust of Greenberg's ethic of survival, I have serious difficulties with many of the concrete ways he interprets it in his essay, "The Ethics of Jewish Power." Though in an earlier publication on the subject he called for the creation of "better mechanisms of self-criticism, correction, and repentance" as the only way to employ power "without being the unwitting slaves of bloodshed or an exploitative status quo" [17] his application (or overall non-application) of this rule to Israeli activities in the West Bank and Gaza since the start of the *intifada* is both puzzling and quite disturbing. At best, his use of this moral principle is extremely superficial as he discusses particular activities. Little or none of the moral agonizing recognized by Greenberg in the original essay is present in this "uprising-era" piece. Such an evident lack of sensitivity gives some credence to Ellis' claim that Greenberg in the end transforms the *Shoah* into a mandate for Jewish survival at any cost.

In addition to the questionable nature of some of Greenberg's specific judgments from a post-Holocaust moral perspective, there are three overarching omissions in his approach. The first is his failure to ask whether there might not be more responsible ways of preserving public order. Even some Jewish supporters of Israel acknowledge that terrible mistakes were made from the standpoint of peacekeeping operations. New techniques have been developed that the Israelis simply ignored. Secondly, and far more importantly, Greenberg fails to realize that preserving public order is not usually best accomplished through the heavy hand of power alone. The words of the leading Catholic thinker Romano Guardini, written out of the personal experience of the Nazi era, need to be seriously weighed by Greenberg: "In the coming epoch, the essential problem will no longer be that of increasing power—though power will continue to increase at an even swifter tempo—but of curbing it. The core of the new epoch's intellectual task will be to integrate power into life in such a way that man can employ power without forfeiting his humanity, or to surrender his humanity to power and perish."[18]

Finally, nowhere in "The Ethics of Power" does Greenberg make a deep commitment to pursue a peaceful resolution of the current conflict with the Palestinians, an essential ingredient of any evaluation of Israel's use of power in the necessary maintenance of public order in the occupied territories. Without such a clear commitment, the misapplications of power that have been part of the Israeli-Palestinian relationship since the *intifada* assume an even greater moral seriousness.

In my judgment the only adequate post-Holocaust morality in terms of the present situation is one that draws on both the ethic of survival and the ethic of solidarity, in fact, one that understands their inherent linkage. While Ellis has either dismissed or assumed Israeli survival needs, a totally inadequate position, his call for Jews to develop a sense of solidarity with the Palestinians cannot go unheeded. One of the profoundest moral lessons that Christians have learned from research into the *Shoah* is how ecclesial self-definitions rendered Jews "unfortunate expendables" who could be cast aside in a situation in which the churches themselves felt under dire threat. If we see any beginnings of a post-Holocaust morality in the churches, it is in the moment towards an ecclesiology that has no room for "expendables," even in circumstances where the challenge to Christian group survival is indeed real. Ellis seems to be urging Jews to learn much the same lesson from the *Shoah* in his plea for an ethic of solidarity, not now to create Palestinian "expendables."

A noted Holocaust survivor and author, Professor Yisrael Gutman of the Hebrew University, spoke words in a similar vein at the Third International Jerusalem Conference on the History and Culture of Polish Jews in February 1988. One of six hundred Israel professionals who signed a letter urging the government to negotiate a peaceful withdrawal from the occupied territories as quickly as possible out of concern for the moral erosion this continued occupation was causing among university students, Gutman said that he better understands how difficult it must have been for Christians to criticize Hitler's Final Solution now that he has witnessed the disappointing reluctance of the Israeli population to criticize its political leadership for unjust activities in the West Bank/Gaza. Gutman added that if Jews are to critique the lack of Christian response to the Jewish tragedy during the Nazi period, they must be ready to receive the critique of Christians and others when they fail to raise a voice in the case of the Palestinian tragedy. By implication, Gutman was advocating an ethic of solidarity. Such solidarity is a requisite for meaningful Jewish survival after the *Shoah*.

An ethic of solidarity, emerging from an affirmation of the continuing centrality of the *Shoah* for Jewish self-identity, must be combined with legitimate aspects of an ethic of survival in any authentic post-Holocaust moral vision. Part of the integration will come from the recognition, recently stressed by the military-based Council for Peace and Security in Israel, that continued occupation will result in Israel's facing an even more destructive war in the future. Reserve General Yosef Geva of the Council defined the alternatives succinctly: "If we do not advance towards peace, we shall deteriorate into war, which is the worst we have ever fought." Another Council spokesperson, Reserve General Shlomo Gazit, saw Israel as facing two options: "(1) to hold on to the territories, to enforce Israeli rule over an alien people rebelling against it, to pay the price, to go to war unavoidably—this is a danger with no favorable prospects; or (2) to strive for peace with a readiness to make territorial concessions, while insisting on security arrangements—these are dangers that nevertheless embody positive prospects."[19]

Addressing the connection between security and solidarity at an even deeper level, Professor David Hartman, an Israeli Orthodox scholar who heads Jerusalem's Hartman Institute, sees a moral imperative for Israeli recognition of Palestinian self-determination. He offers Israelis two options. Either the nation accepts the fundamental needs of the Palestinians and finds ways to accommodate them within the bounds of national security concerns, or it establishes permanent rule over the Palestinians through force and intimidation. Even in the face of arguments showing the military and political feasibility of such ongoing occupation, Israelis need to face up to the fact, Hartman says, that "it would inevitably eat away at and undermine the moral and religious significance of our national renaissance." "We never dreamed of a Jewish nation," he goes on, "that would dehumanize and exploit an entire people. This is not what we prayed for or waited for during the past 2,000 years." Reducing Palestinians to a per-petually subject population gnaws away at all significant links between the moral and spiritual teachings of the Jewish tradition and contemporary Israel. He concludes: "To control the Palestinians permanently will justifi-ably undermine the centrality of Israel for world Jewry. Palestinians will permanently make us feel as strangers and aliens in our own home as long as we are unresponsive to their urgent need for political freedom."[20]

Any just resolution of the Israeli-Palestinian conflict also ultimately must take into account the situation of the so-called Israeli Arabs (some now call themselves Palestinians) who have held Israeli citizenship since 1948. They have generally experienced second-class status as Israeli citizens even though, as Middle Eastern minorities go, their situation has been far superior to most. Certainly any specific injustices they continue to endure must be corrected so long as they choose to retain their citizenship. But apart from particular abuses, the overall significance of their presence in Israel—a growing presence unless a significant number leave for a new Pal-estinian state—becomes a matter of justice for the state as well. This is not an easy issue to resolve if, as I argue, Israel has the right to exist as a funda-mentally Jewish state. But neither can the question be completely buried if full justice is to be accorded to all Israeli citizens.[21]

This essay began with an explicit admission of a pro-Israeli partisanship. It has, within this context, tried to address some of the major moral issues in the current Palestinian-Israeli struggle as objectively and compassion-ately as possible. Someone starting the process from the standpoint of a pro-Palestinian partisanship (and there is nothing wrong with construc-tive, critical partisanship) may well move in somewhat different directions. Hopefully there will be enough of a marriage of minds along the way so that reconciliation may truly commence. Peace is not one of the choices before us in the Middle East today; it is the only road short of destruction for both Israeli Jews and Palestinians. We have failed before.[22] The stakes are even higher now. Hence we cannot do so again without peril to sta-bility in the Middle East and to world peace as well.

The Theological and Ethical Context
for Palestinian-Israeli Peace

MIRIAM WARD

Two basic assumptions underlie this essay. First, the Middle East should not be viewed merely through Western eyes, but must be understood from the standpoint of those living in the region. This holds true for politics and religion, as well as for Middle Eastern culture. Without considering these factors the western world persists in its distorted and myopic view of the conflict in the Middle East. Second, in spite of the fact that the Middle East was the area in which the three great monotheistic religions had their origin, those who share this affirmation of faith have not developed a common theology and ethical context in which to resolve the Palestinian-Israeli conflict. Consequently, one cannot assume that Jews after the Holocaust and Palestinians after the *intifada* can find a basis for peace and reconciliation in their religious and ethical traditions.[1]

These assumptions may lead one to make two inferences. First, one may suppose that consideration of the theological and ethical factors will contribute little to a resolution of the conflict. Those of us in the western world, however, must remember that religion and politics have always been closely related in Middle Eastern life, and that religious ideals and values have frequently been the motivating force for political action. Second, one may suppose that the difference in western and Middle Eastern points of view is so great that the West should refrain from interfering or meddling in Middle Eastern politics. Since, however, the West, and the United States in particular, played a very prominent role in the twentieth century in creating the situation that would lead inevitably to conflict between Palestinians and Israelis, and has continued to increase that tension, the United States and its citizens have the moral responsibility to explore all avenues that will bring about peace with justice to this region. The time for decisive action is now, because ever-increasing inhumane, brutal, and violent incidents have become intolerable and because these have not only produced untold fear and suffering but also are undermining the ideals and character of the Israeli and Palestinian peoples.

At the heart of the Israeli-Palestinian conflict is a basic and simple fact that has been continuously overlooked, denied, or at least submerged in what is surely one of the most successful propaganda efforts in modern times. It can be summed up as follows: The creation of the state of Israel resulted in the dispossession and dispersion of another people, namely, the Palestinians. It is difficult to see how any theological consideration or the ethical imperative arising from such inquiry into the Palestinian-Israeli conflict can sidestep this indisputable fact.

Setting the Theological Context:
Back to the Basics of Theology

My thesis, therefore, is simple: in order that any formula for reconciliation be viable we must return to the very foundations of theology. Whatever the moral imperative, it must rest on justice and truth. Applied to the Israeli-Palestinian conflict we must get beyond the inaccuracies and untruths promulgated so successfully for the past four decades. There can be no durable political solution that does not somehow build on such an ethical foundation. Therefore I choose a theological context that goes to the heart of the issue and to the foundation of theology, one that is shared by the three great monotheistic faiths, and therefore one to which Jews, Palestinian Moslems, and Palestinian Christians can all relate: the meaning of creation.[2]

In its simplest form such a theology sees every human being as created in the image of a loving God. The moral imperative arising from this basic tenet of theology is equally simple, yet deeply profound: one must act in recognition of the sacredness of human life, of the dignity of the human person, of all human persons. In short, all human beings are called to moral accountability before God to see life as the most sacred and basic gift of God. We are all related to one another as brothers and sisters. The subsequent religious praxis flows from this and at the same time underlies and governs relationships among human beings. It demands no less than truth and justice as constitutive for any meaningful interaction among people. Rabbi Akiba sums up the Jewish view of creation when he says: "For this reason a single man only was created, to teach you

172

that if he destroys a single person, the Scripture imputes it to him as though he had destroyed the whole world, and if he saves the life of a single person, the Scripture imputes it to him as though he had saved the whole world."[3]

There is little stress on the concept of creation in the New Testament except in light of God's action in Jesus Christ. In embracing the Hebrew scriptures as part of the Christian canon the early Church accepted the basic idea of human beings created in the image of a loving God and their subsequent freedom. In his beautiful hymn to God's mercy and wisdom the apostle Paul sums up the Christian view: "All that exists comes from him; all is by him and for him. To him be glory forever!" (Rom. 11:36) Paul spells out Jesus' teaching by expressing it in terms of the universality of God's love.

While the Koran has many references to creation, it does not contain a developed or systematic theology of creation. Therefore, in presenting a theology of creation as a context in which one can talk of peace in the Middle East, one must indicate at the outset that while the Koran does not contain a systematic treatment of theological doctrine, the greatness of God and the goodness of creation are pervasive. "Praise be to God, the Creator of heaven and earth . . . God has power over all things" typifies the permeating ideas of creation throughout the Koran. "The Qur'an speaks much of creation, phrasing its message with the simplicity, if not the grandeur, of Genesis: all that is not God is ultimately the work of his power and wisdom."[4]

For Islam it is the Sharia (divinely inspired law) that supplies the theological context and spells out the rules governing interaction of human beings. What is clearly delineated in the Koran and the Sharia is the purpose for which God created. Human beings are created to worship God. Creatures are judged by the fulfillment of their respective inherent purposes. Indirectly, many *suras* suggest that humans must reflect the justice and wisdom of God. The great Muslim advocate of non-violence, Abdul Ghaffar Khan, popularly referred to as Badshah Khan, while proclaiming the necessity of faith in One God, said, "It is my inmost conviction that Islam is *amal, yakeen, muhabat* (work, faith, and love) . . ."[5]

While there may be differences in the particular stress laid on the concept of creation in Judaism, Christianity, and Islam, nevertheless there is solid agreement on the idea that human beings are created in the image of God. Further, the ethical or moral imperative that flows from this is embodied in the notion of freedom and one's call to act responsibly in that freedom. Thus, for Jews there is the covenant between Yahweh and Israel; for Muslims, the call to worship and to reflect the justice of God in one's life; and for Christians, the new covenant realized in Jesus in his bringing the good news to the poor and disenfranchised of this world. Each religion agrees on a call to reflect the justice of God. And from the ancient Greeks through Thomas Aquinas into modern times, an accepted theological as well as philosophical antecedent is that justice rests on truth.

The Human Issues: The Truth of the Matter

A cursory look at the literature on the Israeli-Palestinian problem of the past forty years, in print and other media, reveals a distorted if not out-right false presentation of Arabs, particularly Palestinian Arabs. Distorted myths about Arabs permeate novels, news articles, and analyses of current events in the Middle East. Incredibly, they are accepted with little if any scrutiny even at the university level. Those who dare question are frequently called anti-Semitic. Dissent is stifled.[6]

The negatives have been converted into stereotypes in which, as with all stereotyping, individual characteristics fade. The end result is reduction of all to no one: dehumanization. "Unpleasant" policies are easily justified. Euphemisms conveniently cover the implementation of unjust policies against the Palestinians. The dehumanization of Palestinians is reflected in references made by high level Israeli officials who characterize Palestinians as various kinds of insects or animals. For example, Rafael Eitan, a general in the Israeli Defense Forces who led the Israeli invasion into Lebanon in 1982, likened Palestinians to "drugged cockroaches in a bottle."[7]

The most commonly held stereotype of the Palestinian is that of "terrorist." What is seldom, if ever, discussed is Palestinian non-violent resistance to outside domination. Beginning with the Ottoman Turks, and increasingly so with the British, Jordanian/Egyptian, and Israeli occupations, the Palestinians have used many forms of active non-violence. The weakness and/or ineffectiveness did not lie in its use, but until the *intifada*, in the lack of organization and coordination. That the Israelis understand this well is exemplified in the recent expulsion of Mubarak Awad. Awad publicly proclaimed his goal of teaching active non-violence as the road to a solution to free Palestinians from the dependency into which occupation had forced them, and to self-sufficiency and self-determination. He was branded as subversive by the Israelis.

At the same time, the disparity between acts of institutionalized violence and those of the oppressed who see no alternative to violence is passed over. While terrorism in any form ought to be abhorred and condemned, the condemnation should be commensurate with the act. Killing people on a hijacked airplane or by a Molotov cocktail in a civilian bus, on the one hand, and by dropping bombs on refugee camps and cities or firing live ammunition at a child who breaks curfew on the other, are all indiscriminate taking of human life. None deserves legitimation, but only condemnation, and condemnation proportionate to the act of violence, as well as alternatives open to each party.

Perhaps most destructive of all aspects of the dehumanization of the Palestinians is that in the debate over their land, they have been ignored. From the 1947 partition resolution of the United Nations through the Camp David Accords of 1978, the Palestinians have been excluded from the talks. It was as though they did not exist, or at best, were not mature enough to name their own representatives.

Even during the recent Israeli election the Labor Party proposed talks with King Hussein of Jordan about the plight of the Palestinians. It is incredible for the Israelis to assume they can unilaterally name the representatives of the enemy with whom they will negotiate! How this kind of circumvention of the major party to the peace process can persist remains a mystery. Some recent developments in striving for the truth, however, give reason for hope.

Recent Israeli Appraisals: Setting the Matter Straight

In view of the past dearth of writing in which Israeli Jews have faced the Palestinian issue head-on, current publications come as a sign of hope. The recent declassification of official Israeli documents relating to the foundation of the state of Israel and the "leakage" of others has contributed in no small way to establishing a more accurate picture of reality.[8]

For example, the very existence of *"Plan Dalet"* outlining the Zionist military offensives of April and May, 1948 whose goal was to "accomplish the military *fait accompli* upon which the state of Israel was to be based" was denied until recent writings in English by Israeli Jewish authors. Ironically, the newly released sources, as well as those now available in English, confirm the 1951 findings of the leading Palestinian historian, Walid Khalidi, who published articles on "The Fall of Haifa" and *"Plan Dalet."* Despite the fact that Khalidi examined the *Hebrew* sources available at the time, the counter-propaganda of Zionists prevented widespread acceptance of his conclusions. Khalidi has been vindicated through the recent publications by Israeli Jews who show that indeed *"Plan Dalet"* did exist, and that its aim was the destruction of the Palestinian Arab community mainly through expulsion from their land.[9]

Increasing militarism substituted for diplomacy is another factor that forces Israelis to speak out. Whatever the motivation, the publications by Israeli Jews delineating what really happened to the indigenous Palestinian Arab population during the formation of the state of Israel and in the forty years since are a welcome and necessary contribution to reconciliation between Jew and Arab in the land we call holy. A long-time and fearless champion of truth in the history of the Israeli-Palestinian problem was Simha Flapan, a 1930 Jewish immigrant to Israel from Poland. As one of the founders and first editor of *New Outlook*, he published contributions by prominent Israeli Jewish and Arab thinkers, as well as people of international renown, representing a wide political spectrum. He envisioned a rapproachement of Arab and Jew. His book, *The Birth of Israel*, went to press as his final contribution to the discussion of this issue. He died in March 1987.[10]

Flapan describes the purpose of his book as an attempt to contribute to a better understanding of and more constructive approach to the Palestinian problem. As a peace activist as well as scholar he saw the practical necessity to "undermine the propaganda structures that have so long obstructed the growth of the peace forces in Israel.[11] In his book he examines and debunks seven myths about the creation of the state of Israel. Widely promulgated, particularly in American society, and effectively repeated, these myths seem to be held by many journalists, congresspeople, and intellectuals without question or scrutiny. Because one or another or a combination of these myths has formed the "justification" for many of the injustices against the Palestinians to this day, and because Flapan has drawn attention to the key aspects of disinformation, his summary presentations are most germane and worthy of mention.

MYTH ONE: Zionist acceptance of the United Nations Partition Resolution of November 29, 1947, was a far-reaching compromise by which the Jewish community abandoned the concept of a Jewish state in the whole of Palestine and recognized the right of the Palestinians to their own state. Israel accepted this sacrifice because it anticipated the implementation of the resolutions in peace and cooperation with the Palestinians.

Flapan points out that this was a tactical move by the Zionist leadership rather than an overall strategy. The strategy

aimed first at thwarting the creation of a Palestinian Arab state through a secret agreement with Abdullah of Transjordan, whose annexation of the territory allocated for a Palestinian state was to be the first step in his dream of a Greater Syria. Second, it sought to increase the territory assigned by the UN to the Jewish state.[12]

MYTH TWO: The Palestinian Arabs totally rejected partition and responded to the call of the mufti of Jerusalem to launch an all-out war on the Jewish state, forcing the Jews to depend on a military solution.

Flapan comments:

prior to Israel's Declaration of Independence on May 14, 1948, many Palestinian leaders and groups made efforts to reach a *modus vivendi*. It was only Ben-Gurion's profound opposition to the creation of a Palestinian state that undermined the Palestinian resistance to the mufti's call.[13]

MYTH THREE: The flight of the Palestinians from the country, both before and after the establishment of the state of Israel, came in response to a call by the Arab leadership to leave temporarily, in order to return with the victorious Arab armies. They fled despite the efforts of the Jewish leadership to persuade them to stay.

Flapan writes:

the flight was prompted by Israel's political and military leaders, who believed that Zionist colonization and statehood necessitated the "transfer" of Palestinian Arabs to Arab countries.[14]

MYTH FOUR: All of the Arab states, unified in their determination to destroy the newborn Jewish state, joined together on May 15, 1948 to invade Palestine and expel its Jewish inhabitants.

Flapan continues:

My research indicates that the Arab states aimed not at liquidating the new state, but rather at preventing the implementation of the agreement between the Jewish provisional government and Abdullah for his Greater Syria scheme.

MYTH FIVE: The Arab invasion of Palestine on May 15, in contravention of the UN Partition Resolution, made the 1948 war inevitable.

Flapan observes:

The documents show that war was not inevitable. The Arabs had agreed to a last-minute American proposal for a three-month truce on the condition that Israel temporarily postpone its Declaration of Independence. Israel's provisional government rejected the American proposal by a slim majority of 6 to 4.[15]

MYTH SIX: The tiny, newborn state of Israel faced the onslaught of the Arab armies as David faced Goliath: a numerically inferior, poorly armed people in danger of being overrun by a military giant.

Miriam Ward

Flapan's research disagrees:

> Ben-Gurion himself admits that the war of self-defense lasted only four weeks, until the truce of June 11, when huge quantities of arms reached the country. Israel's better-trained and more experienced armed forces then attained superiority in weapons on land, sea, and air.[16]

> MYTH SEVEN: Israel's hand has always been extended in peace, but since no Arab leaders have ever recognized Israel's right to exist, there has never been anyone to talk to.

Flapan concludes:

> On the contrary, from the end of World War II to 1952, Israel turned down successive proposals made by Arab states and by neutral mediators that might have brought about accommodation.[17]

While it is important for Israelis to face up to the realities surrounding the birth of their state, the same kind of objective evaluation of the Arab leadership of the time by an Arab writer is needed. For instance, what happened to Jews living in Arab countries subsequent to the establishment of Israel ought to be assessed as part of the larger problem. It is only when both sides come to grips with the truth that any kind of reconciliation is possible.

Flapan confined his research to the period of 1948–1952, and studies of how military law was applied to the Arabs of Israel during the subsequent years available in English for a Western readership are few. Although the Arabs remaining within the boundaries of the new state of Israel were granted citizenship, their freedom was curtailed by the continuation of the same military law that was so despised and vociferously denounced by Israeli Jews under the British. This continued until 1966. An entire generation of Palestinians in the occupied territories has come to maturity under a similar twenty-one-year military rule.[18]

To omit Professor Israel Shahak in naming Israeli writers coming to grips with the Palestinian problem would be to fail to mention one of the most consistent and fearless voices on behalf of Palestinians. A survivor of a Nazi concentration camp, Shahak has translated into English for distribution articles appearing in the Hebrew press. In addition, through his lecture tours he has given a glimpse of an Israeli perspective not often heard in the United States.

Shahak's most recent collection of articles, entitled *Report on the Human Rights Violations During the Palestinian Uprising, 1988–1989* covers the first eighteen months of the Palestinian *intifada*, which began December 8,

1987. The articles not only confirm the brutality of Israeli soldiers against defenseless Palestinians but give insights into what is happening to the moral fabric of Israeli society. This should give pause to those seriously concerned about the kind of society Israel is building for its children. For example, Israeli soldiers returning from duty in the West Bank and Gaza report on the way in which following orders to beat up little children and the elderly is brutalizing the soldiers themselves.[19]

From the revisionist history of Simha Flapan and other Israeli writers such as Benny Morris and Tom Segev to the current work of Israel Shahak, Israelis are beginning to address Palestinian suffering. In the theological context, which sees every human being created in the image of a loving God, and the subsequent need for truth apart from which there can be no justice in the affairs of humankind, I have given examples of courageous Israeli Jews who have fearlessly set the record straight vis-a-vis underlying historical assumptions in the Israeli-Palestinian conflict.[20]

The Question of Human Rights: From Theology to *Realpolitik*

To define human rights might at first glance seem trite. However, the fact of the matter is that not everyone agrees on the "who should enjoy them" because not everyone defines the "what" in the same terms. To substantiate this statement, we need simply to review the genesis and composition of the United Nations Universal Declaration of Human Rights.

Agreement on the formulation of the Declaration proclaimed on December 10, 1948 was fairly easy. But when it came to empowering the declaration by means of a covenant or treaty, the ensuing discourse broke down over the definition of rights. Representatives of poor nations stressed the right to eat and support a family, to a dignified existence, while those of well established nations thought in terms of the political and civil rights that are part of the Western system of justice. As a result, two separate covenants were drawn up, the first defining rights in terms of economic freedom and the other political freedom. The United States has never signed the former. As a result of this division, there is no mandate to implement the second Declaration, which the United States did sign, in terms of the economic freedoms implied in political freedom. Thus, the weakness lies not in the Declaration itself, but in those nations such as our own that fail to understand the realities of third world countries where political and civil rights are meaningful only in the context of economic justice.[21]

The selective use by the United States of the Declaration's definition of political rights is germane to a discussion of the Israeli-Palestinian conflict. For example, the US went to war to insure self-determination for Koreans while denying the same right to the Palestinians. The right to self-determination is clearly affirmed in the UN Declaration as well as a second right highly important and applicable in the Palestinian-Israeli conflict, i.e., the right of every person to leave or return to his/her own country. Even though some fifty countries, as of this writing, have recognized the Declaration of Independence made by the Palestine National Council (the parliament of the Palestine Liberation Organization), the United States insists on excepting the Palestinians from enjoying both these rights. Need I mention the hypocrisy in the selective application of a stated position on human rights? It bears repeating that the US is a signatory to the Declaration.

Where Do We Go from Here?

Where do we go from here? I have suggested that consideration of the Palestinian-Israeli conflict should begin with the theological context of God's creation of the world. The affirmation made by the three great monotheistic faiths asserts that God found the creation to be good, and that God continuously sustains it by a power defined by justice and truth. This faith also affirms that when God created the world God placed in the center of its stage a single pair of human beings, and that man and woman were made in God's image. Thereby God gave to this pair and their descendants both unity and dignity. Furthermore, God made clear that they were in a relationship to the Divine. Because they were created by God they would also be accountable and obedient. Metaphorically, this was expressed as relationship between a father and his children, and as the father acts with justice and mercy towards his children, so the children should reflect these qualities in their attitudes and actions towards each other.

This theology defines a social order, but is it sufficient to resolve the present conflict? When the first descendants of the single pair destroyed that unity when one brother killed another, it was clear that more was needed. The murderer became a fugitive from society, condemned by the blood of his victim crying from the ground for justice. Unity and dignity had been violated, and God's command that we all act as one another's keepers had been broken. This is where we turn to our varied religious traditions. The three monotheistic religions have always made a distinction between the ultimate basis on which we build our personal faith, and what others before us have said, done, and accepted as tradition. Without removing ourselves from our traditions or losing ideals and values of these traditions we find ourselves selecting from them enduring and relevant elements that enable us to live constructively and with positive good will for all people. Today these traditions can teach us how to realize the unity of the human race and the dignity of every individual.

While Rabbi Akiba stressed the command to love our neighbors as ourselves, it was Ben Azzai who associated this command with the broader theological principle of the creation, and thus clarified the Jewish understanding of "neighbor." By stating that the generations of the first pair's descendents were made in the likeness of God, he widened the scope of God's human family and explained that the members of this family came from all races of people. In the Christian tradition, Paul made explicit Jesus' teachings and actions that expressed the universality of God's love. Paul affirmed this by stating that Christ recreated the old fractured creation by breaking down the walls of hostility which divided Jew and Greek, slave and free, male and female. (Gal. 6:15; 3:28) Similarly, Islam has at times spread a message of unity and universalism, one based on the freedom and dignity of the individual, throughout diverse cultures of the world.[22]

While justice and truth cry out from the ground because they have been violated, we desperately need a theology that demands the recreation of wholeness and unity among God's vast human family. The way of vengeance that expresses a desire to eliminate either Palestinians or Israelis will not work, for the voices of the victims will still cry out and the victimizers will always be fugitives. God's demand that we love our neighbor keeps that love from trying to create a sentimental utopia, a wishy-washy idea of love. Rather it sets us in the direction of trying to bring about a unity of understanding and reconciliation. We have underestimated the power of love. If we really take God seriously, if we really want to be obedient to an almighty and at the same time beneficent God, then we must strive for reconciliation. We must strive for reform of our inner feelings and attitudes, and work for change.

The theological perspective that I have presented in broad outline is the root and source of inspiration for the United Nations Declaration of Human Rights. That the latter has acquired a moral and political force cannot be questioned. In the words of Pope John XXIII, "There is no doubt that the Document represents an important step on the path towards the juridical-political organization of the world community. For in it, the dignity of a human person is acknowledged in all human beings . . ."[23]

But theology transcends even this declaration, because theology has a much greater dynamic than any human rights platform, however noble the latter. It is love that transforms people and moves nations towards reconciliation. That this is possible has been amply demonstrated in the lives of Mohandas Gandhi, Badshah Khan, Dorothy Day, and Martin Luther King, in the past, and by Dom Helder Camara and the lesser-known Palestinians Elias Chacour, Mubarak Awad, and Kamil Shehadeh of today. These are the voices whose message of brotherhood and sisterhood of humankind, of love and reconciliation, must be heard. For theirs is a message that comes out of a conviction of faith and a theology shared by the three great monotheistic religions. Each affirms the equality and dignity of all human persons made in God's image.

10

The Occupation Must End

ROSEMARY RADFORD RUETHER

This volume is based on the premise that the Israeli occupation of the West Bank and the Gaza Strip must end, that this occupation is creating intolerable violations of the human rights of Palestinians and demoralizing the Israeli people as well. While disagreeing on many matters of fact and interpretation, the Jewish, Christian, and Palestinian contributors to this volume all, in one way or another, accept this judgment that the occupation cannot continue.

But what is not clear in most of these essays is just what is meant by this occupation. Why has it become so intolerable? What are its human costs? I wish to show in this essay that the basic patterns of brutality that have become visible in the treatment of the Palestinians in the occupied territories by the Israeli army are not new. This pattern of brutality has been a part of the occupation for twenty-one years. Indeed the *intifada* can only be understood as a collective response to this pattern to brutality that finally became too much to bear.

The response of the Israeli government and military has been to escalate and greatly intensify the same patterns of brutality that caused the uprising in the first place. The basic assumption behind this response is that enormously increasing Palestinian pain and suffering would cause them to "quiet down." It is generally agreed that this response has been counterproductive. Increasing Palestinian suffering has both prolonged the uprising and created an increasingly united resistance of all Palestinians across classes.[1]

Why has the Israeli government so miscalculated Palestinian response? To answer this question, it is necessary to be clear about the purposes of the occupation. The policies that the Israeli government has adopted toward the land and people of the occupied territories stand in the context of a forty-one year process of expulsion of Palestinians, land confiscation,

183

and Jewish settlement that has sought to reshape the demographic realities of the region which, until May of 1948, was called Palestine.

In 1947, when the United Nations partitioned this region, giving 57 percent of the land for a Jewish state and 43 percent for a Palestinian Arab state, there were some 1.4 million Palestinians dwelling in this area, compared to 600,000 Jews. The Palestinians lived in all parts of the region, including the coastal regions assigned to the Jewish state. In fact, there were slightly more Palestinians than Jews living in the area given for the Jewish state. These Palestinians owned 90 percent of the land, 50 percent of the citrus groves, and 95 percent of the olive groves in the region of the Jewish state.[2] For this reason the Palestinians rejected partition. They wanted a united Palestinian state in which Jews, particularly those resident before the Zionist immigrations, could be citizens.

The Zionists claim that they accepted the partition plan, but this is only half true. What they accepted was that part of the partition plan that gave them the legal basis for a Jewish state. They did not accept the territorial limits of that state, the residence in it of so many Palestinians, nor the existence of a Palestinian state alongside the Jewish state. They intended to change these facts by war.[3]

In the 1948–49 war the Zionists terrorized into leaving or forcibly expelled some 780,000 of the Palestinians. They expanded the borders of the Jewish state by 20 percent, leaving only a remnant of the land allotted to the Palestinians. They secretly negotiated with King Abdullah of Jordan, who wished to annex the West Bank, in order to assure themselves that whatever land of the Palestinian state remained would disappear into Jordan and would not remain as an independent political base for the Palestinians.[4] The consistent policy of all major Zionist leaders from Ben-Gurion to Shamir has been to negate the existence of the Palestinians as a national community with a right to a state and to severely interdict any and all expressions of Palestinian national identity: political, economic, social, or cultural.

After the 1948–49 expulsions, only a remnant of 180,000 Palestinians remained in the expanded Jewish state. All the land of those expelled, and much of the land of those who remained, was confiscated as the permanent patrimony of the Jewish people under the Jewish National Fund. The remaining Palestinians were given citizenship, but few of the privileges enjoyed by Jewish citizens. They were kept under military rule until 1965, unable even to travel outside their village without a special permit. Little of the economic development given the Jewish areas was extended to the Palestinian areas.[5] Still today they cannot serve in the army and so cannot share in the many privileges linked to army service. In a state that defines itself as a Jewish state, they are an anomaly, to be made as much as possible a silent, invisible, landless proletariat.

When Israel conquered the West Bank and Gaza in 1967, the same patterns of expulsion, military rule, land confiscation and Israeli settlement were applied to this region. Some 55 percent of the land in the West Bank and 30 percent of the land in crowded Gaza has been confiscated for Israeli use. The difference is that these regions, with the exception of the Golan Heights and a broad strip of land around Jerusalem, have not been annexed and their people have not been given even the token citizenship accorded the Palestinians within Israel.

The reason for this is that the Israelis fear that the large number of Palestinians in these regions, close to 1.5 million, plus the 780,000 Palestinians now in Israel, totaling altogether 2.28 million, would challenge the demographic control of the 3.5 million Israelis and force the redefinition of Israel. It would eventually become a binational state rather than a Jewish state. Hence the Israeli government adopted toward these Palestinians under occupation a policy of extreme repression of all aspects of their economic, social, and cultural life, together with creeping land confiscations, settlements, and appropriation of the water and infrastructures of the land.[6]

The purpose of this policy was to convince as many Palestinians as possible to leave voluntarily, thus reducing their numbers to the point where part or all of the region could be annexed without diluting the definition of Israel as a Jewish state. "Hawks" in Israel are those who believe in annexing all of the land, keeping Palestinians under permanent military control. Increasingly this group openly advocates mass expulsion along the lines that took place in 1948.

"Doves," by contrast, fear the presence of so many Palestinians in an expanded state and so advocate a new partition, taking over the regions settled by Israelis and carving out a new remnant of land to be given back to the King of Jordan (and perhaps Gaza could go to Egypt). It is assumed that these Palestinians "given back" to Jordan and Egypt will nevertheless still be available as low paid workers in Israel. The unwillingness of Egypt and now Jordan to cooperate with these "peace plans," however, has made these solutions untenable.[7]

Thus we must be clear that neither the "hawks" nor the "doves" of mainstream Israeli politics have included the possibility of a Palestinian state in their plans. The acceptance of a two-state solution has, until now, been advocated only by tiny left-wing Israeli parties such as the Progressive List for Peace.

Meanwhile the Palestinians, under the PLO, have gradually accommodated to the view that a two-state solution with a Palestinian state in the 1967 borders, together with recognition of Israel on the other side of these 1967 borders, is a necessary compromise. This position began to be suggested in meetings of the Palestine National Congress in 1973 and was openly proclaimed at the Algiers meeting of the PNC in November 1988. It was confirmed by Yasir Arafat's speech to the United Nations in Geneva in December of 1988. The *intifada* made the sufferings of the Palestinians under the occupation visible to the outside world, and thus disposed the Western nations, including the United States, to respond positively to these overtures from the PLO.

I have said that the brutal policies of the occupation are not a new policy, but the intensification of a continuous policy. The scale of the repression has also made the injustice much more visible to the outside world, but the veil of secrecy has only partly been lifted. Since the first months of the *intifada*, Israel has made strenuous attempts to deny access to the areas where clashes were taking place to reporters and journalists. The total and systematic pattern of the repression is still a largely untold story in the Western press.

If we are to evaluate the urgency of ending this occupation, it is essential to understand the full scope of its brutality. For the past two years I have been closely monitoring these developments through the information gathered by the Palestine Human Rights Information Center (PHRIC) in Jerusalem with its sister center in Chicago.[8] In December 1988 I spent several weeks on a fact-finding trip during which I was able to see many of the results of the repression in the form of closed universities; banned popular organizations; wounded young people in hospitals; refugee camps under continuous curfew; demolished houses; families with their sons dead, maimed, or expelled; and the like. We also interviewed a number of Israeli peace leaders.

Our group visited Al-Haq, the Human Rights legal research and advocacy center in Ramallah, where we obtained copies of their report, *Punishing a Nation; Human Rights Violations during the Palestinian Uprising, December 1987–December 1988.*[9] We were given a first hand precis of the study from those who had done the research for it. On the basis of the Al-Haq and PHRIC data and analysis, together with my own reading and observation,

I would like to make a summary of these human costs of the occupation. I do so prior to any theological or ethical reflection, since I believe that such theological and ethical reflection will be fallacious unless it is clear what it is we are reflecting upon. No theological or ethical reflections on the occupation can be valid until the reality of the occupation is made visible.

The most visible human costs of the uprising have been deaths by shooting. This has happened on a regular and continuous basis since the beginning of the uprising, despite international outcry. None of those shot has been armed with guns, and many of them have been children. Few, if any, of these shootings have taken place in what could genuinely be called a life-threatening situation for the Israeli soldiers. A number of people shot have been passers-by who were not even involved in demonstrations. Many of the people shot before being apprehended have been shot again and sometimes killed after they were already in the control of the military. There have also been some cases of death squads intentionally targeting persons seen as leaders.[10]

PHRIC, which has gathered the most complete data on killings in both the West Bank and Gaza (Al-Haq's research is limited to the West Bank), lists shooting deaths as of December 8, 1989 as 599, but also lists another 224 who have died from other causes, particularly beatings and tear gas inhalation. The Israeli military regularly kicks and clubs people whom they have arrested. This beating has been done systematically with the intention of inflicting permanent injuries. Kicking and clubbing often is done by a group of soldiers all taking turns assaulting a helpless, prone person. When this turns into frenzied gang beating it is most likely to result in deaths.[11] It is also common for soldiers to rampage through houses and shops, breaking furniture, pouring food on the floor, and slapping and insulting all those present.[12]

The third major cause of death is the inhalation of a type of cyanide tear gas that is lethal, particularly to the young, old, and those with respiratory problems, when set off in enclosed places. Contrary to the instructions on this tear gas (which has been supplied by the United States), it is regularly thrown in such enclosed places, such as shops, homes, and even hospitals. In addition to the eighty-two persons estimated to have died of tear gas inhalation, it has also caused numerous miscarriages, perhaps as many as several hundred.

But these deaths are only a part of the picture of the human costs of the occupation. The next major cost in human suffering is serious injuries.

Many of these injuries will result in lifelong maiming and impairment of health. In our visits to hospitals we saw a number of young people who had been shot or beaten in such a way as to be permanently paralysed. A doctor who is an eye specialist told us that he himself has removed thirty-five eyes injured by rubber bullets, half of them from young children.

There is no way to make an accurate count of the injured and of how many will suffer permanent damage. PHRIC estimates the injured at 80,000, but this is a very rough figure. When we visited Al-Ahli hospital in Gaza, a small private hospital with only eighty beds, the head resident said that their figures, just for their own hospital, were that they had treated 730 cases of gun shot wounds and 7,500 cases of beating. They also estimated 150–200 cases of miscarriages caused by tear gas or by beating. The head resident told us that pregnant women are tied with their hands behind their back and beaten on their backs and abdomens.[13]

We spoke to university and medical committee groups who are making plans for programs to train physiotherapists who can teach family members to help rehabilitate the injured. Since the universities have been officially closed by the Israeli government and popular medical committees banned, I shall not state the sources and location of these plans for physiotherapy programs. What such plans indicate, however, is that the Palestinians are attempting to prepare themselves for a situation in which many thousands of people will have long-term injuries.

The occupation has also seen a number of other kinds of violations of human rights. One of these is deportation, which has generally targeted those perceived to be community leaders. The use of deportation represents a return to policies that were common in the first years of the occupation, when hundreds of Palestinians were deported each year. From 1977–85 there were few deportations, but this form of punishment rose again in 1985 (forty-two between 1985 and 1987). In 1989 fifty-eight persons were deported, with fifty-six cases pending.[14]

There has also been a return to large scale house demolitions as a form of collective punishment. Some 1,225 houses have been demolished or sealed by administrative degree, and several hundreds of others demolished on the grounds that they lacked building permits. (The government makes it extremely difficult to obtain permits, and so many Palestinians build without permits. The decision whether or not to demolish such unlicensed houses then becomes a form of control.)[15] Various forms of resistance to Israeli control can result in house demolition.

The use of administrative detention has also greatly increased since the uprising began. Under administrative detention anyone can be arrested without charge or trial and kept in prison for up to six months, indefinitely renewable. Al-Haq estimated 3,000–4,000 people at present in administrative detention, most of them in the brutal prison, Ansar III, in the Negev, where they are kept in crowded tents without adequate protection from heat and cold, adequate food, or medical facilities. Those under administrative detention are typically journalists, educators, human rights workers, and other community leaders.[16] About 50,000 Palestinians were imprisoned during the two years of the uprising.

One of the major causes of disruption in the daily lives of Palestinians, especially in the refugee camps, has been the use of continuous and prolonged curfews. Many of the refugee camps have been sealed off, with walls built blocking most of the entrances and exits, allowing only one way out, which is controlled by the military. More recently the military has also built high observation towers so they can look down on the camps, thus spotting people crossing roofs or slipping down between the narrow allies separating the refugees' houses, delivering food or other supplies to families who have begun to run out.

Curfews have been imposed on a twenty-four hour basis, during which time no one is allowed to leave the house. Such total curfews have gone on for several days at a time. Curfews that allow an hour or two during which residents may leave their houses to shop have been prolonged in some areas for weeks at a time. Al-Haq estimated 1,600 curfews in one year, 400 of them prolonged.[17] But these figures are only for the West Bank. In Gaza the refugee camps are under almost continuous partial or total curfew.

Curfews bring all normal life to a halt. Breadwinners cannot go to work, and children cannot go to school. Medical help has often been prevented from entering areas under curfew, and the injured not allowed to leave to seek medical attention. In addition, telephones, electricity, and water have been cut off, garbage pick-up stopped, and farmers prevented from tilling and harvesting their fields. Thus, curfews represent a way of holding an entire community hostage, preventing them from meeting their ordinary human needs.

The use of prolonged curfews interconnects with a general repression of the social infrastructures of daily life. A variety of economic sanctions have been used to limit all sources of income. These include new taxes; bans on delivery of fuel, both for homes and vehicles, over periods of time; blocks on marketing local goods in Israel or Jordan; preventing olive harvesting and olive pressing (a chief source of income for most farmers);

severe restrictions on funds sent in from outside sources, either to families or to Palestinian institutions, such as universities, or blocking access to bank accounts outside Israel. In an effort to repress the tax revolt that has been a feature of the uprising, soldiers at check points were stopping Palestinians (identifiable by their license plates) and confiscating the cars of those who had not paid all their taxes.

A major assault on Palestinian cultural development has been the closure of schools, from primary schools through universities. The primary and secondary schools were not closed in Gaza, but here much the same effect was created through curfews. When we were there in December 1988, the primary schools had just begun to open after having been closed for most of the year. The secondary schools were due to open, although there were threats to close them again if there was any "trouble" from the school children, i.e., demonstrations. The universities, which had all been closed for a year (Bethlehem University for thirteen months), had been given no assurance that they would ever be allowed to open again.[18] In January, 1989 the schools in the West Bank were all closed again.

The chief reason given for this policy of school closure is that the gathering of children and youth in schools was a prime source of "unrest." But this argument is belied by the fact that alternative educational programs for small groups in homes, churches, and mosques also were banned by the military. Obviously leaving 300,000 school children and 18,000 college students in the West Bank without schooling for a year is far more likely to cause "unrest" than having them in school.

When the closure of schools and universities first took place, many educators made plans for alternative education. Popular education committees sprang up everywhere and developed programs that could be carried on in homes, churches, and mosques. Many educators saw this as an opportunity to create a much more participatory form of education, preferable to the traditional rote and authoritarian education still found in most schools. These programs were planned for fewer than ten students meeting at any one location, so there could be no question of the classes causing "demonstrations."

However, the military ruled that these alternative education programs were also banned. Teachers were forbidden even to prepare homework that could be picked up by parents to take to children at home. Although some of the alternative education has continued secretly, such banning of home classes throws into serious question the purpose of such school closure. What is its purpose, other than an expression of fundamental animosity toward the cultural development of the Palestinian people as a whole?

There has also been a general repression of Palestinian cultural, social, economic, charitable, and professional institutions, and a ban of all kinds of popular self-help committees. One of the first kinds of organizational activity banned was labor unions. Early in the uprising the labor union offices were closed and labor leaders either deported or imprisoned under administrative detention. Research, professional, and charitable institutions have also been closed for one to two years, their archives confiscated, and their buildings sealed.

The Arab Studies Society, which, among other areas of research, gathered information on destruction of villages over the past forty years, has been closed. Also closed is the largest women's charitable institution, Inash al-Usra (The Society for the Preservation of the Family) that ran a nursery school, an orphanage, women's embroidery and sewing collectives, and training programs for girls. Among the other institutions that have been closed are the General Federation of Trade Unions, The Society of Friends of the Sick, the Federation of Professional Organizations (which organizes doctors, dentists, engineers, lawyers, veterinarians, and pharmacists), and the Organization for the Care of Ecology and Society.[19]

The banning of popular committees in the summer of 1988 represents a new step in the effort to dismantle the development of Palestinian social infrastructures. A host of popular committees had sprung up to organize self-help employment and literacy classes for women; alternative education for youth; agricultural cooperatives, including home gardening; and medical services for those unable or afraid to go to hospitals. (It is common for ambulances to be impeded in their efforts to take the wounded to hospitals or for the wounded to be arrested in hospitals and taken to prison, so many injured people were afraid to go to hospitals.) The declaration that all such popular committees were illegal has not prevented them from carrying on their work, but it gives a blanket law by which their leaders can be arrested.

The general charge leveled at these institutions and groups is that they are fronts for the PLO. But since almost all Palestinians in the occupied territories define themselves as supporters of the PLO as their national representative, this is a charge that can be leveled at any form of Palestinian organizing. The basic purpose for these proscriptions seems to be to prevent Palestinians from developing the infrastructures of autonomous national life. This was openly said to the former President of Bethlehem

University. When he asked the military commander why the universities were closed, the commander replied, "You are trying to help these people do for themselves what we want to do for them."[20]

The soldiers put this more crudely. For example, when a group of teen-aged girls from Beach Camp in Gaza were attempting to leave for school, the soldiers chased them back into their homes, yelling, "You animals. Why do you want to go to school. You can't learn anything anyway." The tears running down the girls' faces as they ran into their homes were as much from the humiliation of these insults as from the tear gas the soldiers were shooting at them.[21]

It should be evident from the above account that this comprehensive and brutal effort to repress the uprising has totally failed. The effect has been to unleash a host of enterprising forms of survival activity and to draw all segments of Palestinian society together in solidarity across class lines, overcoming the individualism and the distinctions of wealth and privilege that formerly divided the elites from the poor, especially from those in the refugee camps.

The Palestinian community in the occupied territories has become united as never before. But the costs have been extreme. This entire community has been subjected to a reign of state terrorism. Community health and the welfare of almost all members of this community has been put at risk. It is the urgent responsibility of the world community to bring a rapid end to this situation of occupation, even before actual negotiations for a final settlement take place.

The world community through the United Nations must insist that the Israelis withdraw their troops from these regions and that they be replaced by a UN peace-keeping force. Since the kind of repression that the Palestinians are experiencing is integral to the occupation itself, it is not possible to alleviate these violations by legal reforms of occupation practices. The only way this violence can be ended is by the withdrawal of the occupation army itself.[22] How can this come about?

Since the United States provides four billion dollars a year in financial aid to Israel, it holds the key to forcing Israel to withdraw from the territories. In 1956, when Israel occupied the Sinai in alliance with Great Britain and France, Eisenhower refused to accept this *fait accompli*. He insisted that Israel withdraw from the territory occupied, and it did so. The United States could have done the same thing when Israel occupied the territories in 1967, but it did not do so. At any time up to the present, if the United States government had insisted that Israel withdraw and had been willing to use its economic aid power to back up this insistence, it could have made Israel withdraw.

Thus American citizens—Christians, Jews, and a growing body of Arab-Americans, both Christian and Muslim—hold a major responsibility for mobilizing the collective will that can force the American government to act decisively in this matter. It is evident that the Israeli government itself is virtually paralysed by its own internal contradictions on this and other issues of importance to its future. It is highly unlikely that the national will to withdraw can come solely from within the Israeli Jewish community itself. There must be a major input from the outside to force Israel to make this decision and perhaps give its leaders the excuse to do what they otherwise could not do on their own.

How can the American Christian community become effective in helping generate the national will to insist that Israel withdraw from the territories? The Christian churches in America have been particularly silent on this issue. They have not taken the role of moral leadership that they have taken in other areas of international injustice, such as Central America and South Africa. The reasons for this have been a combination of ignorance and misinformation about the actual situation, guilt for Christianity's evil history of abuse of the Jewish people, and an identification with Israel on grounds of a shared biblical and Western culture.

While the last two sentiments have merit, ignorance and misinformation have allowed these sentiments to be misused. It is vital that Western Christians become informed about the Palestinian reality. Western Christians need to find the way to think through, theologically and ethically, their relation to the Jewish people, and to that part of it that is the state of Israel, that does justice also to Palestinian human and political rights. We hope that the essays in this book will make some small contribution to this task of providing more information and better theology and ethical practice.

I wish to conclude this essay by discussing two major areas of theological and ethical reflection that seem to me vital to establishing a just practice toward both Israeli Jews and Palestinians. The first area, which has already been well treated by Sister Miriam Ward, is the theological basis for co-humanity. I will not attempt to speak here, as she does, from the basis of all three monotheistic faiths, but only from a Christian context. In what way are we as Christians mandated to love the other as much as ourselves? How are we called to a universal humanity that demands that we be as concerned about violence to Jews as about violence to Christians, and as concerned about violence to Palestinians as about violence to Jews?

193

The second question is related to the first, but will draw Western Christians into less familiar paths of thought. To what extent are distinct and separate national communities mandated by God? Do the Jews as God's "chosen" people have a unique right to be, not only a separate religious community, but also a distinct political community or Jewish state? Or, as South African apartheid theology has argued, are all national (racial-ethnic) groups expressions of God's "orders of creation" and called to live in distinct and separate political communities from each other?[23]

The root of both Christian abuse of the Jewish people (and other groups), and Jewish abuse of Palestinians is the failure of an active ethic of co-humanity. Despite the teachings of all our traditions that we are all God's children, that we are all in God's image, we have in fact acted as if other groups of people were not really human beings with the same feelings, rights, and needs as ourselves.

Particularly in situations where one group assumed power and the other group was stripped of the rights of self-protection, the practices of abusive power have been justified by a cultural ideology that said that these other people were not really human in the same way as we were. They were animals to be worked but denied cultural development, or insects to be exterminated as threatening "pollutants" to our own health and well-being.

Western Christians are familiar with this kind of rhetoric directed against Jews by Nazis. It is startling to see both the rhetoric and the practice of abuse directed against Palestinians by Jews. The name of this kind of abusive ideology and use of power is racism (a term that applies to any inferiorization of one group by another, regardless of whether the two groups belong, from a scientific, anthropological point of view, to distinct "races"). Western Christians, guilty about their own racism toward Jews, have not been able to name the reality of Israeli practices and attitudes toward Palestinians as racism.

When the United Nations, backed by a third world majority, voted in 1975 to condemn Zionism as racism, there was a general outcry from Western Christians and refusal even to consider the possibility that this charge might have some truth.[24] I believe that this UN declaration erred, not in an accurate perception that Israeli practices toward Palestinians are racist, but that it chose to make this judgment as a generic condemnation of Zionism.

Zionism as a movement has many branches, some of which undoubtedly carry attitudes of Jewish and Western superiority to Arabs. Other Zionists are strongly committed to reject such attitudes. Thus to speak of Zionism as racism prevents the discussion from being focused on its real object, namely, the actual legal, social, and cultural policies and attitudes that have developed in the state of Israel, in the project of building a Jewish state and displacing what had formerly been the Palestinian majority in the region. It is this that needs to be named as racist, not as a dogmatic, ideological statement, but rather as a documentable study of actual cultural attitudes and political practices.

It is easy to find examples of abusive anti-Semitic rhetoric from Arab nations, although it is much more difficult to find such statements from Palestinians, who are generally careful to distinguish their critique of Zionism, as an actual policy directed at displacing them and denying their political and human rights, from Jews and Judaism. It is very important, therefore, not to lump Palestinians together with any rhetoric that might be gleaned from other Arab spokespeople.

Most importantly, it is not helpful to talk about this intercommunal antagonism on an ahistorical, archetypal plane, as critics of anti-Semitism have tended to do in the West. In the Israeli-Palestinian conflict, we are talking about a particular abusive power relation. Racist hostility to Palestinians among Israeli Jews has arisen to justify that abusive power relation. Palestinians, and more often, the larger Arab world, have responded by a counter-rhetoric of hatred that expresses its outrage as these actual, historical actions.

Therefore, change in the attitudes of hostility must focus on changing the abusive power relation of Israelis toward Palestinians, while assuring Israelis that their own security will not only not be jeopardized, but in fact promoted by these changes. Where lies the hope that such a transformation from fear and hatred to fellow-feeling and compassion is possible between these two communities?

I believe that there is a great deal of hope that this change is possible from the Palestinian side. One of the astonishing experiences for any Western Christian in talking to any number of Palestinians, from the most educated to grassroots people, is the extent to which they attempt to understand the fear and violence that characterize Israeli Jews. They try to enter somewhat sympathetically into the trauma of genocide that Jews experienced in Europe, the effects of which Palestinians see as being falsely projected upon them, in the entirely different context of the Middle East. It is very common for Palestinians in the occupied territories to say things such as "although we are suffering terribly physically, we think the Israelis are really in worse shape psychologically than we are. They are going to have to deal with their guilt for what they are doing to us for generations to come."[25] One clergyman told some Israeli Knesset members that when the *intifada* was over, "You will have to build another Yad Vashem (monument to the Holocaust) for us."[26]

Obviously Palestinians are not prepared to be "reconciled" to Israelis until the abusive power relation is changed. But once this power is withdrawn, and Israelis accept what Palestinians see as their generous willingness to share their land with Israeli Jews in a two-state solution, then there is no doubt that there are many Palestinians who are willing to work to build community with Jews across these divisions.[27]

The question is much less obvious from the Israeli Jewish side. As a people only recently empowered after a history of victimization, Israeli Jews have a great need to justify the endless consolidation of this power and to believe that Palestinians really "hate" them and want to annihilate them. This belief serves as an excuse for rejecting the possibility of compromise and coexistence. There are, however, an important group of Israelis who have broken through these ideologies and entered into solidarity with Palestinians. These progressive Israelis see themselves as serving the authentic self-interest of Israel as much as the human rights of the Palestinians by such a compromise. It is evident to them that the settlers and maximalists of Greater Israel are, in fact, embarked on a suicidal course. Only by a just compromise with the Palestinians can there be long-term security for Israel.[28]

This brings us to what is perhaps the most crucial question for both Zionism and its Jewish and Christian supporters: to what extent is a separate "Jewish state" desirable, in either theological or pragmatic terms? Is not this idea of a Jewish state the crux of the problem? Can Western Christians really claim, either that all ethnic groups should have distinct nationstates on universal grounds, or that, by some special mandate from heaven, Jews should be granted an ethnic state—although such a state would be unacceptable, let's say, for Anglo-Saxon Protestants in America?

I believe that the Zionist concept of a Jewish state is a remnant of a racist concept of nationalism that arose in Europe in the nineteenth century and has caused havoc around the world wherever it has been exported and taken over by anti-colonialist movements. Palestinians are willing to accept a Palestinian state alongside Israel as a Jewish state only as a compromise that will extract them from the intolerable situation of abuse under which they presently suffer. But it does not reflect their ultimate ideal. Their ultimate ideal remains a united land where Jews, Christians, and Moslems could live together.

This goal does not mean they want to destroy "Israel," in the sense of destroying Jews as human beings or as a collective community. In fact many have come to accept the idea that Jews need a Jewish state for the time being because they have been traumatized by the Holocaust and so cannot trust living in a situation where they do not have the clear monopoly on power. But an exclusivist nationalism, particularly drawn on lines of religious ethnicity, is unappealing to most Palestinians who have generally sought to overcome religious ethnicity and create a common community between Christians and Muslims.

Thus, their future hope is that both Israel and Palestine as separate states, and eventually Israel and Palestine together, can grow beyond ethnic-religious nationalism toward an umbrella identity that can encompass the stories, histories, and cultures of Jews, Christians, and Muslims. I think that this is also the goal to which Christian faith should dispose us. This does not mean that the particularities of national culture and religion are not respected and given their place in shaping identities, loyalties, and even political communities.

But, in relation to the God who loves all peoples and bids us to live together on one earth, these particularities must be seen as penultimate, not as ultimate. They belong to our historical particularities, not to the divine will and purpose. By accepting and affirming our particularities, we are also called to transcend them in mutual affirmation. Such mutual affirmation of our multi-particularities must also be a basis for co-existence in our diversity within political communities and, finally, within this one earth that we all must share as our common "promised land."

PART 3

Palestinian Perspectives

The five authors in this section of the book are among the leading intelligentsia of the American-Palestinian community. Four of them, Ibrahim Abu-Lughod, Muhammad Hallaj, Walid Khalidi, and Ghada Talhami are of Muslim background. Edward Said comes from a Christian Palestinian family, yet he has written more about Islam than about Christianity: a major theme of his writing is the distorted images of Islam and of Arabs in Western literature and media. His book, *Covering Islam: How the Media and the Experts Determine How We See the Rest of the World* (1981) is an example of such writing.

None of these five authors discusses the *intifada* or Israel from a theological or religious perspective, although Walid Khalidi makes the most extensive mention of Islam. He does so primarily as a worrisome problem of growing Muslim fundamentalism, evoked by Jewish Israeli fundamentalism, and not as a positive resource for justice and peace. These five Palestinian-Americans write as ethical humanists trained in social sciences. They were invited to be the dialogue partners for this volume because, in the judgment of its editors, they were the sort of Palestinian-Americans who are the most appropriate counterparts for liberal and liberation-oriented American Jews and Western Christians.

Why not choose Palestinian-Christian and Muslim clergy and theologians? To understand why we did not do so, but instead sought out these five Palestinians who write from a highly ethical and justice-oriented world view, but not from an explicitly religious one, we must be clear about the role that religion plays in the Middle East and how this role shapes a major view-point of Palestinian intellectuals toward religion.

From the Palestinian perspective, religion is a highly problematic point of departure from any discussion of a just resolution of the Israeli-Palestinian conflict because religion operates there primarily as a source of irresolvable conflicts and mystifications. Evocation of the name of God or Allah (the Arabic word for God) generally has negative consequences, for God functions in the Middle East (and not only there) primarily as a tribal deity, One who chooses one religious community in a way that negates the others.

Religion and state are still fused in much of the Middle East in a way that Western Christians and Jews have somewhat forgotten. Both Zionism and Muslim nationalisms or Pan-Islamism are ideologies that seek to be incarnated in confessional states in which religious minorities are second class citizens at best. Secularism and the Enlightenment, which separated church and state in the West in the eighteenth and nineteenth centuries, allowed people from different religious communities to stand on an equal footing with each other as citizens.

Such a legal and cultural development has happened much less in the Middle East. When Muhammad Hallaj says that, as a Palestinian, Zionism appears to him as something anachronistic, as a kind of "medieval" phenomenon, what he has in the back of his mind is a Jewish counterpart to Islamdom, the medieval Islamic system where the *Sharia*, or Koranically derived law, defined the entire social and political order.

Such a medieval world view has been the enemy of Arab secular nationalists, but it is a medieval world that still encroaches very much on the present time. Both fundamentalist religious Zionists and Muslim fundamentalists seek to reinstate those classic religio-political patterns of their traditions again today. The Palestinian intellectual writes as a secularist because secularism is the only way forward to a new social order no longer governed by religious confessional states.

The American Jews and Western Christians in this volume write as people for whom separation of church and state was essentially accomplished two hundred years ago and is taken for granted as the basis of a just social order. Remnants of WASP (White Anglo-Saxon Protestant) privilege, of course, did not entirely disappear with the US Constitution and Bill of Rights. It continued to oppress American Catholics and Jews into the mid-twentieth century. But today the understanding that Catholics, Protestants, and Jews are equal citizens under the American law is so well-established as to be indisputable, although the United States is not without its Christian fundamentalists who call for a renewed "Christian" America.

In the 1950s and 1960s there also emerged in North America a sort of interfaith civil religion that became typical of public life. Catholics, Protestants, and Jews could all appear on the same platform and offer prayers from the same podium or pulpit on the assumption that they were indeed all praying to the same God, the God who united us all in the one American covenant.

No such interfaith political covenants exist either in Israel or in the Islamic world. The God who elected the Jews and promised them the land is the God who did not elect the Palestinians, the God who disenfranchises them, in whose Name the Palestinians are labeled as representatives of the *sitra achra* (the realm of Satan), to be purged out of the land so that God's favored people can occupy it.

The Islamic God also has no place for Jews or for Christians as equal members of the political community. As Westerners, they belong to *dar al-Harb*, the sphere of Holy War in which the true believer must struggle. Arab Jews and Christians, who have long been a part of the Islamic world, are acceptable precisely because they do not seek to dominate or to define the political community in their own terms. Traditionally they were seen as occupying the status of *dhimmi* or protected groups, which had accepted Islamic overlordship and paid a special tax indicating their submission. While such a subordinate status was less oppressive and subject to persecution, for the most part, than the status accorded Jews in Western Christendom, it is hardly a modern ideal of political equality.

In the 1930s and early 1940s, when the Palestinian nationalist movement, led by Muslims, was demanding the granting of a Palestinian Arab state from the British Mandate authorities, this *dhimmi* status was their model for inclusion of Palestinian Jews, including some who had immigrated under the Zionist project, into citizenship in such a state. Ibrahim Abu-Lughod describes this earlier "Muslim version" of Palestinian nationalism in his history of evolving Palestinian options for a state inclusive of both Jews and Palestinians.

Palestinian political ethics have developed radically from that classic Muslim perspective. They have done so by rejecting religious politics and the ideal of the *Sharia* state. In the process many Palestinian nationalists prefer not to discuss religion at all. One quietly seeks to ignore the God of tribal politics because such a God can only be an impediment to a just socio-political order that will allow people of many religions to live together as equal citizens under the same laws of one secular nationality.

For Palestinians, a state where religious differences do not divide and subordinate some groups to others under the law, where there is a national identity that embraces all the people who live in that state, regardless of religion, is still only a "dream," as Muhammad Hallaj so poignantly describes it in his essay. This Palestinian dream remains unattainable in their historical homeland precisely because of Zionism, or the Jewish ethnic and confessional definition of nationalism.

What is extraordinary is that this principle of a secular nationalism, embracing religious pluralism, that American Christians and Jews take for granted for the United States, they refuse even to discuss for the state of Israel. American Jews, who have been leaders of secular pluralism in America, demand an acquiescence, increasingly in explicitly religious terms, to a Jewish state, defined in religious ethnic terms. American Christians, who take for granted a secular, pluralistic nationalism for the United States, generally see no contradiction in accepting an ethnic confessional concept of a Jewish state as appropriate for Israel.

The Palestinian "dream" or ideal solution, beginning in the 1960s with the reemergence of Palestinian nationalism, has been the "secular democratic state for Jews, Christians, and Muslims," basically the same political ideal espoused by American Jews and Christians for the United States, where they recite together their faith in *e pluribus unum*, a secular democratic state where people of all religions can be members of the one national covenant. Why is it that the established norm of political ethics for Americans is undiscussable for Israelis and Palestinians? The different ways in which religion has come to be related to the political order in these two contexts is a key part of the answer to this question.

Palestinian nationalists eschew God-talk precisely for the sake of political ethics. This we believe is key to understanding the silence toward religion in these five authors. And yet ethical values, which are the heritage of Christianity and Islam, shape their values, just as they shaped the values of the Enlightenment intelligentsia in the West who made possible the secular democratic solution to religious differences there.

For example, some readers may be surprised by the essay by Ghada Talhami, which focuses on the role of international law in proving the just cause of the Palestinians. What, Americans are likely to think, does a discussion of international law have to do with theological and ethical dialogue? But Law is the key religious category for Islam, as it is for orthodox Judaism. For Muslims, the *Sharia*, or Koranic Law, traditionally was presented as the key to a just social order.

But a religious law, defined on lines of ethnic communalism, fails to fulfill that promise of justice in modern pluralist societies. So international law, particularly those codes which define common standards of civil and human rights to be accepted by all nations, becomes a kind of "secular *Sharia*," the heir to that quest for a legal system that can define and estab-

lish justice. Ghada Talhami wishes to show that, by the standards of international law, the agreed upon standards for justice within and between nations, accepted by all signatories to the United Nations, the Palestinian
cause must be judged as just.

As international law becomes the modern substitute for the Koranic
Sharia, so also the Arab ethical humanist represents the best of the demands of truth, justice, and righteousness of the biblical and Koranic heri-
tages. But, like Locke and Hume in England, Montesquieu and Voltaire in
France, and Franklin and Jefferson in America, the Palestinian humanist
nationalist knows that sectarian religious divisions have to be put aside if a
new, more just social order is to be built, in which people of all faiths can
be equal members of the same political covenant.

Only when that possibility is accepted as a common basis for Jewish
Israeli, Muslim, and Christian Palestinian political life together, as citizens
of one state, might it then also become possible to imagine and discuss the
nature of God as a unifying basis of such a covenant. Such a God would
unify people across, rather than divide peoples along, religious lines. Such
a God would promote just sharing of the land, rather than favoritism of
one people against the others. Such a God does not yet exist (culturally
speaking) as a shared presupposition of these communities. Thus dialogue
between Jews, Christians, and Palestinians must begin as a dialogue about
historical truth and about humanistic justice, and not yet as a dialogue
about the God of such truth and justice.

11

Toward Peace in the Holy Land

WALID KHALIDI

1

The uprising that began in December 1987 in the territories Israel has occupied for over twenty years ranks as the fourth major attempt by the indigenous inhabitants of Palestine to stem the Zionist colonization of the country. First was the rebellion of 1936–39 against Britain's policy, exercised under its League of Nations mandate, for a Jewish National Home; then came the resistance to the 1947 UN General Assembly resolution to partition Palestine, which developed into a civil war before the regular war that broke out when the British left on May 15, 1948. Third, from 1964–65 onward, came the rise among the Palestinian diaspora of the Palestine Liberation Organization (PLO) and guerrilla movements against the status quo.

Today, in contrast to the three earlier instances, the Palestinians on the West Bank of the Jordan River and in the Gaza Strip are face-to-face with their perceived dispossessors, with no third party or geographic distance intervening. While the Israelis wield all state powers, the chief weapons of the Palestinians are the stones of the countryside. If the areas of Israel proper and those in the occupied territories already colonized, requisitioned, or annexed are subtracted from the total area of historic Palestine, the Palestinians in the occupied territories today stand on no more than 15 percent of the soil of the country.

In a statement read out at a Jerusalem hotel on January 14, 1988, which might be called the Jerusalem Program, leading representatives of the uprising outlined their aspirations and demands for lifting the oppression of the occupation and achieving "real peace" between Israel and the Palestinian people.

A certain Masada-like poignancy attaches to this latest manifestation of the Palestinian collective will, and with it a legitimate claim to the attention and concern of the outside world.

2

The Palestinian national identity had already begun to take shape at the beginning of World War I. It crystallized during the British Mandate (1918–48) in the resistance to Zionism. The notion that the Palestinians were a people and merited a national state of their own was evident to those members of the United Nations, including the United States, that voted in 1947 for the partition of Palestine. Since the beginning of the Palestinian diaspora in 1948 the sense of Palestinian nationality has been vastly strengthened; the rise of the PLO only gave expression to an existing reality.

For four decades since the establishment of Israel, the Palestinians have been pushed and pulled together by a multitude of shared experiences that have created a sense of national community rare in the Middle East and the third world: it has transcended geographic dispersion, village, clan, and sectarian loyalties, as well as the pressures of Arab host governments and Israeli occupiers. Endowed with skills surpassing those of most Arab peoples, the Palestinians long ago crossed the threshold of nationhood, and, like so many other peoples in history, are irreconcilable to living in a limbo of permanent statelessness. It is this, rather than any brilliance in the leadership of Yasir Arafat, which has frustrated all attempts to foist an illegitimate leadership upon the Palestinians or fob them off with substitutes for a sovereign place under the sun. It is this which constitutes the umbilical cord between the Palestinians of the occupied territories and the diaspora.

The Palestinians have more than tripled in number, from 1.3 million in 1948 to 4.5 million in 1988, and their rate of increase is not declining. In the Gaza Strip alone they number some 600,000 and are destined there to reach 900,000 by the end of the century. All the psychological and physical pressures bearing down on them the last twenty years to leave the occupied territories have failed. The Palestinians under occupation have drawn the obvious lesson from the fate of their compatriots who left in 1948 and 1967. Even for those who want to leave, the absorptive capacity for Palestinians in the Arab countries has been strained to the limit: Lebanon and Syria no longer qualify as havens for Palestinians; Jordan's King Hussein is already obsessed with the nightmare of a massive Palestinian influx into his country. Egypt hardly has standing room for its own people, and opportunities in the countries of the Persian Gulf have been circumscribed.

Some Israeli leaders contemplate a policy of thinning out or expelling the Palestinians. But to where? Northward into the Shi'ite heartland of Lebanon or across the Golan Heights toward Damascus? Southward into Sinai? Eastward across the Jordan River? Even hard-liners in Israel might balk at the first two suggestions, and the third is also problematic. It was one thing to drive out a civilian population amid the confusion of large-scale military operations, as happened in 1948; it would be another to do so in an environment where no fighting by regular armies was taking place. It was one thing to drive refugees across the river from their camps in the Jordan Valley in the wake of the retreating Jordanian army, as happened in 1967; it would be another to uproot the inhabitants of the towns and villages of the highlands. Even before the recent events in the occupied territories, Palestinian conduct in Lebanon in the face of siege and bombardment showed that Palestinian civilians do not panic as readily as they did in 1948.

The extraordinary courage displayed in the occupied territories since December 1987, especially by Palestinian youth, is but one indicator of the resistance an Israeli policy of mass expulsion would face. It is therefore reasonable to assume that the bulk of the Palestinians in the occupied territories will remain *in situ*, and that they will increase in number, even as the acreage at their disposal continues to dwindle with Israeli foreclosures, and their political frustrations mount in the absence of a general settlement. Given the resonance between the Palestinians inside and outside the occupied territories, continued denial of Palestinian nationhood is unlikely to lead to the diminution of its intensity or the moderation of its expression. It would therefore seem that, just as Israel is a reality that the Palestinians and the PLO must accept, Palestinian nationhood is a reality that Israel must accept. As Israel is here to stay, the Palestinians are here to stay, too.

3

Over the years the Palestine problem has generated concentric circles of expanding conflict. From the early 1880s to 1948 the conflict was preponderantly between the Jewish community of Palestine and the indigenous Arab Palestinians. From 1948 to 1967 the conflict was preponderantly between Israel and the neighboring Arab countries. In the period since 1967 the struggle has grown to new dimensions despite the Egyptian-Israeli peace treaty signed in 1978. Even a cursory look at this last period would reveal the adverse—and often bizarre—effects of the persistence of this conflict on regional stability, Western interests, and superpower relations.

The rise of Middle Eastern radicalism, for example, is not altogether unconnected with the continued non-resolution of the Palestine problem. Libyan leader Colonel Muammar al-Qaddafi, like most of his Arab contemporaries, was suffused in his youth with anger at the perceived injustices suffered by the Palestinians. The rise of the radical PLO in the mid-1960s was as much a revolt against moderate Arab regimes and their Western sponsors as against Israel. The PLO strategy of seeking bases in the Arab countries for operations against Israel led to the destabilization of Jordan in 1970–71 and contributed to the disintegration of Lebanon. It took the PLO's operations from Lebanon against Israel and Israel's scorched-earth strategy against southern Lebanon (which was designed to pit its Shi'ite inhabitants against the PLO) to make a new breed of Shi'ite militants receptive to Ayatollah Khomeini's message and install Iranian-style fundamentalism on Israel's northern borders. The oil embargo of 1973, with all its consequences, was motivated by the Arab perception of American support for Israel during the Middle East war of that year.

The Israeli hope of dealing a death blow to Palestinian nationalism by the military destruction of the PLO led to the 1982 invasion of Lebanon; for the first time, Israel laid siege to and occupied an Arab capital. The perceived opportunity afforded by the departure of the PLO from Beirut induced the United States (with not a little encouragement from Israel) to assume the anachronistic task of reconstructing Lebanon around the Maronite Christian minority, in colossal disregard of the other Lebanese sects and the heritage of the ancient city of Damascus next door. The result was the tragic loss of American and other lives and the first military skirmish in history between America and Syria, in which two American planes were shot down and an American pilot was taken prisoner.

The bizarre chain of events only grew longer. Lebanon's central institutions broke down totally, creating an ideal environment for anarchy and the unfettered pursuit of vengeance through the taking of American and other Western hostages. Eventually the trail led to White House preoccupation with the release of hostages and to the scandal of the Iran-contra operation.

Israel's need for the mass immigration of Jews to offset Palestinian demographic growth supplies part of the motivation for focusing international attention on the plight of Soviet Jewry. This issue impinges on US–Soviet relations and figured prominently during General Secretary Mikhail Gorbachev's December 1987 visit to Washington. The powerful opposition of the American Jewish establishment toward US arms sales even to moderate Arab countries affects the credibility of the United States with these Arab regimes, as well as the viability of their pro-Western orientation; it drives some of them to seek alternative sources of supply in Moscow, further weakening Western influence.

With competitive support from the two superpowers the arsenals of Israel and some Arab radical countries have grown exponentially. A nuclear alert was declared by the United States in 1973, in response to a threatened Soviet intervention at a time of heightened Arab-Israeli tension. Meanwhile, we have growing reminders that Israel has crossed the atomic, if not the thermonuclear, threshold, while evidence of biological warfare capabilities in the region also mounts.

The likely harvest of human and material devastation in a future Arab-Israeli war is a cogent argument for the need to defuse the Palestinian problem from which the conflict between Israel and the Arab states derives. This need is all the more compelling because of the increasingly religious aspect that the struggle for Palestine is assuming.

Religious undertones have always been present in the Palestine conflict. To be sure, Herzlian Zionism has remained explicitly secular in orientation despite the implicit premise of divine right in Zionist polemics. Palestinian opposition was primarily motivated by the political objectives of Zionism, even though some religious fears were voiced among Palestinians concerning the Muslim sanctuaries of Jerusalem and Hebron. Even after the creation of Israel and the expansion of the conflict to include the Arab states, Arab reaction did not assume a Muslim coloring per se—and this despite the historical analogy uppermost in the Arab mind, of Israel as the reborn Crusader kingdom of medieval times.

The reason for the secular thrust of Arab reaction was the vigor of pan-Arab ideology as preached in the 1950s and the 1960s by the Baath Party from Damascus and Baghdad and the Arab National Movement from Beirut, and the adoption of this ideology by Gamal Abdel Nasser until his death in 1970. Pan-Arabism posited the existence of one multi-state Arab nation to which the peoples of the individual Arab states belong. The components of the nation are a common language and history, and shared sentiments and interests.

As opposed to pan-Arabism, pan-Islamism stresses the unity through faith of all Muslims, whether Arab or not. Religious fundamentalism has been precipitated in the Arab world in the last two to three decades by a number of developments and factors, not least being the growth of Jewish fundamentalism in Israel and the occupied territories. There is also the continuing grinding poverty of tens of millions, despite the oil wealth; there is the profligacy of the lifestyles of the rich and powerful, coupled, especially in Egypt, with claustrophobic demographic pressures. A newly educated and relentlessly growing army of university graduates has emerged with few economic opportunities and little knowledge of the West. Some Arab rulers are perceived as subservient to the United States, particularly in matters pertaining to Israel. And Israel is perceived as enjoying an intolerable freedom of action throughout the Arab world, as when, for example, it launched air raids on Baghdad and Tunis in 1981 and 1985, respectively.

Ultimately, secular pan-Arabism failed to achieve a convincing semblance of unity, and the *raison d'état* of individual Arab states conflicted to the point of causing internecine disputes; these Arab countries seemed powerless in the face of continued Israeli occupation of Palestinian, Syrian, and Lebanese territory.

These are the circumstances in which the appeal of Ayatollah Khomeini resounds. His appeal is not restricted to Shiʿites, but extends to the Sunni masses and intellectuals, inasmuch as his rallying cry is not Shiʿism but Islam, and the targets of his attacks include both the great powers and the Arab dynasts. His constant reference to the liberation of Jerusalem is as effective as it is deliberate.

Religious fundamentalism is both a reactive and assertive phenomenon in the face of challenge and failure. It is partly a search for a bulwark against engulfment by alien values, partly a protest against tyranny whether foreign or indigenous, and partly a revolt against underdog status and frustrated expectations. The context in which religious fundamentalism has taken hold in the Arab world is wider than the Arab-Israeli conflict, but that the conflict exacerbates the pace and intensity of fundamentalism's evolution is undeniable.

Palestinians both inside and outside the occupied territories have been affected by this change in the political climate. The competition between Muslim fundamentalist groups and PLO sympathizers under occupation (which, ironically, was encouraged by Israeli intelligence authorities) has been replaced by growing solidarity and operational coordination between the two groups.

This is in part an index of the general shift in the Middle Eastern political mood away from secularism, but it is also a response to the paramount necessity of closing ranks in the face of escalating Israeli pressures. It is not too difficult to understand why, at times of great adversity or challenge, believers might seek a *deus ex machina* in Allah. The immediate and omnipresent stimulus for such a trend in the occupied territories lies in the biblical pronouncements, posturings, and conduct of the Gush Emunim— the spearhead and the hated symbol of Jewish fundamentalist willfulness, particularly in the ancient quarters adjoining the Muslim sanctuaries of Jerusalem and Hebron. It is perhaps no exaggeration to say that the Palestine problem and the Arab-Israeli conflict may have already crossed the threshold of their metamorphosis into a twenty-first-century version of the Crusades.

4

Within living memory, the United States was looked upon by Arab public opinion as the most friendly and trustworthy Western power. Unlike Britain or France, which took control of much of the region after World War I, the United States was unencumbered by any legacy of imperialism or conflict with any Arab people. But with the assumption by the United States of its new global responsibilities at the end of World War II, this idyllic state of affairs was unlikely to persist, and it did not. Nevertheless the depth of alienation from the United States of contemporary Arab public opinion (among both the masses and the intellectuals), even in moderate states with friendly official relations with Washington, has elicited little concern in the West. This alienation is a grave harbinger of things to come.

What strikes one most about this state of affairs is its sheer gratuitousness: two of the principal objectives of the United States in the Middle East—access to Arab oil and the prevention of Soviet domination of the area—do not necessarily militate against cordial Arab-American relations.

No Arab state wants to see the area dominated by either the United States or the Soviet Union; geographic proximity to Russia argues the prudence of cultivating the friendship of the more distant superpower. Pan-Arab parties have been locked in often mortal combat with the local communist parties, and even in radical Arab countries these parties live at the state's sufferance. The Soviet penetration that has occurred in the Middle East cannot be dissociated from the failure to resolve the Arab-Israeli conflict and the Arab need to balance American support of Israel with support from the Soviet Union. Similarly, with oil, the Arabs need American and Western markets no less than the West needs Arab oil. The most disruptive political impingement so far on the supply of oil to the West has been a result of American policy toward Israel.

For four decades now the Arab world has pondered the nature and motivation of this policy. Probably no other topic has been discussed at greater
length in Arab political literature or debate. Three principal hypotheses
have emerged: (1) US policy in the Arab-Israeli conflict is the reflection of
unchangeable American cultural and religious values; (2) the American
pluralistic political system gives leeway to competing groups, including
the powerful pro-Israel lobby; (3) as a capitalist, imperialistic system the
United States is intrinsically inimical to the interests of the Arabs.

The Arab circles most concerned for the future of Arab-American relations have clung to the second hypothesis; we have come under harsh
attack for the naïveté of our implicit faith in the possibility of a change
for the better in American policy. We have long argued the need to distinguish between harsh-sounding election promises and the policies subsequently pursued, and have stressed the learning potential of political
incumbents and the existence of an institutional memory and regional ex-
pertise in the State Department and other American agencies which tend
to balance domestic political calculation. The experience of the Reagan
Administration—even in a second term when reelection was not a factor—systematically knocked down each of our arguments. To be sure, the
Administration's Middle East diplomatic initiative of September 1982 gave
momentary demonstration of the goodwill of the United States, but unfortunately this effort soon petered out.

The effect of all this on the consciousness of Arab intellectuals has been
a direct identification of the United States with Israel: when Israel confis-
cates, colonizes, or invades, it is the United States that is seen to be behind these actions. Not only does this threaten to eliminate the United
States as a disinterested third party that can mediate, referee, and act as a
court of appeal, but for Arabs it casts the United States in the same mold
as the enemy. The pervasiveness of these perceptions is not annulled by
the comfort taken by some Arab rulers in the presence of American war-
ships on the horizon or AWACS aircraft overhead.

A deep emotional alienation from the United States is developing in the
Arab world, buttressed by a hardening conviction that the US government
is structurally incapable of being fair. The stereotyping of the Arab in US
popular culture and politics grows apace, giving little incentive to American leaders to be more forthcoming toward the Arab world. It is not altogether a coincidence that US citizens have been specifically targeted by
radical Arab groups in these last few years.

A major assumption of American policy has been that a strong Israel is
more likely to make concessions toward a peace settlement. With both

Egypt and Iraq neutralized and Syria bogged down in Lebanon and at log-gerheads with the PLO, Israel is as near the zenith of its military might as it will probably get. Yet the essence of even the Israeli Labor Party's position would seem categorically to preclude accommodation to the minimal demands of the Palestinians and the substance of the consensus forged at the Fez summit of the Arab League in September 1982: a sovereign Palestinian state within the 1967 frontier, in binding, internationally guaranteed coexistence with Israel, a solution that could be fashioned in such a way as to eliminate any threat to the security of Israel, as I have argued previously.[1]

To the best of my knowledge, the furthest the Labor Party seems willing to go would be the creation of Palestinian "enclaves" in the Gaza Strip and the West Bank. These enclaves, separated from one another by Israeli settlements and suburban blocs as well as by various military enclosures, would amount to 60–70 percent of the Gaza Strip and about 40 percent of the West Bank. The Jordan River would constitute the international frontier behind which the Israeli army would remain in control. Municipal or quasi-municipal functions would devolve to local Palestinian representatives in these enclaves, but internal security would remain in Israeli hands. Jordan would be invited to "co-police" the enclaves with Israel and presumably to extend its citizenship to all the inhabitants. This attenuated and selective Jordanian presence would be the justification for calling the arrangement a "territorial compromise." Face-to-face talks with a Jordanian delegation containing local Palestinians virtually chosen by Tel Aviv would negotiate this settlement at an otherwise ceremonial international conference.

This, to the best of my understanding, is the essence of the Jordanian option to which the United States and the Labor Party of Israel seem wedded, as at once a conduit, a repository, and final destination. Strategically it would absolve Israel of acknowledging a Palestinian nationhood, past or present, embracing the occupied territories and the diaspora, with all the attendant political, juridical, and moral implications. Tactically it would keep the PLO, symbol of Palestinian nationhood, out of the peace process, drive a wedge between the PLO and Jordan, present a "conciliatory" Israeli face to the outside world, and throw the burden of rejectionism and "missed opportunities" on the Palestinians.

This Jordanian option is but a latter-day version of an almost hallowed tradition for solving the Palestine problem over the heads of the Palestinians. Theodore Herzl established the tradition in his talks in 1898 with Kaiser Wilhelm II. Chaim Weizmann followed the pattern in his dealings with Lord Balfour (1917) and with Emir (later King) Faisal in 1919. Throughout the 1930s Zionist leaders persisted on this course via non-Palestinian pan-Arab leaders in Damascus, Beirut, and Amman. Like the Balfour Declaration fifty years earlier, UN Resolution 242, passed in 1967, made no reference to the Palestinians, while the Camp David accords settled their future without their participation. With impressive monotony the same recipe is tried again and again despite the catastrophic consequences that each attempt brings in its train, and the invalid arguments heard at each juncture.

Even *full* Jordanian sovereignty over the West Bank (including East Jerusalem) during the period between 1949 and 1967 was not viable. The alleged dichotomy between the Palestinians in the occupied territories and those in the diaspora is in the eye of the beholder; I argue that the bonds between those Palestinians are as intimate and indestructible as the bonds between Jews inside and outside Israel. No West Bank or Gaza "leader" anointed by the United States or Israel could look his compatriots in the eye, much less negotiate away their birthright. Far from stabilizing Jordan, the Jordanian option would strike at the very roots of the regime. It would involve it in mortal combat with all factions of the PLO and pit it against last-ditch Palestinian resistance in the occupied territories. Nor would the détente between Amman and Damascus survive such developments. Syria's Hafez al-Assad may encourage Jordan to isolate Yasir Arafat for his own tactical reasons, but no conceivable consideration of ideology, self-interest, or prudence would lead him to implement the Jordanian option. As the senior statesman of the Arab world, King Hussein must know this, and his sound political instincts will lead him to the obvious conclusion.

5

The sad events in the occupied territories since December 1987 confirm this analysis. And while it is too early to say what new leadership (if any) will emerge, certain assessments can be offered with reasonable assurance.

There is evidence of an extensive organizational infrastructure emerging at the grass roots, an intermeshing of formal and informal groups of the kind described in classical writings on revolutions. The activist leadership seems to be typically diffuse, anonymous, decentralized, and non-pyramidal, with heavy representation from the younger urban, rural, and refugee camp generations in relatively equal proportions. A new psychology seems to have gripped the bulk of the population, partly induced by the anniversaries falling in 1987–88 (the twentieth of the occupation and the fortieth of the establishment of Israel), partly by the immobilism of the Israeli political scene, the ultra-hawkish stance of Prime Minister Yitzhak Shamir, the perceived indifference of Washington, and the loss of momentum in the peace process. The November 1987 Arab League summit in Amman seemed preoccupied with the Iran-Iraq war, and the PLO leadership was locked in its perennial crisis of relations with Assad and Hussein.

Within this psychology, three new elements can be singled out. Factional and ideological differences among Palestinians (e.g., the business sector versus the radicals, secularists versus fundamentalists, some PLO factions against others) are being overcome. These differences had hitherto impaired the effectiveness of resistance but now seem to have been subsumed under a national consensus of unprecedented scope and cohesion.

A barrier of fear has been broken. This is the result of a sense of immunity acquired incrementally over two decades against the worst the occupation could do. Well over half of the entire adult male Palestinian population of the occupied territories must have seen the inside of an Israeli prison. In the extended family networks that prevail in the territories only a minority will not include a relative who has been manhandled, humiliated, injured, imprisoned or exiled, or had his or her home demolished. When every detail of one's daily personal, social, economic, and professional life is governed by one or more of the 1,210 ukases (of competing absurdity) issued so far by the military governors of the occupied territories, one's response is bound to be a deepening contempt for the system and its keepers—as a necessary condition for surmounting one's fear of them.

Finally, we see growing awareness of the need for self-reliance, or rather a compelling realization that in the last analysis salvation is self-generated. This phenomenon should be familiar to Jews in particular. For too long the Palestinians in the occupied territories have waited for St. George to come from across the border. For too long they have seen themselves as minor actors (if actors at all) in the shaping of their own destiny. That the occupation has succeeded in activating the moral outrage of the population is self-evident.

The flavor and weight of this occupation, the motivation and forces behind the current uprising, and the thrust of the population's aspirations may be gathered from the Jerusalem Program—the statement read out at a press conference in January at the National Palace Hotel in Jerusalem by a

214

spokesman for the "Palestinian National Institutions and Personalities from the West Bank and Gaza Strip."

The statement contains a long political preamble and fourteen specific points. Three deal with the immediate crisis: the release of those recently arrested, "especially the children," the return of four Palestinians deported amid wide criticism, and the lifting of the siege of the refugee camps. Five points deal with human rights: they call on Israel to adhere to the fourth Geneva Convention; to release people under administrative detention and house arrest and facilitate the reunion of families; to cease the demolition of houses; to initiate formal inquiries into the behavior of soldiers, settlers, and security men who have "unduly caused death or bodily harm to unarmed civilians"; and to grant the political freedom of meetings and conventions including "free municipal elections" under a neutral authority.

Two points address religious fears: the curtailment of "provocative activities" in the Old City of Jerusalem and the preservation of the status quo of the Muslim and Christian holy sites. Two others address the loss of land and water: they call for the cessation of settlement activity and land confiscation and the release of land confiscated, as well as the rescinding of measures "to deprive the territories of their water resources." Two address taxation issues: the cancellation of the Israeli value-added tax and all other direct taxes, and the release of "monies deducted from the wages of laborers" inside Israel, in the absence of commensurate social services. The statement also calls for the removal of restrictions on building permits, industrial projects, and agricultural development programs, including the digging of artesian wells. Discriminatory trade policies are also addressed: either the free transfer of industrial and agricultural produce from the occupied territories into Israel should be permitted or "comparable restrictions" should be placed on such produce entering the territories from Israel.

The political preamble states the obvious, that the occupation cannot last forever, and that "real peace" can be achieved only through the recognition by Israel of Palestinian national aspirations to which the uprising is committed. These include "the rights of self-determination and the establishment of an independent state on our national soil under the leadership of the PLO as our sole, legitimate representative." Continued occupation will lead to further violence, bloodshed, and the deepening of hatred. The only way "to extricate ourselves from this scenario," the preamble states, is an international conference with the participation of "all concerned parties including the PLO as an equal partner" as well as the five permanent members of the Security Council "under the supervision" of the two superpowers. "To prepare the atmosphere for the conference," Israel is called upon to comply with the demands outlined.

If this statement represents the uprising's demands (and the indications are that it does indeed) no one could accuse the Palestinians under occupation of not knowing what they want; nor do the leaders of the uprising seem to be grooming themselves as substitutes or proxies for the PLO.

The tone of the Jerusalem Program is firm but sober. There are no maximalist territorial demands or flamboyant formulations about an unrealizable democratic secular state. The aim is clearly a negotiated peace with Israel on a nation-to-nation basis. Perhaps the most interesting demand of the Jerusalem Program is for the removal of restrictions on political contacts with the PLO, to allow for "participation of Palestinians from the territories in the proceedings of the Palestinian National Congress in order to ensure a direct input into the decision-making process." Such input is more likely to be in favor of pragmatism than not.

6

Despite Arab disarray and the tumultuous fortunes of the PLO since 1982, the Arab and Palestinian stance today is more propitious for an honorable and viable settlement than ever before. The pity is that neither the Israeli nor the American government yet seems able to see this, or if either does, it has yet to find the way to nurture and build upon it.

In the first place, the resolutions of the September 1982 Arab Fez summit remain a remarkably forthcoming, collectively articulated Arab peace plan, enunciated at the level of the heads of state (only Qaddafi absented himself). Skeptics are invited to compare the resolutions with, say, the pronouncements of the 1967 Khartoum summit to see the political light-years traveled by the Arab countries in the direction of pragmatism. There was absolutely no precedent for the Fez summit in collective Arab diplomacy. Its orientation was unmistakably conciliatory toward a peaceful, non-transitional, and guaranteed settlement on the basis of coexistence with Israel within the 1967 frontiers. There is still nothing like it on the Israeli side at such an authoritative and comprehensive level. Likewise, the PLO position as fashioned under Arafat's leadership has evolved within the framework of the Fez resolutions and reached a new level of refinement during the PLO-Jordanian talks of January–February 1986.

I was but a marginal and informal participant in those talks, but my distinct impression was that they broke down not because Arafat was averse to accepting Resolution 242, negotiating with Israel, or denouncing terrorism—the three conditions set by Washington and relayed by Amman. Arafat specifically accepted Resolution 242 alongside "other pertinent UN resolutions." He specifically mentioned the Israeli government as a party with whom he was willing to negotiate a peaceful settlement within the context of an international peace conference and on the basis of his February 1985 accord with King Hussein. He reaffirmed his denunciation of operations outside the occupied territories and Israel.

There was one fundamental sticking point: Amman absolutely insisted (presumably at the behest of Washington) on a take-it-or-leave-it basis, that acceptance of Resolution 242 should be "without trimmings," i.e., with no qualifications whatsoever. This raised the obvious question of the quid pro quo, which, Arafat was told, was US acquiescence in the participation in a joint Jordanian-Palestinian delegation to the international conference of Palestinians who were not themselves PLO officials but were approved by the PLO. "What about Palestinian self-determination?" the PLO asked. This, Amman replied, was a matter between Jordan and the PLO. Would that it were! In the circumstances Arafat asked that in return for accepting the three conditions, Amman should obtain assurances from Washington (not Tel Aviv) about Palestinian self-determination on the basis of the Jordanian-PLO accord of February 1985. Amman could not see its way to doing that—hence the breakdown of the talks.

Is it really so outrageously perverse of Arafat to have balked at unilateral, unconditional, unreciprocated recognition of Israel, which the Israeli government itself has not solicited and has declared its intention to reject? Or is his perversity more in his hesitation to place his hope blindly in a UN resolution that does not even mention his people by name, to stop resistance to Israeli occupation and to give up PLO presence at the peace conference? Is he so lamentably wrong to hesitate to forget all UN resolutions favorable to his cause, to delegate Palestinian representation to Amman, and to throw himself upon the noblesse oblige of Tel Aviv and the empathy of Washington?

The eighteenth meeting of the Palestine National Congress (PNC) held in April 1987 in Algiers demonstrated, with the return to the fold of the Popular Front for the Liberation of Palestine and the Democratic Front for the Liberation of Palestine, the fundamental solidarity between the central Palestinian factions that constitute the PLO, isolating the dissident fac-

tions sponsored by Syria. The admission for the first time of the representatives of the Palestine Communist Party to the PLO Executive was coun-
terbalanced by the admission of two specifically Muslim representatives to
the General Council, thus broadening the popular base of the PLO. The
Abu Nidal group was denied admission to the various PLO bodies. The
eighteenth PNC meeting confirmed Arafat's status as *primus inter pares*.

The PNC position on Resolution 242 was a retreat from Arafat's specific
but qualified acceptance of it during his talks in Amman. But the Congress's
rejection of the resolution was reasoned rather than categorical, on the
grounds that 242 considered the Palestine problem as a "question of refugees" and ignored the "inalienable national rights" of the Palestinian people. On the other hand, the PNC reaffirmed support of the 1982 Fez summit peace plan and called for the development of relations with "the
democratic forces in Israel" that are against "Israeli occupation and expansion." Equally significant, because of the presence of the Popular Front and
the Democratic Front, was the Congress's readiness to participate in an
international peace conference "on a footing of equality" under the aegis of
the United Nations, with the participation of the permanent members of
the Security Council and "the concerned parties in the region," i.e., Syria
and Israel. The distinctive relations between the Palestinian and Jordanian
peoples were reemphasized, as was "confederation between two independent states" as the principle for future relations between Jordan and a Palestinian state in the occupied territories. In sum, the Algiers PNC meeting
left the door open for peaceful negotiations while specifically acknowledging the need for a constitutional link with Jordan.

Between the PNC meeting in April and the Amman summit in November 1987, several initiatives were undertaken to reduce the tensions between the PLO and Damascus. This was partly necessitated by the fes-
tering wounds in Lebanon, but largely by the need dictated by common
sense to coordinate with the "concerned party" of Syria before any international conference. One early result of the these initiatives was the absence of a PLO-Syrian confrontation at the Amman summit; another has
been the lifting of the siege of the Palestinian refugee camps in Lebanon.

My impression as a participant in these initiatives is that while the gap
in perceptions between Damascus and the PLO is considerable, both parties are equally keen to bridge it. A rapprochement between the PLO and
Damascus is a *sine qua non* for serious Arab preparation for peace talks. Of
the three Arab core parties to the conflict (Syria, Jordan, and the PLO),

Syria is the senior coalition member. This is a function of its geographic position, history, traditional role, and its military strength and preparedness. As to whether President Assad is committed to peace talks, the answer is that he is a signatory to the Fez summit peace plan but, like many others, is very skeptical about the outcome of the negotiations with an Israel that is so preponderant militarily and enjoys perceived unlimited and unconditional American backing. Can anyone credibly blame him for this?

The West has misinterpreted the significance of the Amman summit's preoccupation with the Iran-Iraq war and the green light it gave for the resumption of relations with Egypt. This summit was a special session, summoned specifically to address the Gulf war. No regular Arab summit has been convened since 1982 because of tensions between Syria and the PLO and between Syria and Iraq.

The true significance of the Amman summit, therefore, is that it was held with the presence of Assad, Arafat, and Saddam Hussein of Iraq, and that it paves the way for a regular summit meeting to address the Arab-Israeli conflict—a necessary preparatory step to the peace talks. Egypt's "return" may increase its military, political, and economic role in the Gulf countries, but it does not necessarily enhance its role or credibility in the decisions that have to be taken collectively by the three main Arab parties in the conflict: Syria, Jordan, and the PLO.

7

For several years now much time and energy have been expended on the issue of an international conference versus direct talks. This has been at the expense of any crystallization of substantive principles for the resolution of the conflict. There is little difference between direct talks with or without the umbrella of an international conference if such a conference is purely ceremonial. It is difficult to see what attraction a ceremonial international conference would have to the Syrians, the PLO or, for that matter, the Soviets. Conferences, qua conferences, do not solve conflicts. Surely the key to a successful international conference (ceremonial or not) and even to direct talks is intensive, high-level albeit quiet pre-negotiations with and between all the principal protagonists (Syria, Israel, Jordan, and the PLO) with maximal persuasiveness exerted by the superpowers on their respective friends.

In the light of historical experience accumulated since the Balfour Declaration, the récent uprising in the occupied territories and the configuration of power in the Arab world, the building blocks of what seems to me an honorable and pragmatically just settlement would appear without equivocation to be the following:

—the withdrawal of Israeli forces from southern Lebanon and the Golan Heights to the international frontiers, with demilitarization of the evacuated areas under UN supervisory observers and contingents stationed therein;
—the territorial partition of Mandatory Palestine along the 1967 frontier;
—a Palestinian state on the West Bank and Gaza Strip (linked by a non-extraterritorial road), living in peaceful coexistence alongside Israel. This Palestinian state would be in confederation with Jordan and precluded from entering into military alliances with other countries, whether Arab or not;
—the designation of West Jerusalem as the capital of Israel, East Jerusalem as the capital of Palestine. Extraterritorial status and access to the Jewish holy places would be assured, and a Grand Ecumenical Council formed to represent the three monotheistic faiths (with a rotating chair) to oversee interreligious harmony. Reciprocal rights of movement and residence between the two capitals within agreed-upon limits would be negotiated;
—an agreed limited return of 1948 Palestinian refugees to Israel proper and their unrestricted right of return to the Palestinian state. Those unable or unwilling to return would be compensated;
—agreement that the Jewish settlements existing in the occupied territories in 1948 would remain under Palestinian law, the others to be evacuated but not dismantled;
—explicit reciprocal recognition between Israel, the PLO, Jordan, and Syria;
—Arab summit and Islamic summit guarantees of the settlement as the *point final;*
—superpower and great power guarantees (inside and outside the UN Security Council) with sanctions;
—an interim transitional period of fixed and limited duration.

Important sectors of Israeli public opinion, not only on the left of center but at the center itself, favor a settlement that might be acceptable to most Palestinians. They are aware of the dangers of indefinite domination of another people. However, this is not the thrust of popular Israeli sentiment nor of the thinking of the Israeli leadership. The Israeli scorpion is determinedly uncognizant of the Palestinian fellow creature in the same bottle. Paradoxically, a Palestinian state in the occupied territories within the 1967 frontiers in peaceful coexistence alongside Israel is the only *conceptual* candidate for a historical compromise of this century-old conflict. Without it the conflict will remain an open-ended one between the maximalist concepts of Zionism and those of its Arab and Muslim hinterland, whatever palliative measures are taken in the meantime.

One would have thought the Jewish genius capable of grasping effortlessly the need for an honorable and viable settlement in light of the geographic, demographic, and ideological realities of the Middle East. Even archaeology adds its imperative plea in the form of the debris of so many past regional empires. The path to integration into a region would not seem to be via emphasis on extraneousness and escalating dependence on the outside. The breaking of bones is no passport to peace.

12

The Palestinian Dream:
The Democratic Secular State

MUHAMMAD HALLAJ

In December 1988, I was invited to participate in a conference hosted by the Washington-based Center for Strategic and International Studies on the impact of the Palestinian uprising on the prospects of Arab-Israeli peace. Meron Benvenisti, the former deputy mayor of Jerusalem and currently the director of the West Bank Database project, was my Israeli counterpart on one of the panels of the conference.

Benvenisti is not known as an extremist, and he has frequently spoken out against the continued occupation of the West Bank and Gaza Strip. In fact, he has acquired a reputation—particularly in the United States—for his unsympathetic views of Israel's policies of de facto annexation, even though he argues that, undesirable as the occupation may be, it has become "irreversible."[1]

At the conference, Benvenisti surprised me—and apparently surprised most of the other participants—when he asserted that to reassure Israel of their good intentions, the Palestinians should "recognize Zionism," and not only the state of Israel. Another participant, an American rabbi, wanted to know if the Palestinians were willing to recognize "Israel's moral legitimacy," a point on which I was not able to reassure him.

When the Arab-Zionist conflict over Palestine began in earnest seventy years ago, with the Balfour Declaration of 1917, the Zionists had a tendency to define the conflict primarily in moral terms: in terms of presumed historic and divine rights, and in terms of the right of a threatened Jewish people to shelter and survival. After the Nazi disaster of the 1930s, the establishment of a Jewish state (or a Jewish home, in the parlance of the time) was increasingly viewed in the Christian West as a moral world obligation. When Britain and the United States sent a joint commission (the Anglo-American Commission of Inquiry) to Palestine in 1946 to look into the escalating Arab-Jewish conflict, one of its American members was so devastated after a visit to Europe's concentration camps that he could not wait to reach Palestine to arrive at a conclusion. Europe's Jews have suffered enough, he wrote, and, they ought to be compensated. They "must be permitted to go where they wanted to go, and if that was Palestine, so be it."[2] The Palestinians became invisible and entirely irrelevant, and their concern—later proved to be fully justified—that Jewish immigrants were not going to Palestine to seek haven within an existing society but to replace it, did not matter.

After the establishment of Israel in 1948, the Zionist case increasingly relied on legal and strategic grounds. Certain United Nations resolutions (at first the partition resolution of 1947 and later Security Council Resolution 242 of 1967) became primary weapons in the Zionist arsenal against the Arabs. The series of Arab-Israeli wars of the past four decades were also used to justify Israel's policies and behavior, including its territorial expansion, its refusal to compromise on the question of repatriation of Palestinian refugees, and its subsequent occupation of the rest of Palestine and its refusal to withdraw. Israel even found support for its presumed contribution to Western strategic defense by keeping "the evil empire" at bay.

Security threats to Israel, real and imagined, became the most widely used Israeli-Zionist self-justification. In the 1970s and 1980s, as a corollary to this increased Israeli emphasis on the security argument, the Arabs in general and the Palestinians in particular were subjected to an unparalleled smear campaign depicting them as irrational terrorists, a charge that came to be the equivalent of a "blood libel" against the Palestinians.

At the same time, it became increasingly difficult for Israel to maintain the posture of a threatened society. Its ability to win wars repeatedly, the development of an Israeli nuclear arsenal, and America's inordinate generosity with money, arms, trade, and diplomatic protection have made the security argument less and less convincing. The invasion of Lebanon in the summer of 1982 and the colossal and often brutal destruction that it caused further undermined Israel's argument about the Arab threat.

In addition to Israel's increasingly intolerable behavior in the Middle East, the rise of Jewish fundamentalism and the Zionist right wing to power in Israel in the late 1970s,[3] its close military and economic ties to South Africa,[4] and its emergence as a principal arms merchant and collaborator with oppressive regimes in Central America and other areas of the world have eroded Israel's moral veneer.[5] Israel's friends found themselves lamenting its threatened "moral fiber" and the "endangered Zionist soul."

Then the Palestinian uprising exploded in December 1987, and Israel's brutality reached unprecedented levels and was seen by the entire world. For the first time, comparisons between Israel and South Africa became common in the media. A public opinion poll in the United States showed that a majority of Americans, including more than 40 percent of American Jews, believed that there was an element of racism in Israel's treatment of the Palestinians.[6] Doubts about Israel's much advertised moral stance became widespread. The return to moral terms, usually expressed as demands on the Arabs to recognize not only the state of Israel—which is what state recognition implies—but also Israel's *right* to exist, then its "moral legitimacy" and even its ideology—Zionism—reflected not only suspicion of Arab sincerity but also the Zionists' own doubts about the moral standing of the state that they had created.

Moral Issues

Although Israel, in the 1980s, often revealed chinks in its moral armor, such imperfections were usually viewed in the Christian West as temporary aberrations, usually forced on Israel by security imperatives, and as extra-legal behavior, as the work of deviant fanatics who blemished an otherwise moral Zionist edifice. Thus, Israeli soldiers who were caught engaged in brutal behavior were accused of soiling "the purity of Jewish arms," and Israelis who engaged in undeniably cruel behavior were accused of threatening Israel's "moral fiber." Israel was often pictured as the victim of its own misdeeds.

The Palestinians—the constant and most experienced eyewitness to Israel's misdeeds—find it difficult to accept the view that morally reprehensible deeds are aberrations from the Zionist ethical norm or deviations from the pattern of Israeli behavior. Their experience tells them otherwise.

How do the Palestinians understand Zionist Israel, and how do they see it from a moral perspective?

1. Zionism, the ideology, is seen by the Palestinians as an anachronistic—nearly medieval—world view. They see it as an outdated religious definition of nationhood, an outmoded and dangerous mix of church and state, and as a contradiction of the concept of socio-political pluralism. Its political expression—the establishment of a Jewish state in Palestine—is

understood by the Palestinians as morally reprehensible in a dual sense: as an escapist philosophy that preaches the uprooting and transfer of Jewish communities from their countries to escape rather than struggle against injustice, and as a selfish creed justifying the abuse of one community—the Palestinian Arabs—for the benefit of another.

2. Since Zionism began its political career in 1897, its insensitivity to the impact of its program on the Palestinians was translated into cruelty in dealing with them. It demonized them to justify its disregard of them. It de-legitimized them to justify their displacement and dispossession. As one writer put it: "The dehumanized image of the Palestinians which the Zionists developed and propagated was instrumental in displacing the moral issue and establishing an aura of legal justification around Zionist goals and activity."[7]

3. The Palestinians fault the Zionist movement, and later Israel, for willingness to collaborate with powers with imperialist ambitions in the Middle East. This has been the case since the founder of political Zionism, Theodor Herzl, offered to cooperate with the German expansionist policy toward the east in the late nineteenth and early twentieth centuries in return for German sponsorship of Zionism until this day.[8] Correspondingly, the Arabs fault Zionism, and later Israel, with the sin of siding with the West against Afro-Asian national liberation movements during the era of decolonization struggle. The early convergence of interests between Zionism and British imperialist schemes in the Near East led a British commentator to observe that "it was the fact that the Jews were the stool pigeons of British imperialism that doomed the whole business in Arab eyes from the beginning."[9]

4. The Arabs resent Israel's involvement in what they perceive to be deliberate efforts to destabilize their society by the encouragement of dissident and separatist movements, usually based on ethnic minorities and religious sects, from Iraq to Lebanon to the Sudan. They see it as an effort to "Balkanize" the Arab world, to weaken it through fragmentation as a prerequisite to the imposition of Israeli hegemony over the region.[10]

5. The Arabs fault Israel for its support of authoritarian and other unpopular regimes throughout the world by supplying them with arms and by training and advising their security services. The relation with South Africa is particularly understood as affinity between racist and discriminatory regimes.

Not only the Palestinians, but many Jews throughout this century have been troubled by the idea of a Jewish state. Even before the Zionist "dream has become a nightmare in recent months," as Yehuda Menuhin put it in a recent article critical of Israel's Palestinian policy,[11] Jewish thinkers from Ahad Ha'am, early in the century, until this day have expressed their fear that a national Jewish state would not only impact cruelly on the indigenous Arab society in Palestine but would also have a detrimental effect on the Jewish people and their historic mission in the world.[12]

Regardless of how the conflict over Palestine began, the fact today is that both parties have come to view it as a "zero sum game." The Palestinians believe that Israel's refusal to negotiate its withdrawal from the occupied West Bank and Gaza Strip and its de facto annexation policy are intended to foreclose permanently the option of independent national existence for the Palestinian people. The Israelis, on the other hand, justify their opposition to Palestinian independence on the grounds that a Palestinian state in any part of Palestine would be the opening salvo in the final battle for Israel's existence and a stepping stone to its destruction.

The evidence is more supportive of Palestinian than Israeli fears. Israel's policy is based on the proposition that no one has legitimate sovereignty over the West Bank and Gaza and that, therefore, they are up for grabs. It does not recognize that their Palestinian inhabitants have inherent popular sovereign right to territories which had been part of their homeland since long before Israel itself came into being. Israel has repeatedly made it clear that in any future settlement, it intends to lay claim to sovereignty over the West Bank and Gaza. That is why it has taken the view that Security Council Resolution 242 does not apply to the West Bank and Gaza, and the view that any Palestinian autonomy ought to be for the inhabitants and not for the land.

The Palestinians, on the other hand, are not so exclusivist in their claims. Although they ardently believe in their historic right to Palestine, their political claims have been significantly modified. Their political claim is limited to a range between 22 and 46 percent of the country, between the territory occupied by Israel in 1967 and the territory assigned to the Arab state in General Assembly Resolution 181, the partition resolution of 1947. They have given clear and repeated signals that their actual expectations hover around the lower end of that range, meaning the West Bank and Gaza Strip.

Furthermore, the Palestinians have accepted—in the Rabat Arab summit of 1974 and more recently in the nineteenth session of the Palestine National Council in November 1988—international security arrangements, including the stationing of UN peacekeeping forces on Palestinian soil. Israel has neither offered similar assurances to the Palestinians nor has it offered assurances of its own.

It is obvious that the Palestinians, on the vital issues of geography and security, have done much more to alleviate Israeli fears than Israel has done to alleviate Palestinian fears. The conflict, therefore, remains at its most dangerous level: a conflict over national existence and security.

The "Civilized" Solution

The two-state solution in Palestine has come to be accepted by the world community as the most desirable and likely outcome of the Middle East peace process. It is so perceived because it is understood to satisfy the minimal needs of the Israelis and Palestinians by enabling both to enjoy independent nationhood.

The Palestinians have come to accept the two-state solution as being less iniquitous than the status quo. They have come to accept it as a compromise with injustice rather than a triumph over injustice. They accept it as a tolerable political compromise, defective as it is in several respects:

1. The two-state solution, based as it is on the country's partition between Palestinians and Israelis, makes a part of the country alien territory to each of the two peoples who have the greatest attachment to it.

2. The Palestinian state, restricted as it would most likely be to about one-fifth of the country, would be obviously incapable of accommodating the hundreds of thousands of refugees, those who are in greatest need of a homeland.

3. The two-state solution is a concession to the denial of the possibility of Arab-Jewish coexistence. It institutionalizes the denial of social pluralism in Palestine.

4. It preserves and perpetuates the nationalist nature of the conflict which, because of residual irredentist attitudes on both sides, threatens to subvert the compromise in the future.

That is why the Palestinians came around to the two-state solution, not as a preference, but as recognition of compelling circumstances. The Palestinian preference, their ethical solution, which in their literature they often call the "civilized" solution, is the Palestinian democratic nonsectarian (or secular) state.

It should be pointed out, however, that the fact that the two-state solution is not the preferred solution to the Palestinians, it does not mean that they are not sincere in its acceptance as a way to resolve the conflict with

Israel. The Palestinian attitude can be described by Professor Harkabi's dictum that the Palestinians and the Israelis, to achieve peace, need to distinguish policy from grand design. The democratic secular state is the Palestinian grand design; the two-state solution is their policy.

The Palestinians believe that a day will come when the grand design might become feasible. After a period of living within the framework of the two-state solution, and after fears and apprehensions subside, both sides might come to the conclusion that it is in their mutual interest to go beyond the severe constraints of mini-states and agree, peacefully, to grow together into the unified democratic state, and achieve conciliation and not just compromise.

The Democratic State

Until the 1960s, the Palestinians viewed Jewish presence, and consequently the state of Israel, as an act of foreign aggression, as a colonialist adventure. Israel was a settler state after the model of white settler societies in Africa, based on the dispossession and displacement of an indigenous society by foreign immigrants.[13] They saw it, not as an issue to be addressed, but as an injustice to be redressed. For that reason, Palestinian political thinking during the first two decades of Israel's existence was encapsulated in the twin slogans of "liberation" and "return," signifying the Palestinian right to liberate a territory that had been occupied and usurped, and to repatriate a society that had been dispossessed and displaced.

For the first time since Arab-Jewish conflict over Palestine began early in the century, in the late 1960s the Palestinians came to terms with Jewish presence in Palestine by calling for the establishment of a bi-national Palestinian state in which Palestinian Arabs and Israeli Jews would share sovereignty and citizenship in a common homeland, with equal rights and obligations. This Palestinian proposal, known as the democratic secular (or non-sectarian) state, signified Palestinian acceptance of a Jewish society—though not state—and in that sense it was a profound change of attitude toward Jewish presence in the country.

The democratic non-sectarian state became official Palestinian policy when the Palestine National Council (PNC) adopted it in the late 1960s as the political aim of Palestinian struggle for national rights. It called on the PLO's Executive Committee to study the concept and to develop it into a constitutional plan for the future of the country and its inhabitants.[14]

The director of the PLO's Planning Center, Nabil Shaath, writing under the pseudonym Muhammad Rasheed, did produce a sketchy outline of the vision, published as a pamphlet and widely distributed in Palestinian circles at the time,[15] but it was not pursued beyond reaffirming it in subsequent resolutions as the PLO's future vision for Palestine and Arab-Jewish relations. Palestinian struggle for national rights, said a PNC resolution in 1971, "is not an ethnic or religious struggle against Jews," and it affirmed the commitment to a "Palestinian democratic state in which all those willing to live in peace will enjoy the same rights and obligations."[16]

Israel's immediate and emotional rejection of the idea did not encourage the Palestinians to develop it into a political program. Unfortunately, although Jews felt safe only in democratic secular states everywhere else in the world, they found the idea inappropriate, even suicidal, in Palestine. An Israeli professor wrote that the democratic secular state had "genocidal implications."[17]

Also, the idea found little support in the world because it required too drastic an adjustment of the status quo and, for that reason, was politically not feasible. The Palestinians shelved it and began to call for the two-state solution.

When Yasser Arafat addressed the UN General Assembly in 1974, he regretfully relegated the democratic secular state idea to the status of a "Palestinian dream."[18] In PNC resolutions and in Palestinian literature, the democratic secular state came to be known as the "strategic solution," meaning, in effect, one that is deferred indefinitely, if not abandoned. The PLO began to veer in the direction of the two-state solution as a more viable political compromise. The Palestinian "civilized solution" became, like Plato's virtuous republic, a model to be suspended from the heavens for people to imitate if not to attain.

The essential virtue of the democratic non-sectarian state is in its ethical suppositions and intent. It accepts the possibility and desirability of harmonious coexistence between ethnic and religious communities; it seeks to maximize the self-fulfillment of both communities by extending physical and spiritual contact with the land they both love; and it aspires to reconcile—not just compromise—the conflict between them. As a Palestinian intellectual, the late Dr. Fayez Sayegh once explained the superiority of the democratic secular state over other solutions:

> What is needed is a principled and courageous vision. The required vision must do precisely what a "compromise" cannot. A compromise takes its departure

from the actual positions of the contending parties and seeks to find a solution somewhere *between* them. The needed vision transcends those starting points and looks for a solution *above* them.

Men who cannot or will not surrender to one another may be inspired to surrender to a higher vision—and in that surrender find freedom and fulfillment, as well as reconciliation.[19]

The Palestinians saw the democratic secular state as a historic reconciliation of Arabs and Jews, a synthesis of the Palestinian thesis and the Zionist antithesis.

The division of Palestine—a small country of ten thousand square miles not known to be rich in material resources—into two states may be a necessary interim measure that can answer the immediate needs of personal security and national pride. But if the Palestinians and Israelis aspire to triumph over fear and injustice—and not only contain them—they must see beyond the immediate horizon of their nationalist imperatives. The democratic, non-sectarian republic—though proposed by the Palestinians—is a universalist vision of inter-communal relations. But its virtues go beyond its principles. It promises a more spacious home and a richer life for the two peoples who cherish Palestine most. If the two mini-states of partition reassure the Palestinians and Israelis, the democratic non-sectarian state liberates them.

It may be a dream, but it is not a fantasy. Even Israeli Jews who see sinister implications in this form of Arab-Jewish existence in Palestine indirectly admit its promise. Professor Harkabi, who saw "genocidal implications" in the democratic secular state, also wrote that the "Arabs brandish the slogan of a 'Democratic State' as a means of psychological warfare against us, in order to weaken our determination," suggesting that the idea is not without merit.[20]

Yehuda Menuhin, the well-known British-Jewish concert violinist, proposed a similar future for Palestine to save Israel from the "living nightmare" of occupation and repression of the Palestinians. Obviously unaware that the Palestinians had made such a proposal twenty years before, he wrote in the summer of 1988: "Even if the offer [of an Arab-Jewish federation in Palestine] were at first rejected by the Arabs, I believe it should be determinedly maintained by Israel . . ."[21]

It is not inconceivable that both Arabs and Jews would in the future contest the parentship of the "civilized solution" to the future of Arab-Jewish coexistence in Palestine. Such a contest, unlike the present conflict, would honor them both.

13

Morality and Expediency in the Policies of Zionist Israel

GHADA TALHAMI

Since December of 1987, a civilian uprising in the land the Jordanians call the West Bank, the Israelis the occupied territories, and the Palestinians East Palestine and Gaza has drastically changed the political facts of the Arab-Israeli conflict. What began as pitiful acts of stone-throwing by Palestinian youths, otherwise unarmed, quickly turned into a total civil war that, though fought with unequal armor, proved to be a serious threat to the occupying power. Thus began what has come to be the Palestinians' major rebellion since the 1936 General Strike and Uprising. Unlike the 1936 rebellion, however, the 1987 *intifada* burst on a scene complicated by overlapping laws, conflicting claims of sovereignty and a land fast becoming, at least in its economy, a dependent state, part of Greater Israel. It was not only a wounded cry from a suffering population, but a quest for sovereignty, which the Palestinians had lost in 1948.

By invoking the right to rebel and to resist the occupiers' laws, the Palestinians based their case on a corpus of international laws that came to embody the civilized nations' definition of ethical collective behavior. This corpus of laws and conventions, which, beginning with the Congress of Vienna in 1815, includes such acts as the General Act of the Anti-Slavery Conference of Brussels of 1890, the Protocol of Aachen regulating diplomatic missions and ranks in 1818, a convention recognizing the neutrality of Switzerland in 1815, and the Geneva Convention of 1864, which created the International Red Cross. The most important development to emerge from this collective effort was the work of the two Hague Peace Conferences in 1899 and 1907. These two conferences established a set of laws regulating maritime warfare and setting standards for the conduct of war. The Convention Regarding the Laws and Customs of War on

Land detailed acceptable standards for the treatment of prisoners of war and for the conduct of occupying powers towards the occupied population.[1]

No single case of systematic denial of political rights to a national group rivals that of the Palestinians. Ever since the beginning of this century, the Palestinians have experienced a steady erosion of their status as a political community. This process has culminated in a total loss of autonomy, in physical dispersal, and in absorption and occupation by other political units. Their declining fortunes were directly related to power plays within the world's leading international bodies. The Palestinians suffered the consequences of these struggles, first in the League of Nations, with Britain playing the lead part as the arbiter of international peace and the architect of the new system of mandates, and later in the United Nations, with the US as a guarantor of a new world order. It became the Palestinians' fate to define the fortunes of the weak nations of the world, who had no recourse but to rely on the emerging body of laws enacted by these two international bodies.

Caught between the dismal reality of their condition and the idealism expressed in the new corpus of international laws, Palestinians often expressed their disillusionment by resorting to acts of violent resistance. Their right to resist was based specifically on documents and precepts enacted by the United Nations and on the new morality of national liberation articulated by the new Afro-Asian members of the world body. Both the Afro-Asian nations and the treaties purporting to uphold a higher standard of behavior in times of war bestowed on the Palestinian struggle some form of legitimation. The Palestinians' readiness to take up the armed struggle, on the other hand, was always influenced by their adversary's flagrant disregard for the spirit and content of international agreements. Indeed, the Palestinians' will to resist was the direct outcome of their loss of faith in the ability of international bodies to enforce their own laws on international antagonists. The Palestinians firmly believe that they started out with a strong legal case and that their adversary's case was baseless in law. This conviction alone explains the Palestinians' reluctance to acknowledge the other side's legitimacy and the validity of its laws. This has also earned the Palestinians a "terrorist" label. Yet a growing body of opinion around the world views the excessive penalties meted out by Israel to Palestinian civilians as another variation on the theme of terrorism.

Since the rights of the conquered and the occupied remain ill-defined, and since the international community has not yet restored to the Palestinians their statehood, they remain a menace to organized society. In

Hobbesian language, the stateless person is an *ens completum* (an absolute will), free from any legal strictures. What such a person has is a "natural right" not subject to collective standards. In the words of one expert, the position of the stateless person vis-à-vis organized society is analogous to that of a pirate to the international order. Similarly, the Israeli usurpation of the Palestinian right of statehood constitutes another form of terrorism for it denies them a fundamental and basic human right, namely the right of self-determination.[2]

Palestinian rights in their own homeland were acknowledged by the British Government even as it drafted, in 1917, the secret wartime Balfour Declaration, a tripartite agreement between the British Zionist Organization, the Jews, and the British Government. The British promise of a "national home" for the Jews in Palestine, a territory not yet conquered by the British, was limited by the statement that nothing in that promise shall "prejudice the civil and religious rights of existing non-Jewish communities in Palestine."[3] With the creation of the Mandate system by the League of Nations, the responsibility of the great powers towards the former subjects of the defeated Ottoman and Austro-Hungarian Empires was clearly delineated. Article 22 (1) of the League of Nations Covenant explained the essence of this system and gave these people a provisional promise of independence:

> To those colonies and territories which as a consequence of the late war have ceased to be under the sovereignty of states which formerly governed them and which are inhabited by peoples not yet able to stand by themselves under the strenuous conditions of the modern world, there should be applied the principle that the well-being and development of such peoples form a sacred trust of civilization and that securities for the performance of this trust should be embodied in this Covenant.[4]

Furthermore, the League of Nations' Mandate for Palestine, which was the instrument justifying British rule over Palestine, was based on the Covenant. The British authorities, in essence, accepted the responsibility spelled out in Article 2 of the Mandate Agreement, which promised to develop self-governing institutions for the existing inhabitants of Palestine. They were pledged to work towards realizing independence for the Palestinians as recognized by the Covenant. The Mandate system itself consisted of three classes, ranging in levels according to the estimated degree of political maturity of these populations. The Ottoman territories, including Palestine, were classified as class "A" Mandates, or the most advanced territories. Together, the Mandate Agreement and the Balfour Declaration were written evidence of the status of the Palestinians following the First World War. The subsequent incorporation of the principle of self-determination of peoples in Article 1 of the UN Charter, and the reinstatement of the principle of trusteeship and existing international agreements of members in Articles 37 and 80, qualify the Palestinians for the enjoyment of the principle of self-determination. Since the UN Charter recognizes the right of all peoples to self-determination, it has acquired the force of public international law.[5]

The inclusion of the Balfour Declaration in the Mandate Agreement, however, was the first in a series of blows which jeopardized the Palestinian right of self-determination. British Foreign Secretary, Ernest Bevin, recognized publicly before the House of Commons on February 25, 1947 the tragic consequences of Britain's contradictory and dual obligation to the Arabs and to the Jews:

> There is no denying the fact that the Mandate contained contradictory promises. In the first place it promised the Jews a National Home and in the second place, it declared the rights and position of the Arabs must be protected. Therefore, it provided what was virtually an invasion of the country by thousands of immigrants and, at the same time said that this was not to disturb the people in possession.[6]

The right of self-determination is considered by most to be a customary and general principle of international law. Since it emerged in this century and its general acceptance by the international community, the right of self-determination gave rise to the question of eligibility to peoplehood. Here, it is assumed that those communities who experience permanent bonds of attachment, such as a common language or culture, or those who felt distinct from other groups and had a desire to exercise this right, were probably eligible. The most common and recent application of the principle of self-determination as enunciated in the UN Charter has been in reference to the worldwide process of decolonization.[7]

Since the colonial powers did not challenge the principle, its application was much easier than in the case of two collective groups seeking to qualify for this right in order to affirm their links and permanent status in one single territory. When such a situation developed, as in the case of the Arab-Jewish conflict over Palestine, it became worthwhile to examine each group's national credentials and historic links to the land separately. The crucial historical period is the British Mandate, which preceded the establishment of the state of Israel.

From 1919 until 1948, Palestine was organized as a distinct political unit, with a flag, passport, and currency of its own. Its people were recognized as being Palestinians, and the attachment of people to land made of this territory a state, enjoying a status no different than that of Egypt or India during the same period. In 1948, the bonds of the people to the land were severed when the Palestinians became technically "refugees" and the Palestinian state disappeared. In its place, new immigrants declared themselves a state and refused UN resolutions to readmit the Palestinian refugees to their former homes. This tragic development was not reversed until 1969 when the UN General Assembly adopted the historic resolution 2535 reaffirming the "inalienable rights of the Palestinian people," thereby discarding the refugee status of the Palestinians.[8]

Establishing the juridical link between a given people and a disputed territory is difficult in practice. In the Palestinian case, prior to the UN Partition Resolution of 1947, the determinant of nationality would have to be legal residence (although this by itself does not confer political rights) and nationality where Palestinians resided. When you add the majority rule to these two criteria, the illegality of the UN Partition Resolution that gave rise to the state of Israel becomes obvious. When the Resolution was passed, the total size of the Jewish population in Palestine was around 600,000. One-half of these were neither nationals nor legal residents of the country, but recent immigrants who did not yet meet the nationalization requirements of the government of Palestine.[9]

Legal residence was usually certifiable by the granting of official permits. Indeed, if the wishes of the local Palestinian population, both Jewish and Arab, had been examined, only the adult voters of the 300,000 legal Jewish Palestinians would have voted on the partition question, versus the collective strength of the adult voters of a total of 1,323,434 Arab Palestinians. In flagrant disregard of these facts, the UN passed the Partition Resolution by a vote of outside states, without any due regard to the wishes of the local population, and allotted to the Jewish minority 56 percent of the total land area of Palestine.[10]

In recognition of these facts, Article 6 of the PLO's Covenant in 1968 asserted that only Jews who were nationals of Palestine before "the beginning of the Zionist invasion," would be considered Palestinians. The Palestine Liberation Organization was legally correct in adopting this formula, although pragmatic considerations and international pressure, specifically by the Soviet Union, later forced the PLO's Parliament, the Palestine National Council, to adopt another formula which superseded Article 6. Arafat's 1974 UN speech also pointedly referred to the "Palestine of tomorrow," which would "include all Jews now living in Palestine who chose to live with us there in peace and without discrimination."[11]

Palestinian commentators argue that all of Israel's cabinets since 1948 have, in effect, carried out an Israeli version of Article 6, expelling hundreds of thousands of Palestinians and denying them the right of return. The state has consistently denied those Palestinians living in Israel proper full citizenship rights.[12] Article 6 of the Palestine Covenant was considered a terrorist principle by Israel's defenders, who interpreted it as calling for the dismantling of the state of Israel. In actuality, the Palestine Covenant illustrates the enormous difficulty facing Palestinians whenever they attempt to establish the legitimacy of their case.[13]

Although Israeli sources claimed in later years that the creation of Israel was a legal action sanctioned by the UN, in reality Jews were able to maximize their control over certain areas of Palestine by resorting to terror tactics before the partition plan. They continued to do so by defying UN-arranged truces during the ensuing war. The pre-state Jewish terror campaign, which included deliberate attacks on civilians, is too well-known to merit more than passing mention. Underground para-military organizations like the Haganah (later the core of the Israeli Army), the Irgun and the Stern engaged in a flagrant campaign that included the sinking of the *SS Patria* in 1940, a ship loaded with Jewish refugees, in order to force the lifting of the British ban on illegal Jewish immigration to Palestine. In a little-known article by the current Israeli Prime Minister, Yitzhak Shamir, which appeared in *Hehazi* (Summer 1943), voice of the Stern terrorist gang, Shamir gave a startling justification of terror:

> Neither Jewish ethics nor Jewish traditions can disqualify terrorism as a means of combat. . . . We have before us the command of the Torah, whose morality surpasses that of any other body of laws in the world: 'Ye shall blot them out to the last man.' We are particularly far from having any qualms with regard to the enemy, whose moral degradation is universally admitted here. But first and foremost, terrorism is for us a part of the political battle being conducted under the present circumstances, and it has a great part to play: speaking in a clear voice to the whole world as to our wretched brethren outside this land, it proclaims our war against the occupier.[14]

Incidents targeting unarmed Arab civilians, such as the massacre of Deir Yassin and the forced march of the Arab population of Lydda and Ramallah, illustrate this process. Israel did not abide by the boundaries of the area assigned to it by the UN Partition Resolution but continued to expand its territory, even while negotiating armistice agreements with the various Arab states surrounding its borders.[15]

Israel's greatest disregard for international morality was illustrated by its handling of the Arab refugee problem. When, during the course of the 1948 Arab-Jewish War, a flood of refugees fled their ancestral homes, the new Israeli government refused to permit them to return. This position was defended by reference to the circumstances of this Arab exodus rather than by arguing against the refugees' right of return. The Israelis claimed that the Arabs fled of their own volition, often prodded by broadcast calls by other Arab governments. By taking this step, the Arabs have forfeited their right of return, the Israelis argued. In reality Arab refugees fled as a result of strong provocation by the Israeli armed forces. Recent investigations, such as the one by the noted British journalist Erskine B. Childers, have disproved the allegation of Arab broadcasts.[16]

The refusal of the young state of Israel to abide by a variety of UN resolutions calling for the return of the Arab refugees (beginning with General Assembly Resolution 194 (III), adopted on December 11, 1949) was further violation of the Palestinian individual's right of self-determination. Since the collective right of self-determination presupposes the individual's right to political self-expression and the right to remain and return to one's country, the Palestinians should not have been prevented from returning to a land they left in time of war. The Universal Declaration of Human Rights formalized this right in Article 13 (2) which reads "Everybody has the right to leave any country, including his own, and to return to his country."

The Declaration of Human Rights, which has not been accepted by all as legally binding, is nevertheless acceptable as such by the International Court of Justice. This body views the Declaration as binding on all member states of the UN because the Declaration interprets the principles of the Charter. Moreover, the opinion of Vice-President of the Court Ammoun condemning the presence of South Africa in Namibia incorporated the Declaration into the Charter. This made the Declaration, just like the Charter, binding on all its signatories. Israel was a member of the UN at the time of the passing of General Assembly Resolution 194 and is expected, as a member, to uphold all UN laws, such as the Charter and the Declaration.[17]

Since the Declaration was adopted unanimously, with only eight abstaining countries (who did not reject it in its totality), it acquired great

Ghada Talhami

significance beyond the initial expectations of its authors. The statement
in the preamble describes it "as a common standard of achievement for
all peoples and all nations." The Declaration is often cited in UN resolutions and is considered by many to enjoy the force of customary international law.[18]

After the creation of the state of Israel, both spontaneous and Arab-
sponsored infiltrations of its borders by displaced Palestinian refugees began to occur regularly. The Israeli response to these attacks lacked any
semblance of legality. The Israelis adopted a two-pronged policy: (1) the
by-passing of UN agencies on the scene (such as the Mixed Armistice
Commissions and United Nations Treaty Supervisory Organization) in
favor of a policy of massive retaliation, and (2) a campaign of destabilization, aimed at the heart of Arab regimes supportive of the refugees.

The diaries of Israel's one-time Foreign Minister, Moshe Sharett, provide ample evidence of this policy, which eventually led to the Suez War
of 1956 and the Arab-Israeli War of June 1967. A revealing excerpt from
these diaries exposes Israel's vested interest in pursuing the policy of massive retaliation. After the Israeli attack on Gaza, in response to activities of
Arab infiltrators in 1955, Israel was cautioned by the US against escalating
the violence and was even offered a US security pact. Moshe Dayan, the
Defense Minister, reportedly stated, in a meeting with Israeli ambassadors:

> We do not need a security pact with the US; such a pact will only constitute an
> obstacle for us. We face no danger at all of an Arab advantage of force for the
> next 8–10 years. . . . The security pact will only handcuff us and deny us a
> freedom of action, and this is what we need in the coming years. Reprisal ac-
> tions, which we could not carry out if we were tied to a security pact, are our
> vital lymph. First, they make it imperative for the Arab governments to take
> strong measures to protect the borders. Second, and that's the main thing, they
> make it possible for us to maintain a high level of tension among our population
> and in the army. Without these actions we would have ceased to be a combative
> people and without the discipline of a combative people we are lost.[19]

The total effect of Israel's history of disregard for international conventions, and the world community's readiness to ignore its promises to the
Palestinians, pushed the latter in the direction of third world forms of resistance. Beginning with attacks by guerrilla bands along Israel's borders in
the 1950s, Palestinian resistance metamorphosed as an independent, guer-
rilla-based war of liberation following the defeat in the 1967 War.

The Arab-Israeli War of 1967 not only destroyed the military capabilities of neighboring Arab states, it also shredded the myth of Arab spon-

sorship of the Palestinian cause. The war removed the Jordanian administration as a buffer between Israel and the Palestinian citizens of the
eastern part of Palestine. Israel, overnight, acquired the status of an occupier of large, heavily populated areas. The Palestinians emerged as independent operators, seeking a redefinition of their rights as resistance fighters and political agitators. While the Israelis attempted to establish legal
grounds for their military and administrative methods of control over the
West Bank and Gaza, the PLO, now speaking for all Palestinians, strove
towards some legitimation of its actions.

Emerging in 1964 as a successor to the discredited Egyptian-sponsored
PLO, led by Ahmad Shukairy, the Arafat-led PLO sought its inspiration
from the historic experiences of the Algerian, Cuban, and Chinese revolutions. Viewing its struggle as that of a third world people facing a colonialist beachhead established in its midst by the Western powers, the PLO
adopted the strategy of a popular war. This was based on provisions in the
UN Charter which forbade all kinds of war except the war of self-defense.
The PLO saw no alternative to the principle of armed struggle, since a
national movement facing an occupying power must rely on its military
arms. As one PLO pamphlet put it: "military action is the foundation,
while political action is the upper structure." Because the Zionist occupation cannot be ended merely by weakening the enemy militarily, the liberation force must attack the enemy's means of livelihood, both agricultural
and industrial.[20]

In one PLO study of the rationale for resorting to the armed struggle to
liberate the land, the need to maintain the favor of international world
opinion was also stressed. World public opinion must be apprised of the
solutions used by the liberating forces in order to avoid the accusation of
fascism or anti-Semitism. "Our concern for gaining the favor of international public opinion," the study emphasized, "will be an important element leading to winning the approval of that world opinion for whatever
solutions we choose." "Terrorism" entered the lexicon of Israelis as a general label for Palestinian acts of violence. But this term meant something
quite different to Palestinians. "Several factors may be ascribed to non-
official, political terrorism," wrote Eqbal Ahmad, an expert on third world
resistance movements. "One, the need to be heard, is crucial," he explained. He added: "Terrorism is a violent way of expressing long-felt,
collective grievances. When legal and political means fail over a long period, a minority of the aggrieved community acts out violently, often elic-
iting the sympathy of the majority."[21]

239

As soon as Israel settled down to administering the occupied West Bank and Gaza, it proceeded to devise an iron-clad military regime and to create its own legal argument, justifying its reinstatement of the Emergency Regulations enforced during the British Mandate period. By denying the existence of Palestinian sovereignty over Palestine before 1948, Israel found that it could avoid the application of the Geneva Conventions to that area. A theoretical scheme was devised by Dr. Yehuda Bloom, then a lecturer in International Law at Hebrew University. In an article titled: "The Missing Reversioner: Reflections on the Status of Judea and Samaria," he justified by-passing the Geneva Conventions, since the law of belligerent occupation, or the Geneva Civilian Convention, applies to an occupied area only if its "legitimate sovereign" was terminated by the occupying power. The West Bank and Gaza, which were annexed and administered respectively by Jordan and Egypt after 1948, do not fall under this category, he claimed.[22]

Although this cynical interpretation was condemned by many, even by some within Israel itself, the Israeli Government continued to ignore all the critics. Many experts, inside and outside Israel, voiced the view that the Civilian Convention applied to people, not to territory, and that the Israelis could not compound the misfortunes of the Palestinians under Jordanian and Egyptian rule by installing an occupation regime of their own. The Israeli Government regards the Geneva Civilian Convention as a treaty intended to protect governmental rights, specifically, the right to claim disputed territory. In reality, the Convention's preamble, written by the governments attending the Geneva Diplomatic Conference of 1949, stated that they met "for the purpose of establishing a Convention for the Protection of Civilian Persons in Time of War." No specific mention of governmental rights was made in the Convention by its authors. In its Commentary (on the Convention) the International Committee of the Red Cross referred to the intent of the Convention as "the first time that a set of international regulations has been devoted not to State interests, but solely to the protection of the individual."[23]

The Israelis also claim that they hold the West Bank and Gaza according to the principle of "defensive conquest." But even if one is willing to accept Israel's presentation of its role in the hostilities leading to the June War of 1967 as being wholly defensive, one has to conclude that this concept is groundless in international law. Article 2 (4) of the UN Charter prohibits the threat or use of force against any nation. It does not make any exception to this rule for fear of encouraging expansionist wars.[24]

The Israelis defend the imposition of the British Emergency Regulations on the occupied territories. To understand Israel's elaborate argument, it is necessary to describe the Regulations and their origins. These regulations originated as a Palestine (Defense) Order in Council in 1937. They empowered the British High Commissioner in Palestine to make any necessary regulations in order to meet the emergency of rising violence in the area. The Regulations were eventually used extensively in 1945 against Jewish terrorist groups. Today, Israel contends that the Regulations were incorporated into Jordanian law in 1948 and because the occupied territories are, from the Israeli point of view, still part of Jordan, they must remain the law of the land. A recent study by André Rosenthal, however, proved conclusively that the 1937 Order in Council, on which the Regulations were based, was cancelled on May 12, 1948. Israel, therefore, cannot ratify a non-existent law. However, the Israelis point to the fact that the British Government ceased publication of the official *British Gazette* in Palestine between November 29, 1947 (when the UN Partition Resolution was passed) and May 15, 1948 (the date of actual British withdrawal from Palestine). Because Jewish lawyers were not notified of this cancellation, Israel claims that the law is still valid.[25]

Israel's most vehement argument pertains to the question of incorporating the 1945 Emergency Regulations into Jordanian Law and its enforcement by the Jordanians in the West Bank after 1948. Israel has relied on the Emergency Regulations, particularly the clause sanctioning deportations, in order to control the population of the occupied territories. The Emergency Regulations were even used to deport many Israeli Palestinians (Arabs with Israeli citizenship) in the period between 1948 and 1967. The relevant article in these Regulations, Article 108 of Part 10 ("Restriction Order, Police Supervision, Detention and Deportation") reads as follows:

> An order shall not be made by the High Commissioner or by a Military Commander under this part in respect of any person unless the High Commissioner or the Military Commander, as the case may be, is of the opinion that it is necessary or expedient to make the order for securing the public safety, the defense of Palestine, the maintenance of public order or the suppression of mutiny, rebellion or riot.[26]

During the 1960s and 1970s, when Israel applied this policy to the West Bank and Gaza extensively, many Palestinians were deported without due process and without being able to appeal to the Israeli Supreme Court. In the late 1970s, due to international pressure caused by revelations of the widespread practice of torture in Israeli jails, precise appeal procedures

241

were established to promote the appearance of strict adherence to British laws Israel claimed to be in effect. It was during these appeal hearings that one began to hear arguments questioning the applicability of the British laws. Arguments presented by the Israeli side in the landmark 1979 case of *Abu Awad vs. the Israeli Defense Forces Commander of Judea and Samaria* became a precedent used later to bolster the standing of British law in Jordanian territory. The Israelis claimed that the Jordanian government continued to apply the 1945 British Emergency Regulations through a proclamation to that effect (Proclamation No. 2) made by the Jordanian Military Commander of the Arab Legion, on May 19, 1948, which read:

> All laws and regulations in force in Palestine at the end of the Mandate, on 15 May 1948, shall remain in force throughout the regions occupied by the Arab Jordanian Army . . . , save where that is inconsistent with any provisions of the Defense of Trans-Jordan Law, 1935, or with any Regulations or Orders issued thereunder.[27]

The Israeli Supreme Court held, in this case, that the defense failed to present any evidence supporting the contention that the Defense of Trans-Jordan Law had been contravened, and, therefore, the Emergency Regulations remain valid. The Court further argued that the Jordanian Constitution of 1952 failed to repeal the Emergency Regulations, and that this enabled the Israeli authorities to apply the Regulations by virtue of the Israeli Military Commander's Proclamation No. 2. The aforementioned Israeli proclamation was made on June 7, 1967, and stated that "The law in existence in the Region on June 7, 1967, shall remain in force."[28]

The strongest refutation of this argument was presented by Palestinian advocate Aziz Shehadeh, an authority on Jordanian law, who clarified the status of the 1945 Defense Regulations in Jordanian law during the deportation hearings of Mayors Muhammad Milhem of Halhoul and Fahed Qawasmeh of Hebron. These hearings were held before the Israeli Supreme Court in 1980. Shehadeh claimed that on May 13, 1948, King Abdullah of Jordan extended the provisions of the Trans-Jordan Defense Laws of 1935 to areas that the Jordanian Army will control. In a proclamation issued a few days later by the Jordanian Commander in Palestine, it was clearly stated that the British Regulations would be reinstated, except where they contravene the Trans-Jordan Law of 1935 or "any regulations or Orders issued thereunder." Shehadeh argued that "the regulations that remained in force are those regulations which were issued by virtue of the Palestine ordinances. These regulations, however, do not include those regulations that were put into force by virtue of the Palestine Orders in Council."[29]

Shehadeh also insisted that the Jordanian Constitution of 1952 did not in any way refer to the 1945 Defense Regulations. Neither were the Regulations ever used by the Jordanian Government after 1948, since all defense regulations and orders issued during the Jordanian regime were based on the Jordanian Defense Law of 1935. As stated during the *Abu Awad* case, the Israeli government claimed that Article 9 (1) of the Jordanian Constitution, prohibiting the deportation of Jordanian citizens, cannot supersede a previous emergency regulation. But Shehadeh argued that whenever the Jordanian Supreme Court was confronted with two conflicting laws, it automatically upheld the laws of the higher body. In this case, the higher law would definitely be the Jordanian Constitution.

Summarizing his argument, Shehadeh, the Palestinian advocate, concluded that the Jordanian Defense Law of 1935 applied to the West Bank, but not the Palestine Defense Regulations of 1945. He added that the Jordanian Defense Law does not sanction the deportation of people of the area. This position is strengthened by a similar prohibition in the 1952 Jordanian Constitution. The Israeli authorities, however, deported the two Palestinian mayors on the grounds that emergency regulations can only be cancelled "explicitly and by name."[30] The Israelis conveniently forget the condemnation of the Emergency Regulations levelled by their own experts during the Mandate years. In the words of Dr. Bernard Joseph (later the Israeli Minister of Justice) before a 1946 conference of the Lawyers Association in Tel Aviv: "With regard to the Defense Laws, the question is: Are we all to become the victims of officially licensed terrorism, or will the freedom of the individual prevail?"[31] The use of the word "terrorism" here is to be noted.

Armed with its own interpretation of which laws apply and which do not apply in the occupied territories, Israeli policy towards the occupied West Bank and Gaza (the Syrian Golan Heights were illegally annexed in 1981) evolved as an iron-fisted regime totally in opposition to the spirit of the Geneva Civilian Convention. The four Geneva Conventions were an expansion on the past achievement of the Hague Convention IV of 1907 and its Annexed Regulations which attempted to humanize the law of war. The Conventions consider individuals under the occupation of a foreign state to be "protected persons" (Fourth Convention, Article 4). Under the designation of "protected persons," these people are protected from:

(1) physical pressure for the purpose of obtaining information, (2) collective punishment, (3) individual or mass forcible transfers, (4) destruction of property not necessitated by military operations, and (5) changing the status of public officials.

The Israeli government has denied that the Geneva Conventions are applicable to the occupied territories, but it has permitted the International Committee of the Red Cross to operate "on an *ad hoc* basis." Yet certain articles of those conventions cannot be overlooked. Article 49 of the Fourth Geneva Convention, for instance, prohibits the transfer or deportation of the civilian population in order to discourage actions similar to the mass deportation of Jews during World War II.[32] Yet deportations are a common practice in the occupied territories and are freely acknowledged by the government and its information agencies. During the Palestinian civilian uprising, which began in December of 1987, Israeli Foreign Minister, Shimon Peres, told an interviewer:

> The Israeli government or the Israeli army is operating under two different laws—the Israeli law, that does not permit deportation, and the Jordanian law, which recognizes deportations as a very important punishment. Now since Israel, even in the occupied territories . . . does not use, never, capital punishment, the most we can do is to deport, in accordance with the law of the land, the law of the West Bank.[33]

Deportations, furthermore, have been used as a punishment for political activity and have been employed as a device to remove the leadership ranks of the occupied Palestinian population. Often, the deportees suffer this punishment after having served their prison sentences, thus suffering double punishment. A large number of deportees are expelled merely for the crime of "infiltration," or having missed the registration deadline for the 1967 census. Nor does the deportation policy spare the Palestinian residents of the annexed eastern half of Jerusalem, since they are still technically Jordanians.

The flagrant disregard of international law here can be illustrated by instances when the Israeli Government deported Gaza citizens to Jordan and West Bank citizens to Lebanon. Jordan never ruled Gaza and Lebanon never ruled over the West Bank. Prominent deportees over the years have included the President of the Muslim Supreme Court, a prominent journalist, the Mayor of Jordanian Jerusalem, the President of Birzeit University, the Mayors of Halhoul and Hebron, and prominent union leaders. Along with deportation, some political activists who attempted non-military yet organized resistance to the occupation have suffered imprison-ment and even torture.[34]

Israel's deportation policy, nevertheless, does not prevent it from relying on international law when the need arises. The District Court of Jerusalem invoked certain sections of the Geneva Conventions in its 1961 judgment in the case against Adolf Eichmann, *The Attorney General of the Government of Israel vs. Eichmann.* The Court even stated that Israeli law is not in conflict with the principles of international law. But, in actuality, the Israeli Gov-ernment has found an ingenious way of circumventing the Conventions, by first signing them before an international organization, but then prevent-ing their passage in the Knesset. Deportations are still a common practice, although clearly outlawed by the 1907 Hague Regulations, the 1945 UN Charter, the 1946 Judgment of the Nuremberg Military Tribunal, and the Fourth Geneva Convention, all of which are legally binding on Israel.[35]

The Palestinian civilian uprising, which began in December, 1987, added another twist to this issue. Confronting the prospect of massive and hastily convened trials for those seized during the disturbances, some Is-raeli sectors began to call for civilian trials. Fearful of the international repercussions of continued use of the Defense Regulations in the trials of young and unarmed civilians, some Israelis began to question the wisdom of maintaining this military legal system in the occupied areas. The Israeli Defense Force Judge Advocate, General Amnon Straschnow, responded by warning that holding the trials in civilian courts has great implications for the political status of the territories. To establish a civil judicial system, he maintained, would negate the occupation regime itself.[36] In the eyes of many, Israeli practices are a form of legal terrorism. As Eqbal Ahmad ex-plained the phenomenon of official, state-sponsored terrorism:

> The more serious examples are set by governments. When practiced and sup-ported by powerful states, terrorism is legitimized as an instrument of attaining political objectives. It is no coincidence that international terrorism came in vogue during history's most televised, hence most visible, super-power inter-vention; in Indo-China. But the lessons of Vietnam went unheeded. Today, those who condemn terrorism are among its primary sponsors.[37]

Other forms of illegal behavior on the part of the Israeli authorities have involved various forms of annexation, removal of the original population from their land, collective punishment, massive destruction of property, and the erection of illegal settlements on occupied land. Among the better known acts of annexation was the *de jure* annexation of East Jerusalem in

1967, the *de jure* annexation of the Golan Heights in 1981, and the *de facto* annexation of over 50 percent of land in the occupied territories through the illegal settlement movement. The annexation of land is made possible through the use of Article 125 of the Defense Regulations of 1945, which gives Israeli military governors the power to restrict freedom of movement by declaring certain areas "closed": not to be entered without permission. Articles 109 and 110 of the same Regulations empower the military governor to restrict possession and the right to leave a location.

The Emergency Articles for the Exploitation of Palestinian Lands have been used extensively to expropriate lands in favor of Jewish settlements on the West Bank and Gaza. The Israeli Minister of Agriculture can take possession of uncultivated lands to insure their cultivation. The Minister of Defense assists in this scheme by declaring an area closed for defense purposes or security reasons, sometimes simply because the landowner has been expelled or deported. When the landowner attempts to return, he or she is forbidden to do so without a written permit from the military governor who can deny, and often does so, access to the land for purely military reasons. When the land lies fallow for several years, the Minister of Agriculture then seizes it because it is "uncultivated" and usually hands it over to Israeli settlers.[38]

Among the better known acts of massive destruction of property was the 1967 demolition of Arab homes adjoining the Western Wall (the Wailing Wall) of the Dome of the Rock, which rendered 4,000 Arabs homeless. This act was undertaken in order to create more open space for Jewish worshippers. The 1967 destruction of the Arab villages of Yalu, Imwas, and Beit Nuba (in the Jerusalem area) was followed by the creation of a recreation area in the same vicinity, named Canada Park. The destruction of the Biblical village of Imwas (or Emmaus) caught the attention of British journalist Michael Adams, who recorded its story in *Chaos or Rebirth*. The well-known 1948 dynamiting of the two northern villages of Iqrit and Bir'im was only among the most famous in a series of village destructions spanning the entire history of Israel. The International Committee of the Red Cross has also described, based on eyewitness accounts of its members, the dynamiting of the Syrian town of Quneitra before returning it to the Syrian Government in 1974.[39]

It should be evident from the above that Israel's illegal policies in the occupied West Bank and Gaza are motivated by more than just a desire for strategic security. Israel's penchant for annexation and population removal is clearly related to its determination to create more room for a steady stream of Jewish immigrants. This itself is based on a dubious legal concept known as "the Jewish people entity." A Zionist idea, "the Jewish people" concept was first articulated by the Jewish Agency (the effective government of the Jewish community of Palestine during the Mandate period) before the creation of the state. This Zionist organization succeeded over the years, through Israeli statutes, in transforming the religious meaning of the term "Jewish people" into a secular, juridical term. As such, the term was applied to the "Jewish people" inside Israel, whereby they became the recipients of privileges and rights denied to other non-Jewish Israeli citizens.

When applied to people outside of Israel, the term "Jewish people" became a vehicle for the establishment of a juridical link with the state of Israel, with or without their consent. The concept was used during the Eichmann trial, when the Israeli District Court stated that "the connection between the Jewish people and the state of Israel constitutes an integral part of the law of nations."[40] Should the UN General Assembly recognize this discriminatory concept, it would constitute a violation of Articles 55 and 56 of the UN Charter. Article 55 states that "the United Nations shall promote . . . universal respect for, and observance of, human rights and fundamental freedoms for all without distinction as to race, sex, language or religion." In a letter dated April 20, 1964 from US Secretary Talbot to Dr. Elmer Berger, Executive President of the American Council of Judaism (a non-Zionist body), the American official rejected explicitly the validity of this concept:

> The Department of State recognizes the State of Israel as a Sovereign State and recognizes citizenship of the State of Israel. It recognizes no other sovereignty or citizenship in connection therewith. It does not recognize a legal political relationship based upon the religious identification of American citizens. It does not in any way discriminate among American citizens upon the basis of their religion. Accordingly, it should be clear that the Department of State does not regard the Jewish people concept as a concept of international law.[41]

Israeli domestic legislation bearing on this subject dates to the earliest days of the state, the most important being the following four fundamental laws:

1. The Law of Declaration of the Establishment of the State on May 14, 1948, stating that the state of Israel exists not only for people residing on its territory, but for all Jews.
2. The Law of Return of 1950, which established a perpetual open door for Jews everywhere wishing to return to their "homeland."

3. The Nazi Acts and Nazi Collaboration Punishment Law of 1950, which authorizes punishment by the state of Israel against anyone accused of crimes against *the Jewish nation*. This legislation defines "crimes" as any harm directed at Jews, even the incitement of hatred towards Jews.
4. The Nationality Law of 1952, which sanctions the automatic granting of citizenship to Jews who come to Israel, unless they declare on the day before their arrival their disinterest in exchanging their existing citizenship for an Israeli one.[42]

The vast implications of this doctrine, especially the Law of Return, for the Palestinians cannot be overlooked. It has, over the years, impelled the Israelis to drive out as many Palestinians as possible in order to make room for more Jews. Legislative enactments such as the aforementioned laws illustrate the futility of arguing the finer points of international law protecting an occupied population when the ruling power uses the fiction of legality to achieve its own legal objectives. Shlomo Avineri, Professor of Political Science at Hebrew University, commented recently on Israel's denial of Palestinian rights to a homeland:

> The problem is that when we say 'morality' we have not said anything, for we have no idea what morality is acceptable to the entire world. . . .
>
> The main argument is between universalist views, which contend that there is not one standard for me and another for you, and attitudes which ultimately apply different moral standards towards different people or groups. For example, Golda Meir once said that she did not understand the right of Palestinian refugees to demand their homeland, when some of them were second- or third-generation refugees and had never been in Palestine.
>
> Clearly, Golda did not grasp how untenable this view was on the part of one belonging to a people asking to return to its homeland after 80 generations, not two or three.[43]

The PLO's willingness to trade the status of a rebel movement for that of an internationally recognized national liberation movement has been in evidence since 1974. However, only third world nations inside and outside the UN have accepted this change readily. The PLO's stature within the UN improved dramatically, but the Western powers, primarily the US, have continued to demand total Palestinian surrender to Israel's security needs. The price of accepting the Palestinian people's inalienable right to statehood and security was, literally, nothing less than the voluntary obliteration of the PLO in favor of a tame and pliable Palestinian leadership.

The period of 1974 to 1988 should be viewed as a contest of wills between a seasoned and hardened Palestinian leadership and a Western community of states devoid of any sympathy for anti-colonial struggles. Palestinian gains within the international forum of states were frozen by the reality of Western opposition and resistance. The deadlock was finally broken by the PLO itself, which seized the initiative by unilaterally recognizing Israel in hopes of gaining recognition for itself and sympathy for the unarmed rebels of the *intifada*. Not surprisingly, the US hesitated before finally succumbing to world pressure generated by Arafat's unilateral recognition and unequivocal renunciation of terrorism.

Israel's response to the PLO's bold strategy of peace amounted to insistence on further conditions before accepting the olive branch. One of these conditions was a demand for compliance with its own definition of terrorism. The PLO's reiteration of its right to continue with the armed struggle until the occupation is ended was seized upon as further proof of Palestinian duplicity and treachery. Thus, the issues of who are the terrorists and what is terrorism remain at the root of the conflict. This is despite a large body of international documentation supporting the right of the occupied to resist and carry out "the justifiable war of self-defense."

The Israelis have survived and prospered in direct proportion to their ability to enforce their own laws whenever and wherever possible. Always suspicious of the role of international peace-keeping agencies in the area, the Israelis consistently obstruct the international rule of law. More than any other state alongside its borders, Israel's concern for its strategic security overrides any desire it might have to ingratiate itself to world public opinion. Not since the UN Partition Resolution of 1947 and the subsequent battle for legitimacy and recognition within the UN did Israel attempt reconciling itself to laws other than its own. Its emphasis on maximum security along its borders has led to an active policy of massive retaliations, demolition of homes, and building of illegal settlements on land not yet annexed to them.

Often ignoring laws passed by the UN, of which it is a member, Israel has relied instead on the dubious legality of such concepts as "the Jewish people" and the "Land of Israel." If Israel's short history proves anything, it is that states can often defy UN resolutions and international morality and still retain their membership in the world body. This, of course, does not augur well for the future of the world organization or of the peace-loving nations of the world.

14

Statehood, Recognition, and the Politics of Peace

IBRAHIM ABU-LUGHOD

1

On the seventieth anniversary of Britain's military occupation of Palestine, the Palestinians of **central Palestine** (the so-called West Bank) and Gaza engaged in an *intifada* unprecedented in Palestinian history in its scope, militancy, and comprehensiveness. It was in December 1917 that General Allenby, then commander of the British Forces, who were theoretically "allied" with the Arabs led by the Sharif Husayn of Mecca, victoriously entered Palestine. While the Arabs, acting upon their understanding of the terms of their alliance with Britain, thought that the British would soon hand them the affairs of Palestine, in actuality Britain had already pledged itself (in the Balfour Declaration of November 2, 1917) to support the establishment of a national home for the Jewish people in Palestine. Regardless of the conflicting interpretations attached to that pledge, what became readily obvious to the Palestinians was that their right to self-determination as a national community, acknowledged in the Covenant of the League of Nations in 1919, was not on Britain's agenda.[1] The initial and purposeful British violation of the Palestinian right to self-determination was inherited by Israel when it was proclaimed in 1948 on part of Palestine. As Britain's role in that denial passed into history, Israel, particularly with its 1967 occupation of the West Bank and Gaza, which had remained under Arab control after 1948, became the chief colonial power thwarting Palestinian self-determination. Thus the *intifada* signified once more Palestinian determination to end Israel's colonial control of their lives and land, and achieve independence and sovereignty; equally significantly the *intifada* ushered in an unprecedented era in the politics of the Palestinian-Israeli conflict. It enabled the Palestinian people, acting through their highest legislative authority, the Palestine National Council, to articulate and launch its policy of peace in the new context of statehood

250

and recognition, relying on the politics of mutuality and acceptance of the other. That, broadly speaking, marks a new era in the historic encounter between Palestinian Arab and Israeli Jew. The chief characteristic of this new era is the increasing acceptance and legitimacy being accorded to the Palestinian striving for symmetry in the relationship between Palestine's two hostile communities.

2

Palestine acquired a definite geo-political connotation and status once the British colonial administration assumed full power and control; the new geopolitical status and the exercise of Britain's mandatory control was legitimated by the League of Nations (1922). The Palestinian national movement acquiesced and dealt with the British colonial administration *de facto;* but the Mandate was never accorded *de jure* recognition by the Palestinians nor were its terms or control ever uncontested by the national movement. The initial encounter in Palestine was essentially one between a Palestinian Arab national movement that sought national independence— in that it was similar to all other Afro-Asian independence movements— and the British colonial administration. But it was also more than an ordinary independence movement for the colonizer had already promised to "facilitate the establishment of a national home for the Jewish people"; the promise was enshrined in the terms of the Mandate laid down by the League of Nations. That, in the view of the Palestinians, entailed their permanent subordination by denying them their right to self-determination, including independent statehood. The Palestinian movement, then and later on, was unwilling to accept in any form the Zionist claim of a historic connection between Palestine and the European Jews (which was partially used to rationalize the Balfour Declaration) for whom Zionism spoke. The struggle between the Palestinians and the British colonial administration was thus compounded by the British commitment to Zionism and the Palestinian rejection of both—Britain's control and Zionism. The Palestinian rejection of Zionism and what it entailed in terms of the potential transformation of Palestine to a Jewish national home grew in intensity as the demographic and land ratios—Palestinian Arab to European Jewish—in Palestine began to undergo serious change, especially in the thirties.[2] Whereas the early Palestinian rejection conveyed to the Mandate was premised on an anticipated grave outcome, by the thirties the danger to the Palestinians was more real and concrete. The acuteness of that danger in some measure underlay the last major revolt of the Palestinians, *al-Thawra al-Arabiyya al-Kubra*, the Great Arab Revolt of 1936–39 during the Mandate period. The aim of the revolt was to compel the Mandate administration to rescind the Balfour Declaration, to halt Jewish immigration, to curtail land transfers to Zionists, and of course to declare Palestine an independent sovereign state.

Two issues are important to highlight in connection with that struggle. In view of the serious transformation that occurred already in Palestine, the Palestinian movement attenuated its policy of rejection of Zionism by confining that rejection to the political aspirations of the Jewish community *in situ*. Testifying before the Royal Commission (chaired by Lord Peel) dispatched to Palestine to examine the causes of the revolt, the Palestinian leadership was quite clear about the political objective of the Palestinians and their perspective on the Jews. They sought independence for Palestine and accepted the right of Jews already settled on the land to live in Palestine as citizens of the demanded independent Palestinian state. The leadership then made it abundantly clear that what they had in mind was an Arab state of Palestine in which European Jews who had settled, legally or illegally, on the land—in spite of expressed Palestinian objection—would constitute a confessional minority; their position and status would be similar to that of Jews in other Arab countries. Whether that entailed full equality of citizenship was neither amplified nor ever tested.[3]

Generally speaking, the Palestinian leadership, even after the British army crushed the Arab Revolt of 1936–39, continued to hold on to the major principles of a solution to the conflict premised upon an independent Palestinian state; in that state different ethno/religious communities would coexist but an Arab majority would clearly determine both the character and distribution of power in the state. Only a minority, represented by the bi-national Communist Party of Palestine, advocated early-on a State premised on full equality of individual rights—thus negating a possible national or ethno/religious basis of the potential Palestinian polity.

The second issue about which the leadership was explicit in its statement to the Royal Commission was its perspective on immigration and land transfer. They called for an unconditional termination of all Jewish immigration and requested the Mandate authorities to halt land transfer to Jewish companies or individuals. British failure to do so, the leadership strongly hinted, would entail continuation of the Revolt. It was widely perceived that immigration and land transfer in the final analysis jeopardized the Palestinian right to self-determination. The Zionist perspective on the relationship between Palestine's two communities was clearly much more complex. After all, the Zionists of the Mandate period knew what an earlier generation of European Zionists—external to the land of Palestine—either ignored, pretended to ignore, or deliberately distorted. They knew that the Palestinian Arab community was now conscious of the political implication of the Zionist program, and that the Palestinian community was organized politically and gave every indication of opposing both the Mandate and its Zionist protege. Thus the Zionist solution to the conflict was much more complicated in its public presentation; it had to take into account the Palestinians, the Europeans, including Britain and the League of Nations, as well as Zionism's actual or potential Jewish constituencies. On the one hand the Zionists insisted all along on the need of the Jewish people for "a homeland" in Palestine (which, in their early perspective, included Mandatory Palestine as well as Transjordan). Although they did not, in the early stages, equate a homeland with statehood, all three parties to the conflict understood it that way. On the other hand, the Zionist movement showed considerable tactical flexibility in the presentation of its political program.

From the standpoint of the relationship of the two people on the land it is interesting to note how ambiguously expressed was the Zionist perspective on the role and right of the Palestinian Arabs. The mainstream Zionists—Labor, Mapam, General Zionists, etc.—either ignored or actively opposed altogether the specific political aspirations of the Palestinians for independent statehood; effectively and consistently they opposed the Palestinian right to self-determination. And while they campaigned for a Jewish homeland one searches in vain for a clear statement on the position or status of the Palestine Arabs in that homeland. Of course Herzl's original formulation would have entailed "transfer" of the Palestinians to the adjacent countries.[4] But nowhere did the Zionists actually say that in a projected homeland or state the Palestinians would continue to live on their own land and become, as it were, citizens (equal or otherwise) of the new state. On the other hand, they did not present a scheme for their actual "transfer" as Herzl thought. Still, it should be noted that the Zionist leadership was pleased with the Royal Commission's recommendation that the Palestinian Arabs in the projected Jewish state to be established in partitioned Palestine be "exchanged" for the Jews of the projected Arab state. The reason the Zionist leadership welcomed the proposal was that the exchange would have resulted in the eviction of over 200,000 Palestinian Arabs from the projected Jewish state whereas the Jews who would be removed from the Arab state would hardly exceed two thousand persons! Be that as it may, it is fair to indicate that the Zionist leadership was principally concerned with the Jewish homeland/state. When they spoke of coexistence with Arabs (irrespective of the modality of that coexistence) that did not signify a commitment to coexistence with Palestinian Arabs in the projected Jewish state. All that indicated was coexistence of the projected Jewish state with the Arab countries. The exception to this perspective was that proposed by the Revisionist leader Vladimir Jabotinsky. He was quite clear in his view of the destiny of the Palestinian Arabs. Testifying before the same Royal Commission, he stated publicly and clearly that the Arabs would have to accept their eventual status as a "national" minority in a clearly Jewish state. Interestingly, while he thought that it was a hardship for the Jews to live as a national minority anywhere, he certainly did not consider it a hardship for the Palestinian Arabs to exist as a national minority in the Jewish state (which, according to his testimony, would be established in both Palestine and Transjordan).[5] He confirmed what the Palestinians feared most at that time: that the intention of the Zionists was in fact to ingather Jewish immigrants, acquire sufficient Palestinian land to accommodate the new immigrants, and thus transform the basic character and structure of Palestine and achieve Jewish statehood. The achievement of these would result in the subordination of the Palestinians.

The Palestinians were unable to establish the Palestinian Arab state in 1948; Palestine's Jewish community, with considerable external European/American support, succeeded in proclaiming the state of Israel. The violent encounter in 1948 resulted in the forced exodus of approximately half of Palestine's Arab population (close to 800,000) from its normal places of residence. Only a very small minority of about 150,000 remained within Israel's control.[6] Since then Israel has opposed the repatriation of these expellees; while Palestinians in Israel acquired its nationality, their position and status is clearly one of subordination legally and socioeconomically. Equally important, Israel has maintained and reinforced the historical Zionist rejection of the Palestinian right to self-determination in their own national homeland.

It is now possible to characterize the asymmetrical perspectives that governed the politics of the two communities up to and through the first serious break in Palestinian history, 1948. Each community delegitimized and opposed the specific political aspiration of the other to establish an independent state either in the whole or in part of Palestine. Thus, at the political level, both engaged in what I have described elsewhere as the politics of negation; and in that kind of intercommunal politics there was symmetry. At no point in the period of the Mandate did either community accept the validity of the claim of the other for independence and sovereignty in Palestine. The rejection was mutual.

The relationship was also asymmetrical; the asymmetry applied to the perception of the other as a people, as a cultural community. Whereas the Palestinians gradually adapted to the Jewish presence in Palestine—by 1948 Palestine's Jewish community constituted approximately one third of the total population—and tried to accommodate that presence politically, the Zionists, with some exceptions, either denied the Palestinians their cultural identity as a people or denied the legitimacy of their presence in Palestine. It was the historic Zionist contention that the Arab population of Palestine is part of the Arab people as a whole and thus has a homeland other than Palestine. Its presence in Palestine was directly related to the expanded economic opportunities made possible by Jewish immigration.

3

The emergence of the Arab-Israeli conflict in 1948 and its subsequent development had the effect of politically marginalizing the Palestinians. The discourse on the issue, certainly in Western literature, showed awareness of or sensitivity to the Palestinians specifically as refugees; as such they constituted a "problem" for which a solution should and could be found. Israel insisted throughout that the refugees should be settled elsewhere and denied any responsibility for their fate. For Israel, the refugees were an issue of concern to and for the Arab states. Since 1948, Israel dealt, and insisted on dealing, with various Arab states to resolve any and all issues underlying the Palestine-Israel conflict.[7] Although Israel's historic insistence on dealing with one or another of the Arab states to resolve the question of Palestine could be explained politically, it also reflects the historic Zionist negation of the Palestinians as a people, culture, and potential political community.

The reemergence of the Palestinian as the crucial factor in the Arab-Israeli conflict is associated directly with the first political initiative that the Palestinians undertook in the post 1948 dismemberment of Palestine. That initiative made it possible for the Palestinian people, who by then had come under the control of Israel and of different Arab states, to form the Palestine Liberation Organization in 1964. Within less than ten years the Palestine Liberation Organization acquired national, regional, and international legitimacy as the representative of the Palestinian people.[8] It is to the policies and expressions of the Palestine Liberation Organization that one needs to turn to determine the Palestinian perspective on both Israel and the Israeli Jewish presence in Palestine in the context of a seriously transformed geopolitical reality.

Much has been said about the Palestine National Charter; it will be recalled that the Palestine National Council adopted the Charter in 1964 and slightly amended it in 1969. For all practical purposes the Charter became the basic constitutional document that enabled the Palestine Liberation Organization to pursue its policies to retrieve Palestinian national rights. What concerns us now are those expressions in the Charter that reflect the attitudes, values, and policies of the Palestinians regarding both Israel and the future of Israel's Jewish population in the context of the Palestinian struggle for liberation. Specific articles in the Charter reaffirmed the Palestinian historic negation of the Balfour Declaration, the Mandate, and the entire structure of the Mandatory policies; other articles quite clearly reaffirmed the Palestinian rejection of the results of the Mandate and in particular viewed the establishment of Israel as being contrary to the Palestinian right to self-determination. Thus the call for "liberation" and the possible political transformation of the territory was understood then to imply the establishment of a Palestinian state that would displace the state of Israel—which at that time did not include the so-called West Bank and Gaza—and thus would undo one of the most egregious consequences of the illegally established British Mandate.[9] The Palestinian rejection was and remained a political rejection of Israeli statehood. In other words, the radical transformation of Palestine that produced Israel, a Jordanian West Bank, an Egyptian-administered Gaza Strip, and a Palestinian community in exile had no appreciable impact on the Palestinian political view of their adversary. The Palestinian denial of Israel's legitimacy was of course reciprocated at that time by Israel's denial of the legitimacy of the Palestinian aspiration for statehood and the return of the Palestinians to their homes and lands in Palestine.

Quite clearly there was symmetry in their mutual rejection. Yet the asymmetry noted earlier survived into the new era of the sixties and seventies. The 1969 Palestinian call for a democratic non-confessional state in Palestine and its amplification by Yasser Arafat, Chairman of the Executive Committee of the Palestine Liberation Organization, in his speech before the General Assembly of the United Nations in November 1974 conveyed an entirely new conception of coexistence between the two people; Arafat effectively and clearly called for the peaceful coexistence of all Palestinian Arabs and all Israeli Jews within the same polity, to be established in Palestine. There was no ambiguity about the equal status of all people irrespective of confession in the polity called for by Arafat. It is of course true that Arafat was negating the state of Israel as a Jewish state, but what was new in his appeal was the explicit acceptance of Israeli Jews—irrespective of how they came to reside in Palestine/Israel—as equal citizens in the potential Palestinian polity. It should also be pointed out that the call for a democratic non-confessional state would have the effect of negating any cultural or ethnic character for the projected Palestinian polity.

Despite Israel's strong rejection of both Arafat's statement and the political program upon which it was based, we must accord that statement its due political significance. Had it not been for the gradual acceptance of the Israeli Jewish reality in Palestine, which Mr. Arafat's statement acknowledged, the very specific political programs that were advanced subsequently by the Palestinian national movement would not have been possible. The political programs adopted by the National Council beginning in 1974, and elaborated, specified, and clarified in various sessions between 1977–87, reflect a clear evolution in the Palestinian perspective on Israel and Israeli Jews. This trend led inevitably to the adoption by the Council of the Political Program of 1988 and the Palestinian Declaration of Independence. It is to this very significant evolution and its implications that we should now turn.

4

When the Palestine National Council met in Cairo in the summer of 1974 in the wake of the October 1973 war, it became evident that the Palestine Liberation Organization was prepared to move in political directions that had not previously been contemplated. After considerable and heated debate the Council adopted what came to be known as the Transitional Program,[10] which in its essence came to terms with the reality of Israel without according it legitimacy.

The call for the establishment of a national authority on any territory to be "evacuated" by or "liberation" from Israel was a major policy statement whose political significance was understood by the proponents as well as the opponents of the program. Until then the Palestinians, under the leadership of the Palestine Liberation Organization, had pursued a policy of liberation that was predicated upon a strategy of armed struggle—as the

National Charter ordained—and had affirmed that the only way Palestinian rights could be retrieved was by mass mobilization and protracted war. Palestinians, through organized political/militant movements and parties, engaged in a variety of militant actions that brought considerable international attention to their cause, placing them once more at the center of the Arab-Israeli conflict and obtaining for them international—especially third world—and regional support. Yet it was clear in 1974 that the Palestinians would not be able to achieve their political goals without the active commitment and support of the Arab states. It is important to point out that the Palestine National Council adopted the Transitional Program in 1974 subsequent to and taking into account the revised strategy of the Arab states.

It had become clear, especially in negotiations with the United States, that the Arab states felt confident that in the wake of their credible military and political/economic performance of 1973, they would be able to reach a political settlement of the Arab-Israeli conflict, something that had eluded them since they committed themselves to that course at the Khartoum Summit Conference in 1967. The Arab political strategy, which assumed the possibility of the withdrawal of Israel's army of occupation from the territories occupied in 1967 (and the possible implementation of the "legitimate rights of the Palestinian people") suggested to the Palestinians that their own strategy of "liberation" would have to be seriously revamped and synchronized with the Arab strategy even if they continue to engage in limited guerrilla activity. In an important way, the Transitional Program's adoption by the Palestinian movement reflected their assessment that it was feasible for the Palestinians to reach their political goal of self-determination by a combination of political and militant means.

Such an outcome, if successful, clearly entailed an alteration of the Palestinian perspective not only on the Jewish presence in Palestine, but more significantly on the issue of Israel as a state in part of Palestine. It is important to bear in mind that at that time Israel was in full, even though contested, control of Palestine—Israel, the West Bank, and Gaza. Thus the Transitional Program signalled that the Palestinian movement was willing to discuss and negotiate Israel's withdrawal from the West Bank and Gaza (or any parts thereof), that Israel's consent for withdrawal from Palestinian territory and transfer of power to the Palestinians was necessary and, no matter how ambiguously stated, that the Palestinians were dealing *de facto* with an Israeli state. One cannot understand the subsequent political programs of the Palestine Liberation Organization and its creeping recognition of Israel without understanding the significance of the adoption of the Transitional Program. It was the opening gambit that led inexorably to the politics of acceptance enunciated cautiously by the Palestine National Council in November 1988. Chairman Arafat expressed Palestinian accommodation more explicitly in his address to the General Assembly of the United Nations and in his press conferences in Geneva on December 13 and 14, 1988.[11]

5

A careful reading of the political statements issued by the Palestine National Council at the conclusion of its various sessions held subsequent to the adoption of the Transitional Program clearly reveals the tremendous evolution in the political stance of the Palestinian movement, particularly on the crucial issues of Israel, interaction between Palestinian Arabs and Israeli Jews, and the political aspiration of the Palestinian people. Beginning with the Cairo 1977 session, the Council endorsed the principle of Palestinian independence in the West Bank and Gaza, endorsed positive interaction with Israeli Jews of different political persuasions, including Zionists, and edged toward *de facto* acceptance of the territoriality of Israel. The political formulation of the Council made it possible for Palestinians and others sympathetic to their perspective to claim that the call for the establishment of a Palestinian state in the West Bank and Gaza entailed the acceptance of a political settlement premised on the existence of two states in the land of Palestine—the so-called two-state solution. The same formulation made it possible formally and informally for Palestinians and Israelis to meet and seek means to resolve their historic conflict. The dialogue between officials of the Palestine Liberation Organization and willing Israeli counterparts would not have been possible without the blessing of the Palestine National Council. It is also important to note that the international peace initiatives launched by the Palestine Liberation Organization pursuant to the resolutions adopted by the National Council in Cairo in 1977 were predicated on those principles.

Israel's response to these positive developments within the Palestinian movement reflected its commitment to pursue its historic policy of negation. It held on firmly to its denial of the right of the Palestinians to self-determination; it denied the right of the Palestinians to be represented by the Palestine Liberation Organization, and denied them their right to independence and sovereignty in any part of Palestine. Its proposed alternatives revolved around the achievement of a political settlement with Jordan (the so-called Jordanian option) or the provision of "autonomy" for the inhabitants of the West Bank and Gaza. When Israel did not deny the existence of the Palestinians as a people (as Golda Meir did in 1969) it denied them their right to form an independent political community on their own land. Clearly such a policy of negation could not achieve a settlement; hence Israel's policy of repression of the Palestinians under occupation and its attacks on the Palestinians outside Palestine (the invasion of Lebanon and the air raids against various Palestinian establishments and premises).

The asymmetrical relationship became more glaring as increasing frankness began to characterize official Palestinian policies and expressions prior to the outbreak of the *intifada*. The major policy initiative that the Palestine Liberation Organization undertook after Israel's devastating invasion of Lebanon was connected with the International Conference on Palestine, held in Geneva in 1983. The Conference called for the convening of a United Nations sponsored peace conference to be attended by all parties to the conflict—including the Palestine Liberation Organization on an equal footing. The peace conference would be convened on the basis of all relevant resolutions of the United Nations and would have as its principal aim the achievement of a comprehensive settlement of the Arab-Israeli and Palestinian conflicts. The call for that conference was endorsed by the General Assembly of the United Nations in the fall of 1983. It was understood by all member states of the United Nations—including both friends and opponents of the Palestine Liberation Organization—that such a conference implied a two-state solution to the Palestine-Israel conflict and that the site of the would-be Palestinian state was the West Bank and Gaza. A careful analysis of Yasser Arafat's statements, especially after the Amman Accords with King Hussein and the Algiers 1987 session of the Palestine National Council,[12] clearly reveals the Palestinian commitment to achieve a comprehensive settlement with Israel in the context of an international peace conference and on the basis of internationally accepted resolutions. Arafat's policy pronouncements, which appeared in his interviews published in *The New York Review of Books*,[13] for example, clearly reveal the Palestinian willingness to engage in the politics of mutual acceptance and to reach a peaceful settlement with Israel on the basis of the existence of two states and the implementation of internationally accepted resolutions pertaining to refugees. Arafat's appeal for a peaceful political settlement met with the usual cynical and negative response of Israel.

6

Israel's policy of political negation of any Palestinian initiatives, coupled with a policy of terrible repression, exploitation, and continuing dispossession of the Palestinians, eventually led to the *intifada* of the Palestinians in the West Bank and Gaza. A careful reading of the directives and communiques issued by the leadership of the uprising reveals two important issues: first, the Palestinians' absolute determination to bring Israel's colonial control of their lives and land to an end; second, their wish to be independent on their own land and achieve a political settlement with Israel. Despite Israel's attempts at distorting the political significance of the uprising, it became clear to all parties concerned that a successful political settlement is not only feasible but, perhaps more significantly, the only possible alternative to the current repressive impasse. For a settlement to happen, Israel and its supporters will have to negotiate with the Palestine Liberation Organization. Conscious of the need to stimulate a process of negotiation through an international peace conference, the Palestine National Council, at its session in Algiers in November 1988, adopted the historic Declaration of Independence and the enabling political resolutions.[14] These became the basis for the policy of peace that the Palestine Liberation Organization is actively promoting today. The Palestinian peace policy is predicated upon a mutually acceptable coexistence of two people and two states in the land of Palestine. Only in this manner can the need of the two peoples for secure national and cultural identity, justice, and equality be realized. To break out of its impasse, Israel must finally respond positively to the Palestinian peace policy and enter into the negotiating process envisaged in the International Peace Conference. When that happens, the historic contribution of the *intifada* to peace-making will be complete. And once more the historic role of the victim as the initiator of peace will be reaffirmed.

15

Intifada *and Independence*

EDWARD W. SAID

1

The Palestinian uprising or *intifada* on the West Bank and Gaza is said to have begun on December 9, 1987. A month earlier an Arab summit meeting in Amman had resolved the usual moral support for the cause of Palestine, although the various kings and presidents had also indicated that their primary interest was not Palestine but the Iran-Iraq war. This partial demotion of Palestine was gleefully noted by commentators in the United States, who were led by the usual "experts" (Daniel Pipes, Thomas Friedman, et al.) ever ready to portray Yasser Arafat as a bumbling scoundrel, grinning his way from one failure to another. What seems to have escaped "expert" and official Israeli notice was that the occupied territories had already had twenty years of a regime designed to suppress, humiliate and perpetually disenfranchise Palestinians, and that the likelihood of an outside force actually improving the situation had gradually disappeared. Instead the situation for Palestinians had gotten worse, and their sense of embattled loneliness, even abandonment, had increased. Capitulation was impossible. An intensification of resistance therefore seemed required and with it, greater discipline, more determination, and enhanced independence of method, planning, and action.

In discussing the unfolding *intifada* (note that this is the one of the few Arabic words to enter the vocabulary of twentieth century world politics) we are in fact talking about two dynamics, one internal to Palestinian life under Israeli domination, the other external, in which the Palestinian exile presence has interacted dialectically with regional and international powers. Consider first the internal situation. Alone of the territories occupied by Israel in 1967, the West Bank and Gaza remained in an unforgiving limbo of local repression and frozen political process. Sinai was returned to Egypt in 1980, the Golan Heights and East Jerusalem were formally annexed by Israel, a change in status hardly welcomed by the Syrians and Palestinians who lived in those places, but at least the annexation represented a new dynamic. In the meantime, more settlements were established on the West Bank and Gaza, more land expropriated. After municipal elections on the West Bank (not in Gaza) overwhelmingly returned pro-PLO candidates in the spring of 1976, the officials were summarily dismissed. Whenever leaders emerged they were either imprisoned, killed, or maimed by Jewish terrorists, or they were simply expelled.

And always, the expropriations of land, the increasingly tight control over water, the perpetual encroachments of Jewish settlements pressed down on Palestinians in the territories, which after 1977 became known as "administered" lands, renamed "Judea and Samaria." The Camp David accords as interpreted by the Israelis and the US opened no avenue of independence, only a series of pointless negotiations with phantom Palestinian "inhabitants" from the occupied territories who could never be identified or promised anything. There were occasional, and quite unsuccessful, attempts to empower collaborationist Palestinians (e.g., the Village Leagues) who would perhaps be more amenable to Israeli wishes, but those never acquired anything like the credibility needed to swing a critical mass of Palestinians behind them. After a time they were dropped and forgotten.

Although it was frequently referred to as a benign occupation, the Israeli presence on the West Bank and Gaza hurt more and more people as time passed. Students were forced to endure the extended closing of schools and universities. Workers who depended on intermittent piecework inside Israel for their livelihood faced daily reminders of their subservient status; they were paid less than Jewish workers, they had no union to support them, they were required to be kept under lock and key anytime they stayed overnight inside the Green Line. Some were burned alive as a consequence, many others referred to themselves as "slaves." There was a proliferation of over a thousand laws and regulations designed not only to enforce the subaltern, rightless position of Palestinians under Israeli jurisdiction, but also to rub their noses in the mud, to humiliate and remind them of how they were doomed to less-than-human status. Books by the thousands were banned. The colors of the Palestinian flag were outlawed; even the word "Palestine" could earn its user a jail sentence. Administrative detentions were common, as were the dynamiting of houses, torture, collective punishments and harassments, complete with rituals of dehumanizing behavior forced upon unarmed Palestinians. Yet Palestinians on the

West Bank and Gaza were required to pay Israeli taxes (but had no one to represent them), to submit to the gradually more and more cruel whims of settlers who did what they wanted with impunity, to face their alienation from their own land. To plant a tree required a permit. To hold meetings also required a permit. Entry and exit required permits. To start a well required a permit—one that was never given.

None of these horrific things went completely unnoticed. A fair number of Israelis protested them, and the Israeli press, notable, by and large, for its independence recorded them. Various groupings—the Israeli League for Human Rights, chaired by the unflagging Professor Israel Shahak, the small bands of peace activists sometimes including Peace Now, a handful of writers, academics, intellectuals, Knesset members—signalled the world that outrages were taking place. But the massive political, economic, and military support of the United States enabled things to go on as usual. The outrages continued (in fact they increased) and with them, the powerful propaganda and justifying rhetoric of those whom Noam Chomsky has called "the supporters of Israel" went forward unabated. By the early months of the first Reagan administration it became clear that there was nothing Israel might do, from unmercifully punishing Palestinians under its rule to invading countries all around it, that the US would not support. Aid levels went up tremendously, so that aside from the direct budget-to-budget support that Israel (uniquely of all the countries that receive US foreign aid) was assured of (all of it paid at the beginning of the fiscal year), in amounts that exceeded one third of the total US foreign aid budget ($3 billion in 1988), there were other kinds of unprecedented and blanket deals made. A strategic partnership was devised between the two countries: Israel was accorded favored nation trading status; previous debts were forgiven; a huge variety of intelligence, military, and political liaisons were established; US taxes were waived on Israeli securities, bonds, and funds. Not for nothing, then, did the head of AIPAC, Tom Dine, say in early 1987 that never had the US (and especially the Congress) been more pro-Israeli than now.

People in the US who had made a practice of speaking up for human rights everywhere in the world, and particularly in countries within the Soviet sphere, simply said nothing about the appalling situation created by the Israeli occupation. Yet the alternative sources of information—in contrast to the mainstream US media's shameless pandering to the Israeli lobby, as described by Robert I. Friedman in *Mother Jones*, June 1988—kept up the monitoring of the internal situation. Here mention must be made of local groups such as Law in the Service of Man, a group of Palestinian lawyers; the West Bank Data Project, funded by the Ford Foundation and directed by Meron Benvenisti; the Alternative Information Center in Jerusalem; and Raymonda Tawil's Palestine Press Service, whose courageous and objective efforts to record, and occasionally contest, human rights abuses from murder to land expropriation made it impossible to pretend that no one knew what, in fact, was going on in the name of democratic, freedom-loving Israel.

By the second Reagan administration a sizeable amount of Israeli revisionist historical research had exposed the much longer record of Zionist attitudes and practices toward the Palestinians. As the truth about 1948 and 1949 came to light—thanks to the efforts of Tom Segev, Simha Flapan, Benni Morris, Avi Shlaim and others—a remarkable coincidence between these historians' research and the testimony of three generations of Palestinians was clear. More to the point, there emerged a perceptible continuity between Zionist theories and actions before as well as after 1967. The occupation—for all its deliberate and programmatic humiliation of Palestinians, its bare-knuckled attempts to rob a whole people of nationhood, identity, and history, its systematic assault on civil institutions and vulnerabilities—could be seen as extending the logic of earlier Zionists like Ben-Gurion, Herzl, and Jabotinsky into the present. Far from revealing a defensive strategy of self-protection against extermination and annulment this logic instead showed a political and state philosophy relentlessly on the offensive, spurning Arab overtures for peace, attacking civilians undeterred by compassion or understanding, pretending all along that Israel was engaged in a fight for its survival. In this context, the protestations of Israel's idealistic friends that Zionism's early spirit was being corrupted and betrayed by Israeli occupation methods, sounded both indecent and unconvincing.

It was the terrible force of these realities that Palestinians under occupation resisted; the symbols of the *intifada*—the stone-throwing children—starkly represented the very ground of the Palestinian protest. With their stones and an unbent political will these children stood fearlessly against the rows of well-armed Israeli soldiers, backed up by one of the world's mightiest defense establishments (the Israeli military buying mission in the US alone had a $25 million per annum administrative budget), bank-rolled unflinchingly and unquestioningly by the world's wealthiest nation, supported faithfully and smilingly by a whole apparatus of intellectual lackeys. The occupation had lasted for twenty years without a single change for the better. Life was more difficult. Israelis were less interested in peace and coexistence. The US, the other Arabs, even putative allies like the Soviet Union seemed paralyzed by that mixture of foregone hypocrisy and benevolent hand-wringing that always contributed to sustaining the occupation still longer. Therefore the time had come to start trying to change realities, from the bottom up. On 18 December 1987, the well-known Syrian poet Nizar Qabbani produced his brilliant ode to *Atfal al-Hajarah* (Children of the Stones) and in characterizing their dazzling gesture of revolt, he also pinned down the cafe-haunting, nouveaux-riche merchants, commission-agents, polygamous princes, intellectuals, and rulers whose exploits in London and Cannes had in fact produced the *jil al-khiyanah* (generation of treason) that surrounded and still continued to exploit the Palestinian cause.

But, as I said, the *intifada* also has its antecedents in the external, that is exile, situation of those dispossessed and dispersed Palestinians who were driven from their lands in 1948 and 1967. By 1969 the Palestine Liberation Organization and its constituent groups had emerged as a mobilizing force not only for Palestinians but for a whole generation of Arabs—intellectuals, young people, and politically influential activists, for whom the fall of Abdel Nasser and his unionist style of Arab nationalism had to be replaced with a political vision more capable of implementation and defense after the disasters of 1967. An early motto of the Palestinian movement was the ideal of establishing a secular democratic unitary state in all of Palestine; this attracted much attention in the Arab world, first because of its intrinsic merits as a notion that rose beyond the crippling inhibitions imposed on whole populations by Zionism on the one hand and small-scale state nationalisms in the Arab world on the other. Also implied in the secular-democratic-state concept was a political and social program that would liberate people from the legacy of imperialism, in which partitions, make-shift state boundaries, and top-heavy national security states produced neither the true independence nor the political actualities for which earlier generations had so strenuously fought.

In the period of 1969–74 Palestinians had disastrous encounters with Arab state authority, in Jordan and Lebanon, principally. This revealed the defensiveness of standing regimes as well as uncritical fidelity to ethnic or resurgent religious nationalism. The secular state idea was slowly abandoned. In 1974 at the Palestine National Council (PNC) meeting, a new notion was put forward, first by the Democratic Front. It was then espoused by Fatah, and Arafat in particular. Palestinian nationalism had to be recuperated immediately by a Palestinian national authority; thus, as the PNC resolutions began to put it, any portion of land liberated from Israeli occupation should go directly under the independent jurisdiction of a Palestinian "national authority." Also in 1974 Arafat came to the UN to offer his peace plan, having earlier in the year gained an Arab Summit consensus that the PLO was "the sole legitimate representative of the Palestinian people."

Thus a new trajectory was established toward the idea of partitioning Palestine, although the word *partition* was never uttered, and the program of a two-state solution was frequently both unclear and often diverted. The PLO remained committed to "liberation" at the same time that the highest Palestinian authority—the PNC—had begun to speak of political (as opposed to "military" or "armed struggle") measures in furtherance of its national objectives. While it remained fixed explicitly on the complete liberation of Palestine, the PLO seemed to indicate a preference for the political independence of a Palestinian state. In time the liberation idea almost slipped from sight, although it remained as a historical *cum* rhetorical gesture, for after all, most Palestinians were not from the territories occupied by Israel in 1967, and their loss had to find a commemorative place somewhere in the concrete actualities of Palestinian life. Moreover the UN's General Assembly, the non-aligned movement, the socialist block, and the Islamic conference had begun to show accelerating interest in Palestinian statehood, inalienable rights, and so on. So while the international context showed a clear improvement in the Palestinian national status, and pointed it toward a Palestinian state on a part of Palestine alongside Israel, some Palestinians, some Arab states, Israel, and the US engaged in furious battle in which civil war (Lebanon), invasion (Israel's massive interventions in Lebanon, from the early 1970s until the great campaign of 1982), inter-Arab imbroglios (the aftermath of Camp David, the contest with Syria's Hafez al-Assad from 1976 to the present), and Palestinian insurrections (1983–85), were aimed ultimately at curtailing or on the other hand capturing the still potent symbol of "Palestine," which remained the greatest central foreign policy issue of the entire Arab world. During this period it was the PLO, Fatah, and Yasser Arafat that provided the focus for the gradually emerging and finally unmistakable double-sided idea that Palestinians had to arrive at their vision of their own future *on their own*, and that this vision, while theirs, had also (somehow) to conform to the international consensus (or "international legality" as the going phrase became in 1988).

Any history of the period, then, would have to concentrate on the relentless and unevenly matched fight between Israel and its supporters on the one hand, and Palestinian nationalism and its supporters on the other. At issue were not just the political claims to self-determination of the latter, but the very idea of Palestine itself. The military contours of this fight had immense scope. Thus, for example, when Israel invaded Lebanon in full force in 1982, producing not only the horrors of the siege of Beirut but also the massacres of Sabra and Shatila (described with oxymoronic double-speak by the Israeli court of inquiry as showing the "indirect responsibility" of the Israeli army in charge), it was openly admitted by Israeli spokespeople at the time that (1) the real battle was for the West Bank and Gaza, and that the PLO had to be destroyed utterly because of its representative status and (2) that because it had become internationally "responsible," having observed a UN-monitored truce on the Israeli-Lebanon border for eleven months before June 1982, the PLO had to be attacked. Israel's US-supported attacks on Tunis (October 1985) and its assassination of Abu Jihad (April 1988) in his home there showed the almost limitless extent to which Israel would go in combatting any independent Palestinian force.

Not that there were no defections from the basically hard Likud line, always reinforced with astonishing complaisance by the Reagan administration whose perennial "green light" was never turned off. There were. New configurations appeared within Israel expressing all sorts of doubt about Israeli policy in Lebanon (the southern part of whose territory continued to be occupied even as I write), in the occupied territories, and in the third world generally, in which support for discredited regimes was, it seemed, a vital order of business for the Israeli military-industrial complex. Similarly, in Western Europe and the United States, whose support of Israel had traditionally been one of the cornerstones of liberal and Jewish public opinion after World War II, the less and less friendly questioning of Israeli policy proceeded apace. Important symbols in the erosion of the wholesale approval of Israel were Arafat's meetings with the Pope, the slow but sure support given Palestinian positions by the European Community, and the mounting authority of Zionist Jews critical of Israeli policy (Nahum Goldmann, Pierre Mendes-France, Philip Klutznick, and Bruno Kreisky were early leaders of this trend).

Yet throughout it was the Reagan administration's active cooperation with Israeli intransigence and its hostility to Palestinian aspirations, human rights, and life itself that characterized the environment external to Palestine. Some of the milestones were the moral permissiveness that—from Alexander Haig to George Schultz—the US accorded to Israel's adventures outside its borders; the astounding additions to the US dole to Israel after one or another of that country's particularly horrific exploits ($450 million added immediately after Sabra and Shatila and $180 million on the very day in December 1988 when Reagan admonished the Israelis about expulsion and killing of Palestinians); the almost grotesque congruence between Israeli and US positions on "terrorism," which became the watchword of US policy in the second Reagan administration. In fine, we can say with Christopher Hitchens that the complete "Israelization" of US foreign policy occurred, so that by the penultimate year of Reagan's tenure Israel had become the US's main strategic ally east of the English Channel.

With what horrendous cost to Palestinian civilians—most of them refugees—one can scarcely say even at this point. Over 20,000 Palestinians and Lebanese were killed by Israeli troops in the summer of 1982 alone. How many more in the occupied territories and elsewhere were punished by Israel—the reports of torture were internationally known at least since the mid-1970s—through imprisonment, expulsion, maiming, killing, loss of property and freedom, it is difficult to say, but the figures that now exist are awful. They show something like a ratio of one hundred Palestinians killed for every Israeli killed (this in the midst of an appallingly mindless chorus led by Israel about the scourge of Palestinian "terrorism") and, according to Alexander Cockburn, approximately one out of every sixty-six Palestinians imprisoned (roughly ten times the average figure for blacks under the South African regime). During the *intifada* more Palestinians proportionate to the population were killed by Israeli soldiers than were US soldiers during the Korean and Vietnam wars combined. All of this was part of an orchestrated campaign to exterminate Palestinians as a political presence in Palestine. To Begin they were "two-legged vermin"; to General Eytan they were "drugged roaches in a bottle"; to Shamir they were "grasshoppers"; to politer spokespeople, Palestinians were "the Arabs of Judea and Samaria"; to the New York *Times* they were simply "Arabs."

Even so, the Palestinian political line grew clearer and clearer. This is a major irony. In the US, Arafat and the PLO were remorselessly and repeatedly attacked by a supine media and an Israeli-dominated policy elite for terrorism, extremism, rejectionism, and hostility to democracy; in the Arab world attacks on Arafat (which led to a whole mutinous movement within Fatah ranks in 1983, eagerly financed by Syria) were fueled by charges that he was a capitulationist, that he had conceded too much to his enemies, that he had given up armed for political struggle (the distinction in the Palestinian context was fatuous, but it had great emotional staying power nonetheless). The PNC, for its part, stayed on course. In 1984 it was convened despite enormous Syrian pressure in Amman. Once again the partitionist idea—with Jordanian confederation—was implicitly accepted. A new alliance was forged with Jordan in 1985 and 1986, precisely to accommodate Palestinian nationalism to the international consensus, now unambiguously upheld by Gorbachev's Soviet Union. All the Arab states, with the exception of Syria and Libya, had come around to the two-state view, although few actually said it publicly. Then came the criminal war of the Beirut refugee camps sponsored by Syria between 1985 and 1988. Arafat and his people were being constantly pressured by Syria and its pocket insurgents. Threats from the US (which had aggressed against Libya in 1981 and 1986, as it was to do again in 1989); the deepening Palestinian gloom on the West Bank and Gaza; the indifference of the Arabs, the endless Lebanese crisis; the rise of an anarchical Islamic movement; the hemorrhaging effect of the Iran-Iraq war; the ceaseless enterprise of the Israeli-US axis (as symbolized throughout 1986 and 1987 by Iran-Contra and the campaign against Nicaragua); the absence of reliable Arab and strategic allies: all these took a severe toll from the Palestinian drive led by the PLO.

It remains impressive, I think, that the Palestinian center acquired more, not less, authority from its constituents. In April 1987 a PNC meeting held in Algiers stressed that an international conference and negotiations there were the desired means to end the dispute with Israel. Jordan had already defected from its alliance with the PLO, the result (said Palestinians) of US pressure. At regular intervals, but with sharper clarity after 1984, Arafat stated his willingness to meet with Israelis, to negotiate a peaceful settlement, to end the longstanding conflict. His remarks were either not reported or they were scorned. And meanwhile the situation on the West Bank and Gaza kept getting worse. Talk of "transfer" became widespread. Rabbi Meir Kahane, with his explicitly racist, but unimpeachably frank, claim that Israel couldn't both be Jewish and democratic, attracted attention, grew more popular. Isolated incidents (the moronically criminal hijacking of the *Achille Lauro* in 1985, the Rome and Vienna airport massacres) were treated as "trends," whereas the assault on Palestinian rights literally everywhere, but especially in the US, Lebanon, and the occupied territories were ignored. When it finally erupted, the *intifada* was treated by the media (and the Israelis) as a law and order problem; the historical and political context was refused and unreported.

A number of things occurring in the US stand out as a small part of the international background for the *intifada*. In early 1988 a group of Palestinians in Los Angeles, legal residents all, were indicted under the Smith-McCarran Act for subversion and threatened with expulsion. We must remember that a US-Palestinian citizen, Alex Odeh, had been assassinated in the same area less than three years before, yet none of his well-known assailants were apprehended. During the previous winter, Congress had passed the so-called Grassley Amendment (in effect, a Bill of Attainder) invidiously pointing the finger at the PLO, alone among all world organizations, as "terrorist." It closed the Palestine Information Office in Washington and threatened the PLO's UN observer mission with termination. The Los Angeles indictment and the Grassley Amendment were fought, and were ultimately defeated, but they showed how deep was the official US hatred of the Palestinians, how far the government was willing to go in forgiving Israel everything it did and punishing Palestinians for their mere existence, how arrogantly the administration dismissed the Arab position, and Arab humanity itself.

Despite all the protestations about freedom of the press, public discussion about the Palestinian people dominated and carried by the media remained at a remarkably low and degraded level. Aside from "terrorism," a notion never carefully defined or even reflected upon, Palestinians were described by such basically condemnatory and confining categories as extremist (as opposed to moderates, who never seemed in evidence), rejectionist, and faction-ridden (despite the fact that the overwhelming preponderance of the PLO stood behind the centralist consensus). Israel was routinely referred to in terms indicating morality and flexibility. Among "dovish" Zionists in the West and Israel (chief among them Yehoshofat Harkabi, Arthur Herzberg, and Abba Eban) Palestinians were referred to in the scandalously racist framework of "a demographic problem," the suggestion being that too many Palestinians were a threat to Israel's Jewishness (or "purity," as the more honest of this group put it). In all such instances I am reminded of W. E. B. Dubois's answer to the question put to him as an American Black, "How does it feel to be a problem?" "It is," he said, "a very strange experience." For in fact the entire tenor of Zionist and Western discourse about the Palestinians has been to reduce us to so problematic, eccentric, and unthinkable a level as to make our every effort to appear to

271

be human only a confirmation of our dehumanized, permanently subaltern status. This has been the conceptual coefficient of the war against Palestinians led in the West by the supporters of Israel.

Faced with such an array of pressure, real threats, and actual punishment, the Palestinian will was mobilized, and by the end of 1987 it had reached the threshold of pain it could no longer endure. The shadow line had to be crossed, and whether or not the crossing actually took place on December 9, that quickly became the date when, as the Palestinian journalist Makram Makhoul reported, fear was forbidden, and the stones were taken up. From now on there was to be no turning back, as the Palestinian sense of irreversibility took hold: the occupation had to end, political independence had to be declared, the sacrifice had to be made. After King Hussein had withdrawn his faltering and unpopular claims to the West Bank in late July 1988, the die was cast. A PNC would have to be convened, the Palestinian claims would have to be put forward, not in vague terms but in the accents of a movement bent upon national statehood.

2

The nineteenth session of the Palestine National Council (November 12–15, 1988), formally entitled the *"intifada* meeting," was momentous and in many great and small ways, unprecedented. Held in Algiers, there were fewer hangers-on, groupies, and "observers" than ever before. Security was tighter and more unpleasant than during the 1987 PNC session, also held in Algiers; Algeria had just had its own brutally suppressed *intifada* in the autumn of 1988, so the presence of several hundred Palestinians and at least 1,200 members of the press was not especially welcomed by the Ben Jadid government, which paradoxically needed the event to restore some of its tarnished revolutionary lustre. This was also to be the shortest PNC meeting ever held. Barely three and a half days long, it accomplished more by way of debate, discussion, resolutions, and announcement than any Palestinian meeting in the post-1948 period. Above all, this PNC secured for Yasser Arafat the certainty of his place in Palestinian and world history for, as one member put it, "We're not only living through a Palestinian revolution; it's also Abu Ammar's [Yasser Arafat's] revolution."

None of the approximately 380 members came to Algiers with any illusion that Palestinians could once again get away simply with creative ambiguity or with solid affirmations of the need to struggle. The *intifada's* momentum and its ability to have created a clear civil alternative to the Israeli occupation regime now necessitated a definitive statement by the PNC of support for the *intifada* as an end-to-occupation and relatively non-violent movement. This required an unambiguous claim for Palestinian sovereignty on whatever Palestinian territories were to be vacated by the occupation. Together with this, there also had to be an equally unambiguous statement on peaceful resolution of the conflict between Palestinian Arabs and Israeli Jews based on UN Resolutions 181 (partition), 242, and 338. In short, the PNC was asking of itself nothing less than emphatic transformation: from liberation movement to independence movement. Jordan's recent withdrawal of claims for the West Bank made the need for transformation urgent and compelling.

If you live in the US, participating in Palestinian discussions, debates, and soul-searching reappraisals is particularly poignant. Palestinians meet rarely enough, given the widespread dispersion among our five million people, and the fact that we have no center, no territorial sovereignty of our own, makes our distance from each other in the midst of a US society whose government's hostility to us seems to be limitless, a continuously frustrating experience. Tunis serves the role of occasional headquarters, but since Abu Jihad's assassination, Arafat's presence has necessarily been fitful and erratic. Still, most of us in the PNC made at least one trip there; many documents and drafts went through fax, express mail, or over the phone. The date of the PNC kept getting postponed, but it was definitively set by late October, not without trepidation, since Algeria's internal volatility remained high.

PNC members were to be quartered in bungalows adjacent to the enormous meeting hall set in a conference-cum-vacation center built by Ben Bella in 1965, approximately thirty miles west of Algiers. Four of us travelled together overnight to Paris from New York, transferred from de Gaulle to Orly airport, and arrived in Algiers at 2:00 P.M. on November 11. Ibrahim Abu-Lughod and I were driven off to one bungalow only to find it already occupied; a second choice turned up the same fact, so we settled for a downtown hotel, which came to mean no hot food and hardly any sleep for three and a half days, as we commuted back and forth at the craziest hours. Despite jet lag, we went back to the conference center late that Friday night to call on Arafat, who seemed involved in three concurrently running meetings. He was confident but looked tired. Everyone knew that this was his step, first to articulate, then to persuade everyone to take, then finally to choreograph politically. He handed me the Arabic draft of the declaration of statehood and asked me to render it into English. It had been drafted by committee, then rewritten by Mahmoud Dar-wish, then, alas, covered with often ludicrously clumsy insertions, and in-explicable deletions. Later Darwish told me that the phrase "collective memory" had been struck by the Old Man because, we both opined, he took it for a poetic phrase. "Tell him it has a serious and even scientific meaning," Darwish implored me. "Maybe he'll listen to you." He didn't, and I didn't listen to Arafat when he wanted other phrases from other con-texts inserted.

Nobody was to see these texts until much later, and indeed perhaps the oddest part of this PNC—with its obsessive post-modern rhetorical anx-ieties—was how the two main documents (the declaration of statehood and the political resolutions) were discussed in public debates for hours on end without a piece of paper before us. After the opening ceremonies on Saturday the PNC divided itself into two committees, the Political and the *Intifada*. Arafat had the texts memorized, and Nabil Shaath, adroit chair-man of the Political Committee, had them before him. All significant dis-cussion about what we were doing took place in the riveting atmosphere of that Committee, with speaker after speaker sounding off on what after all was the most significant political moment in Palestinian life since 1948. Words, commas, semicolons, and paragraphs were the common talk of each recess, as if we were attending a convention of grammarians.

The heart of the discussions occurred in the speeches given late Sunday and mid-afternoon on Monday by George Habash and Abu Iyad (Salah Khalaf) respectively, the first an opponent of the by-now well-known sub-stance of the political program, the second, Arafat's key supporter and one of the main leaders of Fatah. Habash's expressed reservations concerned the clear acceptance of 242 and 338, resolutions unfriendly to us not only because they treat us only as "refugees," but also because they contained an implicit pre-negotiating recognition of Israel. This, Habash said, was going too far too soon; there had been agreement that such tough issues as recognition, 242, borders, etc., would be handled at the international conference. Why, Habash asked, was it so necessary to go forward on everything *before* the conference? He spoke passionately and clearly, say-ing without hesitation that he and the Popular Front wished to remain within the PLO, no matter what the outcome or the disagreements. To which, in a meandering and yet always fascinating speech, Abu Iyad re-sponded by saying that decisions had to be made now, in the face of the discouraging realities of the Israeli elections, because our people needed an immediate, concrete statement of our goals. What clinched it for me as

I listened to Abu Iyad was the logic of his thesis that decisive clarity was needed from us principally for ourselves and our friends, not because our enemies kept hectoring us to make more concessions.

Arafat remained throughout the debate, occasionally intervening, and yet maintaining his office, so to speak, from his seat in the house; an endless stream of secretaries, delegates, messengers, and experts came to him, and yet he seemed attuned to every phrase uttered in the hall. He had told me early on that he had planned the Declaration proclamation to occur shortly after midnight on November 15, after a whole night's debate on November 14. By about 9:30 P.M. on Monday November 14, the political program had been passed by large majority in the Political Committee, and immediately afterwards, the whole PNC was reconvened in plenary session. Habash and his supporters fought each sentence almost word by word on the crucial 242/338 paragraph, which was voted on in different forms half a dozen times. The somewhat garbled paragraph that resulted shows the effect of these battles in its ungainly phraseology, although the actual substance remains unmistakable. At one point Arafat stood up and recited the entire program from memory, indicating, as the Chair hadn't done, where the clause, sentence, and paragraph breaks occurred, so that there could be no mistake about meaning, emphasis, or conclusion. For the first time in PNC history, voting by acclamation wasn't going to be enough; Habash insisted on precise tallies, which emerged to his disadvantage, 253 for, 46 against, 10 abstaining. There was a sad nostalgia to what he represented, since in effect by voting against him we were taking leave of the past as embodied in his defiant gestures. The declaration ceremonies that closed the meetings were jubilant, and yet somehow melancholy.

About this break with the past there could be no doubt whatever. Every one of the great events in December 1988—Arafat's meeting in Stockholm with five leading American Jews, his speech and press conference in Geneva at the UN, his explicit recognition of Israel, the beginning of a US-PLO dialogue—was made possible by the PNC's decisions and the break with the past. To declare statehood on the basis of Resolution 181 was first of all to say unequivocally that an Arab Palestinian and an Israeli state should coexist together in a partitioned Palestine. Self-determination would therefore be for two peoples, not just for one. Most of us there had grown up with the reality (lived and remembered) of Palestine as an Arab country, refusing to concede anything more than the exigency of a Jewish state, won at our expense in the loss of our land, our society, and literally uncountable numbers of lives. A million and a half of our compatriots were under brutal military occupation (as we met, the entire 650,000 people of Gaza were under total curfew), fighting tanks and fully armed soldiers with rocks and an unbending will. For the first time also, the declarations were implicitly recognizing a state that had offered us nothing whatever, except the by now empty formulas of Camp David or the openly racist threats of population "transfer."

The declaration of statehood spelled out principles of equality, mutuality, and social justice far in advance of anything in the region. Call them idealistic if you will, but better that than the remorseless sectarianism and xenophobia with which Palestinians have had to contend for these five decades. Then, too, the *principle* of partition was asserted, not the territories specified in the 1947 UN resolution. All of us felt that since Israel had *never* declared its boundaries, we could not declare ours now; better to negotiate the question of boundaries directly with Israel, and of a confederal relationship directly with Jordan, than to spell them out fruitlessly in advance. There was no doubt, however, that we were in fact discussing the territories occupied in 1967.

There was absolute clarity in speaking of a peaceful settlement to the conflict. "Armed struggle" does not appear in the binding Resolutions. Central to the Resolutions is a long and awkward sentence endorsing the international peace conference based on "UN Resolutions 242 and 338." The language surrounding acceptance of the UN Resolutions is a statement of the obvious, not a reservation about acceptance. For example, representation by the PLO on an equal footing with other parties, the aegis of the Security Council, the *implementation* of 242 and 338, the centrality of the Palestinian-Israeli conflict, the inalienable rights of the Palestinian people: all these are mentioned as the *context*, the history, the Palestinian interpretation of what we were accepting. This was especially necessary since 242 and 338 say literally nothing about the political actualities of the Palestinian people, which in 1967 seemed scarcely evident, except as the detritus of the Arab-Israeli June war.

The rejection of terrorism in all its forms (also asseverated in the Declaration) makes an emphatic distinction between resistance to occupation (to which Palestinians are entitled according to the UN Charter and international law) and indiscriminate violence whose aim is to terrorize civilians. Note that no all-purpose definition of terrorism exists today, one that has validity and impartiality of application internationally. Yet the PNC took a step that is unusual in its attempt to make distinctions between legitimate resistance and a proscribed indiscriminate violence of states or of individuals and groups. Also note that Israel has always arrogated to itself the right to attack civilians in the name of its security. These facts highlight the courage of what is ventured in the Palestinian statement.

Finally and most important, all the resolutions, however they are read, clearly intend willingness to *negotiate* directly. There are no disclaimers about the "Zionist entity," or about the legitimacy of Israeli representatives. All of the relevant passages about peace, partition, and statehood in the 1964 Palestinian National Convenant are flatly contradicted by the 1988 PNC Resolutions, which give their statement added, not lessened, force. All the refusals, attacks, and insults heaped on the Council's results, both by Israel and the usual array of US "experts," signifies consternation; clearly, the more Palestinians take responsible and realistic positions, the less acceptable they become, not just because Palestinians want peace, but because official Israel does not know what to do when peace is offered it. There is a dispiriting continuity here between the early days of Israel's existence when Ben-Gurion refused peace with the Arabs, and the all-out rejection trundled out today by Likud and Labor alike.

The point is not that the Council documents are perfect and complete, but that they must be interpreted as everyone in Algiers intended—as a beginning that signals a distinct break with the past, as an assertion of the willingness to make sacrifices in the interests of peace, as a definitive statement of the Palestinian acceptance of the international consensus. A few days before the Algiers meeting, Sharon appeared on Italian television vociferating loudly about the need to kill Arafat. That no comparable sentiment was expressed about Israeli leaders anytime in Algiers is a fact that furnishes its own eloquent comment on the real difference now between Israeli and Palestinian leaders. These are dangerous times for Palestinians; the occupation will get worse, and assassinations and fullscale political war will intensify. For once, however, the record is unmistakable as to who is for peace, who for bloodshed and suffering. But the Palestinian campaign for peace must be joined, since sitting on the sidelines is no longer any excuse.

What is difficult either to understand or condone is how the US media—quite unlike the rest of the world—has internalized the rejectionism promulgated by the Israeli and US establishments. Far from reading the texts as they were meant to be read, commentators persist in suggesting that whatever was said in the texts could not by definition be enough. On November 20 a major *New York Times* editorial accused the Palestinians of "gamesmanship and murkiness" in Algiers. The egregious A. M. Rosenthal ranted on (November 18) about "a cynical continuation of the Arab rejectionism of Israel," and the equally improbable George Will (*Washington Post*, November 20) said that the Algiers meetings were the equivalent of a Final Solution to Israel. Why is not Israel itself asked whether it is willing to coexist with a Palestinian state, or negotiate, or accept 242, or renounce violence, or recognize the PLO, or accept demilitarization, or allay Palestinian fears, or to stop killing civilians, or to end the occupation, or to answer any questions at all? Perhaps the US media will someday break their silence, as Palestinians and the rest of the world already have.

3

What so dramatically transpired after the Algiers PNC was also a direct result of the *intifada*, which in 1989 continues bravely in its second year. But if the political victories of the Palestinian people have been duly noted and even celebrated internationally, the profounder social and moral achievements of this amazingly anti-colonial insurrection require fuller acknowledgment.

People do not get courage to fight continually against as powerful an army as Israel's without some reservoir, some deeply and already present fund of bravery and revolutionary self-sacrifice. Palestinian history furnishes a long tradition of these, and the inhabitants of the West Bank and Gaza have provided themselves generously from it. Yet what is new is the focused will, the creative and voluntary nature of the people themselves. There has been no easy resort to weapons, for example, and no exercise in noisy, even if noble-sounding, rhetoric. Instead the leaflets of the *intifada* have been concise, concrete, and above all, implementable; each was a *nida'* or appeal, and neither an order nor a declaration. Above all the sense that the *intifada* demonstrated of a collectivity or community finding its way together is what was most impressive. The source of this is the organic nationhood that today underlies Palestinian life. For the first time Palestinians exposed themselves to it, allowed themselves to be guided by it directly, offered themselves to its imperatives. Instead of individuals and private interests, the public good and the collective will predominated. Leaders were never identified. Personalities were submerged in the group.

The *intifada* therefore accomplished a number of unprecedented things. In my opinion, the future of the Middle East as a whole is going to be influenced by them, and Palestine and Israel will never be the same again because of them. In the first place, collaborators with the occupation were encircled and gradually rendered ineffective, as the entire mass of people under occupation came together in a block that opposed occupation. Even the class of merchants and shopkeepers played a major role in this transformation. Secondly, the old social organizations that depended on notables, on family, on traditional hierarchy were all largely marginalized. A new set of institutions emerged, and in fields like health, education, food and water supply, and agriculture, these provided an *alternative* social organization to that dominated by the occupation regime. In short the new alternative social situation that emerged was national, independent, and the first step in the appearance of the Palestinian state announced formally in Algiers on November 15. Thirdly, the role of women was substantially altered. The Palestinian woman had been essentially a helper, a housewife, a secondary person in what was in effect a male society, as is the case throughout the Arab and Moslem world. During the *intifada*, however, women came to the fore as equal partners in the struggle. They confronted Israeli (male) troops; they shared in decision-making; they were no longer left at home, or given menial tasks, but they did what the men did, without fear or complexes. Perhaps it would be still more accurate to say that because of the *intifada*, the role of men was altered, from being dominant to becoming equal.

These are momentous changes and, as I said, they will surely have an effect throughout the Middle East as the twentieth century advances towards its end. In the meantime, however, 1989 presented a more concrete challenge. In the immense and understandable wave of euphoria that swept the Palestinian and Arab world as the US-PLO dialogue began, a number of other things were worthy of concern and attention. The Israeli government elected in November 1988 was composed of men whose hostility not just to Palestinian aspirations but to Palestinians as human beings is undying. Men like Rabin, Sharon, Netanyahu, Arens, and Shamir are the inheritors of a tradition of uncompromising brutality and lying, in which *all* means are justified so long as the end—Israeli ascendancy at the expense of Palestinian life itself—can be assured. Under the influence of these men during the last six weeks of 1988, the level of protests and of repression in the occupied territories increased significantly. On the other hand, the media has either been banned from reporting the facts or, as the case appears to be with the *New York Times*, it has deliberately chosen to downplay the ugliness of what is taking place. To fire into a funeral procession and kill four people, to shoot at a group of men quietly observing a moment of silence and kill three, to maim children, to put whole cities like Nablus and Gaza under twenty-four-hour curfew for several consecutive days, to humiliate and beat people at random, to destroy houses— all these are sickening examples of an Israeli policy that has escalated its violence against Palestinians, with insufficient or no notice taken of them by the mainstream influential Western media.

What *has* captured media attention is the process of negotiation by which, for instance, Yasser Arafat pronounced certain phrases and then received American recognition. Since that time Palestinian spokespeople have been on television, have been interviewed by the radio, have been quoted extensively by newspapers. All of that discussion has been political. What has been left out has been the paradox by which Palestinian moderation has been met with increasing Israeli intransigence and actual violence. I myself agree with the policy articulated and voted upon by the PNC. I am a member and I voted enthusiastically for a realistic and, above all, clear policy. I certainly do not advocate any retreat from what we decided to do politically in order to gain the independence of the state of Palestine. But what surprises and worries me is that those of us who live outside the occupied territories have had to minimize a good part of the moral claim on which we stand when, because of the limited opportunities offered us, we neglect to speak in detail about what is happening to our people on the West Bank and Gaza. I do not mean that we should speak only about what is being done to them by Israel but also what heroically they are doing for themselves.

Here is where the difficult and crucial role of detail becomes important. The struggle for Palestine has always been, as Chaim Weizmann once said, over one acre here, one goat there. Struggles are always won by details, by inches, by specifics, not only by big generalizations, large ideas, abstract concepts. Most of what the world now knows about daily life during the *intifada* is the result of (1) what the Palestinians under occupation have experienced minute by minute and (2) what has been reported about those experiences and achievements first by Palestinians and then by international agencies like the UN, Amnesty International, and concerned citizens' groups in Israel, Europe, and North America. Those of us Palestinians and Arabs who live outside Palestine—in exile or dispersion—have not been afforded enough time to testify to the daily details of life under occupation; we have therefore not impressed on the awareness or the conscience of the world what our people are suffering and how cruelly Israel has treated their aspirations. These details are what our struggle is all about: why, for example, should a Palestinian farmer require a permit to plant a new olive tree on his land, whereas a Jewish settler can do what he wishes on land expropriated from the Palestinian? This policy of persecution and discrimination is what we have contested and still do contest. It is more important a fact of our political lives than negotiating with a US ambassador in Tunis.

I am deeply concerned that in the glamorous search for recognition and negotiations we will lose the moral and cultural detail of our cause, which is a cause after all and not just a sordid game to control images, or to say the right phrases, or to meet and talk with the right people. The US (and in particular President Reagan and Secretary Shultz) has been supplying the Israeli army with the bullets that kill Palestinian men, women, and children. It is up to us—Palestinians and supporters of Palestinian rights— to formulate a policy that deals directly with *this* America, as well as the other America, represented by the many people who support Palestinian self-determination. Neither can be neglected. Most important of all, we cannot neglect to register and attest to the suffering and the greatness of the Palestinians under Israeli occupation, which this remarkable collection of essays does so well. Only by doing those two things will we become partners in the common struggle, and not onlookers or mere passive observers. Thus will the inside and outside become one.

PART 4

Concluding Thoughts

16

Solidarity with the Palestinian People: The Challenge to Jewish Theology

MARC H. ELLIS

On my last trip to Israel and Palestine I discovered what might be termed a dangerous and unholy alliance of ideas. The first part of this alliance, despite the overwhelming evidence to the contrary, was a pervasive belief among Jewish Israelis in their essential innocence on the Palestinian question. Though difficulties were admitted and even articulated at great length, the underlying sense, even among people to the left on the political spectrum, was that these errors were abberations to be corrected rather than fundamental questions to be pondered. The second part of this alliance was the belief, still held in the face of the uprising, that somehow the establishment and continuance of the state of Israel was part of the redemptive plan for the Jewish people. This was maintained by religious and secular Jewish Israelis, though articulated in different languages and symbols. There was a decidedly mystical aspect to the redemption: creating a Jewish state out of the barren desert and the ashes of Auschwitz; Jews deciding the fate of the Jewish people for the first time in almost two millennia; Jews speaking their common historical language in courts and classrooms and flying a flag that was distinctly their own.

But beyond the innocence and the redemption lay the third aspect, that is, Israel as the last stand of the Jewish people. This is the most difficult part to describe because in a sense it subverts the first two aspects, though when understood in depth, it stands as complementary rather than subversive. The ingathering of Jews from around the world, though much more limited than hoped for, represents a persistent theme in Jewish history as a movement toward completion and fulfillment of a suffering people. Hence, innocence and redemption. At the same time, though, it confirms another perhaps even deeper strand in the Jewish psyche, the sense of communal isolation in a hostile world, a righteous people embattled with those who dream of a world "cleansed" of Jews.

Thus Israel is seen as the last stand of the Jewish people, an enterprise taken up by the innocent as part of the redemption, yet somehow doomed. Images of Masada are everpresent here, Jews gathering together choosing the time of their own death rather than letting others choose for them, holding off the enemy beyond the appointed time, dying as free men and women rather than as slaves. But in the new scenario the "Romans," symbolically the persecutors of the Jews, die also. Anyone who knows the communal ethos and nuclear capacity of Israel understands the danger of such an image, and also knows that this image permeates Israeli society, religious and secular, conservative and liberal.

Like an unstable chemical compound, this association lurks in the background, often unnoticed and unarticulated, but reenforced by a world view that interprets events through this filter. This is why Prime Minister Shamir could interpret the proposed launching of the Palestinian ship, the Return, symbolizing the refugee status of the Palestinian people, as an act of war. It challenged Israel as innocent and redemptive while reminding Jewish Israelis that the world lacked understanding and was ultimately hostile. Clearly, in the mind of many Jewish Israelis and Jews around the world, Yasser Arafat and the Palestine Liberation Organization assume this symbolic role on a much broader scale. Coming to grips with Arafat and the PLO would be, in some ways, less a military and political reversal of long held views than a renunciation of an understanding of Jewish life that threatens to destroy us as a people: to demonize the Palestinian people reenforces innocence and redemption while continually informing Jews that there is no future for the Jewish people in a hostile world.

What the Jewish essays in this volume point to, without in any sense holding the essayists to this particular interpretation, is that these conceptions of innocence, redemption, and the lack of a future must be critically evaluated before it is too late. The essayists all agree in diverse ways that the first step in this process is admitting that we as a people are no longer innocent. Rabbi Irving Greenberg would place much of the onus for this loss of innocence on the surrounding Arab peoples, while Michael Lerner, Rabbi Arthur Hertzberg, and Judith Plaskow although agreeing in some measure with Greenberg, place more responsibility on a self-generated Israeli culpability. Here Israel is seen as, among many other things, expansionistic and self-serving.

Of course the loss of innocence also affects the sense of Israel as redemptive and here again Lerner, Hertzberg and Plaskow raise questions unspoken in the Jewish community for almost two decades. What if Israel represents less a redemption than a particular example of a Jewish attempt at survival after the Holocaust? Lerner and Hertzberg use strong evocative language in placing Israel in this larger scheme, at the same time asking whether or not the current policies of the Israeli government threaten to break apart the *raison d'être* of the post-Holocaust renewal of Jewish life.

The recognition that we, as Jews, are no longer innocent is linked to a second theme only hinted at in the essays: that we are humiliating a people as we were humiliated. Like the loss of our innocence, this is difficult to admit, for it means that the policies of land expropriation, educational limitations, deportations of Palestinian leadership, imprisonment without trial, the massive arbitrary beatings of youth, are attempts at destroying *and* humiliating a people. The Palestinians are the concrete impediment to the dream of the Greater Israel. Therefore they advise Jewish Israelis and Jews around the world that our redemption is covered with blood. The redemptive aspect of the state—of Jewish empowerment—includes the sinister necessity to humiliate others. Can our conscience be free of what we have done only when the Palestinian people are broken and driven from our sight? Is the innocence of our redemption assured only when the indigenous population is forced into and accepts a form of enslavement that recognizes Jewish Israelis as the sole and legitimate masters?

In a paradoxical way Palestinians are Israel's only bridge into the Middle East, to move a ghetto-like mentality into a larger, more creative framework with the peoples of the Middle East. Could it be, then, that by humiliating Palestinians, Jewish Israelis assume that whatever the political solutions arrived at, they will remain isolated and spurned and therefore within the last part of the unholy and dangerous alliance, the last stand of the Jewish people?

The call to end the occupation is a call to dismantle the trinity of innocence, redemption, and the last stand. Yet creating a framework for peace between Jewish Israelis and Palestinians demands more than critique, and here the essays again only hint at the need for a new foundation—a new way of understanding Jewish life in the Middle East. Jewish theology and ethics come into play, perhaps in a prominent way. If in fact the task of theology is to nurture the questions a people needs to ask about the history it is creating, then the task of Jewish theology is clear: to lay the theological groundwork for Jewish life beyond innocence, redemption, and the last stand. To look toward the end of Israel's sense of isolation and abandonment and toward a future of creative integration and independence is to propose what for most Jews seems to be the most paradoxical of options, that is, solidarity with the Palestinian people. One could go even further by stating that the task of Jewish theology is to lay the groundwork for solidarity with and ultimately an embrace of the Palestinian people. To move in this direction is to come face to face with our own history, perceptions, and symbols. It is to listen to those on the other side of Israeli power as a way of understanding who we have become. Those voices tell us many things we do not want to hear: they plead with us to stop the brutality inherent in occupation. At the same time, Palestinian voices hold open the possibility for Jewish Israelis and Jews around the world to change, to choose a new direction, to review our witness to ourselves and to the world.

Emmanuel Levinas, a French Jewish philosopher, wrote that "ethics arise out of the face of the other." This implies that the critique of the communal ethics arises in the same way, out of the face of the other, in this case, the Palestinian people. Could we say that the healing of our historical traumas might come about when we see in the faces of the Palestinian people our own faces, bloodied, humiliated yet bearing a great hope? This may be what Bishop George Khodre of Lebanon meant when he wrote during the height of the Lebanese war, "If Jews all around the world, could, in an expression of metahistorical generosity, announce the freedom of the Palestinian Arabs, dialogue between peoples of monotheistic faith would gain an opening on an existential level." This act of "metahistorical generosity" would mean the realization that the path we have chosen leads only to tragedy, and that another path is possible and must be chosen despite the crisis and the uncertainty. But it would also mean the realization that the path can be travelled only together with the Palestinian people.

The point here is that Jewish theology needs to affirm that the Palestinians are now a part of our history just as we are a part of the histories of those who in times past persecuted us. The attempt to banish Palestinians, through expulsion or even statehood—if the creation of the state is the way to insure that Jews will never have to see or interact with Palestinians again—is doomed to failure. Even if such banishment could be accomplished, the Jewish people would be left without healing and with a deeper sense of isolation. That the Palestinians are an intimate part of our history is hardly suggested by Greenberg, Lerner, or Hertzberg. Perhaps this is the next stage of Jewish theological expression, which no doubt awaits the end of the occupation.

Beyond Anti-Semitism and Philo-Semitism

ROSEMARY RADFORD RUETHER

In the last few years I have become increasingly involved in work for Palestinian human rights. This has drawn me into a lot of historical research on the history of the Zionist movement and on the state of Israel and its relation to Palestinians. It has also taken me on several trips to Israel-Palestine where I have sought to understand the reality of these two peoples' experiences by listening to their stories. In this process I have become aware of a history of much cruel and unjust treatment of Palestinians by an organized segment of Israeli Jews.

As I try to communicate this reality, and our own complicity in this injustice, to other Western Christians I am struck by the tremendous emotional blocks that these Christians have in confronting bad things done by Jews. I suspect that the reason for this emotional block is that we have not really overcome our own anti-Semitism. Especially liberal Christians, who have become sensitive to and feel guilty about anti-Semitism, tend to compensate for this guilt by idealistic philo-Semitism. Jews and the Jewish tradition have become all-wise and all-good in their minds, an example of superior wisdom and morality to which they can refer to critique the failures of their own tradition.

When faced with the possibility that an organized group of Jews have done some pretty bad things to another group of people, many sensitive "anti-anti-Semites" are thrown into agonized emotional conflict. We fear that we may be slipping back into negative stereotypes of Jews and quickly censor the thought that "maybe those Jews are bad people after all." This suggests to me that we Christians, with our history of negative stereotypes of Jews, have a hard time dealing with Jews as complex human beings like ourselves.

In thinking about Jews we tend to swing between two unrealistic polarities: Jews as superior to us, paragons of wisdom and moral insight, and

Jews as inferior to us, untrustworthy and lacking in true capacity for moral and spiritual life. We can't seem to relate to Jews as simultaneously different from and the same as ourselves, different in having their own particular history and culture, but, within those differences, having the same range of complex human capacities for good and evil, wisdom and foolishness.

Jews have been cruelly victimized as a people who have been on the underside of our unjust power over them. But they are also as capable as ourselves of becoming oppressors of others when they are in the dominant power position. This is not a question of some group of people having a special "nature" to be either victims or oppressors. The problem here is the structure of unjust power between any set of human groups. It is the unjust structuring of power that needs to be changed.

Why is it that we Christians seem to have a hard time dealing with Jews as human beings with the same range of moral and spiritual capacities as ourselves? Perhaps the real issue is that we have a hard time dealing with this complexity in ourselves. We tend to swing between self-congratulation and self-hatred, without coming to a mature self-acceptance. This duality in our relation to ourselves is reflected in the way we deal with others, with those we define as "not-us." We project this same split off duality on the "other."

Greek culture struggled with the relation between the same and the other, and we still seem to find it hard to understand the interaction between the two. We either collapse others into sameness with ourselves and deny their distinctive identity, or else we project onto them the polarized opposites of superiority and inferiority. We see them either in the mirror of our own self-inflation or else in the mirror of our own self-negation. Often both images of the "other" are operative at the same time.

This is true not only of our relation to Jews, but also of our relation to other groups. Native Americans are either the noble innocents of the Garden of Eden or else the devil red man and the "only good one is a dead one." Blacks are either the wise, nurturing Mammy and Uncle Tom or else the slut and the bestial rapist. Depending on the situation, one or another of these polarized images comes to the fore.

My guess is that if Western Christians become sensitive and contrite about our stereotypes and our complicity in the unjust treatment of Palestinians, we will tend to fall into the same unrealistic idealization. As we come to know kind and noble Palestinians, we will generalize this experience into optimistic faith that this is the way "all" Palestinians are. If we then have negative experiences with some Palestinians, we will feel betrayed and fall back into our negative views of Palestinians as "evil, violent Arabs."

The Christians in this collection of essays all, in one way or another, seem to me to be struggling to find the right way of balancing two affirmations: our need to affirm Jewish existence and right to empowerment in the light of an evil Christian history of denial of these rights, and our need to recognize that this power can and has victimized another people, the Palestinians. How can we bring these two affirmations together in a common moral equation?

First of all, we can hardly find the right balance between two realities if we don't really understand one reality, the Israelis, very well, and if we have almost no acquaintance with the other reality, of the Palestinians. With the exception of Sister Miriam Ward, the essays by Christians Robert McAfee Brown and John Pawlikowski suffer from a significant gap of knowledge and experience about the Middle East in general and about Palestinian historical and contemporary reality in particular.

Sister Ward starts her essay by enunciating a basic assumption that must underlie ethical discussion of the Israeli-Palestinian conflict: that this discussion is not to be viewed merely through Western eyes, but must be understood from the standpoint of those living in the region. She further declares that at the heart of the particular conflict of Israel and the Palestinians is a basic fact, continually overlooked, denied, or submerged in what has to be the most successful propaganda effort in modern times, that the creation of the state of Israel resulted in the dispossession and dispersion of another people, namely, the Palestinians.

The chief problem with the other Christian writers mentioned above is that most of their analysis of the situation of Israel comes out of the context of the Holocaust, and of their guilt for this history of extreme victimization of powerless Jews in Christian Europe. Their relation to Jews is not situated in the reality of Israeli Jews today as possessors of the third or fourth strongest army in the world with the capacity of nuclear weapons.

Secondly and most importantly, these Christian writers (as well as Michael Lerner and Irving Greenberg) deny or are oblivious to what is the foundational event that has shaped all Palestinian reality for the past forty-one years, whether they live within Israel, in the occupied territories or in the Palestinian diaspora, namely, the Palestinian "Catastrophe." In 1948 a Jewish majority was created in an expanded Israel (twenty percent more land than what was granted by the 1947 UN partition plan) by systematic terrorization and then direct expulsion of Palestinians. Seven hundred and eighty thousand Palestinians became refugees in order to turn a region that had had a Palestinian majority into a region with only a Palestinian remnant.

The intention was to make Palestinians disappear as a people with a national identity by neutralizing a small remnant in Israel and having the rest disperse into other Arab states. This effort to make Palestinians disappear is the foundational fault and major miscalculation from which all subsequent conflicts with Palestinians and other Arab states have flowed. The Palestinians have maintained their national identity and have continued to struggle for self-determination by various means, including guerrilla war and, more recently, the uprising in the occupied territories (which has been carried on mostly by non-violent non-cooperation).

All moral dialogue between Jews, Western Christians and Palestinians, either in America or the Middle East, will fail to come to an authentic meeting point if this foundational reality of the Palestinian expulsion is denied. In the case of Brown and Pawlikowski, the problem is lack of adequate acquaintance with Palestinians, failure to spend time learning Palestinian history and to enter into dialogue with Palestinians. This results in a rather abstract balancing act between Christian guilt toward Jews in a Western context and the Palestinian right to self-determination. This Western perspective fails to touch either Palestinian experience or the experience of a growing number of Israeli Jews (sixty percent of whom are Sephardic whose families came from Arab lands, not from the West).

There is a tortured reasoning in these essays and others on the subject which seems to suggest that Christians should not speak out in criticism of Israel until there are a substantial number of Israeli and western Jews doing so. This is an odd moral principle. Is it not mostly a strategy for saving oneself from attack as an "anti-Semite"? One can hardly imagine applying such a principle in another context. Would one really wait to criticize American or white South African racism until there was a majority of white Americans or white South Africans doing so?

If Christians had had knowledge of Deir Yassin and of the massacres and expulsions of Palestinians from places such as Lydda in 1948, should they have waited until 1988 to "criticize Israel"? This principle, that Christians should be silent until given permission to criticize Israel by the Jewish community, obscures the fact that Western Christians, such as Brown and myself, simply did not know much about the Middle East until the extremities of the situation forced us to take a look at it. Even now, the assumptions out of which Western Christians make judgments are filled with misinformation.

The position taken by John Pawlikowski is even more problematic. Like Brown, Pawlikowski has been a strong critic of western Christian anti-Semitism, but he has also committed himself to substantial support for the ideological assertions of Zionism against the Palestinians and the Arab world. The historical claims on which much of this propaganda has been based on have turned out to be a tissue of half-truths. The critique of this propaganda has long been present in Palestinian writing, but Pawlikowski follows the lead of Zionist thinkers in refusing to take any writing seriously when it came from a Palestinian or an Arab.

Now, however, a strong school of revisionist Israeli writing is arising that shows that much of the Palestinian critique of Zionist propaganda, especially about the 1948 war, is substantially true. The Palestinians were intentionally expelled by the Israelis in that war in order to create a Jewish state, or a state with an overwhelming Jewish majority. The Israeli army was not outnumbered and facing extermination in that war. Rather, they always significantly outnumbered and outmaneuvered all the Arab armies put together, since the Arab states committed only a small part of their armies to that war and they were largely at cross purposes with each other.[1]

The ideology of Israel's wars with the Arab world as wars of necessity and survival is in jeopardy. It may well be a better historical analysis to ask whether all these wars, beginning with the first one in 1948, could have been avoided if Israel had been really willing to accept both sides of the partition plan, i.e., a Palestinian state alongside Israel and the presence of substantial numbers of Palestinians in Israel, rather than seeking to expel the Palestinians from the Jewish state and to make the remnant of the Palestinian state disappear into Jordan. Much of the rhetoric that Irving Greenberg takes for granted, of Israel with its back against the wall in wars of survival, facing "another Holocaust," assumes extremities which may, in retrospect, be falsifications of the actual Israeli experience of the past forty years.

However one assesses the past, the polarities of demonic Palestinians and Arabs out for another genocide of the Jews, versus Jews in Israel and the world up against another Holocaust, falsify the real alternatives of the present and what must be the path to reconciliation. What finally must be reconciled is the right of two peoples to self-determination in a land they must both share. What can lead to such a reconciliation is temperance on both sides, not images of heroic sanctity and demonic evil arrayed against one another.

Two fallible people need to share, not only a land, but also to share power in a way that gives each sufficient power to govern and protect themselves, but not the power to render the other group helpless and victimized. However much Jews have been in this helpless and victimized position in the past, it is they who are not only brutally oppressing the Palestinians now, but have largely created the conditions that have rendered the Palestinians helpless and victimized.

What is meant by justice (and here I agree with much of Greenberg's moral realism) is not moral perfection that is unable to tolerate ambiguity, but a balancing of power that prevents any people from being either victims or victimizers. This cannot be done simply by moral declamations. It must be a part of the political and legal structuring of power that relates peoples to one another. We need to overcome the unjust structuring of power that magnifies the evil tendencies that we all have as human beings.

How can we find the just and mutual sharing of power that will encourage the generous capacities we all have as human beings? Individuals will always have a range of moral development, some rising to heights of kindness and moral clarity in the worst of circumstances, others seeking unfair advantage in the most ideal situation. But the best way to ensure a modicum of justice in most people is to limit the organized opportunities for injustice between any people. This is essentially the task to be set before a peace conference between the government of Israel and the PLO. It is our job as Americans to use our influence to see that such a peace conference takes place.

18

Christian and Jewish Views of Israel: From Apologia to Realism

GHADA TALHAMI

Five basic ideas, representing a wide spectrum of Christian and Jewish views of Israel, dominate presentations in this volume. Some are reiterated by all writers, while others are the unique contribution of a single author. Among the common and often-repeated arguments are: Christians must tread lightly when criticizing Israel; Christian commitment to the survival of Israel must be openly affirmed; Israel's empowerment is a natural consequence of statehood; Palestinian suffering and right of self-determination cannot be denied; the PLO is responsible for Israel's obsession with security. Among the minority views are Pawlikowski's vehement denial of the religious nationalism of the Israelis and Ellis's emphasis on a need for a Jewish theology of liberation.

The starting point of most of these Western Christian positions on Israel, however, is invariably a reiteration of the historic Christian guilt and responsibility for the humiliation and frequent destruction of the Jews. Most have been moved by Holocaust theology and feel gratified that the homeless Jews are homeless no more. The Holocaust has, if anything, at least impressed on people with a Christian conscience the duty of preserving and supporting this unique state, this Israel. Even though a sizeable number of Christian theologians are increasingly balancing this commitment to Israel with acknowledgment of the immorality of Israel's occupation regime, little guilt exists about the cost to the Palestinians resulting from the creation of a state for the Jews.

What is truly amazing here is the clear and palpable obliviousness to the destruction of the Palestinian community and its ensuing diaspora, which was just as alienating and as devastating as the Jewish diaspora. To Palestinian observers, it is as though the wandering Jew has been replaced by the wandering Palestinian and no one noticed the irony. Indeed, even the belated awakening of some church groups to the plight of the Palestinians did not develop as a result of understanding the tragedy of 1948 but as a result of heightened awareness of third world liberation movements of the 1960s and the 1970s.

Those who wish us to tread lightly when criticizing Israel are amazingly blind to Western complicity in uprooting the Palestinian community. No guilt feelings towards the Palestinians, indeed no sense of responsibility towards those victimized by the victims of the Holocaust is allowed to mar the general Christian admittance of the historic necessity of the state of Israel. It is as if the state of Israel were created by the gentle and persuasive powers of survivors of Auschwitz and Treblinka and not by a hardened leadership, addicted to *realpolitik* and the manipulation of Western public opinion. Christian theologians who interpret the lesson of the Holocaust as the need to provide a state for the remnant of European Jewry at any cost necessary must remember what this meant for the Palestinians. Only when a Christian guilt complex towards the Palestinians is added to the older guilt complex towards the Jews will we begin on the road to justice. This is especially the case when one remembers that, without the collusion and sympathy of Western governments, there would have been no Israel—and no exile and occupation of Palestinians.

Understanding that the natural consequence of Israel's empowerment has been a tendency to commit worldly acts of injustice would have also prepared us for the truth. Instead, some writers, but primarily Irving Greenberg, minimize the seriousness of some of these gross and unethical infringements. To claim, as he does, that the occasional failure of Israel's intelligence-gathering apparatus is expected and normal, is to blind oneself to the racist nature of many of Israel's internal policies. It was no accident, Greenberg must admit, that the Shin Bet victimized only a Circassian Israeli and a Palestinian "terrorist." It is also a falsification of history to portray the judicial picture in the occupied West Bank and Gaza as benign and based on the Arab population's right to free trial and the services of Arab counsel. To do so is to deny the overwhelming weight of international evidence to the contrary, evidence which has proven over and over again that Arab civilians under occupation are routinely beaten and humiliated, occasionally suffer torture, and often do not get to learn the nature of the evidence against them.

Rabbi Greenberg should become aware of other infringements on inter-

national law that shatter his thesis. Most Western readers are now familiar
with such illegal Israeli practices as collective punishment, land expropriation, and expulsion, which target Palestinians in the West Bank and Gaza.
Greenberg's justification of all this as no more than within "the bounds of
an ethic of power," surely flies in the face of common humanity and reason. But Greenberg does not stop here. He goes on to rattle the skeleton
of Arab barbarism when he expresses fears that if Israel loses a war, its
people may face extinction, given "the tender mercies of the Middle East."
Did he ever consider what "the tender mercies of the Israeli Middle East"
meant to Palestinian civilians who endured twenty years of occupation, an
invasion of another Arab country which culminated in massacres, or the
1967 house-to-house combat in Jerusalem?

Father Pawlikowski's quarrel with Rosemary Ruether's equation of religious nationalism with Zionism needs also to be addressed. Because
Pawlikowski narrowly defines religious nationalism as that ideology which
predominates among the religious parties of Israel, such as Herut and Gush
Emunim, he would like us to believe that there is more secular nationalism
in evidence than religious nationalism. Pawlikowski, thus, misses Ruether's
central point, which is that the creation of Israel, and the Zionist ideology,
even as they embraced certain strands of European secular nationalism,
were premised on religious nationalism. How else should one interpret the
substitution of the religious tie for the national tie and calling it nationalism? What of the use of religious symbolism, like Zion and the Star of
David, to create a new/old brand of Jewish nationalism?

Surely, Pawlikowski is aware of the reason behind Israel's refusal to
adopt a written constitution, a document that would necessitate the defining of citizenship and thereby create dilemmas for a state determined to
grant citizenship only to those whose religion is Jewish? No one put it
more eloquently than Yosef Hermoni of the Gush Emunim, who wrote in
the *Jerusalem Post* of 22 June 1976 (the International Edition) insisting that
in Zionist Israel, his party's position was indeed a mainstream position:

> The attempt to present the irrational aspect of our affinity to Eretz Yisrael . . .
> as devoid of significance or even dangerous is one that knows no green lines. . . .
> No intellectual acrobatics can stop Zionism from withering away once it has
> been cut off from its mystical, Messianic dimension, the very root of its exis-
> tence. The profound affinity to Eretz Yisrael, this holy madness with which the
> Jewish people has been sick these twenty-odd centuries, is something the only
> logic of which is illogic. Any attempt to understand the Zionist phenomenon
> without taking into account the "holy madness" of it is a sterile one. Zionism is

mysticism. It is a secular expression of Judaism and the religion of secularists among us. . . . I think that even our sensible people will agree that "the state of Israel is a vision fulfilled."

Hermoni, thus, goes to the root of the problem, and one thinks that Pawlikowski and other Christian theologians should do so also. To view Israel only in the context of the Holocaust is to blind oneself deliberately to the true nature of the terrain. Perhaps Marc Ellis' call for a Jewish theology of liberation should be accompanied by a call for a Christian theology of liberation—only this time, the liberation must be from worn-out concepts and time-honored foci on the European and Western experience, in total blindness to the suffering of weaker people outside the range of the Western historical experience.

Notes

Introduction

1. Yossi Sarid, "The Night of the Broken Clubs," *Ha'aretz*, May 4, 1989.

2. Gideon Spiro, "You Will Get Used to Being a Mengele," *Al Hamishar*, September 19, 1988.

3. Quoted in Alan Cowell, "Three Palestinians Killed in Protests in the Gaza Strip," *New York Times*, June 17, 1989.

4. S. D. Goitein, *Jews and Arabs: Their Contacts through the Ages* (New York: Schocken, 1974), 89–124.

5. See Y. Porath, *The Emergence of the Palestinian-Arab National Movement, 1918–1929* (London: Frank Cass, 1974).

6. Rosemary Ruether, *Faith and Fratricide: The Theological Roots of Anti-Semitism* (New York: Seabury Press, 1974), 185–86.

7. Leon Poliakov, *The History of Anti-Semitism: From Voltaire to Wagner* (New York: Vanguard Press, 1968), 217, 518, n.10.

8. Shlomo Avineri, *The Making of Modern Zionism: The Intellectual Roots of the Jewish State* (New York: Basic Books, 1981), 3–13.

9. Peter Grose, *Israel in the Mind of America* (New York: Knopf, 1983), 41, 51.

10. Rosemary and Herman Ruether, *The Wrath of Jonah: The Crisis of Religious Nationalism in the Israeli-Palestinian Conflict* (San Francisco: Harper and Row, 1989), 138–44.

11. George Antonius, *The Arab Awakening: The Story of the Arab National Movement* (London: Hamish Hamilton, 1938).

12. Walid Khalidi, ed., *From Haven to Conquest: Readings in Zionism and the Palestine Problem until 1948* (Washington, D.C.: Institute for Palestine Studies, 1987), 375–87.

13. Shabtai Teveth, *Ben Gurion and the Palestinian Arabs: From Peace to War* (New York: Oxford University Press, 1988), 179–80.

14. For the relation of the Jewish *Yishuv* in Palestine and the Third Reich in the 1930s, see Edwin Black, *The Transfer Agreement: The Untold Story of the Secret Agreement between the Third Reich and Jewish Palestine* (New York: Macmillan, 1984).

15. Simha Flapan, *The Birth of Israel: Myths and Realities* (New York: Pantheon, 1987).

16. Khalidi, *From Haven to Conquest*, 858–60.

17. Michael Palumbo, *The Palestinian Catastrophe: The 1948 Expulsion of a People from their Homeland* (London: Faber and Faber, 1987).

18. See Janet Abu-Lughod, "The Demographic War for Palestine," *The Link* 19 (December 1986).

Part 1: Jewish Responses to the Uprising

1. Alexander M. Schindler, "Text of a Cable Sent Saturday Night, January 23, 1988 to the President of Israel," *AS Briefings: Commission on Social Action of Reform Judaism*, March 1988, appendix A.

2. See Irving Greenberg, "The Third Great Cycle in Jewish History," *Perspectives* (New York: National Jewish Resource Center, 1981). For an earlier essay see idem, "Cloud of Smoke, Pillar of Fire: Judaism, Christianity and Modernity After the Holocaust," in *Auschwitz: Beginning of a New Era?* ed. Eva Fleischner (New York: KTAV, 1977), 7–55.

Chapter 2: The Illusion of Jewish Unity

1. In keeping with Shamir's decision at the beginning of March, AIPAC has tried to cover some of its tracks. Several of its officials have been making speeches at Jewish meetings in which they have deplored the letter of the thirty senators. However, the most recent fundraising letter circulated by AIPAC simply asserts the hope that some solution will be found for the continuing crisis in the territories; the letter mentions Senator Edward Kennedy and Daniel Patrick Moynihan, who were among the principal signers of the letter of the thirty, as admiring AIPAC's activities. It is worth recalling that in 1984 the pro-Israel Political Action Committees, which are under AIPAC's influence, made intense and successful efforts to defeat Senator Charles Percy of Illinois because he said that while Israel's existence and security must be insured, the Palestinians should be allowed national expression. The Israel lobby is doing no such thing now in any of the campaigns for reelection by the signers of the recent letter.

Chapter 3: Feminist Reflections on the State of Israel

1. Audre Lorde, *Sister Outsider* (Trumansburg, NY: Crossing Press, 1984).
2. Hertzberg's *The Zionist Idea: A Historical Analysis and Reader* (New York: Doubleday and Herzl Press, 1959) provides an excellent discussion of and sourcebook on the important ideological differences among Zionist thinkers. See also, Ben Halpern, *The Idea of the Jewish State*, 2d ed. (Cambridge, MA: Harvard University Press, 1969), chap. 2.
3. Dafna Izraeli, "The Zionist Movement in Palestine, 1911–1927: A Sociological Analysis," *Signs: Journal of Women in Culture and Society* 7 (Autumn 1981): 89; Deborah Bernstein, *The Struggle for Equality: Urban Women Workers in Prestate Israeli Society* (New York: Praeger, 1987), 4–5; Lesley Hazleton, *Israeli Women: The Reality Behind the Myths* (New York: Simon and Schuster, 1977), chap. 1; Natalie Rein *Daughters of Rachel: Women in Israel* (Harmondsworth, England: Penguin Books, 1979), 27–29.
4. Bernstein, *The Struggle for Equality*, 1, 2, 5.
5. Izraeli, "The Zionist Women's Movement in Palestine," 90–95; Bernstein, *The Struggle for Equality*, 16–20; Hazleton, *Israeli Women*, 15–17.
6. Vivian Silver, "Sexual Equality on Kibbutz—Where Did We Go Wrong?" (Unpublished paper delivered at the International Conference "Kibbutz and Communes—Past and Future," May 21, 1985); Naomi Fulop, "Women in the Kibbutz: A Jewish Feminist Utopia?" *Shifra* 3 and 4 (Dec 1986): 33–35; Paula Rayman, *The Kibbutz Community and Nation Building* (Princeton, NJ: Princeton University Press, 1981), 53–54.
7. Tom Segev, *1949: The First Israelis* (New York: The Free Press, 1986), 249–52; Frances Raday, "Equality of Women Under Israeli Law," *The Jerusalem Quarterly* 27 (Spring 1983): 81–83; Hazleton, *Israeli Women*, 22–23.
8. Hazleton, *Israeli Women*, 137–51; Nira Yuval-Davis, "The Israeli Example," *Loaded Questions: Women in the Military*, ed. W. Chapkis (Amsterdam: Transnational Institute, n.d.), 73–77.
9. This term was used by Barbara Welter to describe the nineteenth century Ameri-

Notes

can image of women's nature and role; *Dimity Convictions: The American Woman in the Nineteenth Century* (Athens, Ohio: Ohio University Press, 1976), chap. 2.

10. Yuval-Davis, "The Israeli Example," 76–77; Nira Yuval-Davis, "The Jewish Collectivity and National Reproduction in Israel," *Khamsin* 13 (July 1987): 86–87.

11. Segev, *1949*, 155–61.

12. Sammy Smooha and Yochanan Pere, "The Dynamics of Ethnic Inequalities: The Case of Israel," *Studies of Israeli Society*, vol. I, Migration, Ethnicity and Community (New Brunswick, NJ: Transaction Books, 1980), 167–73; Erik Cohen, "The Black Panthers and Israeli Society," ibid., 147, 149–50.

13. Cohen, "The Black Panthers and Israeli Society," 160–61.

14. Ian Lustick, in *Arabs in the Jewish State: Israel's Control of a National Minority* (Austin: University of Texas Press, 1980), thoroughly analyzes these dynamics. See chap. 3 for discussion of his analytic framework.

15. Ibid., 93–94. Cf. Anton Shammas, "The Morning After," *The New York Review* (September 29, 1988): 49.

16. Abba Eban, "The Central Question," *Tikkun* 1 (1987): 21.

17. Ibid.; Amnon Rubenstein, *The Zionist Dream Revisited: From Herzl to Gush Emunim and Back* (New York: Schocken Books, 1984), chap. 7; Uriel Tal, "Foundations of a Political Messianic Trend in Israel," *The Jerusalem Quarterly* 35 (Spring 1985): 42–45.

18. Mariam M. Mar'i and Sami Kh. Mar'i, "The Role of Women as Change Agents in Arab Society in Israel," *Women's Worlds*, ed. Marilyn Sahr, Martha Mednick, Dafna Israeli, Jessie Bernard (New York: Praeger Special Studies, 1985), 251–58.

19. Hazleton, *Israeli Women*, 143; Davis, "The Israeli Example," 76. Only ten percent of Jewish Israeli men are exempted from military service.

20. Yuval-Davis, "The Jewish Collectivity and National Reproduction in Israel," 60–90, esp. 85.

21. This analogy became clear to me in the course of a conversation with Paula Rayman on July 20, 1987. I am indebted to Paula both for pushing me to deal with the state of Israel and for helping me to organize my thoughts on many of the issues I discuss.

22. I have in mind here the use of the Holocaust to justify almost everything and anything that Israel does, including the occupation and the aggressive response to the Palestinian uprising.

23. Donna Robinson Divine, "Political Discourse in Israel: Literature," *Books in Israel*, vol. 1, ed. Ian Lustick (Albany, NY: SUNY Press, forthcoming).

24. See, e.g., *The New Israel Fund: Annual Report, November 1987* (New York: New Israel Fund, 1987), 8–11, 20–23; Rein's *Daughters of Rachel*, pt. 2 deals with the emergence of the Israeli women's movement.

25. Good sources of information about such groups are *Shalom: Jewish Peace Letter* (published quarterly by the Jewish Peace Fellowship, Box 271 Nyack, NY 10960) and Jay Rothman with Sharon Bray and Mark Neustadt, *A Guide to Arab-Jewish Peacemaking Organizations in Israel* (New York: The New Israel Fund, 1988). (This and other publications and reports of the NIF are available from the NIF, 111 West 40th Street, New York, NY 10018). See also, Saul Perlmutter, "The Light at the End of the Tunnel" (unpublished paper, 1988) and "The Israel Palestinian Center for Research and Information (IPCRI)" (unpublished letter, May 26, 1988).

26. This workshop took place as part of the Non-Governmental Forum at Nairobi. Christie Balka and Reena Bernards, "Israeli and Palestinian Women in Dialogue: A Model for Nairobi. New Jewish Agenda's Role at the U.N. Decade for Women Conference Forum '85 in Nairobi" (unpublished report to New Jewish Agenda), 2–3.

27. Tal, "Foundations of a Political Messianic Trend in Israel," 36–45.

Notes

Chapter 5: The Occupation Is Over

1. For an extended analysis of the themes in Holocaust theology see Marc H. Ellis, *Toward a Jewish Theology of Liberation: The Uprising and the Future* (Maryknoll, NY: Orbis, 1989), 7–24.

2. For an early, radical, and controversial analysis of these themes see Richard L. Rubenstein, *After Auschwitz: Radical Theology and Contemporary Judaism* (New York: Bobbs-Merrill, 1966) and *The Cunning of History: Mass Death and the American Future* (New York: Harper and Row, 1975).

3. Of course, the first priority was to survive as a people so that a future was possible to imagine. This question of survival was described by Emil Fackenheim as the commanding voice of Auschwitz. See Emil Fackenheim, *God's Presence in History: Jewish Affirmation and Philosophical Reflections* (New York: New York University Press, 1970).

4. For an interesting exploration of this new framework see Irving Greenberg, "Cloud of Smoke, Pillar of Fire: Judaism, Christianity and Modernity After the Holocaust," in *Auschwitz: Beginning of a New Era?*, ed. Eva Fleishner (New York: KTAV, 1977), 7–55, and "On the Third Era of Jewish History: Power and Politics," in *Perspectives* (New York: National Jewish Resource Center, 1980).

5. Rubenstein, *Cunning of History*, 28; Greenberg, "Cloud of Smoke," 29.

6. For an extended discussion of Holocaust theology's inability to analyze the case of empowerment see Ellis, *Jewish Theology of Liberation*, 25–37.

7. In effect, a new pragmatism is stressed that allows the "occasional use of immoral strategies to achieve moral ends." With this understanding, the memory of the Holocaust enables Israel to be a "responsible and restrained conqueror." See Irving Greenberg, "The Third Great Cycle in Jewish History," in *Perspectives* (New York: National Jewish Resource Center, 1981), 25, 26. The recent uprising in the occupied territories and the response of Israeli authorities exemplify the difficult position diaspora Jews are in relative to Israel.

8. Ibid., 25. Also see ibid., "Third Era," 6, and ibid., "Power and Peace," *Perspectives* 1 (December 1985): 3, 5.

9. One such attempt to break through the silence is found in David Grossman, *The Yellow Wind*, trans. Haim Watzman (New York: Farrar, Straus and Giroux, 1988).

10. For the first publication of the Committee Confronting the Iron Fist see *We Will Be Free in Our Own Homeland: A Collection of Readings for International Day of Fast and Solidarity with Palestinian Prisoners* (Jerusalem: Committee Confronting the Iron Fist, 1986). A report on Yesh Gvul can be found in "Israeli Doves Arousing Little Response," *New York Times*, 1 March 1988. Also see "A Captain's Ideals Lead Him to Jail," *New York Times* 20 March 1988.

11. For New Jewish Agenda's response to the uprising see Ezra Goldstein and Deena Hurwitz, "No Status Quo Ante," *New Jewish Agenda* 24 (Spring 1988): 1–3. Also see Arthur Hertzberg's "The Uprising," *New York Review of Books*, 4 February 1988, 30–32; and "The Illusion of Jewish Unity" *New York Review of Books* 16 June 1988, 6, 8, 10, 11, 12. For a more personal account see Albert Vorspan, "Soul Searching," *New York Times Magazine*, 8 May 1988, 40, 41, 51, 54.

12. Shamir's response is a prime lesson in Holocaust theology. At a news conference in Jerusalem, Shamir said: "It is the height of temerity and hypocrisy that members of the terrorist organization speak of returning. This boat which loads its decks with murderers, terrorists who sought to murder us—all of us, each of us. They wish to bring them to the land of Israel, and demonstrate that they are returning to the same place in which they wished to slay us. We will and do view this as a hostile act, an act which

endangers the state of Israel." Quoted in "Israel's Furious Over a Palestinian Plan to 'Return' to Haifa by Sail," *New York Times*, 11 February 1988, 15.

13. For an interesting discussion of the theme of excommunication see Roberta Strauss Feuerlicht, *The Fate of the Jews: A People Torn Between Israeli Power and Jewish Ethics* (New York: Times Books, 1983), 281, 282.

14. The strains of this highly problematic and emotional relationship have increasingly come to the surface in recent years. Witness the upheavals in North American Jewish life relating to the Lebanese War, the massacres at Sabra and Shatila, the Pollard spy case and now the uprising. My point is simply that the relationship between Jews in Israel and Jews outside of Israel cannot remain as it is without ultimately dividing the community at its very roots.

15. For Hannah Arendt's prophetic understanding of the choices facing the Jewish settlers in Palestine see a collection of her essays *Hannah Arendt; the Jew as Pariah: Jewish Identity and Politics in the Modern Age*, ed. Ron H. Feldman (New York: Grove Press, 1978).

Part 2: American Christians, Judaism, and the Israeli-Palestinian Conflict

1. The intervention of Middle Eastern Christians in critique of the Vatican II statement on the Jews was widely misinterpreted in this way. See George Irani, *The Papacy and the Middle East: The Role of the Holy See in the Arab-Israel Conflict, 1962–1984* (Notre Dame, IN: Notre Dame University Press, 1986), 17. The first book on Palestinian Christian liberation theology, Naim Ateek's *Justice and Only Justice: A Palestinian Theology of Liberation*, appeared only in April, 1989, published by Orbis Press, Maryknoll, NY.

2. See *The Middle East Policy Statement*, adopted by the governing board of the National Council of Churches of Christ in the U.S.A., November 6, 1980.

3. One of the presidents of the National Christian Leadership Conference for Israel has been David Allen Lewis. See his book on Biblical apocalyptic interpretation of the 1982 war in Lebanon, *Magog 1982 Cancelled* (Harrison AK: New Leaf Press, 1982).

4. The major book on Vatican policy is George Irani's *The Papacy and the Middle East* (see note 1).

5. As an example of the difficulty Christian bodies have in dealing with the issue of mission to the Jews, see Eva Fleischner, *Judaism in German Christian Theology since 1945: Christianity and Israel Considered in Terms of Mission* (Metuchen, NJ: Scarecrow Press, 1975).

6. See "Documents and Statements of the World Council of Churches on the Palestinian Question from Amsterdam, 1948 to Geneva, 1980" in Michael King, *The Palestinians and the Churches, 1940–1956* (Geneva: World Council of Churches, 1989), 130ff.

7. For the development of Christian Zionist theology in American fundamentalism, see David A. Rausch, *Zionism within Early American Fundamentalism, 1878–1918* (New York: Edwin Mellen Press, 1979). For an expression of the alliance of such Christian Zionism with Jewish Zionism in the 1970s, see Merrill Simon, *Jerry Falwell and the Jews* (Middle Village, NY: Jonathan David Publishers, 1984).

Chapter 7: Christians in the West Must Confront the Middle East

1. Gregory Baum, "The Church, Israel and the Palestinians," *The Ecumenist* (November–December 1988): 1–6.

2. For a later printed version of this talk, slightly updated, see "Speaking about Israel: Some Ground Rules," *Christian Century* 105 (6 April 1988): 338–40.

3. See chapter 2 above, p. 75.

4. See chapter 4 above, p. 99.

5. In addition to his essay in this volume, Ellis has argued the point in more detail in *Toward a Jewish Theology of Liberation* (Maryknoll: Orbis Books, 1989); see esp. chap. 6.

6. Elie Wiesel, *The Oath* (New York: Random House, 1973), 214.

7. Ibid.

8. See the helpful historical study by David Biale, *Power and Powerlessness in Jewish History* (New York: Schocken Books, 1986).

9. Ignacio Silone, *Bread and Wine* (New York: Time Incorporated, 1969), 180.

10. See especially Paulo Friere, "Divide and Rule," in *Pedagogy of the Oppressed* (New York: Herder and Herder, 1972), esp. 137ff.

Chapter 8: Ethical Issues in the Israeli-Palestinian Conflict

1. John T. Pawlikowski, "Rethinking the Palestinian Question," *Worldview* 17:10 (October 1974): 41–44.

2. W. D. Davies, *The Gospel and the Land* (Berkeley: University of California Press, 1974), and *The Territorial Dimension of Judaism* (Berkeley, CA: University of California Press, 1982).

3. Walter Brueggemann, *The Land* (Philadelphia: Fortress Press, 1977).

4. For Vatican II's statement on the Jews, see *Nostra Aetate*, in *Stepping Stones to Further Jewish-Christian Relations*, comp. Helga Croner (London: Stimulus Books, 1977), 1–5.

5. Robert McAfee Brown, "Speaking About Israel," *The Christian Century* 105:11 (April 6, 1988): 338–40.

6. Msgr. George G. Higgins, nationally syndicated Catholic column, April 18, 1988.

7. This is a theme in Rosemary Radford Ruether and Harman Ruether, *The Wrath of Jonah: The Crisis of Religious Nationalism in the Israeli-Palestinian Conflict* (San Francisco: Harper & Row, 1989).

8. *The Territorial Dimension*, 121.

9. Benny Morris, *The Birth of the Palestinian Refugee Problem, 1947–1949* (Cambridge/New York: Cambridge University Press, 1987).

10. Simha Flapan, *The Birth of Israel: Myths and Realities* (New York: Pantheon Books, 1987).

11. Michael Palumbo, *The Palestinian Catastrophe: The 1948 Expulsion of a People From Their Homeland* (London/Boston: Faber and Faber, 1987).

12. *The Birth of the Palestinian Refugee Problem*, 294.

13. Joan Peters, *From Time Immemorial* (New York: Harper & Row, 1984).

14. Abraham Heschel, *Israel: An Echo of Eternity* (New York: Farrar, Straus and Giroux, 1969).

15. Manfred Vogel, "The State as Essential Expression of the Faith of Judaism," *Cities of Gods. Faith, Politics and Pluralism in Judaism, Christianity and Islam*, ed. Nigel Biggar, Jamie S. Scott, and William Schweiker (New York/Westport, CT/London: Greenwood Press, 1986), 11–20.

16. Certainly one of the key principles of the 1974 Vatican Guidelines for the implementation of *Nostra Aetate*, the Vatican II document on the Jews, affirmed the need for Christians to understand Jews as they define themselves. The text of the Guidelines

(released in January 1975) can be found in Helga Croner, ed., *Stepping Stones to Further Jewish-Christian Relations* (London/New York: Stimulus Books, 1977), 11–16.

17. Irving Greenberg, "The Third Great Cycle in Jewish History," *Perspectives* (New York: National Jewish Resource Center, 1981), 24–25.

18. Romano Guardini, *Power and Responsibility* (Chicago: Henry Regnery, 1961), xiii.

19. "Peace—Condition of Security," the Jerusalem *Post*, 2 September 1988, 14.

20. David Hartman, "Israel in Gaza: Israelis Speak Out," *Tikkun*, 3:2 (March/April 1988): 19.

21. For more on this issue of Israeli pluralism see my essay "Jewish Approaches to Pluralism: Reflections of a Sympathetic Observer," in Biggar, Scott, and Schweiker, eds., *Cities of Gods*, 55–69.

22. See Ronald J. Young, *Missed Opportunities for Peace: U.S. Middle East Policy 1981–1986* (Philadelphia: American Friends Service Committee, 1987).

Chapter 9: The Theological and Ethical Context for Palestinian–Israeli Peace

1. For a Jewish perspective see Marc H. Ellis, *Toward a Jewish Theology of Liberation: The Uprising and the Future* (Maryknoll: Orbis Books, 1989). For a Palestinian perspective see Naim Ateek, *Justice, Only Justice: A Palestinian Liberation Theology* (Maryknoll: Orbis Books, 1989) is very promising. The author is canon of St. George's Cathedral in Jerusalem.

2. Creation is generally treated within the framework of redemption. In no way do I deny the relationship of creation, redemption, and liberation. My suggested context of a creation-theology is merely used as a starting point where there is agreement by the monotheistic faiths. Many English language commentaries are available on the theme of creation in the Hebrew and Christian scriptures. For Islam an important contribution is Thomas J. O'Shaughnessy, S.J., *Creation and the Teaching of the Qur'an*, Biblica et Orientalia 40 (Rome: Biblical Institute Press, 1985).

3. George Foot Moore, *Judaism* (Cambridge: Harvard University Press, 1944), 1:445.

4. Fazlur Rahman, *Islam* (Chicago: University of Chicago Press, 1979). The author emphasizes that the basic spirit of the Koran is moral, and from that perspective he also emphasizes monotheism. Ideas of social and economic justice flow from these emphases. See also N. J. Dawood, trans., *The Koran* (New York: Penguin Books, 1974), 178, and Thomas J. O'Shaughnessy, *Creation*, 1.

5. Rahman, *Islam*, 100. Also see Eknath Easwaran, *A Man to Match His Mountains* (Petaluma, CA: Nilgiri Press, 1984), 63. The subtitle suggests its contents: "Badshah Khan, Non-violent Soldier of Islam." As the author notes in his preface, Khan, a follower of and co-worker with Gandhi in India "offers the world . . . a way out of the violence that has convulsed the Middle East during the last few decades" (11). Too little is known in the West about Khan, who trained 100,000 Pathans in northern India in an active non-violent resistance against British rule.

6. Joan Peters, *From Time Immemorial: the Origins of the Arab-Jewish Conflict Over Palestine* (New York: Harper & Row, 1984), is a prime example. (For a critical analysis of her position, see Muhammad Hallaj, "From Time Immemorial: The Resurrection of a Myth," *The Link* 18 [January/March]: 1–14.) There should have been an outcry against this book which, in my opinion, is on the same level of historicity as the works claiming the Holocaust never happened. Incredibly, a number of prominent American Jewish authors who gave advance accolades to Peters' book have never withdrawn their

endorsements. Interestingly, Peters' book was dismissed with contempt in Israel and Europe.

7. Jack G. Shaheen, *The TV Arab* (Bowling Green, OH: Bowling Green State University Press, 1984) points to the dangers inherent in stereotyping not only Arabs, but any group. He documents the use of the Arab as "bad guy" in TV sitcoms, children's cartoons, and prime time evening shows. "Most perceptions of Arabs come, not from knowledge, but from faulty and simplistic assumptions." (20).

8. Nur-eldeen Masalha, "On Recent Hebrew and Israeli Sources for the Palestinian Exodus, 1947–49," *Journal of Palestine Studies* 18, no. 1 (Autumn 1988): 121–37.

9. See Walid Khalidi, "Plan Dalet: Master Plan for the Conquest of Palestine," *Journal of Palestine Studies* 18, no. 1 (Autumn 1988), 3–70. Also see Nur-eldeen Masalha, "Sources for the Palestinian Exodus." My focus is on recent Israeli Jewish writings which, by and large, confirm the description given by Palestinian writers as to how the dispossession and dispersion of Palestinians took place as well as the aftermath for those who did not flee. See Fouzi El-Asmar, *To Be an Arab in Israel* (Beirut: Institute for Palestine Studies, 1975); Elias Chacour, *Blood Brothers* (Grand Rapids: Zondervan, 1984); Sabri Jiryis, *The Arabs in Israel* (New York: Monthly Review Press, 1976). Ian Lustick, *Arabs in a Jewish State* (Austin, TX: University of Texas Press, 1980) is a study of how Arabs have been controlled and manipulated, but it is a study done by an outsider, an American.

10. Among the contributors to *New Outlook* have been Albert Schweitzer, Bruno Kreisky, Bertrand Russell, and Jean-Paul Sartre. See Dan Leon, "Book Reviews," *New Outlook* (March–April 1988): 32. Also see Simha Flapan, *The Birth of Israel* (New York: Pantheon Books, 1987).

11. Ibid., 4.

12. Ibid., 8.

13. Ibid., 8–9.

14. Ibid., 9.

15. Ibid., 9.

16. Ibid., 9, 10.

17. Ibid., 10.

18. Ian Lustick, *Arabs in a Jewish State,* is an exception at least in making available a work in English. See note 9 for works by Palestinians. See also Edward Said, *The Question of Palestine* (New York: Times Books, 1979), especially 3–55.

19. Introduction by Israel Shahak, ed. Norton Mez Vinsky (Tel Aviv, Israel: The Israeli League For Human and Civil Rights, P.O.B. 14192, 1989).

20. Masalha, *Sources for the Palestinian Exodus.*

21. See Clark M. Eichelberger, *UN: The First Twenty-Five Years* (New York: Harper & Row, 1970), 70–87.

22. George Foot Moore, *Judaism,* 2:85. Also see Kenneth Morgan, *Islam's Straight Path* (Motilal Barnarsidass: South Asia Books, 1987), 424.

23. *Pacem in Terris,* encyclical by Pope John XXIII, quoted in Joseph Gremillon, *The Gospel of Peace and Justice: Catholic Social Teaching Since Pope John* (Maryknoll: Orbis Books, 1976), 232.

Chapter 10: The Occupation Must End

1. This evaluation is based on several feature articles on the year of the *intifada* in the *Jerusalem Post,* 9–15 December 1988.

2. Uri Davis, *Israel: An Apartheid State* (London: Zed Books, 1987), 20.

3. This view is generally accepted by revisionist Israeli historians, such as Simha Flapan, *The Birth of Israel: Myths and Realities* (New York: Pantheon, 1987), and Benny Morris, *The Birth of the Palestinian Refugee Problem, 1947–49* (Cambridge: Cambridge University Press, 1988).

4. Ibid.; also Michael Palumbo, *The Palestinian Catastrophe: The 1948 Expulsion of a People from Their Homeland* (London: Faber and Faber, 1987).

5. Ian Lustick, *Arabs in the Jewish State: Israel's Control of a National Minority* (Austin, TX: University of Texas Press, 1980).

6. Raja Shehadeh, *Occupier's Law: Israel and the West Bank* (Washington, D.C.: Institute for Palestine Studies, 1985).

7. In the last year quiet overtures have been made by Israel to Egypt to take over responsibility for Gaza, but this has been rejected. In October 1988 King Hussein of Jordan announced that he was severing all ties with and responsibility for the West Bank. See Daoud Kuttab, "The Struggle to Build a Nation," *Nation* 247 (17 October 1988): 336–39.

8. *The Cost of Freedom: Palestinian Human Rights under Israeli Occupation* (Chicago: Data Base Project on Palestinian Human Rights, 1989).

9. *Punishing a Nation* is available from the Palestine Human Rights Campaign, 4753 N. Broadway, suite 930, Chicago, IL 60604; also their update reports through 1989.

10. Ibid., 37.

11. In a particularly shocking case of the gang-beating death of a forty-five-year-old father, Hanni Shammi, first in his own home and then at the military headquarters in Gaza, four soldiers were put on trial but acquitted on the grounds that others also beat Shammi and that they were only following orders. The commanding officer directly responsible testified that "we found relief in beating him and getting ecstatic about it. We kept beating him mindlessly." *PHRC Report,* 31 October 1988, 4; also *PHRC Report,* 8 December 1988.

12. *Punishing a Nation,* 31–32.

13. Interview, Al-Ahli Hospital, Gaza, 17 December 1988.

14. *Punishing a Nation,* 143–46, 163–66.

15. Anita Vitullo, "Israel's War by Bureaucracy: 'We'll Blow Your House Down,'" *PHRC report,* August 1988.

16. *Punishing a Nation,* 147–52.

17. Ibid., 177–96.

18. Ibid., 295–316.

19. Ibid., 317–21.

20. Interview, Brother Joseph Goldstine, Bethlehem University, 16 December 1988.

21. This incident was reported by one of our group, who was with friends in Beach Camp, 18 December 1988.

22. This is the conclusion of the Al-Haq report, *Punishing a Nation,* 133–35.

23. J. W. DeGruchy, *The Church Struggle in South Africa* (Grand Rapids, MI: Eerdmans, 1979).

24. UN General Assembly Resolution #3379 (November 10, 1975). Philip Potter, General Secretary of the World Council of Churches, repudiated the declaration on the grounds that Zionism did not fall within the UNESCO guideline definition of racism: Michael King, *The Palestinians and the Churches* (Geneva: WCC, 1981), 135.

25. Interview with Mary Khass, UNRWA workers, Gaza, 17 December 1988.

26. Interview with Father Riah Abu Al-Assad, Nazareth, 15 December 1988.

27. It is common for Palestinians, in speaking about the possibility of community with Jews, to recall friendships with Jews before 1948 and even intermarriages between the two communities.

28. Interviews with Dan Leon of *New Outlook Magazine*; Adam Keller, Progressive List for Peace; and Gideon Spiro, Yesh Gevul ("There is a Limit," soldiers' resistance group); 21 December 1988.

Chapter 11: Toward Peace in the Holy Land

1. Walid Khalidi, "Thinking the Unthinkable: A Sovereign Palestinian State," *Foreign Affairs* (July 1978): 695–713, and "Regiopolitics: Toward a US Policy on the Palestinian Problem," ibid. (Summer 1981): 1050–63.

Chapter 12: The Palestinian Dream

1. Meron Benvenisti, *The West Bank Data Project: A Survey of Israel's Policies* (Washington: American Enterprise Institute, 1984).

2. Bartley C. Crum, *Behind the Silken Curtain* (New York: Simon and Schuster, 1947), 23.

3. Ian Lustick, *For the Land and the Lord: Jewish Fundamentalism in Israel* (New York: Council on Foreign Relations, 1988).

4. On Israel's relations with South Africa see Jane Hunter, *Undercutting Sanctions* (Washington, D.C.: Washington Middle East Associates, 1986).

5. On Israel's military dealings in Latin America see Bishara Bahbah, *Israel and Latin America: The Military Connection* (New York: St. Martin's Press and Institute for Palestine Studies, 1986). Also see Milton Jamail and Margo Gutierrez, *It's No Secret: Israel's Military Involvement in Central America* (Belmont, MA: Association of Arab-American University Graduates, 1986).

6. *Los Angeles Times* poll conducted March 25–31 and April 4–7, 1988. For summary see Robert Scheer, "US Jews for Peace Talks on Mideast," *The Los Angeles Times*, 12 April 1988.

7. Alan R. Taylor, *The Zionist Mind* (Beirut: Institute for Palestine Studies, 1974). Also see Muhammad Hallaj, "Palestine: The Suppression of an Idea," *The Link* 15:1 (January–March 1982).

8. Marvin Lowenthal, ed., *The Diaries of Theodor Herzl* (London: Victor Gollancz, 1958).

9. John Marlowe, *Rebellion in Palestine* (London: The Cresset Press, 1946), 46.

10. Oded Yinon, "A Strategy for Israel in the Nineteen Eighties," *Kivunim*, February 1982. English translation, Israel Shahak, ed., *The Zionist Plan for the Middle East* (Belmont, MA: Association of Arab-American University Graduates, 1982).

11. *The Washington Post*, 3 July 1988.

12. See Moshe Menuhin, *The Decadence of Judaism in Our Time* (Beirut: Institute for Palestine Studies, 1969), and Roberta Strauss Feuerlicht, *The Fate of the Jews: A People Torn Between Israeli Power and Jewish Ethics* (New York: Time Books, 1983).

13. Ibrahim Abu Lughod and Baha Abu Laban, *Settler Regimes in Africa and the Arab World: The Illusion of Endurance* (Wilmette, IL: Medina Press, 1974).

14. For text of PNC resolutions see Rashid Hamid, *Resolutions of the Palestine National Council, 1964–1974* (Beirut: Palestine Research Center, 1975) (in Arabic).

15. Muhammad Rasheed, *Toward a Democratic State in Palestine* (Beirut: Palestine Research Center, 1970).

16. Hamid, *PNC Resolutions*, 139.

17. Yehoshafat Harkabi, *Palestinians and Israel* (New York: Wiley, 1974), 70.

Notes

18. Arafat's speech can be found in *International Documents on Palestine, 1974* (Beirut: Institute for Palestine Studies, 1977), 134–44.

19. Fayez A. Sayegh, "A Palestinian View," *The Arab World* 16 (February 1970): 18. Emphasis in the original.

20. Harkabi, *Palestinians and Israel*, 81.

21. Yehudi Menuhin, "Mideast Answer: Federation," *The Washington Post*, 3 July 1988, 10.

Chapter 13: Morality and Expediency in the Policies of Zionist Israel

1. Arthur Nussbaum, *A Concise History of the Law of Nations* (New York: Macmillan, 1947), 180–87, 240. These laws, being the work of the concert of European nations and the Russian-led Holy Alliance represented at the Congress of Vienna in 1815, started as a purely European, rather than as an international, effort. When some European states later sided with the Muslim Ottomans against Christian Russia, the Muslim power became an accepted member of this European community and its laws and truly internationalized their nature.

2. Samir N. Anabtawi, "The United Nations, the Palestine Refugees and the Palestinian Revolution," in *The Palestinian Resistance to Israeli Occupation*, ed. Naseer Aruri (Wilmette, IL: Medina Press, 1970), 51–52.

3. W. Thomas Mallison, Jr., "The State of the Palestinian People and the Guerilla Fighters under International Law," ibid., 64.

4. Quoted in ibid., 65.

5. United Nations, the Committee on the Exercise of the Inalienable Rights of the Palestinian People, *The Palestine Question: A Brief History* (New York: United Nations, 1980), 6; see also pp. 65–67. For a discussion of the Charter's significance as a human rights document and as an instrument of positive international law, see Committee to Study the Organization of Peace, *The United Nations and Human Rights*, Eighteenth Report (New York: United Nations, 1967), 12–15.

6. Quoted in Izzat Tannous, *The Enraging Story of Palestine and Its People* (New York: Palestine Liberation Organization, 1965), 11.

7. M. Cherif Bassiouni, *The Palestinians' Rights of Self-Determination and National Independence*, AAUG Information Paper no. 22 (Detroit: Association of Arab-American University Graduates, 1978), 3. See also Ghada Talhami, "From Palestinian Nationhood to Palestinian Nationalism," *Arab Studies Quarterly* 8:4 (Fall 1986): 348.

8. Bassiouni, *Palestinians' Rights*, 2–5.

9. Ibid., 15.

10. Ibid.

11. Ibid., 15–16. The definition of Palestinian nationality is to be found in the British Foreign Office Historical Section, *Handbook on Syria and Palestine*, no. 60 (London: His Majesty's Stationery Office, 1920); see Bassiouni, 34n.120. See also Hisham Sharabi, "Development of PLO Peace Policy," *Palestine/Israel Bulletin* 4:1 (February 1981): 2. This article first appeared in *Al-Fajr* and later in *New Outlook*.

12. *The Palestine Question* (New York: Palestine Information Office, nd).

13. Yehoshafat Harkabi, Israel's authority on the PLO covenant, interpreted the PLO desire to reconstitute historic Palestine as tantamount to a call for the liquidation of all of Israeli society. The Palestinian call for the "liquidation, or the uprooting of the Zionist existence or entity" amounts to a call for destruction, in his view, since Zionism is not only a political regime but is embodied in Israeli society. See Yehoshafat Harkabi, *Fedayeen Action and Arab Strategy*, Adelphi Papers no. 53 (London, 1968), 11.

14. Quoted in *Palestine Perspectives* 34 (March–April 1988): 15.

15. Tannous, *The Enraging Story*, 25; Fred Khouri, *The Arab-Israeli Dilemma*, 3d ed. (Syracuse: Syracuse University Press, 1976), 96–97, 123; Ethel Mannin, *The Road to Beersheba* (Chicago: Henry Regnery, 1964). For the forced march of Lydda, see Maher Abu Khater, "Palestinian Recalls 1948 Lydda Exodus," *Al-Fajr* 7:314 (16 May 1986): 7. The Palestinian in question is the Rev. Oudeh Rantissi, a Palestinian Anglican minister.

16. Childers interviewed Arab leaders, checked records of British and American sources of all Arab broadcasts, and requested the Israelis to furnish proof of their claims, to no avail. See Erskine B. Childers, "The Other Exodus," *The Spectator* (21 May 1961), 672–75. See also the review article commenting on new Israeli scholarship on the Palestinian refugee problem which vindicates Palestinian claims: "Israeli Scholars Dispute Official Record of 1948," *Al-Fajr* 8:314 (16 May 1988): 8–9, 15.

17. Bassiouni, 16–17.

18. Abdeen Jabara, *Israel's Violation of Human Rights in Arab Territories Occupied in June, 1967* (Chicago: National Lawyers Guild, nd), 5.

19. Livia Rokeach, *Israel's Sacred Terrorism* (Belmont, MA: Association of Arab-American University Graduates, 1980), 43–44.

20. PLO/Fateh, *Al-Tajribah al-Kubiyah* (The Cuban experience) (Beirut: Fateh, 1967); idem, *Al-Tajribah al-Siniyah* (The Chinese experience) (Beirut: Fateh, 1967); Leonora Stradalova, *There Will Be Tomorrow* (Beirut: Fateh, 1968). See also PLO/Fateh, *Dirasat wa tajareb thawriyah* (Studies and revolutionary experiences) (Beirut: Fateh, 1967).

21. PLO/Fateh, *Tahrir al-aqtar al-muhtallah* (Liberation of the occupied lands) (Beirut: Fateh, 1967), 16–17.

22. Yehuda Blum, "The Missing Reversioner: Reflections on the Status of Judea and Samaria," *Israel Law Review* 3:279 (April 1968): 279–301.

23. Sally V. Mallison, "The Application of International Law to the Israeli Settlements in Occupied Territory," in *Palestinian Rights: Affirmation and Denial*, ed. Ibrahim Abu-Lughod (Wilmette, IL: Medina Press, 1982), 60–61.

24. Ibid.

25. Ghada Talhami, "The Palestinian Perception of the Human Rights Issue," *Syracuse Journal of International Law and Commerce* 13:3 (Spring 1987): 480–81.

26. Joost R. Hiltermann, *Israel's Deportation Policy*, Occasional Paper no. 2 (Ramallah: Al-Haq, Law in the Service of Man, 1986, 9. Law in the Service of Man is an affiliate of the International Commission of Jurists.

27. Ibid., 11.

28. Ibid., 8–13.

29. Ibid.

30. Ibid., 13–14.

31. Jabara, *Israel's Violation of Human Rights*, 8.

32. Ibid., 9, 13.

33. Jonathan Broder, "Israeli Raids Kill Eighteen Inside Lebanon," *Chicago Tribune*, 4 January 1988, 2.

34. Hiltermann, *Israel's Deportation Policy*, 5–7, 33–34. See also Felicia Langer, "In the Kingdom of Nir," *Samedoun: Friends of Palestinian Prisoners* 1:2 (December 1987): 2, 5, 6; "Israel and Torture," *Sunday Times* (London) (19 June 1977).

35. Hiltermann, 37–38.

36. "Court Keeps No Secrets," *Near East Report* 32:7 (15 February 1988): 2.

37. Eqbal Ahmad, "Comprehending Political Terror," *Al-Fajr* 7:311 (25 April 1986): 6. Ahmad delivered this piece originally as a lecture before the Arab Canadian Center for Development Studies.

38. Bassiouni, 21–22.
39. Jabara, 14–15, 25–26. On the destruction of Imwas, see Khalil Touma, "Imwas, Destruction of a Biblical Village," *Al-Fajr* 7 : 311 (25 April 1986): 8–9.
40. W. Thomas Mallison, Jr., "The Status of the Palestinian People," 24.
41. Fayez Sayegh, *Zionist Propaganda in the United States: An Analysis* (Brattleboro, VT: Fayez Sayegh Foundation, 1983), 46. For an authoritative but opposing view affirming the validity of the "Jewish people" concept, see N. Feinberg, "The Recognition of the Jewish People in International Law," *The Jewish Yearbook of International Law* (Jerusalem: R. Mass, 1948), 1.
42. Sayegh, *Zionist Propaganda*, 38–39.
43. "Morality and Policy: A Symposium," *Jerusalem Post*, International Edition, 27 February 1988, 12.

Chapter 14: Statehood, Recognition, and the Politics of Peace

1. The following works are helpful in relating the issue of British and Israeli occupation of Palestine to that of Palestinian self-determination and the role of the League of Nations, etc.: Henry Cattan, *The Palestine Question* (London: Croom Helm, 1988), and idem, *Palestine and International Law* (London: Longman, 1973); Christopher Sykes, *Crossroads to Israel* (New York: World Publishing, 1965); W. Thomas and Sally Mallison, *The Palestine Problem in International Law and World Order* (London: Longman, 1987).
2. The slow but certain alterations in the land and demographic ratios is carefully and definitively analyzed by Janet Abu-Lughod and John Ruedy in *The Transformation of Palestine*, ed. I. Abu-Lughod (Evanston: Northwestern University Press, 1987), 119–64; see also W. Khalidi, ed., *From Haven to Conquest* (Beirut: Institute of Palestine Studies, 1971), appendix 1.
3. Great Britain, Royal Commission on Palestine, *Report*, presented by the Secretary of State for the Colonies to Parliament, July 1937 (London: His Majesty's Stationery Office); the Palestinian statements were presented by the Hajj Amin al-Husayni, Jamal al-Husayni, Awni abdul Hadi, and others. Their testimonies are part of the public hearings record.
4. Two important studies of the concept of "transfer-expulsion" of Arabs from Palestine as it was elaborated by various Zionist leaders including Herzl should be consulted: Chaim Simon, *International Proposal to Transfer Arabs from Palestine, 1895–1947* (Hoboken, NJ: KTAV, 1988), and Israel Shahak, "A History of the Concept of 'Transfer' in Zionism," *Journal of Palestine Studies* 71 (Spring 1989): 22–37. See also Shabtai Teveth, *Ben-Gurion and the Palestine Arabs* (Oxford: Oxford University Press, 1985), 180–81, which gives Ben-Gurion's reaction to the Royal Commission's recommendation to the idea of "transfer" or "exchange" of population in a partitioned Palestine.
5. Jabotinsky's views of Palestine and the status of Palestinians in the projected Jewish state are to be found in his testimony to the British Royal Commission, reproduced in Arthur Hertzberg, *The Zionist Idea* (New York: Herzl Press, 1960), 556–70.
6. Abu-Lughod, *The Transformation of Palestine*. See also Edward W. Said, *The Question of Palestine* (New York: Times Books, 1987), and Said et al., *A Profile of the Palestinian People* (Chicago: Palestine Human Rights Committee, 1987).
7. The following books are helpful: Simha Flapan, *The Birth of Israel* (New York: Pantheon, 1987), Benny Morris, *The Birth of the Palestine Refugee Problem, 1947–49* (Cam-

bridge: Cambridge University Press, 1988), and Michael Palumbo, *The Palestine Catastrophe* (London: Faber and Faber, 1987).

8. Helena Cobban, *The Palestinian Liberation Organisation* (Cambridge: Cambridge University Press, 1984); Abdallah Franji, *The PLO and Palestine* (London: Zed Books, 1983); and Cheryl Rubenberg, *The Palestine Liberation Organization* (Belmont, MA: Institute of Arab Studies, 1983).

9. Articles 3, 4, 6, 19, and 20 of the Palestine National Charter.

10. The text of the Transitional Program is reproduced in Yehuda Lukacs, ed., *Documents on the Israeli-Palestinian Conflict, 1967–1983* (Cambridge: Cambridge University Press, 1984), 156–58.

11. The text of Arafat's General Assembly speech of November 1974 is reprinted in *Journal of Palestine Studies* 4:2 (1975): 181–92.

12. The text of the Amman Accords is reprinted in *Journal of Palestine Studies* 17 (Winter 1985): 206.

13. Scott Mcleod, "An Interview with Yasser Arafat," *New York Review of Books*, 11 June 1987, 36–40, and idem, "An Interview with Yasser Arafat II," ibid., 25 June 1987, 41–44.

14. The text of the Palestinian Declaration of Independence and Political Resolutions adopted by the Palestine National Council on 15 November can be found in *Journal of Palestine Studies* 8:2 (1989): 213–23.

Chapter 17: Beyond Anti-Semitism and Philo-Semitism

1. For major examples of this revisionist history, see notes 3 and 4 of my article in this volume, p. 183. John Pawlikowski, in his essay in this volume, dismisses my book, *The Wrath of Jonah: The Crisis of Religious Nationalism in the Israeli-Palestinian Conflict* (New York: Harper and Row, 1989), and also Palumbo's study of the Palestinian catastrophe, which uses UN as well as Zionist archives. However it does not seem that Pawlikowski has actually read these books carefully.

On November 13, 1988, Pawlikowski and I had a dialogue on the Palestinian issue at the Catholic Theological Union. At that time he was unacquainted with the revisionist literature by Palumbo, Flapan, or Morris. The advance copy of my book which I had sent him he returned, saying that he had just received it and had not had time to read it. His efforts to come to terms with this new literature in his essay, written in early December 1988, are cursory at best, and does not suggest that he has carefully studied these books or examined their sources. He misstates entirely the thesis of my book and incorrectly uses Morris to shore up the Zionist thesis that the Palestinians left voluntarily and were called out by the Arab states.

This thesis has long been refuted by counter-evidence. See Christopher Hitchens, "Broadcasts," in Edward Said and Christopher Hitchens, eds., *Blaming the Victims: Spurious Scholarship and the Palestinian Question* (London: Verso Press, 1988), 73–83.

Contributors

Ibrahim Abu-Lughod was born in Jaffa, Palestine. After the Palestine War of 1948, he came to the United States, receiving his B.A. and M.A. degrees from the University of Illinois, and his Ph.D. from Princeton University. Abu-Lughod has worked for UNESCO as a social science officer, was an associate professor of government at Smith College, and since 1967 has been a professor of political science at Northwestern University. He was a visiting professor at McGill University and with UNESCO's Center for Educational Planning in Beirut. In 1980, Abu-Lughod headed a team of specialists who prepared for UNESCO *A Feasibility Study for a Palestinian Open University*. Abu-Lughod's books include *Arab Rediscovery of Europe: The Transformation of Palestine; African Themes; Palestinian Rights;* and *A Profile of the Palestinian People*. He has also written many scholarly articles for various scholarly journals in the United States, Europe, and the Middle East.

Robert McAfee Brown is professor emeritus of theology and ethics at Pacific School of Religion in Berkeley, California, where he completed a teaching career that also included professorships at Macalester College, Union Theological Seminary, and Stanford University. He has tried to interpret third world concerns, particularly in relation to "liberation theology," to North Americans through such writings as *Theology in a New Key: Responding to Liberation Themes; Gustavo Gutierrez; Unexpected News: Reading the Bible with Third World Eyes; Religion and Violence;* and *Spirituality and Liberation: Overcoming the Great Fallacy*. He has also confronted the impact of the Holocaust on Christian faith in *Elie Wiesel: Messenger to All Humanity*. He coedited the symposium *A Cry for Justice: The Churches and Synagogues Speak*. He writes frequently for *Christianity and Crisis* and the *Christian Century*.

Marc H. Ellis received his Ph.D. from Marquette University and is at present a professor at the Maryknoll School of Theology, where he directs the

Justice and Peace Program. He has written five books: *A Year at the Catholic Worker; Peter Maurin: Prophet in the Twentieth Century; Faithfulness in an Age of Holocaust; Toward a Jewish Theology of Liberation: The Uprising and the Future;* and *Beyond Innocence and Redemption: Confronting the Holocaust and Israeli Power,* as well as numerous articles. He has also edited a *festschrift* titled *The Future of Liberation Theology: Essays in Honor of Gustavo Gutierrez.* Ellis has been a visiting lecturer at Heythrop College, University of London, and has traveled and lectured extensively in North America, Europe, Latin America, Asia, and the Middle East.

Rabbi Irving Greenberg is the president and co-founder of CLAL, the National Jewish Center for Learning and Leadership. An ordained Orthodox rabbi, a Harvard Ph.D., and scholar, Rabbi Greenberg has published articles and monographs on Jewish thought and religion. His first book, *The Jewish Way: Living the Holidays,* a philosophy of Judaism based on an analysis of the Sabbath and holidays, was published in 1988.

Muhammad Hallaj was born in Palestine and received his Ph.D. from the University of Florida. He taught for sixteen years in universities in the United States and the Middle East, including Birzeit University in the Israeli-occupied West Bank, where he also served as academic vice-president and the director of the Council for Higher Education in the West Bank and Gaza. Hallaj has also been a visiting scholar at Harvard University's Center for International Affairs, and the director of the Institute of Arab Studies in Belmont, Massachusetts. Since 1983 he has been the director of the Palestine Research and Educational Center in Washington, D.C., and the editor of its magazine, *Palestine Perspectives.* He has contributed to several books on the Palestinians and the Arab-Israeli conflict, and has published scores of articles in Arabic and English.

Rabbi Arthur Hertzberg was born in Lubaczow, Poland, in 1921. He received a B.A. from Johns Hopkins University in 1940, an M.H.L. from the Jewish Theological Seminary in 1943, and a Ph.D. from Columbia University in 1966. Since 1956 he has been rabbi of Temple Emanu-El in Englewood, New Jersey. In 1959 he was named lecturer and adjunct professor of history at Columbia University. He is professor of religion at Dartmouth College and has held visiting faculty positions at Rutgers University, Princeton University, and Hebrew University. He served as president of the American Jewish Congress from 1972 to 1978, and he has been vice-president of the World Jewish Congress since 1975.

Contributors

Rabbi Hertzberg's books include *The Zionist Idea* (with Martin Marty and Joseph Moody, 1959), *The Outbursts That Await Us* (1963), *The French Enlightenment and the Jews* (1968), and *Being Jewish in America* (1979).

Walid Khalidi was born in Jerusalem in 1925. He is a graduate of the Universities of London and Oxford, and is currently a research fellow at the Center for Middle Eastern Studies at Harvard. He was professor of political studies at the American University in Beirut, Lebanon, and co-founded the Institute for Palestine Studies in 1963. He has served as general secretary of the Institute since then. He has written and lectured extensively in Arabic and English on the international and regional politics of the Arab world, and on the Palestinian problem and the Arab-Israeli conflict in particular. His articles have appeared in the *Encyclopaedia Britannica, Foreign Affairs,* and the *New York Times.* His books include *From Haven to Conquest; Conflict and Violence in Lebanon;* and *Before Their Diaspora.*

Michael Lerner has a Ph.D. in philosophy from the University of California, Berkeley, and a Ph.D. in social/clinical psychology from the Wright Institute of Psychology. He studied at the Jewish Theological Seminary between 1960 and 1964 while a student at Columbia College. In 1964, he began graduate studies at the University of California and became a national leader of the antiwar movement. In 1977, Lerner founded the Institute for Labor and Mental Health in Oakland, California. Since that time he has served as executive director of the Institute. In 1986, Lerner published *Surplus Powerlessness.* He is editor-in-chief and co-founder of *Tikkun* magazine, a bimonthly Jewish critique of politics, culture, and society. Founder of several *havurot* and active in Jewish communal and religious life, Lerner is both a passionate Zionist and an observant, religious Jew.

John T. Pawlikowski is professor of social ethics and director of the M.A. Program at the Catholic Theological Union, a constituent school of the ecumenical cluster of theological schools at the University of Chicago. He is the author/editor of ten books, including *Christ in the Light of the Christian-Jewish Dialogue; Economic Justice: CTU's Pastoral Commentary on the Bishops' Letter on the Economy; Biblical and Theological Foundations of the Challenge of Peace;* and *The Challenge of the Holocaust for Christian Theology.* He is a member of the Advisory Committee of the National Conference of Catholic Bishops' Secretariat for Catholic-Jewish Relations and the National Council of Churches Committee on Christian-Jewish Relations. He has served by presidential appointment on the U.S. Holocaust Memorial Council since its creation by Congress in 1980. He has visited the Middle East frequently, and at present serves as a member of the Executive Committee of the U.S. Interreligious Committee for Peace in the Middle East.

Judith Plaskow, associate professor of religious studies at Manhattan College, has been learning, teaching, speaking, and writing about feminist theology for almost twenty years. She is co-founder and co-editor of the *Journal of Feminist Studies in Religion,* author of *Sex, Sin, and Grace,* and co-editor (with Carol P. Christ) of *Womanspirit Rising* and *Weaving the Visions.* A New Yorker by birth and conviction, she is a member of two *havurot* (alternative Jewish communities) and of B'not Esh, a Jewish feminist spirituality collective.

Rosemary Radford Ruether received her doctorate from Claremont Graduate School and is at present Georgia Harkness Professor of Applied Theology at Garrett-Evangelical Theological Seminary. She is a prolific author whose many books include *Faith and Fratricide: The Image of the Jews in Early Christianity; Sexism and God-Talk: Toward a Feminist Theology;* and *The Wrath of Jonah: The Crisis of Religious Nationalism in the Israeli-Palestinian Conflict.* She has been active in the Palestinian Human Rights Campaign.

Edward W. Said was born in Jerusalem and received his B.A. from Princeton and his M.A. and Ph.D. from Harvard. He is at present Parr Professor of English and Comparative Literature and chairs the doctoral program in Comparative Literature at Columbia University. He has been a visiting professor at Yale, Harvard, and Johns Hopkins, and has lectured at over one hundred universities in the United States, Canada, Europe, and the Middle East. He is a member of the editorial boards of several literary and philosophic journals in the United States, Europe, and the Middle East, including *Diacritics, Critical Inquiry,* and *Theory and Society.* Between 1980 and 1983 he was chairman of the Board of Directors of the Institute of Arab Studies. He has been a member of the Palestine National Council from 1977 to the present. Said's writings have appeared in twelve languages in several countries. His books include *Joseph Conrad and the Fiction of Autobiography; Beginnings: Intention and Method; Orientalism; The Question of Palestine; Literature and Society; Covering Islam;* and *The World, the Text, and the Critic.*

Ghada Talhami was born in Jerusalem. She received her B.A. from Western College for Women, Oxford, Ohio, her M.A. from the University of

Wisconsin, Milwaukee, and her Ph.D. from the University of Illinois, Chicago. She is associate professor of political science at Lake Forest College, Lake Forest, Illinois, specializing in Mideast and African politics and women's studies. She is the author of *Suakin and Massawa Under Egyptian Rule, 1865–1885,* and of numerous articles on various aspects of the Middle East, especially the Palestine question.

Miriam Ward, Ph.D., is founder and director of the Trinity College Annual Biblical Institute. A member of the Sisters of Mercy, she is also adjunct professor in religious studies at St. Michael's College, and is active in adult education at the parish level. Ward most recently edited and contributed to *A Companion to the Bible.* She has studied several summers in Jerusalem and has led sixteen pilgrimage/study tours to Israel and Palestine. A charter member of Pax Christi, Burlington, and Vermonters for Peace in the Middle East, she has written and lectured on social justice issues in Latin America and the Middle East. She is currently doing research on Palestinian family reunification.

Credits